Iranian Cosmopolitanism

From popular and "New Wave" pre-revolutionary films of Fereydun Goleh and Abbas Kiarostami to post-revolutionary films of Mohsen Makhmalbaf, the Iranian cinema has produced a range of films and directors that have garnered international fame and earned a global following. Golbarg Rekabtalaei takes a unique look at Iranian cosmopolitanism and how it transformed in the Iranian imagination through the cinematic lens. By examining the development of Iranian cinema from the early twentieth century to the revolution, Rekabtalaei locates discussions of modernity in Iranian cinema as rooted within local experiences, rather than being primarily concerned with Western ideals or industrialization. Her research further illustrates how the ethnic, linguistic and religious diversity of Iran's citizenry shaped a heterogeneous culture and a cosmopolitan cinema that was part and parcel of Iran's experience of modernity. In turn, this cosmopolitanism fed into an assertion of sovereignty and national identity in a modernizing Iran in the decades leading up to the revolution.

GOLBARG REKABTALAEI is an assistant professor of Middle East History in the Department of History at Seton Hall University, where she teaches on the modern Middle East. A cultural and social historian of modern Iran, she holds a Ph.D. in Near and Middle Eastern Civilizations from the University of Toronto.

THE GLOBAL MIDDLE EAST

GENERAL EDITORS
Arshin Adib-Moghaddam, *SOAS, University of London*
Ali Mirsepassi, *New York University*

EDITORIAL ADVISORY BOARD
Faisal Devji, *University of Oxford*
John Hobson, *University of Sheffield*
Firoozeh Kashani-Sabet, *University of Pennsylvania*
Zachary Lockman, *New York University*
Madawi Al-Rasheed, *London School of Economics and Political Science*
David Ryan, *University College Cork, Ireland*

The Global Middle East series seeks to broaden and deconstruct the geographical boundaries of the "Middle East" as a concept to include North Africa, Central and South Asia, and diaspora communities in Western Europe and North America. The series features fresh scholarship that employs theoretically rigorous and innovative methodological frameworks resonating across relevant disciplines in the humanities and the social sciences. In particular, the general editors welcome approaches that focus on mobility, the erosion of nation-state structures, travelling ideas and theories, transcendental techno-politics, the decentralisation of grand narratives and the dislocation of ideologies inspired by popular movements. The series will also consider translations of works by authors in these regions whose ideas are salient to global scholarly trends but have yet to be introduced to the Anglophone academy.

Other books in the series:
1. *Transnationalism in Iranian Political Thought: The Life and Times of Ahmad Fardid*, Ali Mirsepassi
2. *Psycho-nationalism: Global Thought, Iranian Imaginations*, Arshin Adib-Moghaddam
3. *Iranian Cosmopolitanism: A Cinematic History*, Golbarg Rekabtalaei
4. *Money, Markets, and Monarchies: The Gulf Cooperation Council and the Political Economy of the Contemporary Middle East*, Adam Hanieh

Iranian Cosmopolitanism

A Cinematic History

GOLBARG REKABTALAEI
Seton Hall University

CAMBRIDGE
UNIVERSITY PRESS

CAMBRIDGE
UNIVERSITY PRESS

University Printing House, Cambridge CB2 8BS, United Kingdom

One Liberty Plaza, 20th Floor, New York, NY 10006, USA

477 Williamstown Road, Port Melbourne, VIC 3207, Australia

314–321, 3rd Floor, Plot 3, Splendor Forum, Jasola District Centre,
New Delhi – 110025, India

79 Anson Road, #06–04/06, Singapore 079906

Cambridge University Press is part of the University of Cambridge.

It furthers the University's mission by disseminating knowledge in the pursuit of
education, learning, and research at the highest international levels of excellence.

www.cambridge.org
Information on this title: www.cambridge.org/9781108418515
DOI: 10.1017/9781108290289

First published 2019

Printed in the United Kingdom by TJ International Ltd, Padstow, Cornwall

A catalogue record for this publication is available from the British Library.

Library of Congress Cataloging-in-Publication Data
Names: Rekabtalaei, Golbarg, 1983– author.
Title: Iranian Cosmopolitanism : a cinematic history / Golbarg Rekabtalaei,
  Seton Hall University.
Description: Cambridge, UK ; New York, NY: Cambridge University Press, 2018. |
  Series: The global Middle East | Based in the author's dissertation (doctoral)–
  University of Toronto, 2015. | Includes bibliographical references and index.
Identifiers: LCCN 2018009863 | ISBN 9781108418515 (hardback : alk. paper)
Subjects: LCSH: Cosmopolitanism in motion pictures. | Motion pictures–Iran–History–
  20th century. | Motion picture industry–Iran–History–20th century.
Classification: LCC PN1995.9.C558 R45 2018 | DDC 791.43/655–dc23
  LC record available at https://lccn.loc.gov/2018009863

ISBN 978-1-108-41851-5 Hardback

For Abbas, Keyhan, and Kiarash

Contents

Notes on Transliteration, Citation, Translation and Dates

In the translation of Persian words, I have adopted the Library of Congress Persian Romanisation Table, but I have applied a more simplified version of the table. To make names easier for the reader, the diacritics indicated in the Library of Congress table for Persian letters such as ث , ح, ذ, ص, ض, ط, and ظ have been dropped. Almost all Persian names (and nouns), including the names of authors, filmmakers and characters in films, have been transliterated according to the simplified version of the Library of Congress table. For the names of renowned authors and/or filmmakers (in the field of Iranian Studies), the common and predominant spelling of the names has been used. Moreover, for the names of famous literary works, such as *Layli and Majnun* or *Shirin and Farhad*, I have dropped all the diacritics indicated in the Library of Congress table for an easier reading of the text. In general matters of citation and footnotes, the 16th edition of *The Chicago Manual of Style* (for footnotes) has been followed. Unless otherwise noted, all translations are my own.

For all dates of events, films and/or publications, I have provided the Gregorian calendar date. Wherever the Persian solar calendar date was indicated in the sources (for example, in newspaper and magazine articles), I have provided both the Gregorian and solar calendar dates. In the case of sources that had only supplied a lunar calendar date, I have supplied both the lunar and Gregorian dates.

Figures

Acknowledgements

The book before you is based on my doctoral dissertation, which I finished in 2015 in the Department of Near and Middle Eastern Civilisations, at the University of Toronto. For the various ways in which they helped to shape its ideas and arguments into the final product at hand, this book is indebted to many people, but especially the following individuals.

Professor Mohamad Tavakoli-Targhi, without whose free-thinking, persistent determination and unconditional support this project would have been impossible. Allowing me to access his astounding library of primary sources has been a unique privilege, for which I will forever be grateful. My less than adequate gratitude to him for the intellectual horizons that he opened up for me during my graduate studies. His unwavering inspiration has been a source of confidence, especially at times when pursuing academic research seemed too arduous a task.

Professor James Reilly, who despite his busy schedule always found time to read my drafts carefully and to provide me with thoughtful and helpful comments. I especially thank him for always pushing me to think and write clearly. His generous attention, words of wisdom and relentless support have been a source of inspiration for me throughout my graduate years and afterwards. My thanks also go to Professor Robert J. King, who always openheartedly afforded me his time, despite the distance, and his eye-opening insights. I am especially indebted to him for introducing me to the world of early cinema, a field that will always be close to my heart.

I am equally indebted to Professors Farzaneh Hemmasi and Madhavi Kale for their participation in my doctoral dissertation committee and for their thought-provoking questions and informative feedback on the manuscript. I especially wish to express my thanks to Farzaneh Hemmasi for her friendship, and for bestowing me with the opportunity to share research ideas, concerns and many enjoyable conversations with her after my defence. I owe a great debt of gratitude to Professor Hamid Naficy of Northwestern University for his careful reading of my manuscript, and his instructive and valuable insight on my project. I would also like to express my gratefulness to the late Professor Amir Hassanpour, my adviser at the Master's level, for inciting my interest in communication media in modern Iran, especially cinema, which became the topic of my doctoral dissertation. His dedication to the issues of social justice and his endless efforts to create a better world for everyone has been and will remain to be a source of inspiration in my academic and personal life.

My time as a Postdoctoral Teaching Scholar in the Department of History at North Carolina State University in Raleigh, North Carolina, from 2015 to 2017, was a formative period in my life where I benefitted from the scholarship and teaching experience of many colleagues. I am indebted to the kindness and generosity of Professor Akram Khater for his mentorship throughout my fellowship. I am equally thankful to Professor David Zonderman for his support. My time in Raleigh would have been impossible without the friendship and care of my colleagues at NCSU, especially Dr Catherine Conner, Dr Sandra Fatoric, Dr Nick Blackwell, Dr Levi McLaughlin, Dr Leif Tornquist, Dr Graham Pitts, Dr Lily Balloffet and Dr Elizabeth Saylor, whose camaraderie I hold very dear.

Since August 2017, the Department of History at Seton Hall University has become my academic home, where I have benefitted immensely from the rigorous scholarship and goodwill of my colleagues, whom I would also like to thank for their friendship. I would like to particularly express my gratitude to Professor Anne Giblin Gedacht for her untiring consideration and thoughtfulness, Professor Kirsten Schultz for her moral encouragement and insights, departmental chairs Professor Nathaniel Knight and Professor Thomas Rzeznik for facilitating a smooth transition for me at Seton Hall University and for assisting me in settling in in South Orange, and Roslyn Jenkins for everything she has done for me behind the scenes. For their support and financial assistance in the progress and completion of this book, I would also like to convey my appreciation to the Dean of the College of Arts and Sciences at Seton Hall University, Dr Peter Shoemaker, and the staff in the Dean's Office, especially Sheila Riley, Brenda Knight and Jean McArthur.

My thanks also go to my colleagues in the Department of Near and Middle Eastern Civilisations at the University of Toronto, for being there and sharing the ups and downs of graduate studies with me.

I would especially like to thank Dr Ida Meftahi, Dr Hamid Rezaeiyazdi, Dr Arshavez Mozaffari and Dr Jairan Gahan for all the invigorating discussions that we had at Robarts Library and outside, on cultural categories of fukulī, jāhil, mutribī, dance, music, the red-light district and all other understudied aspects of Iranian social and cultural history. I have also benefitted greatly from consultation with Mohammad Tahaminejad, Dr Behrooz Mahmoodi-Bakhtiari, Naser Hassanzaadeh and Mr Shahbazi, whose help I would like to acknowledge.

I am also grateful to the wonderful administrative staff in the Department of Near and Middle Eastern Civilisations at University of Toronto, and the Department of History at North Carolina State University, who tirelessly and meticulously worked behind the scenes to ensure that my administrative tasks were completed hassle-free. I am equally indebted to the kind staff at the National State Archives, National Library of Iran, National Film Institute, as well as the Parliament Library, who greatly assisted me in my graduate research in Iran. Some of the photographs used in this book were found in the archives of the National Library of Iran and the Institute for Iranian Contemporary Historical Studies, both of whom I would like to acknowledge and thank. I would also like to extend my sincere gratitude to Mr Pedram Misaqi for his guidance and Ms Sahar Atefmehr for her help in finding some of the old photographs featured in this book.

My doctoral research was supported by Roshan Cultural Heritage Institute, whose generous financial endorsement I appreciatively acknowledge and thank. I am especially grateful to Dr Elahe Omidyar Mir-Djalali for her support and consideration of my project.

I would also like to express my deep appreciation to the editors of the Global Middle East book series, Professor Ali Mirsepassi and Professor Arshin Adib-Moghadam. In addition to the inspiration I have received from his work on cosmopolitanism and intellectual thought in Iran, I am indebted to Professor Mirsepassi for his careful reading of my manuscript and his valuable feedback on the book. I hope to continue to benefit from his scholarship and friendship in the future. I would also like to extend my gratitude to Maria Marsh, the Commissioning Editor of Cambridge University Press, Content Managers, Daniel Brown and Thomas Haynes, Project Manager, Divya Mathesh, the Senior Editorial Assistant, Abigail Walkington and others involved in the publication of this book at Cambridge University Press for their tremendous help in completing and polishing this project. I would also like to express my gratitude to Sophie Rosinke for her help in copy-editing this book.

Nooshin Neirami, Upa Mesbahian, Mehrdad Nadimi, Iman Roshan, Nogol Taheri and Mona Kheradmand, perhaps I don't express my gratefulness in words frequently enough, but suffice it to say that this book would have not been finished if it were not for your care and presence in my life.

Last, but certainly not least, I am beyond grateful to my loving parents, Keyhan and Abbas, and my dear brother, Kiarash, for believing in me when it was difficult for me to believe in myself. Thank you for picking me up every time I stumbled. No words could ever express my gratitude for your unending love, affection and patience, despite all circumstances.

Introduction

A Klee painting named Angelus Novus shows an angel looking as though he is about to move away from something he is fixedly contemplating. His eyes are staring, his mouth is open, his wings are spread. This is how one pictures the angel of history. His face is turned toward the past. Where we perceive a chain of events, he sees one single catastrophe which keeps piling wreckage upon wreckage and hurls it in front of his feet. The angel would like to stay, awaken the dead, and make whole what has been smashed. But a storm is blowing from Paradise; it has got caught in his wings with such violence that the angel can no longer close them. The storm irresistibly propels him into the future to which his back is turned, while the pile of debris before him grows skyward. This storm is what we call progress.

Walter Benjamin, *On the Concept of History*[1]

The book at hand is a study of Iran's experience of modernity through cinema from its inception in Iran in the early 1900s to the Iranian Revolution of 1979. Iranian modernity in the early twentieth century was inadvertently tied to socio-cultural and political conditions that evoked cosmopolitan practices and experiences – conditions that cinema, as a modern technology and space that allowed for the inter-action of cultures and transformation of identities, intensified and transfigured in the decades that followed. As a history of cinematic modernity, then, this book offers a promising way to link cosmopolit-anism to the ethos of modernity in Iran. "Cinematic modernity" is a term that I use to denote the kind of modernity that was shaped by the technology of cinema, the space that it fostered and the visual content that it projected. It is also used to highlight the societal transformations that allowed for cinema's transfiguration (both in its filmic content and

---

[1] Thesis IX in Walter Benjamin's *On the Concept of History*, often referred to as *Theses on the Philosophy of History*. See Thesis IX in Walter Benjamin, *Selected Writings: On the Concept of History*, vol. 4: *1938–1940* (Cambridge, MA: The Belknap Press of Harvard University Press, 2003).

1

spatial form), and the imaginations that cinema's morphogenesis conjured from the turn of the twentieth century to the late 1970s.

Similar to what has been argued for early cinema in the West, in early twentieth-century Iran, film and screening spaces were implicated in a temporality that – similar to Walter Benjamin's description of Angelus Novus – was propelled into the future, while its gaze was toward an ever-present past. This intrinsic cinematic temporality, like the illusion of a continuous image created through the fast-paced passing of celluloid frames, evokes Marx's description of modernity, "all that is solid melts into air."[2] The novelty of the technology of the cinematograph that not only embodied speed and depicted movement, but also portrayed images that had previously been inaccessible, the new spaces of sociability that it facilitated, as well as the new imaginaries that it prompted, all allude to the temporality, the "new time," that cinema engendered in its early years. It was through the sensationally felt everyday changes brought about by this phenomenon in the "new time" that urban Iranians further experienced modernity.

In the field of Iranian Studies, cinema's extrinsic temporality – that is, the periodicity of the activities and culture surrounding cinema – has been almost fully overlooked, and has instead been overdetermined by the country's political and economic periodicity. Iran's geopolitical significance in the region, the repeated intervention of international powers in its domestic and international policies, years of political turmoil, social movements and revolutions have all facilitated conventional historical narratives that explain social and cultural developments in terms of Iran's political history. Such a homogenous conception of historical time, therefore, does not differentiate between the temporality of the political from the temporality of the cultural. What is at stake in this "homogenous time" is the autonomy of cultural temporality. Following Nietzsche in writing against a "monumental narrative," that is, a history that forgets the visible burden of

---

[2] "All fixed, fast frozen relations, with their train of ancient and venerable prejudices and opinions, are swept away, all new-formed ones become antiquated before they can ossify. All that is solid melts into air, all that is holy is profaned." Karl Marx and Frederick Engels, *Communist Manifesto* (New York: New York Labor News Co., 1908), section 1, para. 18, accessed August 24, 2014, http://web.b.ebscohost.com.myaccess.library.utoronto.ca/ehost/ebookviewer/ebook/bmxlYmtfXzEwODYxOTlfX0FO0?sid=6556af4e-22d3–45db-abc3–4ebc8160 dbd3@sessionmgr113&vid=3&format=EK&lpid=np-1&rid=0.

the past by selectively recollecting the past based on present circumstances, I contend that the conventional "history" of pre-revolutionary cinema has been altered not only by the politics of the present, but also by an overarching political history. John Orr argues for viewing modern artworks, including films, as "processes which come into being in a Nietzschean sense by coming *back* into being," and "which move forward by echoing the past."[3] My attempt in this project has been to capture the echoes of the past by investigating ruptures and continuities in the history of pre-revolutionary cinema, independent from and yet connected to socio-political conditions that fashioned them. Upholding a heterogeneous conception of history that examines multiple layers of time, the book at hand studies cinema from the vantage point of cinematic temporality; in doing so, it unearths cinema's autonomous history in terms of reception, propagation, institutionalisation and industrial transformations, and then explores this history in relation to the multiple layers of social and political events that, at times, shaped cinema's morphogenesis.

The basic tenet of modernity as self-confrontation signals a transformative condition. Most scholars of modern Iran have located Iranian modernity in the encounter of Iranians with the Persian translation of works by Western philosophers such as Descartes in the latter half of the nineteenth century, or alternatively in the encounters of Iranians with their "others" through political strife.[4] Some scholars argue for an importation of a wholesale "modernity" from the West or, alternatively, allude to the existence of an abstract form of modernity, to which

---

[3] John Orr, *Cinema and Modernity* (Cambridge: Polity Press, 1993), 1 (emphasis in the original).

[4] For example, Mehrzad Boroujerdi argues for a modernity that was shaped by Iranian intellectuals through their consultation of European texts toward the end of the nineteenth century. See Mehrzad Boroujerdi, *Iranian Intellectuals and the West: The Tormented Triumph of Nativism* (Syracuse University Press, 1996). Ramin Jahanbegloo contends Iranian modernity to have been shaped through the semi-colonisation of the country. See Ramin Jahanbegloo, "Introduction," in Ramin Jahanbegloo (ed.), *Iran: Between Tradition and Modernity* (Toronto: Lexington Books, 2004). Farzin Vahdat contends for the shaping of Iranian modernity through the encounters of Iranian intellectuals with Western modernity in the mid nineteenth century through Russian and British imperialism. He considers the experience of Iranian modernity to have been in terms of a philosophical dilemma informed of the works of Kant and Hegel. See Farzin Vahdat, *God and Juggernaut: Iran's Intellectual Encounter with Modernity* (Syracuse University Press, 2002).

Iranian intellectuals found access from the early nineteenth to the early twentieth centuries.[5] In such scholarship, a concentration on philosophical and cultural notions of rationality, secularism and individualism compels understandings of modernity that situate its origins in the West, and theorises its "arrival" in Iran as a belated phenomenon. In this study, I investigate modernity in local material conditions of everyday life and posit it as part of a simultaneous "global process" that allowed for the "hybridisation of cultures" and refashioning of "national selves."[6]

Considering modernity not as a well-defined period marked by conditions of Western modernity (i.e. industrialisation), but as a futural ethos that hinged upon various and wide-ranging societal transformations that began in nineteenth-century Iran, one comes to discover a close relationship between cinema and Iranian vernacular modernity. In the early twentieth century, Iran was already undergoing societal transformations that can be interpreted within the larger understandings of multiple alternative modernities – the idea that modernity unfolds within specific cultural contexts and that "different starting points for the transition to modernity lead to different outcomes."[7] The establishment of new public spaces, such as hotels, theatres, public squares and reading houses, as well as the paving of roads and the beautification of streets, exposed unprecedented sights, practices and cultural modes in urban centres. During this period of transformation, cinema's novel site of sociability, its "self-transforming" character, its "inherent and ruthless dynamisms,"[8] and its fascination with speed and movement, contributed significantly to the experience of novelty and change in urban centres such as Tehran.

An integral part of the experience of modernity in Tehran, as I demonstrate in the following chapters, was social cosmopolitanism. Following Gerrard Delanty, social cosmopolitanism refers to the social world shaped through cultural modes of mediation, created out of the

---

[5] Hamid Dabashi, for instance, sees modernity as a project (involving the rise of the bourgeoisie, enlightenment, and Industrial Revolution) to which Iranians were exposed through the cinema screen. See Hamid Dabashi, *Close Up: Iranian Cinema, Past, Present, and Future* (London: Verso, 2001), 15.

[6] Mohamad Tavakoli-Targhi, *Refashioning Iran: Orientalism, Occidentalism, and Historiography* (New York: Palgrave Macmillan, 2001), x.

[7] Dilip Parameshwar Goankar, "On Alternative Modernities," in Dilip Parameshwar Goankar (ed.), *Alternative Modernities* (Durham, NC: Duke University Press, 2001), 17.

[8] Orr, *Cinema and Modernity*, 1.

encounters and dialogue of the local with the global in "moments of world openness."[9] An empire at the turn of the century, Iran was home to various ethnic groups such as (Azerbaijani) Turks, Kurds, Lurs, Baluchis and Arabs and different religious communities, such as Muslims, Jews, Zoroastrians and Christians, who lived under the sovereignty of the Persian Empire. Nevertheless, toward the end of the nineteenth century and in the early twentieth century, ever-increasing numbers of war-ridden neighbouring communities chose Iran as their new national home, while a large number of Iranian merchants, political figures, students, journalists and workers also travelled back and forth to the neighbouring regions and beyond. Many members of ethnic, religious and linguistic groups, such as Armenian, Azerbaijani, Georgian and Russian communities, along with Indian, American, French, German and British peoples, congregated in Tehran. The aforementioned groups conceived the growing urban centre as either a safe haven from socio-political pressures that had compelled them to migrate from the empires or newly founded states in which they previously resided, or as a suitable centre for cultural and commercial activities, or alternatively as a fertile locus for the actualisation of colonial and imperial aspirations. The increased assembly and interaction of these communities in Tehran turned the city into a diasporic hub of highly diverse national, ethnic, religious and linguistic communities. I call Tehran "diasporic" to highlight it as a "site for mixed and hybrid identities"; to bring to the foreground the conditions made possible for "mobility and mobilisation," "trade and merchants," "migrants and diasporas" and "travellers and communication,"[10] conditions that allowed for novel encounters and practices. The social and cultural exchanges of diverse groups led to the formation of experiences that, following Stuart Hall, could only be defined "by the recognition of a necessary heterogeneity and diversity; by a conception of 'identity' which lives through, not despite, difference; by *hybridity*."[11] The diasporic communities who resided in Tehran had

[9] Gerrard Delanty, "The Cosmopolitan Imagination: Critical Cosmopolitanism and Social Theory," *British Journal of Sociology* 57(1) (2006): 27.

[10] Michael Geyer and Charles Bright, "World History in a Global Age," *American Historical Review* 100(4) (October 1995): 1040.

[11] Stuart Hall, "Cultural Identity and Diaspora," in Padmini Mongia (ed.), *Contemporary Postcolonial Theory: A Reader* (London: Arnold, 1996), 120 (emphasis in the original).

diverse, urban, middle-class cultural habits which included a vigorous engagement with newspapers, photography, theatre, music gatherings, conferences and charity events – societal conventions that further contributed to the city's cultural assortment at the turn of the century. Such social and cultural heterogeneity, to borrow from Gerrard Delanty, was not reducible to "cultural diversity," but was a "product of transnational movements" of people, cultures and ideas, and was marked by "hybridity."[12]

I choose Tehran as the site of my social and cinematic analysis largely because it was arguably the Bombay of Bollywood or Hindi Cinema. It was the location of many of the sustained film productions that began in the late 1940s, as well as the hub for the publication of film journals, the organisation of film festivals and cinematic activities that shaped the "national" cinema of the country. Furthermore, as mentioned above, it hosted a large number of people from different ethno-religious and cultural groups, and facilitated "geographies of coexistence,"[13] which all together conjured conditions of social cosmopolitanism in the city and beyond.

When considering its connection to early-twentieth-century societal changes in Tehran, cinema proves to be an ideal form to investigate cosmopolitanism. Early cinematograph owners and operators were members of diasporic communities and/or merchants, who by virtue of their trade and travels were informed of the latest technological devices and gadgets outside Iran. The early cinematographic screenings organised by these trendsetters in urban districts facilitated interactions between Tehran's diverse communities. Moreover, the images projected by films provided opportunities to encounter and register difference. Cinema's technology, moreover, allowed for the articulation of local experiences that could speak on a global level. As a cultural "site of tension," a "space of new dynamics, interactive moments, and conflicting principles and orientations,"[14] a site where traumas of

---

[12] Delanty, "The Cosmopolitan Imagination," 16.

[13] Asef Bayat, *Life as Politics: How Ordinary People Change the Middle East* (Stanford University Press, 2010), 187.

[14] In his book, Gerrard Delanty describes cosmopolitanism as a "site of tension" and "a space of new dynamics, interactive moments, and conflicting principles and orientations," but his conception correlates with my arguments for cinema in Iran, and for that reason I used the same wording to theorise cinema as a cosmopolitan space in early-twentieth-century Iran. See Delanty, "The Cosmopolitan Imagination," 15.

and negotiations with modernity could be recorded and staged, early cinema opened new avenues to perceive the world and understand the self. This quality of cinema is indicative of its "reflexive relation" with Iranian cosmopolitan modernity, especially in the context of early-twentieth-century Tehran.[15]

In European and North American contexts where vigorous film industries existed, the year 1915 is considered as the boundary that terminates the period denoted by the term "early" in early cinema. Such periodisations have led to a disregard for cinematic practices outside those geographic borderlines. To account for these shortcomings, scholars have recently acknowledged the uneven development of cinema on a global level and have called for a re-evaluation and expansion of the period.[16] The conditions of filmmaking and film exhibition in cities across Iran where early cinema spaces, presentation practices and distribution networks "constantly comingled past and present, challenging any singular timeline of film's development," beg us to consider early cinematic practices to have surpassed the year 1915.[17] In this book, I consider early cinematic practices to have endured until the late 1930s.[18]

The cosmopolitan cinematic culture that was engendered through the dynamic activities of the early cinematograph operator-merchants came to bear a cosmo-national character upon the first Persian-language films that were produced and screened in Iranian theatres in the 1930s. The emergent cinema of the 1930s was shaped by cosmopolitan filmmakers who entertained nationalist sentiments in their visual offerings. The subsequent "national" cinema that emerged in the late 1940s, after World War II, and continued to the late 1970s was likewise informed by Iran's heterogeneous culture, insofar as it engaged cosmopolitan filmmakers and conversed with international cinematic trends. By probing into the early cinema's cultural practices, cosmo-national film industry of the 1930s and cinematic productions

---

[15] Miriam Hansen, "The Mass Production of the Senses: Classical Cinema as Vernacular Modernism," *Modernism/Modernity* 6, no. 2 (1999), 69.

[16] See, e.g., Kaveh Askari, "Early Cinema in South Asia: The Problem of the Archive: Introduction," *Framework: The Journal of Cinema and Media* 54(2) (2013): 130–135; and Neepa Majumdar, "What is 'Early' Cinema?" *Framework: The Journal of Cinema and Media* 54(2) (2013): 136–139.

[17] Askari, "Early Cinema in South Asia," 133.

[18] Hamid Naficy suggests the year 1941 to be the end of Iranian cinema's artisanal era. See Hamid Naficy, *A Social History of Iranian Cinema*, vol. 1: *The Artisanal Era, 1897–1941* (Durham, NC: Duke University Press, 2011).

that ensued in the decades prior to the 1979 revolution, this book
shows that cinema is an advantageous form to investigate Iranian
cosmopolitanism; on the other hand, cosmopolitanism is a valuable
interpretive category through which one could interrogate Iranian
modernity. Viewed through the prism of cinema, for much of the
twentieth century, Iranian modernity was the sum of contentious
viewpoints that negotiated and competed between local/global, trad-
itional/modern, old/new, ideological/spiritual and national/inter-
national tendencies.

Although commonly and sometimes haphazardly used in academia
and popular narratives, cosmopolitanism escapes easy definition.[19]
The cosmopolitanism of interest to this project cannot be seen in light
of globalisation, especially since, in the context of Iran, cosmopolitanism was a socio-cultural agent in societal transformations before the
processes of globalisation were at play. It is neither associated with
political accounts nor with a Universalist culture as originally set out
by the tradition of Kant in modern cosmopolitan thought. I am interested in a cosmopolitanism that "takes as its point of departure different kinds of modernity and processes of societal transformation" that
do not "postulate a single world culture."[20] Not defined in terms of a
single notion of (European) modernity, this cosmopolitanism rejects
theories of "Westernisation." Upholding "the temporal assumption of
the non-contemporaneity of European and non-European societies,"[21]
Eurocentric accounts associate modernity with a "European narrative
of progress" that overlooks local experiences, "ideas, institutions,
intellectuals, and processes which function as a bridge between the
local and global, tradition and change."[22] On the other hand, when
conceived as "an opening to the world," a process in which the
universal and the particular, the similar and dissimilar, the global

---

[19] Zlatko Skrbiš and Ian Woodward, *Cosmopolitanism: Uses of the Idea* (London: Sage Publications, 2013), 2.

[20] Delanty, "The Cosmopolitan Imagination," 27.

[21] Tavakoli-Targhi, *Refashioning Iran*, ix–x.

[22] In his book, Ali Mirsepassi has a comprehensive discussion on Orientalist intellectuals and historians of the Middle East, particularly Iran, who uphold the grand narrative of European progress and modernity when theorising modernity (or rather modernisation) in societies such as Iran, and therefore reproduce the binaries of East/West and traditional/modern. See Ali Mirsepassi, *Intellectual Discourse and the Politics of Modernization: Negotiating Modernity in Iran* (Cambridge University Press, 2000), 54.

and the local are to be conceived as interrelated and reciprocally interpenetrating principles, cosmopolitanism demands "the opening up of normative questions."[23] Considering it not as an "orientation" that focuses on a specific social form, but as an imagination that can take the shape of "many different forms," cosmopolitanism provides an avenue to analyze the interstitial spaces and practices that defined the contestatory and competing experiences of modernity in Iran.[24]

An inquiry into conditions of cosmopolitanism underpinned by cinematic experiences also offers a stimulating foray into the shaping of nationalism and national imagination in Iran. No matter how "educationally, genetically, economically, juridicially, socially, militarily, cartographically, or otherwise imposed or inculcated" nationalism and national identity are, David Yaghoubian reminds us, it is the people from different classes, races, ethnicities, religious and linguistic backgrounds who are "the producers, bearers, and interpreters" of these concepts.[25] As the following chapters demonstrate, the experience of compound identities, their quotidian cultural practices and their ways of life become indispensable to the configuration of nationalism, especially in early-twentieth-century cosmopolitan Tehran. As cultural products, Iranian filmic offerings drew on global tropes, figures, icons, visual grammar and motifs in the creation of national, and at times, nationalist, films. In other words, Iran's national cinema was arguably a cosmopolitan construct; by facilitating encounters with difference and interactions with global cinematic cultures, it opened up new outlooks on the world and new opportunities for understanding national selves. Cosmopolitanism, I demonstrate throughout this book, was arguably a style of national imagination.

Skrbiš and Woodward attribute four dimensions to a study of cosmopolitanism.[26] Cultural dimension indicates an epistemological disposition of openness to the world around us. The political dimension of cosmopolitanism suggests it to be a political commitment "which encourages us to appreciate and recognise difference, embed our politics in universal principles and commit ourselves to the

---

[23] Gerard Delanty, *The Cosmopolitan Imagination: The Renewal of Critical Social Theory* (Cambridge University Press, 2009), 14.
[24] *Ibid.*
[25] David Yaghoubian, *Ethnicity, Identity, and the Development of Nationalism in Iran* (Syracuse University Press, 2014), xxv.
[26] Skrbiš and Woodward, *Cosmopolitanism*, 2.

dethronement of one's unique cultural identity"; this dimension
extends to political commitments that aim beyond the local and change
into institutionally cosmopolitan principles, ambitions of supra-
national state-building, such as regimes of global governance and
legal-institutional frameworks.[27] The ethical dimension of cosmopolitanism refers to an inclusive ethical core that highlights "worldliness,
hospitality and communitarianism."[28] The methodological dimension
of cosmopolitanism points to its analytical framework, which does not
necessarily reject the nation-state's importance, but rather embraces "a
post-national and transnational perspective"; in other words, such a
cosmopolitan social analysis opens up to "the relational processes
which bind local and global, universal and particular, familiar and
other."[29] Skrbiš and Woodward believe that, in practice, the four
dimensions are closely intertwined, interdependent and largely insepar-
able. My analysis of the Iranian cosmopolitan society of the early
twentieth century will draw from the diverse dimensions of the processes of cosmopolitanism without isolating them, as they cannot be
limited to distinguished categories.[30]

In the context of the Middle East, Sami Zubaida postulates the
conditions of social cosmopolitanism to entail "the weakening of
communal boundaries, the creation of institutions, milieus and means
of communication outside communal and religious authority, in which
individuals from diverse backgrounds and cultures can participate."[31]
Arab and Muslim empires brought together different peoples and
cultures, which allowed for the creation of cultural, literary and commercial diversity, which were confined to the higher echelons of imperial centres.[32] Starting in the nineteenth century, the attempt of the
Ottoman Empire at what Zubaida considers to be "catching up" with
European technico-military and economic superiority, compelled the
facilitation of European education and training, which then led to the
formation of cosmopolitan elites, "who are deracinated from confident
traditional perspectives on the world, yet unhappy with dominant

---

[27] *Ibid.*   [28] *Ibid.*, 3.   [29] *Ibid.*
[30] It is undeniably challenging to distinguish where one dimension begins and
another ends.
[31] Sami Zubaida, "Cosmopolitanism and the Middle East," in Roel Meijer (ed.),
Cosmopolitanism, Identity, and Authenticity in the Middle East (Richmond:
Curzon Press, 1999), 19.
[32] *Ibid.*, 21.

European perspectives," intellectuals who try "to invent their own world, but in the middle of socio-political upheavals in which they actively participate."[33]

In a critique of current historiographies of Middle Eastern cosmopolitanism, Will Hanley takes issue with the elitist and nostalgic designations attributed to the concept, and the fact that it privileges labels over content.[34] Challenging Zubaida's emphasis on qualifications of form, such as mobility, polyglossia and class, in lieu of content, in certifying cosmopolitanism Hanley argues that Zubaida's cosmopolitanism is a "category of exception" rather than "conventional living"; in Zubaida's formulation cosmopolitan milieus are created *outside* religious and communal environments where everyday people of diverse backgrounds usually interact.[35] In other words, cosmopolitanism becomes an exclusive category, as a "plebian majority" is necessary in order for cosmopolitan elites to exist.[36] Asef Bayat, similar to Hanley, points out that cosmopolitanism, as far it concerns a form of lifestyle, has been argued to be the prerogative of the elites.[37] What is ignored, then, he contends, is the cosmopolitanism of the subaltern, "the ordinary members of different religious communities – Muslims, Jews, Christians, Shi'is, or Sunnis," who by virtue of engaging in "intense intercommunal exchange and shared lives in neighborhoods or at work" engaged in everyday cosmopolitanism.[38] "Proximity and interaction" between diverse groups in urban centres, Bayat believes, could provide prospects for diverse groups to "experience trust between them and coexistence in daily life."[39]

Avoiding an elite-centric historical narrative, Chapter 1 of this book, "Cinematic Imaginaries and Cosmopolitanism in the Early Twentieth Century," attends to the ways in which ordinary residents of different ethnic, linguistic, religious and ideological persuasions mingled, interacted and lived together, shaping Tehran's social cosmopolitanism at

---

[33] *Ibid.*, 22.
[34] Will Hanley, "Grieving Cosmopolitanism in Middle East Studies," *History Compass* 6(5) (2008): 1348.
[35] *Ibid.*, 1350.   [36] *Ibid.*
[37] Asef Bayat, *Life as Politics: How Ordinary People Change the Middle East* (Amsterdam University Press, 2010), 186.
[38] *Ibid.*, 187.
[39] *Ibid.*, 188. Here, Bayat is also quick to remind us that in urban conditions, such interactions facilitated by modern urbanity do not necessarily fashion cosmopolitan coexistence, but could also prompt "communal identities."

the "level of the everyday."[40] The congregation of Tehran's diverse communities necessitated the formation of new urban spaces for entertainment, assembly and education, which further promoted new practices, novel spectacles and customs. These conditions were predominant in urban centres and prevalent in places and routes exposed to the urban public in Tehran. Multidimensional communication in urban sites of sociability points to cosmopolitanism as part of a spatial production,[41] which also marked conditions of Iranian modernity in that it had facilitated circumstances for change through the expansion and exchange of imaginations. One can infer that the encounter, socialisation and mingling of such a smorgasbord of communities in these newly established sites of sociability further facilitated conditions of heterogeneity and engendered cosmopolitan identities. To avoid the fault of painting social cosmopolitanism as essentially "European" or as "the experience of a European elite over the whole of the city's social history,"[42] in this chapter, I primarily focus on the social and cultural activities of non-West agents, ordinary residents and hybrid identities.

While it would be short-sighted to conceive of cosmopolitanism only as an analytical category without grounding it in lived reality or practices, it would be simplistic to consider an adoption or acceptance of a – perhaps previously unfamiliar – practice as a marker of cosmopolitanism. What seems to constrain some scholars' cases for a rethinking of cosmopolitanism in the Middle East is a presumption that the formation of hybrid identities/societies entails full openness and total

---

[40] *Ibid.*, 187.

[41] I borrow the term "spatial production" from André Jansson, who, drawing on Ulrich Beck and Lefebvre, employs a spatial approach in studying communication, and posits communication as a multidimensional process of spatial production (i.e. produced within spaces of interaction). See André Jansson, "Beyond 'Other Spaces': Media Studies and the Cosmopolitan Vision," *The Communication Review* 12(4) (2009): 305–312.

[42] Hanley, "Grieving Cosmopolitanism," 1353. Hanley's critique becomes problematic in that he considers cosmopolitanism as "European," as a concept, practice and identity constructed through interactions with the West. How, then, is one to conceive of practices in Iran that were informed by interactions with the non-West or ethnic groups from neighbouring regions, namely, Georgians, Azerbaijanis, Armenians, Russians and Indians? What also limits Hanley's critique of the notion of cosmopolitanism, is his failure to explicate "content" as a qualification for cosmopolitanism: what would *he* include as cosmopolitan content?

espousal of difference or cosmopolitan criteria.[43] Skrbiš and Woodward also argue that encounters with difference, "underpinned by an
attitude of openness within spaces of cultural flows," marked by a
"willingness to *change*"[44] or openness to "being changed," character-
ises cosmopolitan identity. In early-twentieth-century Iran, however,
such encounters did not necessarily prompt a "willingness to
change";[45] in fact, cosmopolitan identities were marked by contestations, negotiations, refutations and, at times, suppression of local and/
or global customs, social norms and ideologies.

This chapter demonstrates that the employment of early cinematographic devices by worldly merchants, many of whom were of diverse
religious and ethno-linguistic backgrounds, engendered the possibility
for the creation of a "cosmopolitan cinematic culture." During this
period, heterotopic cinema screens created a space "located outside or
beyond the conventional moral orders of society"[46] through the portrayal of different cities, lifestyles, peoples and moral orders in silent
international films. Film screenings, in the absence of Iranian film
productions up until the 1930s, therefore significantly added to the
modern experience in Tehran. Jansson posits heterotopia to be a
mental category that explains how individuals and groups "gain moral
and cultural confirmation in relation to the (re)articulation of myths
and images."[47] In light of that, one can argue cinematic heterotopia to
be the imagination articulated in the space of cinema, as "spaces that
obey their own rules, but that through their very otherness reproduce
the dominant sense of 'normality.'"[48] In simpler terms, spaces that
would normally be considered as unfamiliar, that is, "other spaces,"
arguably became increasingly familiar and entangled with everyday
activities in urban Tehran, as they were shown on cinema screens
through international silent actualités, newsreels and short films.
Cinema, as an important facilitator of cosmopolitanism, then, became
an "increasingly *contradictory spatial order.*"[49]

While scholars of modern Iran are now increasingly exploring the
role of intellectuals and political activists from ethno-linguistic and
religious minorities in the formation of nationalist sentiments in the

---

[43] See, e.g., Hanley, "Grieving Cosmopolitanism."
[44] Emphasis in the original.
[45] Skrbiš and Woodward, *Cosmopolitanism*, 10–11.
[46] Jansson, "Beyond 'Other Spaces,'" 305.   [47] *Ibid.*, 306.   [48] *Ibid.*, 305.
[49] *Ibid.*, 306 (emphasis in the original).

twentieth century, very few have attended to the cultural activities of the non-elites in the figuration of national identity. Chapter 1 demonstrates that cinema and its practitioners provided a horizon of expectation for what the future of Iran should hold. Images of national progress and scientific advancement projected in international films, as well as scenes of devastation from war-torn cities, envisaged imaginations for a progressive, sovereign and moral Iran. Cinema trendsetters employed film screenings not only to create a source of revenue, but to inspire patriotic sentiments. Not everyone agreed on how such nationalist aspirations should be actualised. While one may have had access to difference as a spectator in cinema or as a bystander on the street, one may have rejected and challenged that which lied beyond. But would it be wrong to perceive of those nationalists who made such conscious decisions based on social class, religion, education, gender and other criteria as individuals without cosmopolitan imaginations? Does not one by virtue of encounter with difference become cognizant of difference?[50]

Far from engendering "a utopian, borderless and free-floating world,"[51] by the early twentieth century, the encounters and exchanges of multiple peoples in Tehran's neighbourhoods, and the heterotopic spatial and illusory conditions that cinema engendered, stimulated a national imagination that was riddled with multiple and competing ideas. Cosmopolitanism in the early twentieth century, therefore, did not necessarily act in opposition to nationalism. As Chapter 1 and subsequent chapters demonstrate, cosmopolitanism in fact worked alongside nationalism, "sometimes as complementary and sometimes as competitor."[52]

[50] Perhaps it would be worthy to ask: is cosmopolitanism a conscious decision? Is it a self-assigned title by historical actors or one assigned retrospectively? Hanley questions if Middle Eastern cosmopolitanism is "a mental or a material condition." This book is an attempt to think through some of these questions. The cosmopolitan attitudes and imaginations that are of interest to this project are treated as mental conditions that were informed by the cosmopolitan material conditions already embedded in the changing fabric of Tehran since the nineteenth century – a form of mental cosmopolitanism predicated on material social cosmopolitanism associated with everyday life. See Hanley, "Grieving Cosmopolitanism," 1349.

[51] Skrbiš and Woodward, *Cosmopolitanism*, 7.

[52] *Ibid.* The following passage by Skrbiš and Woodward would perhaps be of interest to the issue at hand. "With the term 'being cosmopolitan', we can refer to a set of outlooks and practices, a dispositional repertoire, increasingly

Chapter 2, "Cinematic Education, Cinematic Sovereignty: The Creation of a Cosmonational Cinema," tackles the ways in which the newly established Pahlavi state (1925–1979), having investigated the importance of cinema in terms of national propaganda and commercial revenue, came to appropriate it as an institution and an extension of the government's technology of power to discipline the society. The reign of the first Pahlavi King, Reza Shah (1925–1941), has been generally known as a time of vigorous nation- and state-building – an era in which a discourse of ideological nationalism overdetermines all socio-political and cultural events. During this time, cinema was also co-opted for statist nationalist projects. In attempts to centralise authority, the government codified "public spaces" in the late 1920s, and regulated cinematic spaces, film screening and filmmaking in the 1930s. In other words, the government attempted to take over decentralised cinematic activities that were previously taken up by cosmopolitan cinematograph owners/operators and that had contributed to the formation of nationalist sentiments. This took place while the elite and nationalists highlighted the importance of cinematic education and the central role of visual pedagogy in national "progress" and "advancement," similar to what was happening in international countries.

Amid the blend of discourses surrounding patriotism, economic sovereignty, and national advancement in the 1920s and 1930s, social critics, journalists and cinema enthusiasts also expressed their aspirations for *cinematic sovereignty*; such objectives became even stronger with the making of the first Persian-language silent films in the late 1920s and early 1930s. This emergent cinema first started in Bandar Pahlavi in 1928, then spread to Tehran in 1930, and encompassed the production of a series of silent and talking films with Persian-language intertitles and dialogues that were based on Iranian everyday lives, national figures and Indo-Persian fables. The desire for cinematic

available – yet not guaranteed – to individuals for the purposes of dealing with cultural diversity, hybridity and otherness. We see these outlooks as flexible, and sometimes contradictory. They are discursive, practical resources available to social actors to deal with emergent, everyday global agendas and issues, related to things like cultural diversity, the global and otherness. Yet, we do not see such cosmopolitan values expressed fully, or at all times, and on all issues" (Skrbiš and Woodward, *Cosmopolitanism*, 27). We should also bear in mind that aside from working alongside or against nationalism, cosmopolitanism may also give rise to what Bayat calls "communal identities." See Bayat, *Life as Politics*, 188.

sovereignty could be conveyed through film reviews, in which film critics increasingly expressed enthusiasm about and/or concerns with the "Iranianness" of the films, most importantly manifested in the usage of the language. The Persian language became a fundamental signifier of the nationality of these films, in addition to the costumes, make-up, mise-en-scène and accents used in the motion pictures. The cosmopolitan directors, actors, producers, cinematographers, cinema owners and operators of this movement were involved in a cinematic praxis that increasingly aspired to be "national,"[53] thereby crafting a cosmo-national construct.

I borrow the term "cosmo-national" from Michel Laguerre's "cosmo-national" theory of ethnic neighbourhoods. The local immigrant neighbourhood, according to Laguerre, not a recent phenomenon, is a cosmo-national social formation.[54] This social construct extends beyond the jurisdictional boundaries of the state and includes "the homeland nation and each of its diasporic sites," whereas the diaspora engages with homeland and other diasporic sites (and vice versa).[55] Although Laguerre uses the concept of cosmo-national to describe immigrant neighbourhoods, his critique of alternative concepts used for the enclave is worthy of attention in this historical inquiry. The conceptualisation of the neighbourhood as a "foreign" colony, according to him, does not consider the "presumed reality of the relations of the enclave with the sending country," so much so that the enclave is global by the default that it is not local.[56] On the other hand, framing the global neighbourhood in terms of transnationalism – transnational lives and practices – highlights the relations of the immigrant enclave with the country of origin; this approach is problematic in that it underscores diaspora-homeland relations and downplays diaspora-diaspora relations of the immigrant community, therefore overlooking the multidimensional network of relations that concern the community.[57] In this book, I have attempted to stay away from referring to the emergent cinema of the 1930s as a transnational construct for the reason that transnational cinema, following Laguerre's critique, would accentuate the cinematic relations of the

[53] This is in spite of the fact that a majority of the films of this period were filmed and produced in India.
[54] Michel S. Laguerre, "A Cosmonational Theory of Global Neighborhoods," *Amerasia Journal* 36(3) (2010): xv–xxxiii.
[55] *Ibid.*, xx.   [56] *Ibid.*, xvi–xvii.   [57] *Ibid.*, xvii.

host land to the homeland, but not the cinematic relations of different diasporas in Iran, or the impact of the emergent cinema on the local and the region at large. Moreover, transnationalism is commonly used to refer to "a series of assumptions about the networked and globalised realities that are those of a contemporary situation."[58] Despite the significance of the term in the field of film studies, the broad referential scope of the term transnationalism, as Hjort discusses, has allowed it to encompass processes that are more interesting for their differences than their similarities, thus lending itself to hold a rather homogenising role.[59]

My use of the notion of "cosmo-national" cinema (as a hyphenated construct) is informed by Laguerre's conceptualisation, in that it underlines the multilateral interactions of homeland and diaspora sites; the way I use the term is, nevertheless, different in that it also highlights the emergence of a cinema that increasingly spoke to the social thinkers' aspirations for cinematic sovereignty and attended to national everyday lives, narratives and figures, while relying on the participation of diasporic communities in Iran and cosmopolitan Iranians in the diaspora for its production, distribution and reception. The cosmo-national conception of the emergent cinema of the 1930s refutes the shortcomings of theories of national cinema that do not compensate for the participation of diasporic communities and cosmopolitan identities that shaped this cultural form. Karl Deutsch argues that nations and nation-states are joined together by socially communicative structures that create social closure and a sense of belonging.[60] Such communicative integration of nations would then lead to the exclusion of "foreigners." In these societies, Ernest Gellner contends, cultural boundaries become delineated by national cultures, in turn defined by a central education system.[61] Following Philip Schlesinger, these theories of the nation and nationalism, then, are less concerned with internal differentiation, diversity and conflicts and more with the

---

[58] Mette Hjort, "On the Plurality of Cinematic Transnationalism," in Nataša Ďurovičová and Kathleen Newman (eds), *World Cinemas, Transnational Perspectives* (New York: Routledge, 2010), 30.
[59] *Ibid.*
[60] Karl Wolfgang Deutsch, *Nationalism and Social Communication: An Inquiry into the Foundations of Nationality* (Cambridge, MA: MIT Press, 1966).
[61] Ernest Gellner, *Nations and Nationalism* (Oxford: Blackwell, 1983).

social and cultural forces that bound a nation (or people as a nation).[62] In his seminal book, *Imagined Communities: Reflections on the Origins and Spread of Nationalism*, Benedict Anderson also argues that cultural mediated communication engenders imagined communities such as the nation.[63] "National" cinema, in this light, is a singular construct that embodies the cinematographic productions of a country (i.e. domestic productions), defined against the dominant Hollywood cinema.

The more recent theorisations of national cinema underline diverse representations of the nation, promote more heterogeneous conceptions of national cinema and downplay the role of state in national cinema.[64] In this chapter, I have employed the hyphenated concept of "cosmo-national" cinema as an alternative to conceptualisations that highlight processes of homogenisation of a nation or domesticity of productions. Cosmo-national cinema was national to the extent that it displayed nationalist sentiments, and that Iranian critics identified with it, especially through the category of Persian language. The films of this cinema were also cosmopolitan to the extent that they not only included the participation of cosmopolitan and international figures in their making, but many of them were financially produced by institutions outside the country. Although many of the era's films were produced outside Iran, I have refrained from using the concept of diasporic or "accented" cinema, since film productions of this era were not necessarily concerned with topics pertaining to nostalgia (for homeland), nurturing of a collective memory, territoriality or displacement.[65] The Iranian elite were increasingly motivated to distribute this linguistically sovereign cinema on an international level in order to

---

[62] Philip Schlesinger, "The Sociological Scope of 'National Cinema,'" in Mette Hjort and Scott Machenzie (eds), *Cinema and Nation* (London: Routledge, 2000), 19.

[63] Benedict Anderson, *Imagined Communities: Reflections on the Origin and Spread of Nationalism* (London: Verso, 1983).

[64] For information on British national cinema as a heterogeneous construct, see John Hill, "The Issue of National Cinema and British Film Production," in Duncan J. Petrie (ed.), *New Questions of British Cinema* (London: British Film Institute, 1992). For works that further problematise the conventional usages of the notion of "national cinema," see Andrew Higson, "The Limiting Imagination of National Cinema," in Mette Hjort and Scott Machenzie (eds), *Cinema and Nation* (London: Routledge, 2000), 57–68.

[65] Hamid Naficy theorises "accented cinema" as a diasporic cinema concerned with displacement, memory and nostalgia for a homeland. See Hamid Naficy,

showcase the country as a "modernising" country (with a "glorious ancient past"), one that was now industrially on a par with film-producing international communities. As I demonstrate in this chapter, the nationalists and social thinkers aspired to stage Iran on the silver screen in the 1930s, especially in reaction to the productions of certain international communities who had already taken part in displaying biased and stereotypical representations of Iran on the silver screen.

Chapter 3, "Industrial Professionalisation: The Emergence of a 'National' Commercial Cinema," briefly explores the decade-long hiatus in Persian-language feature-film production from the late 1930s to the late 1940s. During this period, the Allied forces competed in distributing educational and propagandist films in Iran through various cultural channels. Much of this decade was concomitant with the bolstering of an image culture through the circulation and recycling of images of Hollywood, Egyptian and Indian stars, which arguably shaped an esthetic standard for future Iranian cinema stars. In spite of the absence of feature-length-fiction film production, this period witnessed the professionalisation of the industry, which entailed a rapid growth of cinema establishments, stage artists joining dubbing studios and cinema productions and a significant increase in the number of film journals and magazines, as well as film critics who, now having access to more modes of communication, functioned to *direct* the course of cinema industry and culture in Iran. Responding to post–World War II anxieties, Iranian film journals and the popular press increasingly circulated Persian serial fictions and commentaries that featured repeated tropes and social stereotypes – these narratives later re-emerged and were reiterated in the plotline of many future commercial film productions. While this chapter briefly examines some of these tropes, an in-depth analysis of the popular literature in the so-called "yellow press" is required to provide a fresh insight into the moulding of Iran's pre-revolutionary mainstream film industry – a topic that is out of the present project's scope. During this decade-long period, diasporic Iranians engaged in dubbing foreign films into the Persian language, a practice that worked to attract audiences and engendered more revenue for those involved in the industry. The professional film critics, stage actors, technicians and documentary filmmakers of this

An Accented Cinema: Exilic and Diasporic Filmmaking (Princeton University Press, 2001).

period acted as cultural trendsetters who envisioned a horizon of expectation for Iran's future film industry. Their vigorous cultural activities paved the way for the emergence of a commercial cinema in the late 1940s that was endorsed by diverse Iranians in its production and distribution – an enterprise that solidified into a fully-fledged industry in the 1950s.

Chapter 4, "'Film-Farsi': Everyday Constituencies of a Cosmopolitan Commercial Cinema," examines some of the commercial films of this sustained national industry from the late 1940s to the 1970s that were born out of the cultural dynamism of the 1940s. While it drew on the prevalent image culture that preceded it, as well as contemporary international popular films to which it had been exposed, the productions of this cinema enterprise came to be prevalently characterised as "imitative," "futile," "degenerative" and "cheap." Engaging in cinematic cosmopolitanism – as a cinematic praxis – the filmmakers of this mainstream industry, who were cognizant of and in conversation with the narratives and visual motifs of Hollywood, Arab and Indian commercial cinematic productions, shaped a cinema that provided an "aesthetic horizon" for the time's social changes, albeit in entertaining cinematic forms.[66] While being informed of Iranian "moral" values in everyday-life settings, as this chapter shows, commercial films were vernacular offerings that drew on international films' content, mise-en-scène, titles, techniques and characters in forms that maximised profits. These commercial films were significant in registering, contemplating and negotiating the politics of modernisation in a rapidly changing society, in hybrid genres that frequently entailed a blend of slapstick comedy, melodrama, action and musical genres. Exhibiting the interplays and cross-breeding of lowbrow/highbrow culture, modern/traditional, urban/rural and the everyday social issues, the "traumatic effects of modernity" were "reflected, rejected or disavowed, transmutated or negotiated" in these visual offerings.[67] The commercialisation of artistic offerings and the entertaining quality of the films, however, were not to the liking of the intellectual film critics, who advocated artistic visual offerings. In a stance against commercially cosmopolitan film productions, these socially and politically conscious critics encouraged a kind of filmmaking that was committed to social realism. In other words, while cosmopolitan commercial filmmakers created vernacular films for the domestic

---

[66] Hansen, "The Mass Production of the Senses."   [67] *Ibid.*, 69.

audience that gave esthetic expression to social changes in the realm of everyday social experience, cosmopolitan film critics pursued a national cinema that aimed to resituate Iran on the global map.

Having made connections between the Iranian and international popular cinemas (i.e. Egyptian and Bollywood), these film critics deemed the local industry to have only incorporated the "Persian language" as the sole signifier of this cinema's Iranianness; hence, they employed the term "Film-Farsi" (Persian-Film) in a derogative manner to refer to the film industry as a whole. This chapter elaborates on the debates surrounding "Film-Farsi" and the critics' narratives that aimed to *direct* what Iranian cinema "ought to be." Surveying films from the 1950s to the 1970s, I trace and unearth subtle shifts in narratives – even though the themes and concerns of the films overlapped for the most part. While in the 1950s, much emphasis was placed on films that attended to the migration of people from rural areas (moralist and "pure" regions) into the cities (dystopic centres), with the overpopulation of cities the social problems of urban areas were accented in films of the 1960s and 1970s. Moreover, as Iran gained more (economic) prestige among the international community and became a tourist destination from the late 1960s onward, the films of the era increasingly featured international figures in film plots. In order to highlight the local and global connections, I consider popular films as vernacular-cosmopolitan constructs that spoke to popular taste, but that were strongly ostracised by the socially committed film critics.

The aspirations of cosmopolitan cineastes and film critics (in the 1950s and 1960s) for an Iranian cinema that was on a par with global trends of the time, namely, Italian neorealism, French New Wave and the Third Cinema of the 1960s and 1970s (or, in other words, art-house and/or intellectual cinematic productions that lined up with socio-political conditions of the era), were concomitant with cinematic activities of a group of politically minded young Iranian directors. Starting in the late 1950s, as Chapter 5, "Cinematic Revolution: Cosmopolitan Alter-Cinema of Pre-Revolutionary Iran," demonstrates, a number of internationally educated and cosmopolitan young directors attempted to stage Iranian everyday lives on cinema screens, albeit in social realist, philosophically sophisticated, symbolic, metaphorical and intellectual forms that resonated with international critics and audiences. Employing modes of representation and production that were alternative to the "Film-Farsi" industry, the young directors of this era crafted,

what I call, an alter(native)-cinema. Many scholars have used the term
"New Wave Cinema" to refer to this cinematic trend. Paying close
attention to how historical actors identified this movement, I have
adopted the term "alternative cinema" to highlight this trend's formation in variance to what was perceived as the "Film-Farsi" industry.
Incorporating the critics' and the elite's calls for a cinematic revolution
(in form and content) to break away from the "Film-Farsi" trend, as
I argue in this chapter, the young directors embarked upon making
cosmopolitan alternative films and screening them at international film
festivals. A major concern for many films of this time related to the
realist capturing of lifestyles, neighbourhoods, customs and traditions
that filmmakers felt were vanishing rapidly due to modernisation and
urbanisation. Despite their differences, especially in cinematic form,
many alternative films engaged the actors, popular tropes and narratives
for which the popular cinema was shunned. A focus on the temporality
of cinema, autonomous from Iran's political temporality, reveals that a
revolution of expectations, a *cinematic revolution*, presaged the political
revolution of 1979. Toward the 1970s, as more revolutionary fervour
was brewing among the public, alternative films incorporated a more
revolutionary tempo in content – so much so that revolutions were
actually projected on cinema screens before the 1978–1979 uprising.

The book before you does not attempt to provide another history of
Iranian cinema – a task that is impossible given the length and scope of
the project. Instead, this book will provide snippets and examples from
the history of cinema in Iran that explore and unfold cultural debates
in relation to larger national discourses and attest to the cosmopolitan
character of Iranian cinema. In this project, I explore the sustained
refiguration of cinematic cosmopolitan outlooks throughout the pre-
revolutionary era, a cinematic culture punctuated with various forms.
Although the book at hand is not an institutional history of cinema,
I demonstrate the ways in which the institutionalisation of cinema
played a role in how cosmopolitans envisaged Iran's sovereign cinema
as being on a par with those in Europe and the West. While this work is
not a solely social history of cinema, I show how the cosmopolitan
composition of the society and hybrid identities of cinema trendsetters
played a part in the solidification and transformation of cinema in Iran.
Nor is this book an exclusive history of production or reception;
however, it does provide examples as to how a close examination of
film production and reception through the prism of cosmopolitanism

provides a window onto the heterogeneous elements involved in the creation of films and the contestatory reception of such visual offerings. In other words, what makes the historiographical framework of this book unique is its function as an opening into the social, institutional and political histories and national debates through the historiographical category of cinematic cosmopolitanism.

Upholding Miriam Hansen's arguments for cinema's "reflexive relation with modernity," I show that cinema not only represented a "specifically modern type of public sphere," but that it also provided a "discursive form" that allowed for the experience of the mass society to be articulated and recognised.[68] Highlighting a largely neglected heterogeneous society and culture, the following chapters explore the ways in which cosmopolitanism was rendered through cinematic imaginaries (shaped through the technology and the space), and the ways in which the "self-transforming" nature of cinema shaped the contours of cosmopolitanism in relation to modernity, nationalism and revolutions from 1900 to 1979. *Iranian Cosmopolitanism* will further contribute to the historiography of cosmopolitanism in the modern Middle East. Focusing on cinematic activities in Tehran, this book works to decentre Bombay and Cairo as the forefronts of "Oriental" cinematic modernities in West and South Asia; it will thus provide different sets of social and cultural networks to rethink the "Middle East" and the centres and peripheries of modernities in the twentieth century.

---

[68] Here, Hansen specifically defines the public as a "social horizon of experience." See Hansen, "The Mass Production of the Senses," 69.

1 | Cinematic Imaginaries and Cosmopolitanism in the Early Twentieth Century

With the emergence of new communication technologies, social spaces, novel practices, domestic conflicts, revolution and international wars in the first two decades of the twentieth century, the space of experience in Iran was constantly transforming.[1] During this "new time," cinema propelled a horizon of expectation, and in fact, a wide range of possibilities and futures for cinema audiences. Through cinema, actions in the present were informed by the past, and motivated by future expectations. As documents from the first two and a half decades of the twentieth century reveal, Iranian movie theatres predominantly featured international motion pictures in their programs, as no Persian-language short or feature film had yet been produced. Keeping in mind the "reflexive" quality of cinema that provided a cultural horizon in which the traumatic effects of modernity and modernisation were registered and articulated, one could extrapolate that the "aesthetic and sensorial" dimensions of cinema, processed through the act of spectatorship, inspired attitudes for the articulation and negotiation of national imaginations.[2] The international moving pictures screened in Iran evoked a futural prospect of what Iran could and ought to be – a temporalisation of historical time on screen and in cinema space that characterised modernity in the early twentieth century. Much of the literature on early cinema in Iran has attended, in a rather dismissive tone, to the inundation of Iranian cinemas with international films, cinematic colonisation and henceforth the non-existence of an Iranian cinema industry; very little has been expressed in terms of the cinema culture that such cinematic events engraved in the Iranian imaginaries and cinematic visions. Through a genealogical investigation of cinematic activities during that era, this chapter argues for the

---

[1] It should be noted that the early years of cinema in Iran coincided with the onset of the Constitutional Revolution (1906–1911) and thus its history was much informed by the day-to-day goings-on of the conflicts.

[2] Miriam Bratu Hansen, "The Mass Production of the Senses: Classical Cinema as Vernacular Modernism," *Modernism/Modernity* 6(2) (1999): 69, 70.

shaping of a cinema culture that, relating to conditions of Iranian modernity, functioned to embody the global cosmos in its vernacular morphogenesis – a trait that came to bear upon Iranian cinema in various forms in the following decades.

To recover a cinema history that has been buried under the temporality of politics in Iran, this chapter will first explore the socio-cultural heterogeneity that marked the experience of Iranian modernity in the early twentieth century. Highlighting ethnic, religious, ideological, political and cultural diversity in Tehran, the following pages argue for the existence of a cosmopolitan urban society at the turn of the century. The inauguration of cinematographic screenings and the gradual inception of a cinematic culture in the first decades of the twentieth century were much indebted to the diasporic groups and/or cosmopolitan merchants and intellectuals residing in Iran. Prompting new spaces for the socialisation of diverse residents, as well as projecting heterotopic images – of other lifestyles, peoples, cultures, landscapes, wars and practices – cinema further facilitated the creation of cosmopolitan imaginaries. With the growing popularity of cinematographic screenings and their accompanying leisure activities, cinemas became concentrated in certain areas of the city, thus further prompting the urbanisation of Tehran and the city's compartmentalisation.

As this chapter will demonstrate, cinema's newly found position elicited various reactions from the diverse residents of Iran. Amid the brewing of nationalist sentiments, the cosmopolitan intellectuals and the elite seem not only to have accepted cinema as a medium that projected "moral" social norms, but to have adopted it as an effective tool in the education of the public (especially students) and in the service of the nation. Therefore, film screenings were included in school and conference programs, and the masses were encouraged to attend "moral" and "scientific" film screenings. Inspired by the technology, some cosmopolitan film enthusiasts engaged in creating the first newsreels and documentaries that depicted the Iranian empire and local practices of the people in attempts to imagine and stage Iran as contemporaneous with its global counterparts. As this chapter will show, merchants, cinema patrons and social critics associated films with moral edification and national progress, and provoked national consciousness among the public in the first two decades of the twentieth century.

* * *

In the literature on early cinema, some scholars argue for a rethinking of cinema's "emergence within the sensory environment of urban modernity"; much of this scholarship also draws a connection between cinema and "late nineteenth-century technologies of space and time," as well as the "adjacent elements in the new visual culture of advanced capitalism."[3] Such Eurocentric theories are lacking, nevertheless, in that they are based on early Western cinema and its relation to "Western" modernities, industrialisation and modes of capitalism; they thus neglect the analysis of such relationships in societies with alternative histories and modernities. The literature on the history of Iranian cinema, too, is wanting in that it has mainly dealt with the fascination of the Qajar court, especially Muzaffar al-Din Shah (r. 1896–1907), with the cinematograph. The dearth of documents and scholarship on Iranian film productions (and the absence of Persian-language narrative films) in the first two and a half decades of the twentieth century has compelled scholars to overlook the highly dynamic cinematic activities of this era and their contribution to Iran's experience of modernity;[4] even when attended to, these activities have been discussed in terms of their political implications, especially with regard to the role that cinema sponsorship by foreign forces had in disseminating propaganda in the country.[5] On the other hand, some scholars of Iranian cinema have considered it as a royal private enterprise, inaccessible to the public,[6] thus neglecting the role of merchants and tradespeople in the promotion of cinema culture. Such literature has, for the most part, disregarded the significance of cinema in the shaping of Iranian imaginations in such a historically eventful era.

In this chapter, I intend only to scratch the surface and recover a brief history of early cinema in Iran through primary sources such as

---

[3] Ben Singer, *Melodrama and Modernity: Early Sensational Cinema and Its Contexts* (New York: Columbia University Press, 2001), 102.

[4] See, e.g., Hamid Dabashi, *Close Up: Iranian Cinema, Past, Present, and Future* (London: Verso, 2001), 12–18; and Hamid Reza Sadr, *Iranian Cinema: A Political History* (London: I. B. Tauris & Co., 2006).

[5] See, Dabashi, *Close Up*, 17; and Sadr, *Iranian Cinema*, 9–10.

[6] Some examples include: Sadr, *Iranian Cinema*, 8–9; Hamid Naficy, *A Social History of Iranian Cinema*, vol. 1: *The Artisanal Era, 1897–1941* (Durham, NC: Duke University Press, 2011), 39; and Masoud Mehrabi, *Tārīkh-i Sīnamā-yi Īrān: Az Āghāz tā Sāl-i 1357* [*A History of Iran's Cinema: From the Beginning to the Year 1979*] (Tehran: Mu'allif, 1992), 15.

journals, autobiographies, memoirs, travelogues, official documents and newspaper articles, and then analyse, not necessarily in a chronological order, my findings in relation to Iranian modernity from 1900 to the mid-1920s through the prism of cinema. I attend to the imaginaries that international films and hybrid cinema spaces rendered in the context of early-twentieth-century Iran. I argue that in this era, the Iranian modern subject was shaped through the negotiations that occurred through cinematic experiences, either in accepting or rejecting globally informed narratives or in receiving those narratives through multiple and hybrid experiences conveyed through spectatorship in the space of cinema. I contend that the cinema was a heterotopic site, a site of hybridity, both through the concrete public space of sociability that it entailed, and through imaging Iran's Others on its screens. I specifically argue that cinematic encounters in the heterotopic space of cinema in the twentieth century allowed for the formation of cosmopolitan identities; informed by global cinematic imaginations, Iranians further refashioned themselves within their local particularities, and became participants in the twentieth century. Iran's experience of modernity, I contend, was shaped by cosmopolitan cinematic imaginations that envisioned a horizon of expectation for what the future of Iran ought to be: progressive, moral and sovereign. I also rely on extant short actualités and newsreels filmed in Iran (mostly Tehran) by national and international agents as primary sources, to investigate the interactions of ordinary residents – i.e. the train passenger, bystander, horse rider, woman, musician, etc. – in new urban spaces and settings that were captured in these films to comment on the experience of urban modernity.[7] It should be mentioned that this study will only focus on *cinematic* affairs during this period, and

---

[7] Hanley mentions that "evidence from memoirs, films, and literature is always relevant, but never sufficient, to social history," and therefore encourages reliance on "conventional sources, such as administrative, economic, and legal records" as sources to unearth the lives of "lower class" population in shaping Middle East cosmopolitanism. See Will Hanley, "Grieving Cosmopolitanism in Middle East Studies," *History Compass* 6(5) (2008): 1348, 1352. While Hanley's assertion is indispensable and necessary in a historical inquiry, it leaves me with one question: how does one trace everyday modes of living and theorise routine exchanges between ethnically, religiously and linguistically diverse ordinary artists, merchants and shop owners that occurred outside the confines of official economic interactions or administrative records? Is one to consider film as an outcome of history or as a historical source?

will regretfully eschew discussing the usage of other image projectors such as the magic lantern, the kinetoscope and its Iranian equivalent, *Shahr-i Farang*.

In this chapter, I consider an Iranian vernacular modernity that was shaped through local social changes which began to take place in the nineteenth century. Situating Iranian modernity in complex and widespread social transformations that engendered new practices and novel spectacles provides a different outlook on Iran's experience of a "new time." Such conceptualisation allows one to stay away from discussions of Iranian modernity that equate it with processes of state modernisation, and it dissociates modernity from notions of Westernisation and/or industrialisation. When investigating the unfolding of Iranian modernity within local settings and examining its multifaceted transitions from different starting points, one also comes to realise the indispensable significance of cinema to the history of modernity in Iran. In the nineteenth century, the daily life experiences of Iranians underwent many changes. This was especially the case with the spread of epidemic diseases, as well as the means to prevent the propagation of such illnesses in that era. The government-led means to forestall the multiplication and spread of diseases, namely cholera, malaria and black death, engendered the establishment of hygienic measures such as a city piping system, public washrooms, the publication of guidelines on good hygiene, the paving of roads, supervision of mortuaries and cemeteries, beautification of streets and planting of trees alongside roads. In addition, urban centres witnessed a propagation of public spaces such as hospitals, schools, embassies, theatres, public squares, reading-houses, cinemas, hotels and guesthouses. Altogether, these novel features brought unprecedented life experiences to the everyday lives of urban residents of Iran – experiences that could be regarded as part and parcel of the ethos of Iranian urban modernity; the ethos of a new time that prompted the imagination of a progressive Iran, devoid of corporeal diseases.

It was within such urban transformations that a culture of movie-going was engendered – a culture that encompassed various reactions, including acceptance of and objections to this new communication medium. The technology of cinema which shifted notions of time and space, the moving images that it projected and the space that it occupied in Tehran's changing urban setting all allude to the novelties that cinematic modernity conjured as part of the larger transformations in the early twentieth century. Cinema itself was a public space, the organisation, location and management of which further shaped the Iranian urban environment. Cinema introduced a public practice that shifted away from the private consumption of print media, and as such facilitated opportunities for the public to socialise and formulate critical opinions. Cinematic images further provided moments of world openness for Iran's diverse inhabitants to further refashion themselves into cosmopolitan participants of the twentieth century.

1.1 Cinematic Heterotopia in Early-Twentieth-Century Tehran

At the turn of the century, Iran was a diasporic hub for many of the diverse communities who congregated in urban centres for commerce, or political or artistic endeavours. Many of these communities took refuge in Iran away from the chaos of wars and conflicts in their homelands. Armenians, Azerbaijanis, Georgians, Assyrians, Germans, Russians, Indians, Americans, French and British had come together in cities such as Tehran. Such an extensive network of immigrants, religions and ideologies engendered a culture in flux that included a multiplicity of experiences, socio-cultural norms and practices.

Russian activities in Azerbaijan, on the north-western frontier of Iran, had disgruntled the Azerbaijani populations since the early nineteenth century, and drove many Azerbaijani khans[8] into exile – some of whom came to Iran – throughout a quarter-century of Russian domination.[9] The Russo-Persian conflicts which concluded in the Gulistan Treaty (1812) and the Turkmanchai Treaty (1828) also opened a weakened Persia to Russian commercial and political influences, allowing many Russian merchants, activists and political figures of Azerbaijani, Armenian and Georgian descent to immigrate to Iran. By the same token, many Iranians also lived in the Russian Empire. In 1900, this number reached 200,000, the majority of whom were concentrated in the South Caucasus.[10] In fact, a large population of

---

[8] Khan is a title given to leaders of tribes, clans, and sometimes military rulers.

[9] Tadeusz Swietochowski, *Russian Azerbaijan, 1905–1920: The Shaping of National Identity in a Muslim Community* (Cambridge University Press, 1985), 5.

[10] Marina Alexidze, "Persians in Georgia," *Journal of Persianate Studies* 1 (2008): 257.

Iranians resided in Tbilisi (Tiflis), Georgia, in the nineteenth and twentieth centuries.[11] From the late Middle Ages to the nineteenth century, most of these Iranian immigrants dwelled in the Seidabad District and the territory adjacent to the Narikala Citadel, forming the largest professional groups of tradesmen, hawkers, builders and shopkeepers (especially involved in the trade of rugs).[12] Tiflis, moreover, became one of the centres of Persian intellectuals and free-thinkers.[13]

In Iran, on the other hand, at the turn of the century, the Armenian-Iranian merchants were at the forefront of Iran's trade with Europe.[14] The confiscation of Armenian Church properties in 1903 by Tsar Nicholas II, the participation of Armenians in the peasant uprisings – as well as the worker and student strikes of the Russian Revolution of 1905, and the conflicts between Caucasian Muslims and Christian Armenians from 1905 to 1907, led to a crack-down in 1908 by the Russian government on all revolutionary activities.[15] As a result, many revolutionaries were killed, arrested or exiled, while many sought refuge and free expression in Iran.[16] The Russian Revolution of 1905 also had a great impact along the north-western frontier of Iran, especially since Iranian migrant workers constituted a large part of the population in that region, namely in Azerbaijan's Baku; these migrant labourers, many of whom worked in oilfields, became involved in local and regional political activities.[17] These workers who returned to Iran brought with them revolutionary ideas, which significantly contributed to the ideologies behind the Constitutional Revolution of Iran

[11] *Ibid.*, 254.   [12] *Ibid.*, 254.

[13] "The Persian intellectuals who permanently or temporarily lived in Tbilisi were distinguished for their anticlerical intentions and opposition to the Iranian political establishment of that time. Their circle also included Azerbaijani men of letters, Mirzā Shāfiʻ and Mirzā Fath-ʻAli Akhundov. Mirzā Shāfiʻ established Dīvān-i Hikmat, in Tbilis, which organised literary and philosophic meetings." *Ibid.*, 259.

[14] Cosroe Chaqueri, "Introduction to the Armenians of Iran: A Historical Perusal," in Cosroe Chaqueri (ed.), *The Armenians of Iran* (Cambridge, MA: Harvard University Press, 1998), 5.

[15] Houri Berberian, *Armenians and the Iranian Constitutional Revolution of 1905–1911* (Boulder, CO: Westview Press, 2001), 5.

[16] *Ibid.*

[17] For more information on the political activities of Iranian oil workers in Baku, see Sohrab Yazdani, "The Question of the Iranian Ijtimaʻiyun-i Amiuyn Party," in Stephanie Cronin (ed.), *Iranian-Russian Encounters: Empires and Revolutions Since 1800* (London: Routledge, 2013), 189–206.

(1906–1911).[18] Moreover, the contraction of the Ottoman Empire and its eventual collapse in the early 1920s, and the 1915 genocide of Armenians in the Ottoman Empire, led to emigration, exile and forcible displacement of many Christians and Muslims from their Ottoman homeland to various countries, including Iran. Therefore, at a time of heightened national solidification among Azerbaijanis, Armenians and Georgians in various Russian regions, as well as in Ottoman Turkey, the borders of Iran and its north-western neighbours had become increasingly indistinct due to the influx and outflow of populations and commercial contacts, as well as the cohabitation of these communities. As is evident in the news reports and articles of the time, and as this chapter will attempt to show, the multiplicity and coexistence of various populations in the above-mentioned regions prompted a traversing of national, ethnic, religious and ideological identities, as different communities engaged in the same activities, or came together in political and ideological movements. For Armenians, as Houri Berberian discusses, "internal and external political, intellectual, and social circumstances" in the early twentieth century had created a "multiplicity of identities, coexisting and competing for primacy."[19] In other words, during this time, identities were impacted by "setting and context," and were thus "'highly situational,' multiple, fluid, and negotiable."[20] In the case of Armenians, Berberian specifically suggests that the nineteenth- and twentieth-century Armenians of the Caucasus, Ottoman Empire and Iran were transnational communities, consisting of workers and activists that maintained contact with their homeland and other diasporic communities, while also travelling in more than one community.[21] The collaboration of Iranians and Armenians was especially evident during the Constitutional Revolution of 1906–1911, making the

---

[18] Berberian, *Armenians and the Iranian Constitutional Revolution*, 2. Also see Swietochowski, *Russian Azerbaijan*, 64–65. For more information on Transcaucasian and particularly Georgian activities, in relation to the Constitutional Revolution of Iran, see also Iago Gocheleishvili, "Georgian Sources on the Iranian Constitutional Revolution, 1905–1911: Sergo Gamdlishvili's Memoirs of the Gilan Resistance," in Cronin (ed.), *Iranian-Russian Encounters*, 207–230.
[19] Houri Berberian, "Traversing Boundaries and Selves: Iranian-Armenian Identities during the Iranian Constitutional Revolution," *Comparative Studies of South Asia, Africa and the Middle East* 25(2) (2005): 279.
[20] *Ibid.*, 280.   [21] *Ibid.*, 282.

Iranian province of Azerbaijan (and especially the city of Tabriz, where many Armenians resided) the centre of resistance.[22]

In Iran, the transnational flow of migrants into and out of the country, and the increase in population of urban cities such as Tehran and Tabriz, necessitated the fostering of facilities such as guesthouses, hotels, theatres, teashops, restaurants, cafés, stores, schools and other spaces for public congregation, education and entertainment of various communities; so much so that in the first decades of the twentieth century, the number and variety of such public spaces increased dramatically. The building of guest/traveller lodges such as the Grand Hotel on Lālahzār Avenue, the Paris Guesthouse (Mihmān-khānah-'i Pārīs), the Iran Guesthouse and the Hôtel de France, as well as the opening of new shops, such as New Spring (Naw Bahār), Azerbaijan, Bon Marché (named after the famous department store in Paris) and Bon Jour Boutique, in the first two decades of the twentieth century point to the proliferation of such public places. Many of these sites of sociability were in turn owned and operated by members of the diasporic communities living in urban centres.

In terms of public performances, the number of theatrical spectacles and plays performed by residents of Iran and the artists who passed through or toured the country grew significantly. The theatrical play, "Three Fiancés and One Bride," by the Armenian actor-director Monsieur Gustanian and Miss Gul-Sabā,[23] the historical "Eastern dance" piece of "Kay-Khusraw," about the "moral grandeur and power of ancient Persia" conducted by a famous Russian ballet dancer and four European women,[24] and the "historically important piece" of "Nadir Shah of Afshār" conducted under the supervision of "Ghulām-Rizā Sharīf-Zādah (the Head of the Republic of Azerbaijan State Theatre)"[25] are among some of the performances that were staged in Iran during this era. Many of these theatrical performances were co-productions between Iranians and the diasporic communities. To name a few, the "Firdawsi" spectacle (a play about the life and work of the

---

[22] *Ibid.*, 283.

[23] "Faqat Yik Daf'ah" [Only One Time], *Īrān*, yr 4, no. 695 (Saratān 10, 1299 [June 30, 1920]), 4.

[24] "Namāyish-i Tārīkhī-yi Bāshukūh" [Glorious Historical Performance], *Īrān*, yr 4, no. 126 (Sunbulah 8, 1299 [September 1, 1920]), 4.

[25] "Pīs-i Ma'rūf-i Tārīkhī-yi Nādir Shāh-i Afshār" [The Famous Historical Piece of Nader Shah of Afshar], *Īrān*, yr 5, no. 884 (Sawr 12, 1300 [May 2, 1921]), 4.

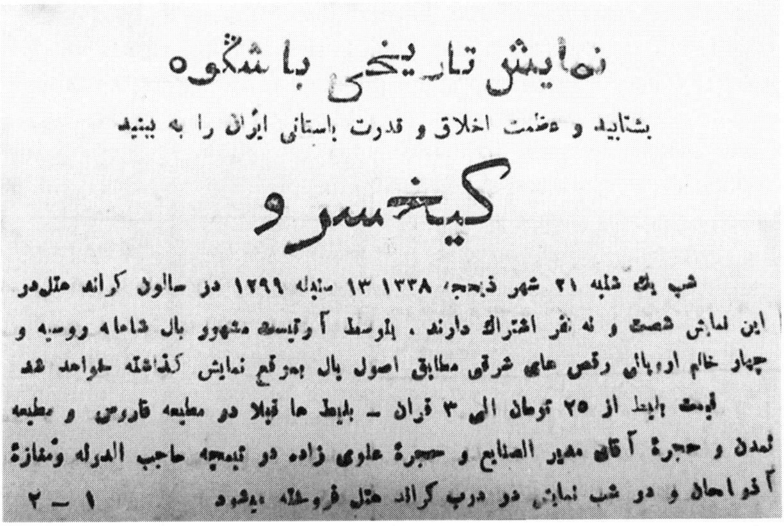

Figure 1.1 An example of a newspaper advertisement for a cultural event in 1920

highly revered Iranian poet of *Shahnamah*, the Book of Kings, the national epic of Iran and its neighbours) was sponsored by the American School of Higher Education (Madrasah-'i ʿĀlī-yi Āmrīkāyī), was performed by "the most famous Iranian actors" and included Caucasian and European music with Iranian anthems.[26] An "Iranian concert and European ballet by the famous Russian actor of the Imperial Ballet, Monsieur Ruba, in unison with other European actors and actresses,"[27] is another example of such co-productions. It is easy to imagine how the advertisement of such performances appealed to the various communities that lived in Iran (Figure 1.1). In terms of education, the number of pedagogical institutions also flourished in the first two decades of the twentieth century. In addition to Tehran's School of Higher Education, Dār al-Funūn, schools such as Iran's Civilisation (Tamaddun-i Irān), the Charitable Boarding School for Orphans (Madrasah-'i Shabānah-Rūzī-yi Khayrīyah-'i Ītām), the School of the Sun of Schools (Madrasah-'i Shams al-Madāris), the School for Armenians (Madrasah-'i Arāmanah) and the Music School

---

[26] "Namāyish-i Bā Shukūh-i Firdawsī" [The Glorious Spectacle of Firdawsi], *Irān*, yr 6, no. 1035 (Qaws 20, 1300 [December 22, 1922]), 4.

[27] "Sālun-i Girānd Hutil" [Grand Hotel Hall], *Irān*, yr 5, no. 884 (Sawr 12, 1300 [May 2, 1921]), 4.

were already established and in operation by the early 1920s.[28] The number of drugstores, health clinics, shops, book stores, reading houses, concerts, conferences and public lectures also increased considerably throughout this period. The German Doctor Kopeliowitch,[29] Mademoiselle Dermis,[30] Doctor Khudzā[31] and the French Doctor Wilholm[32] were among the international practitioners who continuously advertised their clinics in the newspapers of the time. Many of the newly established boutiques and dress shops were also owned and operated by the diasporic communities. A Zoroastrian shop in front of the Shams al-'Imārah building in Tehran, for example, sold "excellent textiles,"[33] while an Armenian merchant, Armenak Aghassian, traded the "latest fashion English women's shoes and men's boots and Parisian cravats" in his English shop on Lālahzār Avenue;[34] it should be mentioned here that to compete with foreign textile imports, Iranian residents also advertised the Iranian handmade fabrics and artifacts sold in their shops. It is within such heterogeneity in material form and experiential quality that one needs to examine the emergence of cinema as a modern technology, and a sensory mode and practice.

---

[28] For "Tamaddun-i Īrān" [Iranian civilisation], see "Avvalīn va Bihtarīn Gārdin Partī" [First and Best Garden Party], *Īrān*, yr 4, no. 741 (Shahrīvar 17, 1299 [September 9, 1920]), 4. For Madrasah-'i Shabānah-Rūzī-yi Khayrīyah-'i Ītām [Charity Borading School for Orphans], see "Bihtarin Namayishhā-yi Akhlāghī" [Best Moral Performances], *Īrān*, yr 4, no. 713 (Asad 4, 1299 [July 26, 1920]), 2. For Madrasah-'i Shams al-Madāris [the School of Shams al-Madāris], see "Dar Madrasah-'i Shams al-Madāris" [In the School of Shams al-Madāris], *Īrān*, yr 7, no. 2264 (Qaws 4, 1301 [November 26, 1922]), 4. For the School for Armenians, see "Sīnamā-yi Fārūs: Bimanfi'at-i Madrasah-'i Arāmanah" [Farus Cinema: for the Benefit of the Armenian School], *Shafaq-i Surkh*, no. 99 (Āzar 20, 1301 [December 12, 1922]), 4. For a brief history of the Iranian Music School, see "Madrasah-'i Mūzīk" [The Music School], *Īrān*, yr 6, no. 1124 (Sūr 5, 1301 [April 25, 1922]), 3. In fact, the Music School had been operating for nine years (as a school dedicated to the education of music) by the time this article had been written.

[29] "Dr. Kopeliowitch," *Īrān*, yr 6, no. 1030 (Tūs 13, 1300 [December 5, 1921]), 4.

[30] "I'lān" [Advertisement], *Īrān*, yr 4, no. 741 (Shahrīvar 17, 1299 [September 9, 1920]), 4.

[31] "Duktur Khudzā" [Doctor Khudza], *Īrān*, yr 4, no. 693 (Saratān 7, 1299 [June 28, 1920]), 4.

[32] "Duktur Vīlhulm" [Doctor Wilholm], *Īrān*, yr 5, no. 794 (Qaws 18, 1299 [December 10, 1920]), 4.

[33] "Pārchah-hā-yi Mumtāz Barā-yi Libās-i 'Ayd" [Excellent Fabrics for Eid Clothes], *Īrān*, yr 6, no. 1089 (Hūt 11, 1300 [March 2, 1922]), 4.

[34] "I'lān" [Advertisement], *Īrān*, yr 5, no. 854 (Hūt 28, 1299 [March 18, 1921]), 4.

The first spaces that began to project cinematographic films in Tehran were commercial spaces such as shops, studios, hotels and coffee houses that were both private (in that they were owned by individual merchants) and public (in that they were spaces of assembly and interaction for urban residents). As film screenings became more popular and more cinematographic devices were imported from Europe by merchants, these ad hoc spaces gave way to more formal and professional cinema spaces. Many of the theatres, hotels and/or locations where films were screened in the first few years after the inception of the technology of cinema were run by Armenian, Russian, Georgian and Azerbaijani émigrés, who thus became the first public cinematograph operators. To name a few, Russi Khan (1875–1967), an immigrant under Russian patronage, also known as Mihdi Ivanov or alternatively as Georgian Fyodorovich, was one of the court photographers of the Qajar Dynasty, who later opened and operated a number of theatres around the city.[35] Two months after opening his personal photography studio,[36] Russi Khan started to screen films in his shop.[37] Aghayev, of Azeri descent, was another cinematograph owner who operated the cinematograph at the same time as Russi Khan in the 1910s. The famous Armenian-Georgian photographer who was born in Iran during the Qajar Dynasty, Antoin Sevruguin (late 1830s–1933), also opened several movie theatres in the 1910s. Ardashes Patmagerian (1963–1928),[38] an Armenian merchant, also known as Ardishīr Khan, was another important figure in establishing cinema and a culture of movie-going in the early twentieth century. In the late 1920s and early 1930s, a certain "Monsieur Levine," the manager of Iran Cinema (Sīnamāy-i Īrān), and "Parī Āqā-Bāyūff" (Pari Aqabayev or Aqababian), or Madame Parī, an Armenian-Iranian woman who had received her

---

[35] It is commonly held that Russi Khan's father was English and his mother was a Tatar Russian.

[36] "Russi Khan, the famous photographer has recently set up a photography studio in European [Franc] style at the beginning of 'Alā' al-Dawlah Avenue, in front of the Ministry of the Military's (Vazir-i Nizām) house ..." See *Tamaddun*, no. 32 (Rajab 20, 1325 [August 29, 1907]), 4.

[37] "I'lān" [Advertisement], *Habl al-Matin*, no. 141 (Mīzān 21, 1286 [October 14, 1907]), 4.

[38] Jamal Umid, *Tārīkh-i Sīnamā-yi Īrān: 1279–1357 [The History of Iranian Cinema: 1900–1979]* (Tehran: Rawzanah Publications, 1995), 27.

education outside Iran and had been active in both theatre and cinema in the 1910s in Tehran, were among cinema owners too.[39]

In addition to the diasporic communities who were involved in the business of cinema, the activities of cosmopolitan locals in the operation of cinematographs and/or conducting film screenings should not be underestimated. Mīrzā Ibrāhīm Khān-i Sahhāf-Bāshī, for example, was one of the first Iranian merchants who brought the cinematograph to Iran and made use of it as a commercial enterprise in his shop in 1903. According to his memoirs, Sahhāf-Bāshī, who travelled extensively around the world, saw "a recently invented electric device," i.e. the cinematograph, at the "Pālās Sīnamā" (Palace Cinema) in Paris for the first time in 1897 after he had "walked in the public park" in the evening.[40] Interestingly, a cinema by the same name, Sīnamā Pālās (Palace Cinema), was established by a Russian immigrant, Monsieur Tāmbūr, in the Grand Hotel on Lālahzār Avenue in the late 1910s.[41]

Around the same time as Russi Khan and Antoin Sevreguin, Hājī Nāyib Muʿīlī, another Iranian merchant, was known to have operated a cinematographic device in his café on Lālahzār Avenue in Tehran in the early twentieth century.[42] Moreover, as has already been discussed by many Iranian cinema scholars, Mīrzā Ibrāhīm Khān-i ʿAkkāsbāshī (1874–1915), the photographer and cinematographer of Muzaffar al-Din Shah, was perhaps the first Iranian documentary filmmaker.[43] After accompanying the Shah to the Paris Exposition in 1900 and seeing the Lumière cinematographic exhibit, ʿAkkāsbāshī, by order of the Shah, purchased a few cinematographic devices, brought them to Iran for the use of the Qajar court and filmed a few royal events; some

---

[39] "Sīnamā dar Īrān" [Cinema in Iran], _Sīnamā va Namāyishāt_, yr 1, no. 1 (Murdād 1309 [July 1930]), 7. It could be that the manager to whom the author in this journal is referring is a person by the name of Monsieur Lūban. The name is not very clear in the publication.

[40] Ibrāhim Sahhāf-Bāshī Tihrānī, _Safarnāmah-'i Ibrāhim Sahhāf-Bāshī Tihrānī_ [_The Travelogue of Ibrāhīm Sahaf-Bashi Tihrānī_], comp. Muhammad Mushīrī (Tehran: The Institution of Writers and Translators of Iran, 1978), 39–40.

[41] "Rafʿ-i Ishtibāh – Sīnamā Pālās" [Correction – Palace Cinema], _Raʿd_, yr 10, no. 124 (Zi-Hajjah 8, 1337 [September 4, 1919]), 2.

[42] Abbas Baharloo, _Rūzshumār-i Sīnamā-yi Īrān az Āghāz tā Inqirāz-i Qājāriyah_ [_The Chronology of Cinema in Iran from Its Inception to the Fall of the Qajars_] (Tehran: Taʿlif Institution, 2010), 43.

[43] See, e.g., Naficy, _A Social History of Iranian Cinema_, vol. 1, 44. Hamid Naficy speaks of cinema during the Qajar period in terms of a pre-capitalist artisanal mode.

of these included Muzaffar al-Din Shah at the Festival of Flowers in Belgium in 1900, some scenes from the Shah's second European visit and 'Āshūrā mourning processions in Tehran.[44]

Operated by people from a variety of backgrounds, Iranian cinemas became the space of socialisation for the Iranian and diasporic communities. As early as 1903, Sahhāf-Bāshī's cinema, according to the memoirs of Ghulām 'Alī khān-i 'Azīz al-Sultān (1878–1940), the second Malījak of the Qajar court,[45] hosted "foreigners" on "Sunday mornings" and the public on "Sunday evenings."[46] According to the same account, on some nights, "Antoin Sevreguin's cinema hosted only Armenians, and turned away Muslims."[47] The Grand Hotel (Girānd Hutil) of Lālahzār, the Fārūs Publishing House (Matba'ah-'i Fārūs), where many public gatherings ensued, and early public movie theatres such as Sun Cinema (Sīnamā Khurshīd) and Pathé Cinema (Sīnamā Pātah) also facilitated the physical encounters of Iranians with people from a multitude of ethnicities and nationalities in such spaces. These cinemas and film-screening venues themselves were located in the commercial and tourist centres of urban cities, where the assemblage and interactions of Iranian merchants, students, passers-by and diasporic communities were further facilitated. Russi Khan, for instance, launched his first public cinema on 'Alā' al-Dawlah Avenue, previously known as Ambassador Avenue (Khīyābān-i Sufarā) – home to the embassies of countries such as Germany, Belgium, Ottoman Turkey and Britain, as well as the Russian Loan Bank and Paris Guesthouse.[48] In 1909, Antoin Sevreguin, in collaboration with Ardishīr Khan and Pathé Institution, opened a new public cinema on "'Alā' al-Dawlah Avenue, in front of the Loan Bank" of Russia, in the personal apartment of Ardishīr Khan.[49] Cinema business was so good on this street

---

[44] This latter event will be discussed below.

[45] As a young boy, Ghulām 'Alī khān-i 'Azīz al-Sultān (1878–1940) was very precious to Muzafar al-Din Shah and was therefore granted the title, "'Azīz al-Sultān" (Dear to the Sultan). He usually accompanied the Shah in court or on hunting trips to entertain him. He was known as the second Malījak, since his father was the first Malījak during the time of Nasir al-Din Shah.

[46] Ghulām 'Alī Khān-i 'Aziz al-Sultān, *Ruznāmayah Khātirāt-i Qulām Alī Khān-i Aziz al-Sultān (Malījak-i Sānī)* [*The Diary of Ghulām 'Alī Khān-i 'Aziz al-Sultān (the Second Jester)*], comp. Muhsin Mīrzāyī (Tehran: Zaryāb, 1997), 533.

[47] *Ibid.*, 1656.   [48] Baharloo, *Rūzshumār-i Sīnamā-yi Īrān*, 42.

[49] "I'lān" [Advertisement], *Īrān-i Naw*, no. 15 (Shahrīvar 19, 1288 [September 10, 1909]), 1.

that later, in 1917, Ardishīr Khan opened another cinema by the name of Sun Cinema in the same thoroughfare.[50] In 1908, Aghayev also advertised "new worth-seeing cinematographic films that portrayed the foreign worlds in motion" in a merchant's shop on the Nāsirī Avenue, thus bringing the global into the local shops of Tehran, where many gathered and socialised.[51] The propagation of cinemas in such areas of Tehran further prompted the mingling and interactions of heterogeneous communities, and shaped a culture that was informed by various ideologies and opinions. Russi Khan later opened more cinemas at some of Tehran's significant landmarks: one on Nāsirī Avenue, in the yard of the famous Iranian institution of higher education, Dār al-Funūn,[52] and another on the upper level of the Fārūs Publishing House on Lālahzār Avenue, home to many of the newly founded hotels, motels, theatres and touristic attractions in the city of Tehran.[53]

The physical spaces of cinema, as unexampled public spaces that facilitated a familiarisation with previously unfamiliar practices, lifestyles and ideologies in the urban sites (through encounters of diverse people), thus also forged a hybrid character upon the cityscape that closely matched Iran's experience of modernity. Such proliferation of public spaces further configured the compartmentalisation of the city, giving rise to some districts in the city that became the centres of socialisation, critical thinking and entertainment. In fact, Lālahzār Avenue soon served as the main location for many more theatres, public spectacles and cinemas in Tehran. The implantation of cinema in this avenue was a product of Tehran's new metropolitan constitution, and it became a terrain for the reproduction of the city's popular culture for many years to come. Excellent Cinema (Sīnamā-yi ʿĀlī), Casino Hall (Sālun-i Kāzīnaw) and Palace Cinema, all established in the second half of the 1910s in Tehran, were among the movie theatres that were established in this street, increasing its urbanite character even further (Figure 1.2).

---

[50] "Sīnamā Khurshīd" [Sun Cinema], *Īrān*, no. 90 (Khurdād 29, 1296 [June 19, 1917]), 4.

[51] "Iʿlān" [Advertisement], *Sūr-i Isrāfīl*, no. 26 (Urdībihisht 3, 1287 [April 23, 1908]), 8.

[52] Baharloo, *Rūzshumār-i Sīnamā-yi Īrān*, 46.

[53] Ghulām ʿAlī khān-i ʿAzīz al-Sultān, *Ruznāmayah Khātirāt-i Ghulām ʿAlī Khān*, 1656.

Figure 1.2 A photo of Palace Hotel and Palace Cinema on Istanbul Crossroad

Other than screening films in public places, many enthusiasts started to rent or sell cinematographic devices for projection at weddings and other festivities, or to hold private film screenings for families and relatives. The famous Qajar court photographer, 'Abdullāh Mīrzā, advertised the sale of one complete set of cinematographic equipment at his shop in 1907.[54] In an announcement in the *New Iran* (*Irān-i Naw*) publication, the Spectacle House of Monsieur Būmir and Russi Khan also advertised the rent and sale of cinematographic devices, especially since "a number of devices" were available at their theatre by that time.[55] In fact, cinemas had become so popular among the Iranian urban populations that, by the 1920s, many restaurants, cafés and other sites of sociability were equipped with instruments required for film projection. Economy Guest House

[54] "One complete cinematograph device in the Navvāb Photography Studio of 'Abdullāh Mīrzā, adjacent to the door of Dār al-Funūn School, has been purchased by receipt, and will be sold." See "I'lān" [Advertisement], *Majlis*, yr 1, no. 55 (Muharram 30, 1325 [March 25, 1907]), 4.

[55] "Pirugrām" [Program], *Irān-i Naw*, yr 1, no. 39 (Mīzān 19, 1288 [October 12, 1909]), 4.

(Mihmān-Khānah-'i Iqtiṣād) specifically advertised "very cheap" accommodation where specialised spaces and technological instruments had also been provided for the welfare of its guests, namely "electric lights, a space for gymnastic [activities], cinematograph [screenings] and [stage] performances."[56] Similarly, the Office for Welfare Work (or Charitable Affairs) of Tehran Municipality (Idārah-'i Umūr-i Khayrīyah-'i Baladīyah-'i Tihrān), in charge of "the establishment of various institutions" for people who were "deprived of the means of subsistence," declared one of its responsibilities to be "the establishment of a home for the afflicted," which was to include "a library, reading room, cinematograph, theatrical [stage], kitchen and cheap coffeehouse."[57] Such a proliferation of cinematographic projection venues must also be viewed in light of nationalist and modernist discourses that viewed cinema and film as media for the moral edification of the audiences and the promotion of patriotism and advancement of the country – topics which will be discussed further below and in the following chapter.

Aside from the actual spaces of cinema and film screenings, the moving images themselves, their origins and their channels of distribution are also worthy of attention in this historical overview. From the beginning, many of the motion pictures screened in Iranian movie theatres or informal movie gatherings were in fact short feature films imported from countries such as France, the United States, Russia, Azerbaijan, India, Germany, Italy and Arab-speaking countries. Many of the films that were showcased in Iran in the 1910s were imported from Russia and, based on newspaper advertisements, they had Russian intertitles. However, with the coming of the Pahlavi Dynasty and its consolidation in the late 1920s, the variety of films screened in Iran changed. Early short films made in the Russian Empire,[58] comedies in

---

[56] "Zindigānī-yi Khaylī Arzān" [A Very Cheap Lifestyle], *Īrān*, yr 6, no. 1030 (Qaws 13, 1300 [December 5, 1921]), 4.

[57] "Idārah-'i Umūr-i Khayrīyah-'i Baladīyah-'i Tihrān" [The Office for the Welfare Work of Tehran Municipality], *Īrān*, yr 5, no. 880 (Sawr 7, 1300 [April 27, 1921]), 3.

[58] "Savār-i Niẓām-i Rūs dar Jang" [The Russian Cavalry in War], for example, was the name of one of the short newsreels screened in 1915. "Sīnamā-yi Jadīd" [New Cinema], *Ra'd*, yr 6, no. 159 (Asad 19, 1294 [August 11, 1915]), 2. Other Russian short films/newsreels included scenes from Saint Petersburg (then Petrograd) and/or the Imperial Russian Army.

the Turkish language (most likely from Azerbaijan),[59] newsreels about World War I (mainly distributed by Russia, France, the United Kingdom and Germany), the Italian silent film of *Salammbo* (based on the novel by Flaubert),[60] *Maciste*, in French,[61] and the American film, *The Count of Monte Cristo*, based on the novel by Alexander Dumas,[62] were among the films that were featured in Iranian theatres in the 1910s and early 1920s. The international motion pictures projected on Iranian screens acted as mediators between competing conceptions of the social world for the audiences. The sites of film screenings rendered visible the parallel alternative spaces of Iran's contemporaries; these images included global urban cities, cultures, narratives, individuals and social conducts that may have previously been inaccessible to the public. Iranians' first recordings of their cinematic impressions are suggestive of such novel experiences. Sahhāf-Bāshī's first film-related experiences illuminate his astonishment at seeing spaces of 'Otherness' on the screen, as the cinematograph recreated "the American Falls exactly as is," and demonstrated "the soldier regiment in motion, and a train at full speed."[63] In his first trip to Europe in 1900, Muzaffar al-Din Shah, too, was amazed by the way in which the cinematograph reproduced "the pictures of most places . . . in an astonishingly vivid manner," namely, "landscapes and exposition monuments, the falling rain, the flow of the Seine, and so

[59] "Tamāshā-yi Shab" [Tonight's Program/Screening], *Īrān-i Naw*, yr 1, no. 104 (Zī-Hajjah 20, 1327 [January 2, 1910]), 1.
[60] The announcement for Palace Cinema mentions that "soon the splendid film of Salammbo written by Flaubert will be screened." See "I'lān" [Advertisement], *Ra'd*, yr 10, no. 153 (Mizān 23, 1298 [October 16, 1919]), 3.
[61] The film *Maciste*, screened in Tehran's cinemas, could refer to any of the following films: the 1914 Italian film, *Cabiria*, the 1916 Italian film, *Maciste Alpino* (or *The Warrior*), or the 1917 *Maciste the Athlete*. Since in the Persian announcement, the film is advertised as "Maciste the Champion," the 1916 and 1917 films are most probable. See, "Sīnamā-yi Khurshīd" [Sun Cinema], *Ra'd*, yr 11, no. 7 (Haml 18, 1299 [April 7, 1920]), 4.
[62] It is not clear which film production of *The Count of Monte Cristo* was screened in Iran; the 1913 version seems most probable. See "Sīnamā Pālās" [Palace Cinema] *Ra'd*, yr 11, no. 32 (Sawr 20, 1299 [May 10, 1920]), 3.
[63] Interestingly, as the following chapter will demonstrate, these are scenes and events that were captured by the first Iranian cinematographers too. Tihrānī, *Safarnāmah-'i Ibrāhim Sahhāf-Bāshī Tihrānī*, 39–40.

forth."[64] Public cinemas arguably worked to elicit such sentiments from the average spectator.

Cinema, as Larkin argues, is modern because of its ability to "destabilise and make mobile people, ideas, and commodities."[65] Following Larkin, then, newsreels from international wars arguably functioned to displace audiences from their local settings and transport them to global locations. In the late 1900s, Aghayev and Russi Khan both worked to project "emergent films" or *pardah* (curtain) from international war scenes, "such as the Russia Japan War,"[66] some of which – according to Russi Khan's announcement – had been "imported by mail."[67] Furthermore, in 1909, the Spectacle House of Mr Būmir and Russi Khan (Tamāshā-khānah-'i Būmir va Rūssī Khān) screened "two comic" films in the "Turkish language," which were most likely imported from Azerbaijan.[68] The advertisement for the New Theatre (Ti'ātr-i Jadīd) which was operated by Antoin Sevreguin, in collaboration with Ardashes Patmagerian and Monsieur Pathé, promised to show films that were directly imported from France and had not been seen before – especially since "Monsieur Pathé, himself, was the first to invent this affair."[69] The novelty of experiences associated with such an array of alterities projected on screen could be best reflected in a 1916 Persian prose piece, which described the cinematic images on Iranian "curtains" as bearing "No stable essence, no spatial or temporal permanency," both symbolically and materially.[70]

---

[64] Muzaffar al-Din Shāh-i Qājār, *Safarnāmah-'i Mubārakah-'i Shāhanshāhī* [*The Blessed Travelogue of the Shah*] (Tehran: Matba'ah-'i Khāsah-'i Mubārakah-'i Shāhanshāhī, 1319; Hijrī Qamarī, 1900), 100–101.

[65] Brian Larkin, "Colonialism and the Built Space of Cinema in Nigeria," in Preben Kaarsholm (ed.), *City Flicks: Indian Cinema and the Urban Experience* (Calcutta: Seagull Books, 2004), 184.

[66] *Subh-i Sādiq*, yr 1, no. 166 (Ramadan 23, 1325 [October 31, 1907]), 4.

[67] *Ibid.*

[68] "Tamāshā-yi Shab" [Tonight's Program/Screening], *Īrān-i Naw*, yr 1, no. 104 (Zi-Hajjah 20, 1327 [January 2, 1910]), 1.

[69] "I'lān" [Advertisement], *Īrān-i Naw*, no. 15 (Shahrīvar 19, 1288 [September 10, 1909]), 1.

[70] Mīrzā Hasan Khān Ansārī, *Nūsh Dārū yā Dāvāy-i Dard-i Īrānīyān* [*The Remedy or the Medicine for the Ailments of Iranians*] (Isfahan, 1912). The "munāzirah" is compiled in Mūsā Najafī, comp., *Bunyād-i Falsafah-'i Sīyāsī dar Īrān* ('Asr-i Mashrūtīyyat): *Talāqqī-yi Andishah-'i Islām va Īrān bā Gharb* [*The Foundation of Political Philosophy in Iran (Constitutional Era): The Intersection of Islamic and Iranian Thought with the West*] (Tehran: University Publishing Centre, 1997), 486.

In fact, the international wars of the early twentieth century had become raging topics in the cinemas of Iran which attracted audiences and were sources of commercial profit for cinematograph-owners. In the years following the Russo-Japanese War (1904–1905), and during World War I, many of the films that were included in cinema programs pertained to the topic of international wars. In 1915, for example, Ardishīr Khan inaugurated his cinema on 'Alā' al-Dawlah (in front of the Russian Bank) with new "international war films" specifically pertaining to the First World War.[71] Many other film projectionists included war newsreels along with comic and moral films in their programs. Excellent Cinema in 1916, for example, advertised war newsreels that portrayed the German invasion of France, in addition to a "drama in three acts" and a "comic" film.[72] The popularity of war newsreels, some scholars have argued, could be attributed to the sponsorship of many of the theatres by various international forces such as the Russians, French or British in different periods. The fact that many of the films projected on Iranian screens during the early years of the twentieth century were produced in countries deeply involved in the race to become "world powers" (i.e. Russia, France, Britain, Germany and the United States), has led many to regard early film screenings in Iran as propaganda strategies strictly designed for political reasons – which may have been the original intention by these Great Powers. For instance, Theodore Rothstein (1871–1953), the first Soviet Ambassador to Persia (1920–1921), inaugurated his mission in Iran by an announcement that the open space in front of the Soviet Embassy would be allocated to the public and Iranian workers on Fridays (the last day of the Persian week), and that Soviet films would be screened there for free.[73] The variety of imported films (i.e. news-reels, comedy, drama, action, actualité, etc.) and the nationality of their origins, as well as the spaces that were allocated for cinemato-graphic screenings, however, implore a more nuanced and multifaceted reading of such claims. Many cinema programs in early-twentieth-century Iran showcased a variety of films where a war newsreel would

---

[71] "Pardah-hā-yi Jangī" [War Curtains/Newsreels], *Ra'd*, yr 7, no. 53 (Āzar 12, 1294 [December 5, 1915]), 4.

[72] "Ikhtār" [Warning], *Ra'd*, yr 7, no. 182 (Khurdād 1, 1295 [May 23, 1916]), 4.

[73] Majid Tafrishi, "Nukhustīn Namāyandigān-i Sīyāsī-yi Ittihād-i Shawravī dar Īrān" [The First Political Representatives of the Soviet Union in Iran], *Ganjīnah-'i Asnād*, yr 2, nos 7 and 8 (Pāyīz va Zimistān 1371 [Fall and Winter 1992]), 43.

be screened before a comedy or vice versa. In 1915, for example, the Spectacle House of Ardishīr Khān advertised "five [international] War Acts (films)," after which "Comic Acts (films)" would be screened.[74] In 1916, Excellent Cinema of Iran (Sīnamā-yi 'Ālī-yi Īrān) also advertised new films of "the world's international wars, moral acts (dramas), and entertaining acts (comedy)," all in one night.[75]

The abundance of war newsreels in cinema programs of this period leaves no doubt that these films were well received by the audiences, and that such films transported Iranian and diasporic audiences to the battlefields and positioned them as contemporaneous participants of the twentieth century.[76] The screening of foreign films would attract the diasporic communities in Iran and inform them of the state of affairs in their home countries. Alternatively, one could even argue that the popularity of the Russo-Japanese war films in Iranian cinemas was based on a sense of hope raised among Iranians of diverse backgrounds that the Japanese triumph over the Russians marked the triumph of a developing country over an imperial force. The Pathé Institution had in fact distributed the Russo-Japanese war film with two titles, one being *Long Live Russia* and the other being *Long Live Japan*, which were alternately selected by the cinema owners to interchangeably play to the varied sentiments of audiences.[77] The contemporaneity of the screening of the Russo-Japanese war with the onset of the Constitutional Revolution in 1906 is perhaps noteworthy in this

[74] "Purugrām Barā-yi Sah Shab" [The Program for the [Next] Three Nights], *Ra'd*, yr 7, no. 59 (Qaws 19, 1294 [December 12, 1915]), 4.
[75] "I'lān" [Advertisement], *Ra'd*, yr 7, no. 165 (Sawr 10, 1295 [April 30, 1916]), 4.
[76] On the effects of war films/newsreels on American audiences, see Kristen Whissel, *Picturing American Modernity: Traffic, Technology and the Silent Cinema* (Durham, NC: Duke University Press, 2008).
[77] The Pathé Institution has published the information pertaining to the production of both films on its website. The website, however, does not publish information on the distribution of the films in different countries. For further information, see: "Événements Russo-Japonais: 'Vive la Russie!' – Lucien Nonguet – 1904," Foundation Jérôme Seydoux-Pathé, accessed September 17, 2012, http://filmographie.fondation-jeromeseydoux-pathe.com/index.php?id=5247; and "Événements Russo-Japonais: Titre: 'Vive le Japon!' – Lucien Nonguet – 1904," accessed September 17, 2012, http://filmographie.fondation-jeromeseydoux-pathe.com/index.php?id=5249. Also, Abbas Baharloo holds that the two versions of the film were distributed in Iran. For more information, see Baharloo, *Rūzshumār-i Sīnamā-yi Īrān*, 43.

historical inquiry.[78] The Russo-Japanese war, as a global event projected many times on Iranian cinema screens, in a sense became the
"future past" of Iran in 1906, in that the war against an imperial
power – captured in moving images – provided a horizon of expectation for Iranians during the Constitutional Revolution. Despite the
intentions of the cinematograph owners and patrons, the reception of
films in Iran by diverse audiences, as well as their reactions, was
naturally far from homogeneous.

The international motion pictures, one could contend, characterised
heterotopic spaces that created spatial and temporal simultaneity with
Iran's others. Cinemas became "places outside of all places," in that
sites captured in films "simultaneously represented, contested, and
inverted" the Iranian space of experience.[79] The images portrayed on
screen were "a mirror," in the words of Foucault, that reflected all that
was not in the Iranian space of experience.[80] The gaze directed toward
Iranians in the previous centuries through various European travelogues and photographs[81] was now redirected toward the Self through
comparison on the cinema screen. This interplay of gazes functioned to
"reconstitute" Iranianness through the imaginations that foreign films
had fostered, and the horizon of expectation that they had shaped. The
imagination of Iran's space of experience against the multiple possibilities showcased on screen propelled nationalist discourses that envisioned Iran as progressive, scientific, moral and war-free. Cinema
screens allowed for the juxtaposition of the "absolutely real" Iranian
local life and "absolutely unreal"[82] virtual images of other places; films
allowed for a relocation of the Self, and for a "contestation" of the
space of living. For the spectator, as Rushton argues, cinema became a
matter of "placing oneself where one is not, of becoming someone or

---

[78] The Constitutional Revolution is a significant event in the history of modern Iran
that functioned to engender a parliamentary system and limit the royal power
which previously gave, almost readily, numerous concessions to the foreign
forces at the expense of the country.
[79] Michel Foucault, "Of Other Spaces," *Diacritics* 16(1) (1986): 24.   [80] *Ibid.*
[81] For more information on the gaze directed toward Iranians in the eighteenth
and nineteenth centuries in travelogues, read Mohamad Tavakoli-Targhi,
Refashioning Iran: Orientalism, Occidentalism, and Historiography
(New York: Palgrave Macmillan, 2001).
[82] Foucault, "Of Other Spaces," 24.

something one is not."[83] The cinema screen engendered a "moment of vision" in its intrinsic temporality; through capturing a moment, "the present" could only be acknowledged once "it had become the past" in the moving images.[84] This moment of vision allowed the subject to be "carried away to whatever possibilities and circumstances are encountered" in films, namely to the multiple lifestyles, cities, battle fronts, cultures and imaginations captured in the moving images.[85] In other words, for Iranian cosmopolitans, cinematic spectatorship prompted possibilities of linking the Others' past with the Self's future, and thus facilitated the imagination of a nation: moral, educated, advanced and on a par with Europe, and now Japan.

The nationality or origins of the international films that were screened in cinemas have led some scholars to consider early cinematic experiences in Iran to have been purely for the international elites, and has inclined them to overlook the significance of cinematic encounters in the formation of cosmopolitan individuals, and disregard the formation of a cinema culture (Figure 1.3). As mentioned before, the screening of international war films encouraged the attendance of the diasporic residents of Tehran, namely, Russian, Armenian, French and British officials who were frequently spotted in the main streets of the city. The encounters of Iranians with global Others through the heterotopic site of cinema, either in its concrete space or on screen, allowed for further refashioning of Iranians into modern cosmopolitan individuals of the twentieth century. At a time when national borders were becoming consolidated, cinema screenings shifted the interior/exterior boundary by making it possible for diverse middle-class and urban groups of people to mingle in heterogeneous sites of sociability and to be exposed to images to which they had no access before. Although movie theatres were privately owned and hence exclusionary to a certain extent, the sense of spectacle created by movie houses, film posters and the loitering of people of diverse ethno-linguistic and religious backgrounds along streets in this district even exposed the urban poor to a world that was previously concealed from them. The cosmopolitanism of the early twentieth century thus emphasised

---

[83] Richard Rushton, "Deleuzian Spectatorship," *Screen* 50(1) (Spring 2009): 51.
[84] Martin Heidegger, *Being and Time*, trans. John Macquarrie and Edward Robinson (New York: Harper & Row, 1962), 388.
[85] Heidegger, *Being and Time*, 387.

Figure 1.3 Sīnamā Īrān advertising *The Mark of Zorro* (1920) in 1308 (1929)

"moments of openness" created through this cultural site, when "new relations between Self, Other and World" developed,[86] and Iranian modern subjectivity was taking shape.

[86] Gerard Delanty, *The Cosmopolitan Imagination: The Renewal of Critical Social Theory* (Cambridge University Press, 2009), 53.

1.2 Francotopic City: Early Cinema Culture and Urbanisation

Aside from the attractions that cinema created for its audiences, the expansion of public transportation such as tramways, trains and cars created new sensory experiences. With the propagation of mechanical speed such as that experienced through the Shāh 'Abdul-'Azīm railroad that extended from Tehran to Shāh 'Abdul-'Azīm Shrine, as opposed to donkey and horse riding, as well as streetcar (or tramline) tracks in heavy traffic areas – namely two parallel North–South and two East–West lines in Tehran – engendered novel spatial and temporal sensations among the public.[87] Moreover, the creation of municipalities, expansion of streets, building of roundabouts (maydān), establishment of shops outside the bazaar and the unprecedented crowding of main streets such as Chirāghgāz and Lālahzār Avenues created a more tangible experience of urban transformation.

In a 1924 article entitled "The Country Has Become Francotopic" (Mamlikat Farangistān Shudah), the *Nāhīd* publication surveyed a range of developments in the city that did not "exist in Tehran a few years back" – namely, "electrical lights ... beautiful shops, chic hairdressing salons, music and orchestra at the upper-levels of Grand Hotel, the sight of Armenian and European women with appealing clothes ... Muslim and European men, scented, with faux-col (bow tie) and ties, the passing ... of electrical cars with the speed of electricity, the flying of airplanes in the sky of Tehran, and etc."[88] The article then remarked, with sarcasm, that "our old *Karbalāyīs*"[89] see such novelties "and tell one another, the world has rotted and the country has become Francotopic [or like the Occident] altogether."[90] As such, the city and its infrastructure fostered modern practices and new human interactions. Tehran engendered, in the words of Henri Lefebvre, "a

---

[87] For more information on the experience of public transportation in Tehran and the experience of railway space (as a microcosm of the nation) in Iran, see Mikiya Koyagi, "The Vernacular Journey: Railway Travelers in Early Pahlavi Iran, 1925–1950," *International Journal of Middle East Studies* 47(4) (2015): 745–763.

[88] "Mamlikat Farangistān Shudah" [The Country Has Become Francotopic (literal translation: The Country Has Become Like the Occident)], *Nāhīd*, yr. 3, no. 9 (Shawwāl 26, 1342 [May 31, 1924]), 1.

[89] *Karbalāyī* is a common title granted to those who make pilgrimages to the holy city of Karbala in Iraq.

[90] "Mamlikat Farangistān Shudah," 1.

place of encounter, assembly, and simultaneity" among its diverse religious, ethnic, political and ideological communities.[91] Following Lefebvre, the city centralised "creation" through its heterogeneous interactions, especially because nothing could exist "without exchange, without union, without proximity, that is without relationships."[92]

Noting the urban changes in Tehran in 1921, the correspondent of *National Geographic* magazine – which had dedicated a whole issue to "Modern Pêrsia and Its Capital" – commented on the "sudden transition from desert to city" while travelling through from Resht to Tehran.[93] The reporter, F. L. Bird, remarked that his first experience of Tehran called for a modification of Kipling's oft-quoted line; "for here East and West have met, but have not mixed."[94] Calling the northern portion of Tehran – built up largely by "the last generation" – a "product of western influence," Bird pointed out the well-graded streets, "some of them lined with elms and plane trees."[95] He further commented on the modern city of Tehran boasting "a tramway, electric lights, motion-picture theatres, hotels and restaurants, European shops, and numerous respectable buildings of semi-Western architecture."[96] It is because of such new developments that Bird deemed it "incorrect to speak of present-day Persia as unchanging."[97] Meanwhile, the *Nāhīd* weekly publication, commenting on the new urban developments and changes in a satirical style, pointed out the dangers associated with tram tracks and the speed of cars on the streets, thus illustrating previously unheard-of feelings and sensations.[98] An article in *Iran* newspaper in 1920, entitled "Donkey-Automobile" (ulāgh-utumubīl), remarked on the new life changes as seen on Iranian streets. The author, writing on behalf of "Modern Nationalists" (millīyūn-i mutijadid), compared the two modes of transportation in terms of "power and impotence," "slowness and speed." Noting a changing society, the author commented on how "the horse succeeds the donkey, the carriage replaces the horse, the automobile replaces the

---

[91] Henri Lefebvre, *The Urban Revolution*, trans. R. Bononno (Minneapolis, MN: University of Minnesota Press, 2003), 191.
[92] Lefebvre, *The Urban Revolution*, 191.
[93] F. L. Bird, "Modern Pêrsia and Its Capital: And an Account of an Ascent of Mount Demavend, the Persian Olumpus," *The National Geographic Magazine*, April 1921, 371.
[94] *Ibid.*   [95] *Ibid.*   [96] *Ibid.*   [97] *Ibid.*, 375.
[98] "Utumubīl-Savārī yā Qaymat-i Khūn-i Insān" [Automobile-Rides or the Price of Human Blood], *Nāhīd*, yr 1, no. 4 (Sha'bān 23, 1339 [May 2, 1921]), 8.

carriage, [and then since] the velocity of the train is deemed insufficient ... airplanes and space-craft are invented."[99] Similarly in 1922, an article in the same publication regarded the propagation of means of public transportation, such as "paved roads, bridges" and tunnels as agents of progress in need of architectural and engineering skills if they were to contribute to a progressive Iran.[100]

During this time, cinema expanded sensory experiences of time and space. The new urban transformations, concomitant with the inception of cinematographic and movie theatres, engendered new temporal experiences in the early twentieth century. Iran's experience of modernity was thus manifested in the streets of Tehran, in movie theatres across the city and registered in film. The early films recorded in Iran – somewhat recently unearthed from the Gulistan Palace – attest to the rapid changes in Tehran's space of experience. Two of the short reels, dating back to the early twentieth century,[101] depict wide and spacious paved roads as they capture images from military or official parades in the city. One of these documentary-style films shows the street on the northern side of the Tūpkhānah (artillery) Square with the backdrop of the modern building of the Office of the Municipality, and the other captures images from a parade on the eastern side of the square with the picturesque British Imperial Bank of Persia in the background. In both of these documentary style films, the street is crowded with pedestrians who are watching horse-riders (perhaps government officials) as they pass down the street. These *actualités* arguably portray the marriage of Tehran's urbanity to its political history, while they reveal the significant place taken by films and film recording (or filmmaking) in relation to this history.[102] Another film presents what seems to be a newly established bridge connecting two sections of a road, thus alleviating the passage of travellers. What is of significance

---

[99] "Ulāgh-Utumubīl" [Donkey-Automobile], *Īrān*, yr 5, no. 798 (Qaws 24, 1299 [December 16, 1920]), 1.

[100] "Īrān va Sanāya'-i Mustazrafah" [Cultural Industries], *Īrān*, yr 6, no. 1130 (Ramadan al-Mubārak 6, 1340 [May 4, 1922]).

[101] These newly found films, unfortunately, have no specific dates, and have not yet been catalogued by the National Film Archive of Iran.

[102] The combination of the attire of the people in the parade, the excitement of the onlookers and the proximity of these streets to the Gulistan Royal Palace urges one to assume that these films depict a royal entourage and the escorting of a high-ranking official or even the Shah. One of these films could arguably date back to the time of the Constitutional Revolution too.

in these films is not a question of the intention of the cameraman or the reception of the films by audiences – especially since many of these films were perhaps not even known to the everyday Iranian audience. Instead, the question as to *why* such sites were selected for recording can perhaps better guide us toward the importance of these new developments in the urban everyday life of Iranians. The filming of a train arriving at the Shāh 'Abdul-'Azīm station, and the passing of veiled women toward it, would at once capture the advances of the country in technological aspects, and place it in spatial and temporal contemporaneity with Iran's counterparts – especially since this documentary-style film appears to be an Iranian version of the Lumière Brothers' *Arrival of a Train to La Ciotat* (1895).[103] The moving images of veiled women (in their 1900s–1910s fashion) in the streets of Tehran and in the Shāh 'Abdul-'Azīm station, too, are significant as they function to place women in temporal and spatial simultaneity with men.

Filming Tehran in this way then transformed the city from "a passive setting of the action into a major agent of the plot."[104] Through the framing process and the subsequent screening, according to François Penz and Andlong Lu, even the most anonymous and banal city location is transformed from "an unconsciously recorded space" to "a consciously recorded space that becomes an expressive space."[105] The capturing of the city in moving images is, in other words, chronicling the bits of the city that disappear forever, becoming part of Tehran's cinematic urban archeology. In a sense, the train passenger, car driver, the woman on the street, the police officer, the

---

[103] This film is most likely recorded by a filmmaker for two reasons: (1) the depiction of the train and the space of the station would be of significance to Iranian nationalists of the time, who were especially eager to extend the train-track lines and also to complete the Iranian railway that connected the north to the south; and (2) the film shows the flocking of women toward the train, images that most international filmmakers would refrain from capturing, considering the social and cultural conditions of the time.

[104] Yve-Alain Bois made this remark about early films of the Soviet filmmaker, Sergei Eisenstein, who made architecture and buildings an integral part of his filmmaking style in the early twentieth century. See Sergei Eisenstein, Yve-Alain Bois and Michael Glenny, "Montage and Architecture," *Assemblage*, no. 10 (December 1989), 113.

[105] François Penz and Andlong Lu, *Urban Cinematic: Understanding Urban Phenomena through the Moving Image* (Bristol: Intellect, 2011), 9.

clergy, the horse-back rider, the dandy and the average passer-by are "emblematic of modernity," both urban and cinematic.[106]

The transformations of the actual spaces of the movie theatres in early-twentieth-century Iran may illuminate better the experiences enacted in such places of exchange and sociability. As mentioned before, the earliest cinemas in Tehran were mainly centralised in the urban, commercial and touristic centres of the city, inhabited mostly by politicians, foreign officials and merchants. In fact, the three streets of 'Alā' al-Dawlah, Lālahzār and Nāsirīyah, which constituted the cosmopolitan spaces of Tehran, were home to most of the early public theatres in that city. This vicinity, as the allegorical emblem of urban modernity, further prompted the regeneration of an urban popular culture. In the words of Giuliana Bruno, cinema housed in this area was "grounded in a locus of spectacle and circulation of people and goods," in a "metropolitan site of" hybrid social configurations, that ranged from "a social elite and intelligentsia" to the average passer-by who was an observer of such spaces.[107]

Much of the scholarship on cinema in Iran has deemed early cinema to have been a private undertaking, only accessible to the nobility and Qajar court. The existence of documents containing the orders of Muzaffar al-Din Shah to import cinematographic machines from Europe, as well as a number of films pertaining to and/or involving the activities of the Shah, indeed, make it almost too easy to reckon the practices of film-watching solely as a courtly leisure.[108] The locations of Iranian movie theatres in the big cities such as Tehran and Tabriz, as well as the operators of cinematographs, however, beg us to consider another standpoint. From its very early days, film screenings in Iran were conducted in public sites of sociability, although perhaps in spaces that were not necessarily intended for such activities – either due to the uncertainty with regard to the reception of the cinemato-graph by the public and/or the unavailability of spaces required for film projection. For example, Mīrzā Ibrāhīm khān Sahhāf-Bāshī's first cine-matograph operated in the inner court (hayāt) of his antique shop,

---

[106] See Scott Lash and John Urry, *Economies of Signs and Space* (London: Sage, 1994), 252.

[107] Giuliana Bruno, *Streetwalking on a Ruined Map: Cultural Theory and the City Films of Elvira Notari* (Princeton University Press, 1993), 43.

[108] See Mehrabi, *Tārīkh-i Sīnamā-yi Īrān*, 15; Sadr, *Iranian Cinema*, 8–10; and Naficy, *A Social History of Iranian Cinema*, vol. 1, 39.

while other merchants in Tehran showed cinematographic films in the spaces of their coffee houses or shops or on the second levels of buildings that lined the main streets of the city. With the eventual propagation of cinema, specific locations were built and/or assigned to the practice of cinematograph spectatorship. The Moving Picture Spectacle House (Tamāshā Khānah-'i 'Aks-i Mutiharrik) of Russi Khan in fact operated in his photography studio, which was well known to both the court and the Iranian public.[109] As mentioned above, many film screenings were held in guest houses (mihmān khānah), hotels and coffee shops. Aghayev, for example, selected his Zargarabād café on Chirāghgāz Avenue as the venue for his public film screenings.[110] Some also considered conferences and schools as suitable places for film projection.[111]

Many screening sessions were organised for charities, the poor and those struck by natural disasters, such as earthquakes. Excellent Cinema conducted a cinematographic screening "for the benefit of fire-victims" of Āmul (a city in Northern Iran) in Iran Motel on Lālah-zār Avenue.[112] New Cinema (Sīnamā-yi Jadīd) offered a "festive night for the benefit of the poor in Tehran," in which the net profit attained from the selling of tickets was allocated for the purchase of bread for the poor.[113] Fārūs Cinema (Sīnamā-yi Fārūs), likewise, organised a cinematographic screening "for the benefit of the Armenian School" in 1922, hinting furthermore at the way in which the Iranian cinematic culture emerged out of hybrid interactions of various communities in urban sites.[114] The programs of film screenings were planned to

---

[109] "I'lān" [Advertisement], *Habl al-Matīn*, no. 141 (Ramazān 6, 1325 [October 13, 1907]), 4.

[110] *Subh-i Sādiq*, no. 166 (Ramadān 23, 1325 [October 31, 1907]), 4. "In the Zargarabād coffee shop on Chirāghgāz Avenue, a cinematograph device has been installed, and new emerging acts (i.e. films) such as the Russo-Japan War are available."

[111] "Az Taraf-i Shirkat-i Kunfirāns" [On behalf of Conference Company], *Īrān-i Naw*, yr 2, no. 140 (Safar 11, 1328 [February 22, 1922]), 1.

[112] "Sīnamā-yi 'Ālī-yi Īrān: Bi-manfi'at-i Harīqzadigān-i Āmul" [Excellent Cinema of Iran: For the Benefits of Fire Victims of Amul], *Īrān*, no. 69 (Rajab 8, 1335 [April 30, 1917]), 2.

[113] "Sīnamā-yi Jadīd" [New Cinema], *Naw Bahār*, no. 225 (Sunbulah 8, 1294 [August 31, 1915]), 4.

[114] "Sīnamā-yi Fārūs: Bi-manfi'at-i Madrasah-'i Arāmanah" [Farus Cinema: For the Benefit of the Armenian School], *Shafaq-i Surkh*, no. 99 (Āzar 20, 1301 [December 12, 1922]), 4.

accommodate the schedules of the urban public and thus to maximise ticket-sale profits. In 1915, for example, New Cinema screened films on "all nights," starting from "seven thirty" in the evening (although sometimes their program actually started at 8.30 pm).[115]

While many film screenings continued to be conducted in various public sites of sociability, in the 1910s theatres and film-screening venues increasingly began to adopt the term "cinema" or culturally similar titles as appropriate designations for the space where they projected films for public audiences. Cinematograph Spectacle House (Tamāshākhānah-'i Sīnamātugrāf), New Cinema – the name of which later changed to Modern Cinema (Sīnamā-yi Mudirn), Sun Cinema and Excellent Cinema are some examples from this period.[116] Regardless of the actual space where films were showcased, these venues engaged in engendering and expanding an urban cinematic culture. The launch announcement of the Grand Hotel of Tehran, which was to open in 1916 on Lālahzār Avenue especially for "the reception of men and honorable guests," boasted that the hotel was "the first new and beautiful building of Tehran."[117] The fact that the advert attended to the functionality of the hotel as both "theatre and cinema" hints to the manner in which the propagation of cinema and theatre was embedded in the urbanisation and the expansion of sites of sociability in Tehran (Figure 1.4).[118]

Many hotels and guesthouses engaged in practices that not only worked to attract audiences from diverse backgrounds, but also functioned to associate leisure and pleasure with the practice of film spectatorship. In these newly established venues, specific provisions were considered for the comfort and wellness of guests and travellers. Gradually, live music would come to be used to accompany the film. To meet the satisfaction of audiences, on some nights, for example, New

---

[115] "Sīnamā-yi Jadīd" [New Cinema], *Ra'd*, yr 6, no. 152 (Saratān 30, 1294 [July 22, 1915]), 1.

[116] Cinematograph Spectacle House (Tamāshākhānah-'i Sīnamātugrāf), Modern Cinema (Sīnamā-yi Mudirn) and Sun Cinema were operated by Ardishīr Khān. He initially collaborated with Antoin Sevreguin in operating Cinematograph Spectacle House.

[117] "Girānd Hutil" [Grand Hotel], *Ra'd*, yr 7, no. 143 (Jamādī al-Awwal 28, 1334 [April 2, 1916]), 4.

[118] *Ibid.*

Figure 1.4 Lālahzār Avenue in the early Pahlavi era

Cinema would play "military [march] music" during the program break.[119] Excellent Cinema, too, would usually include an orchestra (*urkist*) in its programs.[120] Soon, snacks also came to occupy an important place in the cinematic experience, during and in between film screenings. New Cinema, for example, advertised buffet food and beverages that would be served during film screenings every night,[121] and the playing of military music during intermission for special occasions.[122] Café Lālahzār, too, advertised the provision of certain "means of welfare" and the "preparation of the means of comfort" for guests.[123] The Casino (Kāzīnaw) guesthouse on Lālahzār Avenue

[119] "Sīnamā-yi Jadīd" [New Cinema], *Naw Bahār*, no. 225 (Sunbulah 8, 1294 [August 31, 1915]), 4.
[120] "... buffet [and] orchestra are also available." See "Taghyīr-i Makān" [A Change in Location], *Ra'd*, yr 7, no. 202 (Saratān 4, 1295 [June 25, 1916]), 4.
[121] "Sīnamā-yi Jadīd" [New Cinema], *Ra'd*, yr 6, no. 152 (Ramazān 9, 1333 [July 21, 1915]), 1.
[122] "Sīnamā-yi Jadīd" [New Cinema], *Naw Bahār*, no. 225 (Shawwāl 19, 1333 [August 30, 1915]), 4.
[123] "Kāfah Lālahzār Maftūh Shud" [Café Lālahzār Has Been Launched], *Ra'd*, yr 7, no. 136 (Hūt 27, 1294 [March 17, 1916]), 4.

provided travellers with clean "single rooms and sleeping beds" that followed "health provisions," in addition to other "items of comfort": these included serving of food and cinematographic screenings, as well as nightly, Iranian music performances, free of charge.[124] European dishes, such as "Gigot, cutlet, ragout, omelette, soup," were sold at reasonable prices alongside Iranian dishes, such as "Rice-Kebab with side plates (eggs, Lavash bread, yogurt drink, cheese, herbs, fruit)," thus catering to the tastes of diverse clients. During the 1910s, then, the "oral nature of cinematic pleasure" was acknowledged in an "imaginary assimilation to eating," and was actualised in the buying/selling of snacks and food during film screenings during this period.[125] The Casino also had a "reading room" (utāq-i qarā'at-khānah), which featured new newspapers from Iranian and non-Iranian publications.[126] Cinematic experiences in such venues, then, were not necessarily organised around the practice of watching a film, but around socialisation and larger leisure activities that emerged with urban modernity.

The elements of performance in the art of projection were, undoubtedly, crucial in the shaping of this culture. According to 'Abdullāh Bahrāmī, Ardishīr Khan, who was a "sturdy" Armenian – and a spectacle himself – "would stand at the top of the room with a serious and solemn attitude, to give necessary explanations with regard to the acting and its actors." At the same time, a string-player (*Tār-zan*) (i.e. a musician that plays the traditional Iranian instrument, *Tār*) would accompany a percussionist (*dunbak* – i.e. another traditional Iranian instrument) in performing "national songs" (*āhanghā-yi vatanī*), in order to "excite" the audience.[127] Later on, Khān Bābā Khān Mu'tazidī, a French-trained cinematographer and cinema owner, would hire live translators to interpret foreign film intertitles for the local Persian-speaking audience.[128] His partner, 'Alī Vakīlī, a cinema owner,

---

[124] "Kāzīnaw – Casino," *Īrān*, no. 120 (Qa'dah 17, 1335 [September 4, 1917]), 4.

[125] Bruno, *Streetwalking on a Ruined Map*, 44.

[126] See "Kāzīnaw – Casino," *Īrān*, no. 120 (Dhu al-Qa'dah 17, 1335 [September 4, 1917]), 4.

[127] 'Abdullāh Bahrāmī, *Khātirāt-i 'Abdullāh Bahrāmī: Az Ākhar-i Saltanat-i Nāsir al-Dīn Shāh tā Avval-i Kūditā* [*The Memoirs of 'Abdullāh Bahrāmī: From the End of Nasir al-Din Shah's Reign to the Beginning of Coup d'Etat*], (Tehran: Intishārāt-i 'Ilmī, 1984), 42.

[128] According to Umid, and also mentioned by Naficy, Khān Bābā Khān Mu'tazidī was first enrolled in the Alliance Française School in Tehran, but then

operator, author and representative in the Majlis (parliament), would also engage in activities that attracted audiences, such as including live orchestra and adding Persian-language intertitles to celluloid films.[129]

Such new developments, it seems, gave way to the shaping of a culture of film spectatorship that paralleled Iran's emergent consumer culture – one that at once ensured means for business competition and commercial return for cinema/cinematograph owners, enabled possibilities for heterotopic experiences and cosmopolitan encounters, and facilitated the means to regulate and define cinematic culture and the audience in general (Figure 1.5). The culture of spectatorship was further transformed when cinemas began to classify seats in the theatres. New Cinema, for example, advertised three different ticket prices according to the three categories of seats – First Class 8 Qirān (an Iranian currency during the Qajar period), Second Class 5 Qirān and Third Class 2 Qirān – assigned by the cinema owner, and hinting at social stratification in such spaces.[130] On the other hand, "in consideration of workers and students," Excellent Cinema charged "the lowest amounts" for film spectatorship.[131] The physical space that the cinema occupied in cities such as Tehran was, of course, also reminiscent of social divisions. The gradual commercialisation and profiteering of cinema and cinematic practices did not go unnoticed or unchallenged. In 1920, *Iran* newspaper, for example, took issue with Palace Cinema, which had "indicated high prices for its tickets" and delegated "less than half of its seats to class one [seats]." The article moreover criticised the staff of the movie theatre for not providing the best experience; for example, they "showed only a few short acts" of *Monte Cristo* by intentionally ringing "the intermission bell" a few times during the course of the film.[132]

continued his education in Switzerland and France. In Paris, he met Léon Gaumont's son, and through him he found employment in the Gaumont film factory, and thus learned the art of filmmaking there. See Umid, Tārīkh-i Sīnamā-yi Īrān; and Naficy, *A Social History of Iranian Cinema*, vol. 1, 68–69.

129 Naficy, *A Social History of Iranian Cinema*, vol. 1, 69–70.
130 "Sīnamā-yi Jadīd" [New Cinema], *R'ad*, yr 6, no. 159 (Murdād 19, 1294 [August 11, 1915]), 2.
131 "I'lān" [Advertisement], *Ra'd*, yr 7, no. 165 (Sawr 10, 1295 [April 30, 1916]), 4.
132 "Mukhbir-i Mā dar Sīnamā Pālās" [Our Reporter in Cinema Palace], *Īrān*, yr 4, no. 674 (Ramadān 7, 1338 [May 25, 1920]), 2.

Figure 1.5 Sīnamā Millī's advertisement for *Just Imagine* (1930), in Tehran streets. Photo by Austrian Archives (S)/Imagno/Getty Images.

Amid the increasing popularity of cinema in the first two decades of the twentieth century, numerous articles were published in the press in various cities that aimed to introduce the projection device to the people, educate them on the technical and educational aspects of the cinematograph, and/or offer training as regards the "proper" practices for the screening and watching of films. In 1907, in the city of Baku in Azerbaijan – a cosmopolitan city, home to many Iranian immigrants, as well as Azerbaijanis who were fluent in the Persian language and informed of goings-on in Iran – the monthly Persian publication of *Facts* (Haqāyiq) published an article on the "entertaining tool of

Sīnu-mu tigrāf" (cinematograph) or the "moving pictures," which had "recently entered the city and attracted everyone's attention."[133] After having introduced the modern medium, the article then attended to the technicalities of the device and its functions using a picture that showed the inside of a cinematograph.[134] *Chihrah-Namā* periodical, likewise, published an article to introduce the invention of cinematograph to the readers who had already been very familiar with "new inventions such as saucers, wireless telegraph, wireless telephone, and dictograph"; the article further anticipated the cinematograph "to become widespread," similar to other inventions.[135] *Tabriz* newspaper (Rūznāmah-'i Tabrīz), published in the city of Tabriz, also issued an article in March 1911 on cinematograph or moving pictures (Sīnamātugrāf yā 'Aks-i Mutiharrik), which discussed the details involved in the functioning of the cinematographic device and the sensory processes that watching moving pictures entailed.[136] *Luminosity of Education* (Furūq-i Tarbīyat) magazine in 1921 published an extensive article on the new cinematographic and gramophone technologies in Germany and France, such as the creation of phonocinema in the latter.[137] The article, furthermore, descibed new techniques that stop the vibration of the image on screen through the usage of multiple moving mirrors that are rotated at the same rate as the cinematographic film.[138] The author also wrote about the importance of cinematographic screenings in schools and educational institutions.[139] Touching upon the advancement of cinema technology in 1925, *Iran* newspaper published a translated article (from a "French scientific journal") on the new developments in "colour" motion picture film.[140] Moreover, the same

---

[133] "Sīnu-mu tigrāf" [cinematograph], *Haqāyiq*, no. 1 (Safar 7, 1325 [March 22, 1907]), 14.

[134] *Ibid.*

[135] "Sīnamātugrāf-Shab Pardah" [Cinematograph-Dark Screen], *Chihrah-Namā*, yr 7, no. 20 (Zī-Qa'da 1, 1328 [November 5, 1910]), 16.

[136] Abū al-Qāsim, "Sīnamātugrāf yā 'Aks-i Mutiharrik" [Cinematograph or Moving Picture], *Tabrīz*, yr 1, no. 34 (Rabi'al-Awwal 23, 1329 [March 25, 1911]), 4.

[137] "Takmīl-i Sīnamātugrāf va Grāmfun" [The Completion of Cinematograph and Gramaphone], *Furūgh-i Tarbīyat*, yr 1, no. 2 (Urdībihisht 1300 [April 1921]), 19–20. Most likely, the author is referring to the coupling of cinematographic projections with phonographs during screenings.

[138] *Ibid.*, 19.   [139] *Ibid.*, 19–20.

[140] "Sīnamā-yi Rangī" [Colour Cinema], *Īrān*, yr 9, no. 1793 (Hūt 25, 1303 [March 15, 1925]), 3.

publication in 1925 published another extensive article on the emergence and development of "talking cinema" (sīnamā-yi nātiq).[141]

An examination of the newspapers and journals of the time reveals that cinema (or the venue for cinematographic screening) had become a common spectacle by the 1920s. In the early 1920s, the satirical *Nāhīd* journal touched upon the social and cultural phenomena that aroused disputes and tension among the public, namely cinema. In a column entitled "Shahr-i Farang,"[142] the *Nāhīd* publication used satirical cinematic language to survey and grapple with certain issues related to the urban and social affairs in Tehran. Starting its columns with "Injā Tihrān ast" (This is Tehran), the author especially brought to light the transformations of a dynamic Tehran that were increasingly sensationally felt in everyday life. The use of the title "Shahr-i Farang" itself, as a familiar visual medium that portrayed pictures from around the globe while an accompanying narrator explicated and perhaps embellished the scenes with familiar cultural symbols and stories, is revealing in this instance. Operating as a cheap portable medium that brought the global into Iranian localities, Shahr-i Farang was already well known among Iranians who were especially zealous to discover the spaces beyond their own.

Sarcastically referring to Shahr-i Farang as National Cinema (sīnamā-yi vatanī) in his column,[143] the *Nāhīd* author ridiculed the imaginary operator of the device, "Ali, the Blind" (Alī Kūrī), for having imitated other cinema institutions and creating his "national" version.[144] The author, furthermore, poked fun at the national device for operating in neighbourhoods such as Sabzah Maydān (close to the bazar) and the Tūpkhānah Square (Artillary Square), and hence for lagging behind actual cinemas that operated in the upper-class neighbourhoods, such as Lālahzār Avenue. One could even suggest that the author meant to draw comparisons between Shahr-i Farang and Iran, in that they were both functional, but behind the times. For example, in addressing a complaint letter by a woman who took

---

[141] "Sīnamā-yi Nātiq" [Talkie Cinema], *Īrān*, yr 9, no. 1861 (Tir 24, 1304 [July 15, 1925]), 1.

[142] Shahr-i Farang (Francotopic/Frankish city) is an Iranian form of a peep box that was carried around the town by travelling showmen to show images from around the world. Shahr-i Farang is very similar to a stereoscope in function.

[143] "Shahr-i Farang yā Sīnamā-yi Vatanī" [Peep Box or National Cinema], *Nāhīd*, no. 2 (Sha'bān 9, 1339 [April 18, 1921]), 3.

[144] "Shahr-i Farang: Shab-i Jum'ah-'i Duzdhā" [Shahr-i Farang: The Friday Night of Thieves], *Nāhīd*, yr 8, no. 5 (Murdād 10, 1307 [August 1, 1928]), 2.

issue with the lack of movie theatres for women in Tehran, the author jestingly remarked that in the absence of such entertainment forms, women "went to Sabzah Maydān," a neighbourhood devoid of the glamour of Lālahzār, to watch the Iranian version of the visual spectacle "Shahr-i Farang."[145] One could readily read this article as a critique that took issue with the lack of educational media such as cinema for Iranian women, especially in locations that were easily accessible to various audiences. One could also read the article as a social commentary on the compartmentalisation of the city into affluent and poor or modern and traditional districts. In another instance, the author jestingly reiterated some of the points of "the municipal announcement" distributed at Tūpkhānah Square,[146] which stated that "national works [i.e. Shahr-i Farang] in the upper parts of the city" were "harmful" for the public; "There, [one can only find] Pathé Cinema, Sun Cinema and Grand Hotel."[147] The public announcement then instructed audiences "to go downtown" (i.e. to the south of the entertainment centre of Tehran, or the more traditional and less privileged areas of the city) for national artifacts such as Shahr-i Farang.[148] Such comments reveal once again the ways in which cinema (and its Iranian competitor Shahr-i Farang) came to compartmentalise urban cities such as Tehran into contradictory, conflicting and contestatory spheres as part and parcel of the processes of urbanisation.

Having a love and hate relationship with cinema, the Shahr-i Farang columnist interchangeably used the two names, Shahr-i Farang and (National) Cinema, to refer to this local device. In one of his columns, for example, he wrote that "Ali Kūrī" (Ali, the Blind) "had recently

---

[145] Kaminah 'Iffat Samī'ī, "Shahr-i Farang," *Nāhīd*, yr 2, no. 39 (Rajab 11, 1342 [February 17, 1924]), 6–7.

[146] Based on the articles and commentaries published in the press, Tūpkhānah Square used to be one of the original homes of the Shahr-i Farang devices. According to the narratives found in this column, in the mid-1920s, the Tūpkhānah Square, considered as a modern landmark of Tehran, was the dividing line between the more affluent entertainment district in the north from the more traditional district in the south of the city (e.g. Sabzah Maydān).

[147] "Shahr-i Farang: bā yik Tīr Sah Nishān" [Shahr-i Farahng: One Stone Three Birds], *Nāhīd*, no. 5 (Ramazān 28, 1341[May 14, 1923]), 6–7. According to the narratives found in this column, in the mid-1920s, the Tūpkhānah Square, considered as a modern landmark of Tehran, was the dividing line between the more affluent entertainment district in the north from the more traditional district in the south of the city (e.g. Sabzah Maydān).

[148] Moreover, the same article writes, "On the wall of Tūpkhānah Square, it was posted that national cinema or shahr-i Farang has been moved from Tūpkhānah Square to Sabzah Square." See "Shahr-i Farang: bā yik Tīr Sah Nishān," 6–7.

prepared beautiful new acts (films)," and so the author "went to the cinema" (rather than Shahr-i Farang) to prepare reports on those films for *Nāhīd* readers.[149] Ridiculing Iranians who had not caught up with the pace of the Westerners, the author inverted the situation, and remarked – sarcastically – that "the arrogant foreigners" would never amount to the likes of "Karbalā-yī Rajab ʿAlī, the inventor of National Cinema" (i.e. Shahr-i Farang in this case).[150] One could perhaps decipher from such instances that cinema, by the 1920s, had attained a sense of everydayness, albeit disputed, for urban residents. In fact, since cinema was considered by the Iranian middle-class to be an effective device in "not only the well-passing" of time, but also in "scientific education," and moral disciplining of Iranian residents, its aggregation in the urban centres was a given.[151] This is especially of interest if viewed in parallel to the blooming of nationalist sentiments in the early twentieth century. What is meant by nationalist sentiments here are opinions that (even though they are cosmopolitan in origin)[152] negated "Western" domination in the country, while at the same time seeking technological progress flourishing in those countries that helped to achieve the realisation of an "Iranian" progressive and advanced nation. Cinema was reckoned to be a medium that assisted in repelling social maladies brought on by European intrusion and the discolouring of Iranian values.[153] In guiding Iranians toward a futural moral Iran, its propagation in hybrid urban spaces was deemed necessary by Iranian nationalists for solidifying the notion of an independent/sovereign Iran.

1.3 Early Cinema and National Consciousness in Iran

Tehran's rapid societal and cultural transformations in the first two decades of the twentieth century invoked sensory experiences which,

---

[149] "Shahr-i Farang," *Nāhīd*, yr 2, no. 4 (Ramazān 7, 1342 [April 12, 1924]), 6.
[150] "Shahr-i Farang yā Sīnamā-yi Vatanī" [Shahr-i Farang or National Cinema], *Nāhīd*, yr 1, no. 2 (Shaʿbān 9, 1339 [April 18, 1921]), 3.
[151] "Favāʾid-i Sīnamātugrāf" [The Benefits of Cinematograph], *Īrān-i Naw*, yr 1, no. 84 (Āzar 16, 1288 [December 8, 1909]), 3.
[152] It must be kept in mind that many of the nationalist perspectives that flourished in Iran in the early twentieth century (especially before and after the Constitutional Revolution) were shaped by the fluid ideological and intellectual interchanges between Iranians, Armenians, Ottomans/Turkish Republicans, Russians, Azeris, Georgians and others.
[153] "Favāʾid-i Sīnamātugrāf," 3.

aside from wonderment and reverence, also gave way to concerns and fear in response to dealing with such changes. Cyrus Schayegh explicates some of the anxieties that specifically arose from the use of modern technologies, mechanised transport and the shrinking of notions of time and space in the early twentieth century; some of these included concerns about the rapid spread of epidemic diseases and an increase in stress levels that led to mental diseases, and by consequence to moral vice and social ailments.[154]

The modern Iranian imaginary, which prognosticated a healthy Iran devoid of bodily illnesses, soon cultivated feelings for a progressive Iran that was free of "social maladies" and its manifested traits of "lying" and "cheating."[155] In such circumstances of commotion and stir, during a period of governmental decentralisation, education and moral instruction were seen as indispensable to attempts at disciplining the self, enlightening society, advancing the country and locating Iran on the global map. The function of cinema as a public mode of communication became noteworthy here.

Because of its potential role in "moral" instruction, as discussed below and in the following chapter, cosmopolitan nationalists drew links between cinema, education and the materialisation of nationalist sentiments. At a time when it was not yet centralised or officially absorbed by the state, cinema became a medium in the service of the technologies of selfhood, i.e. the means for governing oneself to become a member of civil society. Cinema was imagined to refashion subjectivities in line with the demands of the new time, and to stir patriotic sentiments at a time of national turmoil. In Tehran, patriotic and nationalist sensibilities were shaped during a period that was riddled with a dynamic and interactive diversity; cinema and the culture surrounding it provided a space and a mode of communication for these cosmopolitan interactions and identities that were now increasingly patriotic. In cinema, then, cosmopolitanism was arguably *a style of national imagination.*[156]

---

[154] For a detailed analysis of the importance of sciences in early-twentieth-century Iran, and the medicalised language that was used to cure social maladies, refer to Cyrus Schayegh, *Who Is Knowledgeable Is Strong: Science, Class, and the Formation Modern Iranian Society (1900–1950)* (Berkeley, CA: University of California Press, 2009).

[155] "Nukāt va Mulāhizāt" [Tips and Considerations], *Kāvah*, yr 2, no. 3 (Aban 4, 1290 [March 11, 1921]), 1.

[156] Very few scholars of modern Iran have worked to refine theories of nationalism to include the histories of Iran's minority groups. Although he does not use the

As early as 1907, *Tamaddun* newspaper characterised "theatres and movie houses" as increasingly progressive factors in the future of Iran, especially by exciting and inciting sentiments for national advancement.[157] In 1909, in the midst of the Constitutional Revolution, *New Iran* (*Iran-i Naw*) newspaper published an article entitled "The Benefits of the Cinematograph," which pointed out the ways through which the cinematograph displayed the "microbes of various diseases."[158] In this article, Ghulām-Rizā, the author, claimed that "to repel the enemies of humanity," it was now possible "to take good measures against the microbes that have entered the blood" and that have "fully deteriorated the health" of societies.[159] The cinematograph, the author continued, "magnifies these microbes," makes them visible to the public, and thereby provides the consciousness to avert them.[160] Throughout the article, Ghulām-Rizā encouraged the use of the cinematograph not only for the passing of time (or entertainment), but also for the "scientific instruction" of students.[161] He urged urban schools to include film screenings in their curriculum since the projection of images was "better for the comprehension of students than the explanations of the most capable of teachers."[162]

In a 1910 report on the "Conference against Loan," which was organised in Russi Khan's movie theatre, and was conducted in between "beautiful and excellent electrobiograph" film screenings, the author expressed that the conference speaker saw the solution against foreign loans – and *British Times* magazine's suggestion to hire Europeans for Iranian affairs – to rest in "patriotism."[163] "Would an Iranian acquiesce [if] his/her taxes were in the … hands of foreigners? Would an Iranian … tolerate seeing the dominance of foreigners in his/

---

notion of cosmopolitanism or cosmopolitan identities to refer to ethnoreligious minorities and their activities in Iran, David Yaghoubian looks into the everyday lives of ordinary Armenian residents of Iran and how they acted as co-participants in the creation and shaping of nationalism in twentieth-century Iran. See David Yaghoubian, *Ethnicity, Identity, and the Development of Nationalism in Iran* (Syracuse University Press, 2014).

[157] "Lāyah'-i yikī az Namāyindigān-i Jāpun" [The Bill of One of the Representatives of Japan], *Tamaddun*, no. 36 (Sha'ban al-Muazzam 14, 1325 [September 22, 1907]).

[158] "Favāid-i Sīnamātugrāf," 3.   [159] *Ibid.*   [160] *Ibid.*   [161] *Ibid.*

[162] *Ibid.*, 4.

[163] "Mas'alah-'i Istiqrāz va Kunfarāns Bar 'Alayh-i Istiqrāz" [The Issue of Loans and the Conference against Loans], *Īrān-i Naw*, yr 2, no. 144 (Safar 16, 1328 [February 27, 1910]), 1–2.

her country?" asked the speaker – questions to which he himself responded, "No, no, it will not be permitted."[164] This instance is especially revealing in that it points to the emergence of cinema as a political site that engendered debates on Iranian and global affairs and enabled conversations surrounding national sentiments.

Holding a similar perspective on the significance of cinematic education for the time, Berlin-based *Irānshahr* monthly magazine lamented that Iranians had not yet "discovered the current importance of theatre and cinema"; Murtizā Mushfiq Kāzimī complained that "the higher-ranks and intellectuals of the country are still reluctant about going to cinemas" and that they only prescribed "cinema-going" for their children when they cried on a whim.[165] When "the excitement and inclination for recreation and free-studies have been obliterated," the article insisted, "one cannot hope for progress" in the country; thus directly linking the creation of an Iranian cinema culture to a progressive Iran.[166] Mushfiq Kāzimī further recommended that cinema owners establish "a company for the importation of translated American and German films," so that they could be "screened for women in private spaces," and that the audiences would become familiar with the "awe-inspiring events" of European civilisations.[167] This prescription for the establishment of an exclusive company for the importation of foreign films, in fact, presaged the establishment of Iran Film Company (Shirkat-i Film-i Iran), the first film company dedicated to the importation of films, by more than a decade. To give another example of how the elite stressed the implication of cinema in public edification, in March 1926, 'Alīqulī Mahmūdī in an article in the *Shafaq-i Surkh* (Red Aurora) periodical expressed his regrets that cinema in Iran had gained insufficient attention, despite it being "the best device for education and moral instruction."[168] *Cinema and Screenings (Sīnamā va Namāyishāt)* magazine published in 1930 by the cinema entrepreneur, 'Alī Vakīlī, addressed the importance of cinema in achieving "progress and eminence" in Iran. One article specifically proclaimed cinema to be

---

[164] *Ibid.*
[165] Murtiza Mushfiq Kāzimī, "Ma'ārif dar Īrān: Ti'ātr va Mūsīghī dar Īrān" [Education in Iran: Theatre and Music in Iran], *Irānshahr*, yr 2, nos 5–6 (Isfand 2, 1292 [February 21, 1924]), 326.
[166] *Ibid.*   [167] *Ibid.*, 330.
[168] 'Alīqulī Mahmūdī, "Taraqqī-yi sīnamā dar Tihrān" [The Advancement of Cinema in Tehran], *Īrān*, yr 10, no. 2064 (Isfand 27, 1304 [March 18, 1926]).

a "new born child" that "this age of fortune and blissfulness" had engendered and the "disciplining and maintenance of which" it had "bestowed upon the inhabitants" of that country.[169] Cinemas, then, similar to many other cultural sites of sociability, facilitated spaces where critical debates would be conducted and national fervour spawned. The establishment and appropriation of cinema as a means of education and moral guidance thus operated to morph cinema into a medium, the capacity of which was not limited to entertainment.

It was perhaps for these reasons that as early as 1909, announcements for cinematographic screenings advertised "moral acts/films" (pardah-hā-yi Akhlāqī) – cinematic moral instructions that worked to discipline Iranian imaginations.[170] Many movie theatres, such as Casino Cinema (Sīnamā Kazīnaw), Sun Cinema of Lālahzār Avenue (Sīnamā Khurshīd-i Lālahzār)[171] and Palace Cinema, advertised moral, scientific, historic and war films in their film announcements. In a 1919 film advertisement in *Ra'd* (Thunder) newspaper, Palace Cinema specifically claimed the purpose of cinema to be "the rectification of public morale."[172] In 1923, Sun Cinema (Sīnamā-yi Khurshīd) of Fārūs Publishing House commented on the benefits of cinema for students in Iran, and advocated its use for pedagogical reasons as it was "customary in all of Farangistān [the Occident/Eurotopia]."[173] Such accounts attest to the ways in which some envisioned the future of Iran as commensurate with more advanced countries, in terms of the employment of cinema spaces, as well as visual offerings projected on screen.

To better grasp the early-twentieth-century association between cinema and education, one could perhaps also point to the fact that a

---

[169] "Sīnamā dar Īrān," *Sīnamā va Namāyishāt*, no. 1, 4.

[170] As early as the late 1900s, advertisements for discounted film tickets appeared in Iranian newspapers. In 1909, *New Iran* publication advertised "half-price tickets for students" if they obtained the signature of their school principal. To give another example from the 1910s, Excellent Cinema in a 1916 announcement in *Ra'd* newspaper also advertised "moral acts/films" (pardah-hā-yi Akhlāqī) for students for the "lowest of prices." See: "I'lān-i Tamāshākhānah-'i Jadīd-i Nāsirīyyah" [The Announcement for the Nasiriyyah Spectacle House], *Īrān-i Naw*, yr 1, no. 23 (Sunbulah 28, 1288 [September 20, 1909]), 1; and, "I'lān," *Ra'd*, yr 7, no. 165 (Sawr 10, 1295 [April 30, 1916]), 4.

[171] Not to be confused with Ardishīr Khān's Sun Cinema.

[172] "Raf'-i Ishtibāh – Sīnamā Pālās," *Ra'd*, no. 124, 2.

[173] Not to be confused with the Sun Cinema on Lālahzār Avenue. See "Sīnamā-yi Khurshid" [The Sun Cinema], *Sitārah-'i Īrān*, yr 9, no. 114 (Bahman 11, 1302 [January 31, 1923]).

number of movie theatres were established on Nāsirī (or Nāsirīyah) Avenue, home to the famous school of Dār al-Funūn; Aghayev's 1908 cinematographic screening venue was located in front of this higher education institution,[174] while one of Russi Khan's cinemas was situated in the yard of Dār al-Funūn.[175] As already mentioned above, film gatherings were also sometimes held as seminars and conferences, where diverse residents of Iran congregated. The Conference Company (Shirkat-i Kunfarāns), for example, organised a conference and cinematographic screening in the upper level of Fārūs Publishing House in 1910.[176] In the 1920s, some films and newsreels were also showcased in the Military School (Madrisah-'i Nizām).

Students were specifically targeted in the cosmopolitan nationalists' campaign in promoting cinematic instruction. In 1915, New Cinema allocated 200 free tickets for students in Tehran to watch a film that was of such importance that it was intended to be the only film included in the program of that night (rather than the usual two to three different films that would be included in each program).[177] Other cities such as Tabriz, Mashhad, Rasht and Simnan also participated in the expansion and diversification of sites of sociability, as well as joining in the movement toward public moral edification through cinema. The launch announcement of Iran's Illusion Cinema (Īlīzīyūn-i Irān), which opened in Tabriz in 1910, for example, specifically advertised films that mainly pertained to "science, history, geography of the globe, relating to schools and publications, ethics, light comedies et al."[178] The same movie theatre also offered discounted tickets for students in Tabriz. It thus seems that the cosmopolitan middle-class, who by virtue of their professions had intellectual and commercial contacts with the diasporic communities in Iran and neighbouring countries, understood the significance of cinema in "public" enlightenment as opposed to private consumption of books and publications; they took pride in its potential role in the service of

---

[174] "I'lān" [Advertisement], Sūr-i Isrāfīl, yr 1, no. 26 (Urdībihisht 3, 1287 [April 23, 1908]), 8.

[175] Baharloo, Rūzshumār-i Sīnamā-yi Īrān, 46.

[176] "Az Taraf-i Shirkat-i Kunfirāns" [On Behalf of Conference Company], Īrān-i Naw, yr 2, no. 140 (Safar 11, 1328 [February 22, 1922]), 1.

[177] "Sīnamā-yi Jadīd" [New Cinema], Naw Bahār, no. 221 (Murdād 24, 1294 [August 16, 1915]), 4.

[178] Baharloo, Rūzshumār-i Sīnamā-yi Īrān, 94. The advertisement of interest was in fact a flyer that was dedicated to the Iranian Cinema Museum by Yahyā Zukā.

the technologies of the self and guiding of imaginations toward visions of what Iran ought to be.

The films that have survived from the early twentieth century increasingly point to the shaping of national consciousness in that age. Actualité or documentary films of the Iranian regiment marching in the streets, in military fields and in front of dignitaries, for example, can very well point to an Iran that is militaristically and nationally representable on a global level – an Iran that is arguably "modern" (*mutijaddid*). In Marshall Berman's reading of Baudelaire's poems, "armies on parade" in Paris played "a central role in the pastoral vision of modernity: glittering hardware, gaudy colors, flowing lines, fast and graceful movements," depicting a form of "modernity without tears."[179] In Iran, too, these films captured visions of modernity that were meant to be registered in the visual archive of the twentieth century. The recording of urban landmarks, national holiday ceremonies and cultural signifiers points to a sense of national fervour, evident in films that were either made or ordered to be made by Muzaffar al-Din Shah himself during his lifetime. The chronicling of special occasions on celluloid such as the 'Āshūrā/Tāsū'ā mourning ceremonies and the lions in Dūshān Tappah, the filming of which as Chahryar Adle argues was most probably carried out by Akkāsbāshī (the court's photographer and cinematographer) on the order of Muzaffar al-Din Shah some time between 1901 and 1906,[180] points to the significance of the camera and cinema in recording national, historical and Islamic ceremonies, and in imagining Iran on par with its European neighbours. Other films that Adle considers to have been recorded by Iranian filmmakers – based on the labels and documents

---

[179] Through this passage, Berman brings attention to the preoccupation of Baudelaire's poetry/prose with modern life; for example, "the tremendous importance of military display – psychological as well as political importance – and its power to captivate even the freest spirits." See Marshall Berman, *All That Is Solid Melts into Air: The Experience of Modernity* (New York: Penguin Books, 1988), 137.

[180] Adle mentions that in the existing documents, the name of the cinematographer is not mentioned; however, since 'Akkāsbāshī was the official photographer and cinematographer of Muzaffar al-Din Shah, it is very probable that he filmed the event, making him the first Iranian documentary maker. It should be mentioned that the film has not yet been found. See Chahryar Adle, "Acquaintance with Cinema and the First Steps of Filming and Filmmaking in Iran: 1899–1907," *Tāvūs Quarterly* 5 & 6 (2000–2001): 20, accessed April 16, 2018, www.tavoosonline.com/Articles/ArticleDetailFa.aspx?src=68&Page=20.

that pertain to the films found at Gulistan Palace – include the filming of the pilgrims at the courtyard of Hazrat Maʿsūmah's (a Shiʾi Saint) shrine and the coronation of Ahmad Shah.[181]

The importance of these films lies in their expression of events and locations that portray the nation in moments of advancement and pride. Such settings portray the temporality of an ever-changing Iran. They depict the "future-past" of Iran as a nation that is "becoming"; a changing nation, according to Kosseleck, the future of which would consider its present state already as past. One could think of these films as an attempt to stage the nation in the same manner that European countries represented themselves on the silver screen. Highlighting the time period of such events, it becomes even more interesting to note that these nationally conscious films or newsreels almost accompanied, temporally, a crisis of governance in the first decades of the twentieth century.[182] The potential of cinema for creating state propaganda was also revealed by the 1920s, since an announcement for a film screening in Grand Hotel in 1922 advertised a film depicting "The signing of the Russia and Iran Treaty," in addition to "other important historical films."[183] These newsreels and documentaries were a visual portrayal of "the Iran of Yesterday and the Iran of Today," which later became the subtitle of one of the first Iranian talking (or talkie) films, *The Lur Girl* (*Dukhtar-i Lur*, 1933), and again marked the ethos of modernity in early-twentieth-century Iran. It is also probable that these short documentary films were projected before the actual programs of cinema screenings; or alternatively, they were screened for the royal family, servants and the military, or at public ceremonies and weddings.

National sentiments were in turn heightened in the early twentieth century as cinema created spaces in which males and females came to imagine themselves utilising same public spaces, and later began to actually socialise in them – sites where males and females came to consciously consider themselves as *national* brothers and sisters, as participants in the fashioning of modern Iranian imaginaries. The gender segregation in

---

[181] Adle argues that the former was also most likely the work of ʿAkkāsbāshī. Adle, "Acquaintance with Cinema 1899–1907," 23, accessed April 16, 2018, www.tavoosonline.com/Articles/ArticleDetailFa.aspx?src=68&Page=23.

[182] Here, I am referring to the Constitutional Revolution.

[183] "Muʿāhidah-ʾi Rūs va Īrān Barā-yi Namāyish-i Fīlm" [The Treaty of Russia and Iran for Film Screening], *Shafaq-i Surkh*, no. 27 (Khurdād 2, 1301 [May 23, 1922]), 1.

cinema spaces perhaps allowed for the voluntary participation of women in such sites of sociability. The female audience's utility of the space for screenings, which was perceived to be exclusive to male audiences, further prompted the redrawing of male and female boundaries and their consequently gendered spaces. As Tavakoli-Targhi argues, the expanding public space provided sites for national imaginations where familial relationships of males and females as national brothers and sisters were made possible.[184] Moreover, the mere images of women on the Iranian public cinema screens, arguably, worked to further shift the private/public (andarūnī/bīrūnī) boundaries that configured the movement of women around the city and defined their position in social functions. Women's demand for participation in what were announced as "educational" and "moral" programs of cinema – especially encouraged in film-screening advertisements – attest to the increased desire for participation of males and females in national progress.

In response to an article written by a man in the daily *Iran*, which reprimanded women for participating in gatherings of voodoo and fortune telling, a female writer responded by asking "which one of you sensitive men have ever established a movie theatre, a union, [or] a guesthouse for women that we [i.e. women] instead of [doing activities such as engaging in fortune telling and voodooism], have not attended?"[185] Such instances illustrating women's demands for inclusion in sites of sociability such as movie theatres reveal calls by women for an increased participation in the national affairs. Believing that "in such matters, too, one must think anew," authors and social critics such as Mushfiq Kāzimī emphasised the engagement of women in the production of theatrical performances, and their participation in theatrical and cinema audiences, to rectify "the tired and dust-covered soul of Iran."[186] In that spirit, by the late 1920s, women gained the opportunity to participate in film screenings that were intended solely for women audiences. In 1924, for example, *Iran* newspaper advertised "(film) Screening for Women Only" for two consecutive nights on

---

[184] Tavakoli-Targhi, *Refashioning Iran*, 113–114.
[185] "Javāb-i Barzigar," *Īrān*, yr 6, no. 1233 (Safar 27, 1341 [October 19, 1922]).
[186] Mushfiq Kāzimī, "Mūsīqī va Ti'ātr" [Music and Theatre], *Nāmah-'i Farangistān*, yr 1, no. 3 (July 1, 1924), 140–141. It is important to note here that Mushfiq Kāzimī is specifically referring to the participation of Muslim women in such productions. By 1924, many non-Muslim women had already engaged in the organisation and staging of public performances.

Amīrīyah Street; women were asked to rush to the venue, since they "had never seen anything like [the films] before."[187] In 1930, Alī Vakīlī also established "Zoroastrian Cinema (Sīnamā-yi Zartushtīyān) for the sake of women," where he screened films, for women exclusively, free of charge for two months just to attract a greater female audience to the cinema and engender "a cinema spirit" in women and local families.[188] The entry ticket to the theatre was an issue of *Iran* newspaper; as long as that issue of the newspaper "was made available to women," the theatre was full of women.[189]

Cinema's full potential in the enlightenment of the public, the elite believed, could be exploited better if the public understood the intertitles of international silent films. As such, by 1917, cinemas would screen "new films from the war front," in addition to "comical, historical, and moral dramas," which had their intertitles "written in Persian";[190] a practice that many other theatres soon followed. In 1923, *Star of Iran* (*Sitārah-'i Irān*) publication, advertising for Cinema Pathé of Grand Hotel, mentioned that the progress of cinema in the world was due to "people's awareness of the content of the programs" and the inclusion of "intertitles in the language of the country" in which they resided.[191] Following that, the newspaper advertised for the film *999 Nights*, which had been imported from Berlin, and not surprisingly had its intertitles translated into Persian.[192] In the same year, *Iran* newspaper issued an advertisement for Farus Cinema under the subtitle, "What was the subject of last night's film? – I did not understand since it was not in Persian," assuring the audiences that, from then on, the cinema would rectify the shortcomings of its past by translating the intertitles of the films that were to be screened there "from English and Russian into Persian."[193] Such instances are also significant as they point to the

[187] "Namāyish Makhsūs-i Khānūm-hā" [Screening for Women Only], *Irān*, yr 9, no. 1863 (Tīr 26, 1304 [July 17, 1925]), 2. By this time, some women were also involved in the cinema business. Pari Aqababian (Madame Parī or Satopari Aqababov), an Armenian actress and singer, and her husband, Satenik Aqababian, launched Parī (Fairy) Cinema on Mukhbir al-Dawlah Square in 1928. See Naficy, *A Social History of Iranian Cinema*, vol. 1, 265.

[188] "Sīnamā dar Īrān," *Sīnamā va Namāyishāt*, no. 1, 6.   [189] *Ibid.*

[190] "Sīnamā-yi Khurshīd" [The Sun Cinema], *Ra'd*, yr 9, no. 2 (Safar 2, 1336 [November 17, 1917]), 4.

[191] "I'lān" [Advertisement], *Sitārah-'i Īrān*, yr 9, no. 93 (Day 15, 1302 [January 6, 1923]), 4.

[192] *Ibid.*

[193] "Sīnamā Fārūs" [Farus Cinema], *Irān*, yr 7, no. 1374 (Jawza 6, 1302 [May 27, 1923]), 4.

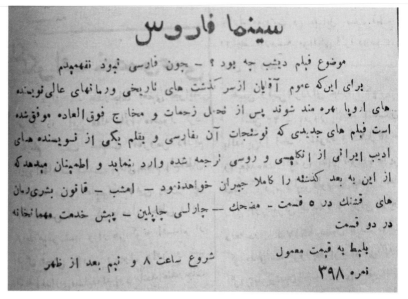

Figure 1.6 An advertisement in *Iran* for the translation of film intertitles into Persian (1923)

importance of cinema as a public communication medium that engendered Iranian national consciousness in the early twentieth century, by claiming the language of the intertitles and incorporating Persian translations, and thus new meanings, into foreign films (Figure 1.6).

Cinema, as a site of sociability, unlike other popular public spaces of mosques, religious seminaries and commissions (*hay'at*), did not include a single preacher; this characteristic in particular allowed for a more critical and democratic engagement of the audience members, and between the audience and the films. As such, one could argue that devoid of a single authoritative figure, the Iranian cinema spaces that were not only sites for the co-presence of various diasporic communities, but also for the infusion of global and local settings, in a sense enabled diverse vernacular imaginations that were at once national and international. It would be, again, more revealing to embed this transformation in the political shift that occurred almost simultaneously in the Constitutional Revolution, where the royal sovereignty of the Qajar ruler mutated into popular sovereignty.

While recent studies have increasingly attempted to make up for the gaps in the narratives of nationalism in modern Iran, much of the literature in the field still attributes the shaping of national consciousness and Iranian nationalism to the post-Pahlavi (post-1925) era. When examined in retrospect, it is undeniably easy to assume that cinema, a cultural "product" of the West, was received with dismay in early-twentieth-century Iran at a time of heightened national consciousness. A close study of the material relating to this era, however, points in a different direction. Cinema's potential in (mass) pedagogy and hence its implication in national consciousness made this medium popular among cosmopolitan nationalists, and its presence in Tehran and other urban centres almost indispensible.

1.4 Competing Reactions to Early Cinema

Despite its endorsement by cosmopolitan figures of diverse ethnic, religious, linguistic and social backgrounds, reactions to cinema's spatial experience and the heterotopic imaginary that it expressed were varied among the urban population. Some scholars argue that negative reactions to cinema had started from very early on.[194] Sahhāf-Bāshī's cinema, many argue, was shut down shortly after it had started to operate. One conjecture is that this occurred after Shaykh Fazlullāh Nūrī (1843–1909), a prominent religious leader of the time, issued a religious decree (*fatwā*) against cinema after attending a show in Qazvin.[195] According to different sources, this was either due to the fact that Sahhāf-Bāshī's cinematograph projected images of unveiled women,[196] or that it was seen by the "traditional Muslim clerics" as polluted devices of foreigners.[197] Another offered explanation is that Sahhāf-Bāshī's theatre was closed down by courtiers due to his involvement in the Constitutional Revolution.[198] It seems that the line of speculation discussed by many scholars of Iranian cinema with regard to Muslim clerics' antagonism to cinema in the early twentieth century is a symptom of an orientalist line of thinking that even today considers the clerics as opposed to "modernity" and its products. Contrary to this line of speculation, however, no written documents from this era (i.e. with regard to the fatwa and/or its reflection in the publications of

---

[194] See, e.g., Naficy, *A Social History of Iranian Cinema*, vol. 1, 59.
[195] Adle, "Acquaintance with Cinema 1899–1907," 9, accessed April 16, 2018, www.tavoosonline.com/Articles/ArticleDetailEn.aspx?src=68&Page=9. See also Naficy, *A Social History of Iranian Cinema*, vol. 1, 59–60.
[196] Baharloo, *Rūzshumār-i Sīnamā-yi Īrān*, 37–38.
[197] Naficy, *A Social History of Iranian Cinema*, vol. 1, 59.   [198] *Ibid.*

the time) have yet been found that suggest the level of religious antagonism one would assume necessary to shut down such an establishment, at least in the first two decades of the twentieth century. It is
perhaps noteworthy to mention here that Russi Khan's cinematographic screenings in his photography studio in 1907 were conducted
during the month of Ramadan and seemed not to have elicited any
reactions from the religious clerics.[199] The Spectacle House of Nāsirīyyah (Tamāshākhanah-'i Nāsirīyyah), operated by Amīr Khān Javān-
shīr, also featured new films in the month of Ramadan.[200]

This is not to say that all religious clerics wholeheartedly accepted
cinema and the culture that surrounded it, but to argue that our
presentist reading of such narratives must be problematised, and reactions to cinema must be historically contextualised. In 1921, for
example, the establishment of a cinema in Hamadan by a British
subject, "'Monsieur' Churchill," had become the target of discontent
by some religious figures in that city. The discontented clergymen, who
considered Monsieur Churchill's movie theatre to be "against religious
laws," wrote to the Ministry of Education of the time[201] and called for
the Ministry to prohibit the cinema from functioning in that city. Such
protests against the showing of foreign films gradually intensified by
the early 1930s. Objections to cinemas by clerics, nevertheless, should
not be taken at face value. The expression of opposition by the clerics
and secular social critics could perhaps be rationalised more by political intentions than religious obligations, a development that became
increasingly evident in cultural and social commentaries in the 1930s
and 1940s.

Very few memoirs or travelogues of Iranians from lower-income and
working classes are available from the early-twentieth-century era to

---

[199] "I'lān" [Advertisement], *Habl al-Matin*, no. 141 (Mīzān 21, 1286 [October 14,
1907]), 4.
[200] "Tamāshākhānah-'i Jadīd-i Nāsirīyyah" [The New Spectacle House of
Nasirīyyah], *Īrān*, yr 1, no. 23 (Ramazān 4, 1327 [September 19, 1909]), 1.
[201] "Mukhālifat-i 'Ulamā-yi Hamidān bā Dāyir Nimūdan-i Dastgāh-i
Sināmātugāph dar Hamadān Tavasut-i Mūsīū Chirchīll: Sanad-i Shumārah-'i
1" [The Opposition of Hamedani Clerics to the Establishing of a Cinema in
Hamedan by Monsieur Churchill: Document Number 1]," in *Asnādī az Mūsīqī,
Tiātr va Sīnamā dar Īrān (1300–1357)* [*Documents on Music, Theatre and
Cinema in Iran (1921–1978 Sh.)*] (Tehran: The Press and Publication
Organisation of the Ministry of Culture and Islamic Guidance, 2000),
vol. 1, 2–4.

attest to diverse reactions of the general public to cinema. What are available for our use, nevertheless, are the memoirs of Iranian nobility, elites and middle-class merchants that were composed in that period, in addition to a few accounts that were compiled later on. Qahrimān Mīrzā 'Ayn al-Saltanah (a Qajar prince), in his memoirs of 1909, for example, proclaimed that the cinematograph had "evolved since the last time" he had seen it and that "people went there (to the cinema) in crowds from dusk to dawn."[202] In his memoir of the same year, he especially expressed his feelings toward cinema when he wrote that the cinematograph "is truly spectacular and it is a good industry (san'at-i khūbīst)."[203] Moreover, he elaborates on his experiences on Lālahzār Avenue, when "in the afternoon . . . women . . . in droshkies . . . traverse the street from bottom to the top and from the top to the bottom."[204] According to the same memoir, Russi Khan's movie theatre on the "second-level of Fārūs Publication House," where "ice-cream, fruit and beer" were served despite the "expensiveness of beer," had become known as the "the court of bow-tie-clad dandies" (darbār-i fukulī-hā).[205]

On the other hand, in his memoirs of 1908, 'Imād al-Saltanah Sālūr – another Qajar prince (and brother of 'Ayn al-Saltanah) – wrote that he "went to the cinematograph the night before."[206] The venue "showed meaningless films," including "an assembly of people from

---

[202] 'Ayn al-Saltanah, "Sīnamātugrāf [Cinematograph]," in *Rūznamiy-i Khātirāt-i 'Ayn al-Saltanah: Rūzigār-i Pādishāhī-yi Muhammad 'Alī Shāh va Inghilāb-i Mashrūtah [Journal Memoirs of 'Ayn al-Saltanah: The Time of the Reign of Muhammad Ali Shah and the Constitutional Revolution]*, comp. Mas'ūd Sālūr and Iraj Afshār (Tehran: Asātīr, 1998), 2185.

[203] "Sīnamātugrāf [Cinematograph]," in *Rūznāmah-'i Khātirāt 'Ayn al-Saltanah*, 2185. It is interesting to note that two princes at the Qajar court have such different conceptions of the cinematograph.

[204] "Sīnamātugrāf [Cinematograph]," *Rūznamah-'i Khātirāt*, 2801.

[205] *Ibid.*, 2801–2802. "Fukulī" was a term that was derogatively used by many Iranians to address people who had travelled around the world (especially Europe) and had adopted modern clothing, especially featuring a faux-col (*fukul* in Persian), as opposed to the Iranian traditional clothing. Faux-col is the French word for a fake collar; nevertheless, according to the Persian dictionary of Dehkhoda, the word "faux-col/fukul" was used to signify a bow tie worn by cosmopolitans in the popular culture of the early twentieth century.

[206] Mansūrah Ittihādīyah, *Injā Tihrān Ast: Majmū'ah Maghālātī darbarah-'i Tihrān 1269–1344 [This is Tehran: A Collection of Articles from Tehran 1890–1965]* (Tehran: Nashr-i Tarikh-i Iran, 1998), 290.

Tabriz in the [military] training field."[207] This entry is especially significant as it points to another film (most likely a short actualité) that was made in Tabriz – a north-western city in Iran – at the time of an uprising led by constitutional revolutionaries. The memoir then describes 'Imād al-Saltanah Sālūr's discontent with the "strange circumstances" of the time, since the clerics of Najaf (a Shi'i holy city in Iraq) do not contest the "unveiling of women, the selling of alcoholic drinks ... the opening of several guesthouses that [allow for] the consumption of alcohol during the day in the open"; "apparently," he proclaimed after observing the transformations of the time, "Tehran has been liberated."[208] Such instances elucidate the contradictory reactions that Iranian urban residents expressed toward cinema and what it came to represent in Iran. It is noteworthy here to also attend to an account in 'Abdulrahīm Tālibuf's 1915 book, *Ahmad's Book* (Kitāb-i Ahmad), where he expressed his antagonism toward the presence of foreign forces in Iran by dismissing "bāzīgar khānah [playhouses]" as the cultural capital of the West: "If we don't have the capacity to preserve our own homeland and our ancestral tombs, the foreign powers will unearth the bones of our ancestors before our eyes and erect playhouses in its place."[209] On the other hand, just before the start of the Islamic sacred month of Muharram (when Muslims are urged to abstain from joyous activities), *Nāhīd* publication criticised the authorities for the closing of all theatres and cinemas "in an attempt to pre-empt the excuses of certain detractors" (i.e. perhaps religious authorities and/or social critics) "even before the start of the month Muharram."[210]

Cinema in Iran emerged within existing gender hierarchies; public cinema screenings, for the first decade of the twentieth century, were limited to the male audiences. On the other hand, however, cinematographic devices were used and/or rented for private screenings in the court for female princesses and Qajar nobility, in private houses for women and children, or at weddings or other ceremonies.[211] However, by 1910, the opportunity to participate in gender-segregated

---

[207] *Ibid.*   [208] *Ibid.*
[209] 'Abdulrahim Talibuf, *Kitab-i Ahmad* [*Ahmad's Book*], ed. Bagher Momeni (Tehran: Farus Publishing House, 1915), 99.
[210] "Shahr-i Farang," *Nāhīd*, yr 3, no. 25 (Asad 28, 1303 [August 19, 1924]), 7.
[211] Russi Khan used to rent his cinematograph to the public, while also putting up another cinematograph for sale, as early as 1907. See *Subh-i Sādiq*, yr 1, no. 166 (Ramaddān 23, 1325 [October 31, 1907]), 4.

public film screenings had become possible for women. In 1910, the Iranian Women's Charity Institution announced "a conference and cinematograph [screening]" gathering for women, the proceeds of which were to go to "orphanages, infirmaries and girl schools."[212] The fact that the event included a conference and its advertisement asked women "not to bring young children" to the event hints at its the exclusivity in the early years of cinema for educated middle-class women who could afford to leave their children with caregivers at home.

The eagerness of women to participate in cinematographic screenings could also be traced in some of the publications of the time. In *Nāhīd*'s "Shahr-i Farang" column of 1924, for example, a woman by the name of Kamīnah 'Iffat Samī'ī protested that "means of recreation and diversion" did not exist for women; she furthermore objected that women did not have "the permission to enter cinemas, and public places such as cafés and national parks," and "exclusive" public sites of sociability did not exist for women's excursion.[213] Similarly, in 1924, writing under the pseudonym of "Your National Sister," a woman remonstrated against the banning of "moral" cinematographic screenings at a women's wedding ceremony in Tehran – especially when women had "not yet seen such moral screenings" and wished "to benefit from such blessing" – while at another wedding, "three immoral '*taqlīds*' [a Persian form of folk theatre] were played without any problems" from the authorities.[214]

As briefly mentioned above, according to 'Alī Vakīlī's film magazine, *Cinema and Screenings*, during the time period that Vakīlī specifically targeted women in advertisements for his Zoroastrian Cinema, movie houses were inundated by women. In the words of the article, it was thanks to the endurance of such "troubles and ... losses" by Vakīlī that "the ethos of modernity and the inclination and zest were instilled in men and respectful women," "participation in social gatherings and

---

[212] "Shirkat-i Khayrīyah-'i Khavātīn-i Īrānī" [Charity Institution for Iranian Women], *Īrān-i Naw*, yr 2, no. 175 (Rabi' al-Awwal 30, 1328 [April 11, 1910]), 1.

[213] Kaminah 'Iffat Samī'ī, "Shahr-i Farang," *Nāhīd*, yr 2, no. 39 (Rajab 11, 1342 [February 17, 1924]), 6–7.

[214] "Sīnamā Man' Ast, Taqlīd Āzād" [Cinematograph is Banned, *Taqlīd* is Free], *Nāhīd*, yr 3, no. 45 ('Aqrab 23, 1303 [November 14, 1924]), 7.

assemblages," was facilitated and "finally the excitement and interest that is demonstrated by people towards cinema" were engendered.[215]

* * *

The heterogeneous context within which cinema emerged in Iran, and the diversity – in form, content and organisation – that further contributed to such heterogeneity, inspired a cosmopolitan imagination that in the words of Delanty could be described as "an ongoing process of self-constitution."[216] The distance between the local experience and the globality perceived on the screens, one could argue, was temporally managed by drawing close the images seen in international films – i.e. as images of advanced countries – to Iran's space of experience. Iran of the early twentieth century can be explained in terms of "a system of social relations, of debates, and conflicts, of political initiatives and claims, of ideologies and alienation,"[217] a system that was in a continual process of refashioning enabled through its encounter with heterogeneity – first social heterogeneity, and then cinematic cosmopolitanism. Through processes of "transgression and negotiation" manifested in discourses surrounding cinema, one can argue that cosmopolitan identities were formed alongside national identities in the early twentieth century, and that the two went hand in hand.[218]

As this chapter has attempted to demonstrate, cinema facilitated instances of world openness through which different modernities communicated and mutually exchanged information. Through the plurality of its interactive logics – i.e. the intermingling of local and global – cosmopolitan cinematic culture provided an impetus for refashioning – "the belief that human agency can radically transform the present in the image of an imagined future."[219] Then one can contend that the imagination fostered through cinema – an imagination of the Iranian horizon of expectation – was a cosmopolitan expression in that it sought to change the local space of experience in relation to the global nexus. In other words, through the multiple interactions of *"being"* with *"that which is not"* (i.e. international images seen on

[215] "Sīnamā dar Īrān," *Sīnamā va Namāyishāt*, no. 1, 6–7.
[216] Delanty, The Cosmopolitan Imagination, 73.
[217] Alan Touraine, *The Self-Production of Society* (University of Chicago Press, 1977), 30.
[218] Delanty, *The Cosmopolitan Imagination*, 75.   [219] *Ibid.*, 71.

cinema screens), heterotopic cinema worked to relocate Iran from its local surroundings to the space of possible futures – futures that entailed an advanced and morally disciplined nation.

To sum up, averting from the predominant Eurocentric conceptions of modernity that consider industrialisation as a primary tenet, but instead conceiving societal transformations as the primary dynamic of alternative modernities, one comes to understand the implication of cinema in Iranian modernity and urbanisation in the early twentieth century. The heterotopic space of cinema which represented parallel global universes, and the hybrid culture that boosted it, worked to create a critical cosmopolitan consciousness that marked early-twentieth-century Iran. In envisaging modern societal transformations, cinema furthermore shaped a modern Iranian subjectivity that in its national consciousness retained the past and looked to the future.

2 | Cinematic Education, Cinematic Sovereignty

The Creation of a Cosmo-National Cinema

Chapter 1 touched upon the importance that Iranian cosmopolitans in the 1910s and early 1920s attached to cinema as a medium for the moral edification of the public in the service of national advancement, despite the absence of a centralised cinema institution. The praising of cinema's didactic potential in the education of children and enlightenment of society, as indicated in newspaper articles and film announcements from the late 1920s to mid-1930s, attests to a more formal approval of cinema as a pedagogical medium in this era. Just as print had transferred singular authority of individuals to texts, in the absence of a state-sponsored cinema institution, the authority of individuals was transferred to heterogeneous cinema in the early twentieth century, thus occasioning democratic imaginings in late Qajar Iran (also manifested in the Constitutional Revolution and social movements of this era). As this chapter will demonstrate, with the coming of the Pahlavi Dynasty (1925–1979) and the solidification of an ideological nationalism, cinema was taken over by statist nationalism and became increasingly regulated and controlled by the state.

The institutionalisation of cinema and its endorsement by the government of Reza Pahlavi (r. 1925–1941) worked to shape cinema as a disciplinary tool that was especially in the service of the processes of statist modernisation in the 1930s. In other words, the state co-opted cinema as part of its nationalist didactic agenda, in attempts at what Foucault calls the "Governmentalisation of the State."[1] To this end, cinema spaces were increasingly supervised film programs regulated and conduct in movie theatres controlled. On the other hand, aspirations for cinematic sovereignty put forward by nationalists, film critics and intellectual elites by the way of film reviews and essays

---

[1] Michel Foucault, "Governmentality," in Graham Burchell, Colin Gordon and Peter Miller (eds), *The Foucault Effect: Studies in Governmentality, with Two Lectures by and One Interview with Michel Foucault* (London: Harvester Wheatsheaf, 1991), 103.

inspired the establishment of a cinema industry that – in line with discourses surrounding national and economic sovereignty – showcased the history, customs and "progresses" of the country in moving images; an industry that was predominantly organised around the usage of "Persian language" in films, and believed that language granted a form of sovereignty to the industry in a modernising Iran. The emergence of this Persian-language cinema in the 1930s entailed engagement with international elements and figures, nationalist narratives, ancient fables and, at times, statist rhetoric. This emergent "cosmo-national" cinema prompted nationalist sentiments that imagined Iran, at least cinematically, as contemporaneous with European, advanced countries, while it employed international directors, producers, actors and cosmopolitan figures in its productions. Film critics and the elite were eager to stage the films of this emergent cosmo-national cinema on an international level, perhaps in a reactionary stance against the orientalist international films and newsreels that were produced and disseminated around the world, some of which attended to the history of and life in Iran. While Persian-language films sometimes tapped into self-orientalising narratives that circulated in newspapers and public discourse of the time, glorifying the ancient Iranian past and idealising the rich Indo-Persian literary culture, their form of orientalism was much different from international orientalist cinematic offerings. The films of this era co-opted orientalist discourses, not to situate Iran as a primitive, backward or stagnant country, but to promote it as a progressive, moral and changing nation. In other words, cosmopolitan filmmakers *and* the state capitalised on orientalist discourses and academic scholarship on "ancient Persia" to push for the bolstering of nationalist sensibilities.

2.1 Screen Education during the Reign of Reza Pahlavi

While discussions and debates surrounding Iranian nationalism and nationalist sentiments had become rampant among cosmopolitan thinkers, writers, artists and constitutionalists from the mid eighteenth century to the first decades of the twentieth century, the first Pahlavi government became increasingly invested in solidifying and promoting a unified national identity, especially through culture. Reza Khan, a Cossack military leader during the Qajar period, became Minister of War in 1921 and Prime Minister in 1923. In 1925, he deposed the last king of the Qajar Dynasty, claimed himself a Shah, and founded the Pahlavi Dynasty – a dynasty that drew a connection between the newly established state and pre-Islamic Persian Empire, also evident in its name. While engaging in centralisation and modernisation policies from the time of his ascension to official power in 1925 to his abdication in 1941, Reza Pahlavi's government borrowed from nationalist ideas and sentiments of his time to instigate nationalist policies, especially in the realm of culture, that aimed to crystallise a uniform Iranian identity and discipline a multi-confessional society. The swapping of the Islamic lunar calendar for a solar calendar, altering dress codes and changing the educational system were among some of the official cultural policies of Reza Shah. Cinema, as a public mode and medium of education, was not immune to such policies.[2]

Following the debates on cinematic education that cosmopolitan merchants and thinkers of the first two decades of the twentieth century had generated, with the centralisation of the state in the mid-1920s, state officials took over the debates on cinematic education and promoted the official adoption of cinema as a pedagogic tool. As early as 1925, the monthly magazine of *Education and Pedagogy (Ta'līm va Tarbīyat)*, the official publication of the Ministry of Education, began to publish a series of articles on the importance of cinema in education, as well as the institutionalisation of cinema in various countries. In an article from the September of that year entitled "Variety: Primary School Education in France," the magazine investigated the modes of pedagogy in both France and England.[3] The article specifically looked into the role of cinema not only for "recreation and amusement," but as a means "to disseminate knowledge and develop cognition,"

---

[2] For more information on nationalist discourse and sentiments in the eighteenth century and the statist nationalism of Reza Pahlavi's Dynasty, see, e.g., Afshin Marashi, *Nationalizing Iran: Culture, Power, and the State, 1870–1940* (Seattle: University of Washington Press, 2008); Mohamad Tavakoli-Targhi, *Refashioning Iran: Orientalism, Occidentalism, and Historiography* (New York: Palgrave Macmillan, 2001); Reza Zia-Ebrahimi, *The Emergence of Iranian Nationalism: Race and the Politics of Dislocation* (New York: Columbia University Press, 2016); and Parts II and III in Bianca Devos and Christoph Werner (eds), *Culture and Cultural Politics under Reza Shah: The Pahlavi State, the New Bourgeoisie, and the Creation of a Modern Society in Iran* (London: Routledge, 2013).

[3] "Mutinavva'ah: Ta'līmāt-i Ibtidāyī dar Farānsah" [Variety: Primary School Education in France], *Ta'līm va Tarbīyat* [Education and Pedagogy], yr 1, nos 3–4 (Khurdād-Tīr 1304 [May–June 1921]), 75.

especially in the fields of "scientific-geographic facts, life sciences, history, and technological exhibition and industries."[4] With moving pictures, the article stated, "the most important events that take place on earth" were projected onto screens; so "similar to a newspaper," cinema brought "the world news to the view of spectators."[5] In an article entitled "Education in Others' Countries," the publication further explored the conditions of education in Russia. "The higher education authority of Russia," according to the article, had become "centralised" in the Commission of Education of that country, the responsibilities of which had expanded to include the administering of "state theatres," "Academy of Fine Arts," "other . . . music and artistic industries," "educational organisations" that had previously been under the supervision of other ministries and state institutions" and "local and town schools."[6] The Commission of Education in Russia, according to the article, was divided into the three general branches of "pedagogic department," "scientific department" and "department of art industry," the latter of which included the administering of theatres and cinemas. The awareness of such developments in a neighbouring country provided incentives for the state endorsement of cinema (especially as an educational tool) in Iran and its centralisation in the late 1930s, a topic that will be dealt with below.

Elaborating on its significance in 1933, Muhammad Husayn Āyram, the Chairman of the National Police Establishment (Tashkīlāt-i Kull-i Nazmīyyah-'i Mamlikatī), described cinema as a "crucial cornerstone" for "the changing of social mentality" and "the enlightening of students' reasoning," and a communication form that acted as a "representative of the national progress of any state."[7] According to the Chairman, through cinema one could "familiarise public opinion"

---

[4] *Ibid.*, 78.   [5] *Ibid.*

[6] "Ma'ārif dar Mamālik-i Dīgarān" [Education in Other Countries], *Ta'līm va Tarbīyat*, yr 1, no. 7 (Mihr 1304 [September 1921]), 29.

[7] "Pīshnahād-i Muhammad Husayn Āyram (Ra'īs-i Tashkīlāt-i Kull-i Nazmīyah-'i Mamlikatī) Mabnī bar Ta'sīs-i yik Madrasah barā-yi Ta'līm va Tarbīyat-i Hunarpishah-'i Sīnamā va Vārid Kardan-i Lavāzim-i Fīlm-bardārī: Sanad-i Shumārah-'i 33/1" [The Suggestion of Muhammad Hussayn Ayram (the Head of National Police Establishment) about the Establishment of a School for the Instruction and Training of Cinema Actors and the Importation of Filming Equipment: Document Number 33/1] in *Asnādī az Mūsīqī, Ti'ātr va Sīnamā dar Īrān (1300–1357)* [*Documents on Music, Theatre and Cinema in Iran (1921–1978)*] (Tehran: The Press and Publication Organisation of the Ministry of Culture and Islamic Guidance, 2000), vol. 1, 103.

with "necessary principles" of moral social norms, and direct the attention of "foreign spectators" to advancements in the country.[8] *Education and Pedagogy* published another article in 1934, "Teaching with the Use of Cinema," which described how in "civilised" (i.e. modernised) countries, "teaching with cinema" was "one of the most common methods in schools."[9] Keeping with such trends, the article then heralded that "one device of educative cinema" had been recently installed in the hall of Dār al-Funūn School of Higher Education, which was programmed to show "historical, scientific, and pedagogical films based on a specific schedule."[10] The Ministry of Education, the article mentioned, was seeking to install cinematic apparatuses in other high schools in Tehran and provinces, therefore maintaining the contemporaneity of Iranian educational tools with those of the "civilised" world.[11] In fact, the 1934 Annual Report of the Department of Publications' Operations (functioning under the Ministry of Education) affirmed that, in that year, an accord had been arranged for the establishment of a "scientific/educational cinema" (sīnamā-yi 'ilmī), which was followed by the installment of one cinematographic device in Dār al-Funūn School of Higher Education, which was utilised by the students of the said institution at the time of the report.[12] Attesting to the first instances of Pahlavi state's interference in film screenings, the report further remarked that all films that were "considered for projection were appraised in terms of their literary/didactic and technical qualities by the Department of Publications" before their display.[13] "More than half of the pieces," according to the report, were banned from screening at the school due to their "lack of technical benefits."[14] In addition to the review of films before projection, the article also stated that the department had taken some measures in "publicising the subject in newspapers and encouraging litterateurs to write articles on the topic," efforts which had already yielded some positive results.[15] In fact, in the same year, the government had asked Ibrāhīm

---

[8] *Ibid.*

[9] "Tadrīs bah vasīlah-'i Sīnamā" [Teaching with the Use of Cinema], *Ta'līm va Tarbīyat*, yr 4, no. 10 (Day 1313 [December 1934]), 619.

[10] *Ibid.*   [11] *Ibid.*

[12] "Rāpurt-i 'Amalīyāt-i Sālīyānah-'i Idārah-'i Intibā'āt" [Annual Report of the Department of Publications Operations], *Ta'līm va Tarbīyat*, yr 5, no. 4 (Tīr 1314 [June 1935]), 220.

[13] *Ibid.*   [14] *Ibid.*   [15] *Ibid.*

Murādī (1899–1976), an Iranian cosmopolitan filmmaker, film critic and screenwriter, to assess the state of the cinematographic device and film screenings at Dār al-Funūn. Upon examining the hall and cinema area of the school on November 15, 1934, Ibrāhīm Murādī expressed his recommendations with regard to the supplies and repairs necessary for the development of a more appropriate cinema space for students, to the Ministry of Education, Endowments and Fine Arts. Murādī's list included "the wiring" of the movie theatre and the covering of windows with black or brown curtains that would allow for screenings during the day.[16] He further suggested that instead of magic lantern projections, "scientific films" (*filmhā-yi sīyāntīfīk*) be imported from Europe for the utility of the students.[17] Until such films were imported to the country, Murādī advised the Ministry to use the "16 scientific film reels" which had been in use at the Military High School Laboratory.[18] The activities and film productions of Murādī will be dealt with in more depth later in this chapter.

In line with the Pahlavi state's mission to discipline an Iranian society through cinema, in 1934, the Ministry of Education designated Muhsin 'Azīzī (b. 1905) – from the Iranian Embassy in Paris – to participate in the "Rome International Congress on Education and Pedagogy through Film," in which authoritative representatives from

---

[16] "Guzārishhā-yi Bāzdīd-i Ibrāhīm Murādī az Sīnamā-yi Dār al-Funūn va Pīshnahād-i Nāmburdah Mabnī bar Vārid Kardan-i Fīlmhā-yī az Khārij barā-yi Dānish Āmūzān: Sanad-i Shumārah-'i 34/2" [Reports of Ibrāhīm Murādī's visits to Dar al-Funun cinema and the suggestion of the aforementioned in regard to the imporation of films from outside the country for students: Document Number 34/2], in *Asnādī az Mūsīqī, Tiātr va Sīnamā dar Īrān (1300–1357)*, vol. 1, 111–112.

[17] "Guzārishhā-yi Bāzdīd-i Ibrāhīm Murādī az Sīnamā-yi Dār al-Funūn va Pīshnahād-i Nāmburdah Mabnī bar Vārid Kardan-i Fīlmhā-yī az Khārij Barā-yi Dānish Āmūzān: Sanad-i Shumārah-'i 34/1" [Reports of Ibrāhīm Murādī's visits to Dar al-Funun cinema and the suggestion of the aforementioned in regard to the importation of films from outside the country for students: Document Number 34/1], in *Asnādī az Mūsīqī, Tiātr va Sīnamā dar Īrān (1300–1357)*, vol. 1, 110. It is interesting to note here that one can confer from this statement that by 1934, Iranian screening venues (and schools) would still use magic lantern slides for the purpose of entertainment and education as part of the visual culture of the time.

[18] "Guzārishhā-yi Bāzdīd-i Ibrāhīm Murādī az Sīnamā-yi Dār al-Funūn: Sanad-i Shumārah-'i 34/1," 111.

forty-five member countries were to participate.[19] Muhsin ʿAzīzī's report on the proceedings of the meeting specifically included a brief history of the Congress, and an exploration of its goals and its structural framework. The Congress, the report stated, was divided into various branches that explored the role of film and cinema in "the maintenance of individual hygiene" and thus "the preservation of [the health of] the society," and "the pedagogy of the masses"; the account further reported that the Congress examined the relation of "the state to educational cinematography." Specific attention was given to various laws that governed state intervention in the management of cinemas, technical aspects of the technology and the role of cinema in the "disciplining of the nation"[20] – all topics that were or came to be of interest to the Pahlavi state.

In April 1935, Nasrullāh Falsafī, the editor-in-chief of *Education and Pedagogy*, published an extensive article in the same magazine that explored various "Tools for Education," including "Oral Lectures," "Books" and the "Use of Cinema in Schools."[21] In the section pertaining to cinema, the article recommended the use of films in schools so that the visual repertoire of students would be developed in addition to their learning abilities attained through hearing. He, however, suggested a limited utilisation of cinema in schools since the speed of moving images would not allow for students to pay close attention to the subject or to remember many of the details.[22] Similarly, an article published in *Mihr* (*The Sun*) journal in 1937 explored the "Services of Cinema in the Progress of Education."[23] "A writer, no matter how knowledgeable and professional," the article stated, "cannot fully describe the civilisation, habits, traditions, actions and tense moments of a nation and people"; there, "cinema comes to the help of publications," for the reason that "cinema illustrates buildings and constructions, the fashion of walking and speaking, [and] the laughter of people

---

[19] Muhsin ʿAzīzī, "Kungirah-'i Bayn al-Milalī-yi Rum Rajaʿ bah Taʿlīm va Tabīyat bah vasīlah-'i Fīlm," [The International Congress of Rome on Education and Pedagogy through Film], *Taʿlīm va Tarbīyat*, yr 4, no. 4 (Tīr 1313 [June 1934]), 230.

[20] *Ibid.*, 231–232.

[21] Nasrullāh Falsafī, "Vasāyil-i Taʿlīm" [Tools for Education], *Taʿlīm va Tarbīyat*, yr 5, no. 2 (Urdībihisht 1314 [April 1935]), 22.

[22] *Ibid.*, 23.

[23] "Khadamāt-i Sīnamā dar Pīshraft-i Maʿārif" [The Services of Cinema in the Progress of Education], *Mihr*, yr 5, no. 3 (Murdād 1316 [July 1937]), 307.

who live in the most distant parts of the world ... and because cinema is the best interpreter of nature, and is nature itself."[24]

Cinema's employment by international forces in the distribution of filmic propaganda also compelled some thinkers to advocate the technology in the service of the nation. In a letter to the editor of *Iran* periodical in 1934, an author observed that after "European countries did not find their propagandist tools such as public speeches, newspaper, radio, etc. as sufficient for the progress of their goals," they began to showcase their "national artifacts, love for [their] country ... and the ever-increasing advancements of their country such as [their] fine arts, factories, and ways of creating gravel roads" on cinema screens for "friend and foe."[25] Continuing to comment on the merits of cinema for reasons of propaganda, as well as education, especially in the absence of other entertainment forms, the author urged managers of cinemas in Tehran to feature "moral and instructional films" that were especially beneficial to "children, women, and school students."[26]

Aside from cosmopolitan educators who advocated the use of cinema in public education, the Pahlavi State also co-opted the notion of cinematic pedagogy, therefore taking over activities that cosmopolitan merchants and thinkers had initiated outside the jurisdiction of the state in the 1910s and 1920s in the service of national advancement. By regulating and codifying cinemas and related activities, the government attempted to direct cinema's didactic potential and align it with its own political agenda. Act 35 in the State Budget's Amendment Act, issued on 17 March 1935 by the Ministry of Finance, is noteworthy here if one is to better understand the role of films in the project of state education and modernisation. The Act stated that "cinematograph films that have pedagogical, instructive, and technical aspects, and that are imported by government institutions are exempt from customs and transportation tolls/taxes,"[27] thus highlighting the importance that the Pahlavi government ascribed to the role of cinematic education.

---

[24] *Ibid.*
[25] H. M., "Sīnamā dar Īrān" [Cinema in Iran], *Īrān*, yr 18, no. 4350 (Farvardīn 13, 1313 [April 2, 1934]), 2.
[26] *Ibid.*
[27] "Qānūn-i Mutammam-i Būdjah-'i Sāl-i 1313 Mamlikatī" [Amendment Act in 1934 State Budget], *Pāygāh-i Ghavānīn va Mugharrarāt-i Kishvar* [State Laws and Regulations Database], accessed May 15, 2013, www.dastour.ir/brows/? lid=19273.

The large number of international films that were imported to Iran by the late 1920s also propelled social critics and later the Pahlavi government to take a stronger stance against the uninhibited import-ation of international films or the projection of uncensored foreign motion pictures in Iran. The origins of these films and the route they took to enter Iran, as Kaveh Askari argues, tell us much about the politics and national debates of the time.[28] While in the 1900s and 1910s, Russian films (or films with Russian intertitles) were easily imported to Iran through Russia, in the late 1920s, political tensions in both Russia and Iran seem to have influenced film distribution in the country. In 1928, for example, out of the 305 motion pictures that were imported to Iran, 133 were American, 100 were French and only 30 were Russian; most of these films were 8- to 10-year-old serial film "junk prints," and were therefore more easily imported to Iran, even from Russia.[29] The increase in the number of imported American films may also be attributed to the growth and export of Hollywood film productions in the late 1920s. In 1930, while the total number of imported films increased, the number of American, French and Russian films decreased and the quantity of German film imports increased.[30] This shift could perhaps be accounted for by the flourishing of eco-nomic and cultural relations between Germany and Iran in the 1930s.[31] Despite their origins, the rise in the number of international films that were featured in national movie theatres garnered social anxiety among social thinkers.

Aside from the number of international films, the screening of uncensored international films also added to the vexation of critics. For instance, in an *Iran* newspaper review of a German film entitled *Paprika* (1932), a film critic specifically took issue with some sexually evocative scenes in the film, the redaction of which, the author empha-sised, would not have detracted from the film's success. The critic mentioned that many newspapers and journals in Iran had already

---

[28] Kaveh Askari, "An Afterlife for Junk Prints: Serials and Other 'Classics' in Late-1920s Tehran," in Laura Horak, Anupama Kapse and Jennifer M. Bearn (eds), *Silent Cinema and the Politics of Space* (Bloomington, IN: Indiana University Press, 2014), 69–70.

[29] *Ibid.*, 70.   [30] *Ibid.*, 69–70.

[31] For more information on the economic relations between Iran and Germany during the time of Reza Shah, see Jennifer Jenkins, "Iran in the Nazi New Order, 1933 to 1941," *Iranian Studies* 49(5) (September 2016): 727–751.

attended to the ways in which the "righteous class and those concerned about social morality" outside Iran had obliged the exercise of "strict control" over film production and screening.[32] The showing of "naked breasts," "revealing of legs above the knee," indecently acting women, kisses and embraces that were "very visible" and other similar scenes, the author held, had been removed from many films and banned from public screenings in the United States of America and Germany. "Truthfully," the author added, such means of control had to be implemented; if not a "school for the refinement of morality," cinema was surely not a school for the "teaching of debauchery." Similar to other foreign nations, film control had to be imposed in countries such as Iran where people who advocated "social morality" and "family" values were in the majority.[33] The film critic, therefore, prescribed the direct intervention of governmental and non-governmental institutions in the censoring and controlling of films.

With the increase in the number of international films and movie theatres in the late 1920s and 1930s in Tehran, and growing pressure from social and cultural critics for strict control over movie screenings, the Pahlavi government began to introduce official regulations for cinema programs and film projections. During this period, as the following paragraphs demonstrate, cosmopolitan filmmakers and the state also engaged in initiatives to create Persian-language films that aimed to craft and promote a national cinema that could compete with international visual offerings.

2.2 Regulating Cinema Programs and Cinema Spaces

In 1930, a set of regulations entitled "Code of Film Recording and Cinema Screening" (Nizām-nāmah-'i Bardāshtan-i Fīlm va Namāyish-i Sīnamā) was submitted to the Ministry of the State (or Ministry of the Interior) for ratification.[34] The first chapter of the Code was dedicated

---

[32] "Sīnamā-Ti'ātr: dar Sīnamā Īrān-*Pāprīkā*" [Cinema-Theatre: in Iran Cinema-Paprika], *Īrān*, yr 18, no. 4500 (Mihr 12, 1313 [October 4, 1934]), 3.

[33] *Ibid.*

[34] "Nizām-Nāmah-'i Marbūt bah Fīlm-Bardārī va Namāyish-i Fīlmhā-yi Sīnamāyī: Sanad-i Shumārah-'i 19" [The Code Pertaining to the Recording of Film and Screening of Cinema Films: Document Number 19], in *Asnādī az Mūsīqī, Ti'ātr va Sīnamā dar Īrān (1300–1357)*, vol. 1, 51–54. It is not clear which institution and/or individuals were behind collecting the set of codes that were given to the Ministry of State for filmmaking.

to the regulation of on-location film-recording in the city of Tehran. According to the Code, there were two forms of film-recording: (1) "Shooting a cinematic film [i.e., filming] based on a script that has been written before" (i.e. narrative films); and (2) "Shooting locations, buildings, and social lives" (i.e. documentary/newsreel films).[35] The second chapter of the Code attended to the various technicalities associated with film screenings, such as "the distance between the cinematograph device and film reel," the number of exit doors for movie theatres, and the distance between theatre seats and the film screen.[36] These measurements intended to prevent the break out of major fires in cinemas, mostly resulting from the combustion of nitrate film. This set of regulations was further expanded in 1935 to include all matters that were related to the structure and building of cinemas, and was ratified by the Ministry of the State under a new title, "The Code for Cinemas" (Nizām-nāmah-'i Sīnamāhā). According to this law, the establishment of any cinema building was premised on the attainment of an "official permit" from the Police Office of the city of interest, "registration in the municipality" upon the receipt of the permit and the surveillance of the establishment by that city's munici-pality.[37] The spatial positioning of cinema buildings within the city and the hygienic and sanitary practices of the movie theatres also required the ratification of the city's municipal office before any permits were issued. In other words, in comparison to the decentral-ised screening practices in the first two decades of the twentieth century where films would be projected in cafés, restaurants and hotels, in the third decade of the century the government administered cinematic regulations, thereby facilitating the state surveillance of cinema as a disciplinary corpus.

The centralisation of cinematic practices was concomitant with the control of cinema's programs and the stratification of movie theatres (according to cinema ranks and the audience), which would further compartmentalise cities and also indirectly govern the socialisation of audience members. The 1935 legal code for cinemas demanded the categorisation of movie theatres into three grades, each with its own set

---

[35] *Ibid.*, 52.   [36] *Ibid.*, 53.
[37] "Nizām-Nāmah-'i Sīnamāhā" [The Code for Cinema], Pāygāh-i Ittilāʿāt-i Qavānīn va Mugharrarāt-i Kishvar [National's Laws and Regulations Information Database] (1314 [1935]), accessed May 17, 2013, www.dastour.ir/brows/?lid=22666.

of criteria, providing an official evidence of social stratification. Grade one cinemas, for example, were required to screen at least three films in each program that had to be arranged in the following specific order: "1. Newsreels of events that are no more than two months old, 2. Scientific, industrial, geographic, or athletic films, 3. Major film productions, the production of which are no more than one year old, and their length is no less than two thousand meters."[38] The code was flexible enough to allow cinemas to screen films of major film companies up to two years after their production, and also to replace scientific, industrial, geographic and athletic films with other kinds of films.[39] The concern over hygienic measures was also manifest in the regulations for grade one and two movie theatres, where devices for air purification were mandatory.[40] While grade one and two cinemas were devoted to at least one feature film – mostly talkies by the early 1930s – and several short reels, grade three cinemas were exclusively reserved for silent films.[41] Price differentiation was consequently applied to the three kinds of cinema, as well as to the seats in each theatre. Although written on paper, the regulations were not always necessarily applied or strictly followed; however, the state systematisation of cinemas, again, points to an official attempt at centralisation, rationalisation and order in a modernising Iran, while reflecting social stratification in different neighbourhoods.

According to the official state records of the Ministry of Education, Religious Affairs and Fine Arts from the year 1935, more than fifty-four "pieces" (i.e. films and theatrical performances of all sorts) were submitted to the Ministry to acquire permission for screening/performance; out of the fifty-four, however, the Ministry issued permissions for only forty-five pieces, thus abstaining from supplying permits for performances/screenings that lacked "technical and literary value."[42] According to the same report, certain measures had been taken to "promote theatre (namāyish) in schools and to introduce students to the benefits and basics of this technology"; the Ministry had specifically encouraged the adoption of "national stories especially from

---

[38] *Ibid.*   [39] *Ibid.*   [40] *Ibid.*   [41] *Ibid.*
[42] Office of Publications – Office of Census, "Khulāsah-'i 'Amalīyāt-i Vizārat-i Ma'ārif va Awqāf dar Sāl-i 1314" [A Summary of the Work of the Ministry of Education and Religious Affairs in the year 1935], *Annual Report and Census 1312–1313 [1933–1934] and 1313–1314 [1934–1935]*, Ministry of Education and Religious Affairs and Fine Arts, 23.

تدریس بوسیلهٔ سینما

درممالك متمدنه تدریس بوسیلهٔ سینما یکی ازطرق بسیار معمول مدارس
است . وزارت معارف از چندی پیش برای تأسیس اینگونه سینماها درمدارس مشغول
مطالعهوتهیهٔ وسائل بود . اخیراً یك دستگاه سینمای تربیتی درتالار دبیرستان دارالفنون
نصب کردیدهاست که تدریج اًمطابق برو گرام معنی بردهای تاریخی وعلمی وتربیتی
را برای محصلین نمایش خواهد داد ووزارتخانه در صدد است که بتدریج دستگاههای
دیگری نیز درسایر دبیرستانهای طهران وولایات نصب نماید و این موضوع مفید را
بیشتر تعمیم دهد .

Figure 2.1 The 1934 report of the Department of Publications' Operations (of
the Ministry of Education) on the state of cinematic education in Iran

Shahnamah" for performances and screenings – thus once again
underscoring the state's newly found interest in theatre and cinema,
and their employment for the promotion of nationalist narratives
(Figure 2.1).[43]

The promulgation of cinema as an educational tool by the state in
the early Pahlavi years also points to the transformation of cinema into
a disciplinary tool. Aside from its entertaining and esthetic appeals,
cinema was also seen as an instrument for the containment of society.
Pahlavi's conception of educational cinema is similar to what Wassan
and Acland conceptualise as "useful cinema," that is "a body of films
and technologies that performs tasks and serve as instruments in an
ongoing struggle for aesthetic, social, and political capital."[44]
The authors distinguish between useful cinema and educational cinema
in that the former includes experimental, fictional and non-fictional
didactic films. In the context of Pahlavi era Iran, however, one can
observe the conflation of the two forms of cinema, not only in
the range of films that were shown in cinemas and educational venues
(i.e. schools, conferences, etc.), but also in that education identified

[43] *Ibid.*
[44] Charles R. Acland and Haidee Wasson, "Introduction: Utility and Cinema," in
Charles R. Acland and Haidee Wasson (eds), *Useful Cinema* (Durham, NC:
Duke University Press, 2011), 3.

"a disposition, an outlook, and an approach toward a medium on the part of institutions and institutional agents."[45]

The propagation of cinema, as in the previous decades, evoked a plethora of reactions in the 1930s. In 1933, the author and editor-in-chief of *Armaghān* (*Gift*) magazine, Vahīd Dastgirdī (1879–1942), took issue with cinema and lamented that "the effective, wise advice and philosophical and literary sermons had been washed off from the world repository," and were instead replaced by "the advice of novels, cinema, and newspaper."[46] In a clear stance against the widespread discourse surrounding "moral cinema," Dastgirdī inquired, "Which moral cinema is there that does not display lust … in front of the youth's vision?"[47] Dastgirdī could not help but deem the space "that incarnated the love-making of unchaste impure Europeans in sight of inexperienced … youth" as "the house of indecency" (*dār al-fahshā*, i.e. brothels) and "the locus of decay" (*markaz-i kharābī*) of chastity and honour.[48] Dastgirdī did not believe in the total obliteration of cinemas, novels and newspapers; in fact, he encouraged their multiplication in number. Rather, he believed in the annihilation of "lies" that promoted the widely disseminated international cultural products of the time as "moral" as opposed to "the enemy of [public] morale."[49]

'Alī Akbar Hakamīzādah (d. 1987) also took issue with the space that cinema engendered in the sociocultural context of Iran. In 1935, Hakamīzādah believed that although "women and men are of the same kind (jins)," their "mingling" in spaces such as cinemas was "more harmful than the mixing of wolves and sheep," especially since the latter "takes life at once," but the former obliterates "existence, gradually."[50] Touching upon an already commercialised cinema culture in Iran, Hakamīzādah reprimanded "ignorant people" who posted pictures of "ill-behaving women" (zanhā-yi nābikār) with "erotic poses" (hālat-hā-yi shahvat-angīz) on the walls of their rooms, warning that their children could "from an early age, learn the ways of

---

[45] *Ibid.*, 4.
[46] Vahīd Dastgirdī, "Durūgh" [Lies], *Armaghān*, yr 14, no. 10 (Day 1312 [January 1933]), 676.
[47] *Ibid.*   [48] *Ibid.*, 677.   [49] *Ibid.*
[50] 'Alī Akbar Hakamīzādah, "Tablīghāt" [Advertisements], *Humāyūn*, yr 1, no. 7 (Farvardīn 1314 [March 1935]), 31.

adultery and lust."[51] Proclamations against the images of unveiled women in the mid-1930s were concomitant with the increasing appearance of veiled and unveiled European and Iranian women in urban streets and on cinema screens, and were simultaneous with the general commotion around the unveiling of women in Iran promoted by Reza Shah.[52] A poem by the name of "Book of Chastity" published in *Armaghān* magazine in 1934 explored themes that related to unfavourable repercussions of women's unveiling in public. Some of the verses of this poem included:

Ārī ān zan kah bīhijāb āmad   'Āqibat khānimān kharāb āmad[53]

Aye, that woman who egresses unveiled
A broken home she ultimately garnered

and

Balkah az rukh chaw pardah bugshāyad   Yikjahān fitnah az pīsh āyad[54]

Once she removes her veil from her face
A world of sedition follows

The same poem then connected women's unveiling to notions of "Westernisation":

Har kah yik rah safar bi-maghrib kard   Bā khud āvard ānchah rā kah āvard
Tā bah 'ādāt-i dīgarān pay burd   'Ādāt-i khvīsh rā haghīr shimurd[55]

Whoever went once on a journey to the West
Brought with them whatever they could bring
Once they became familiar with the others' conducts
They denigrated their own habits

and

Az urūpā hamīn hunar āmūkht   vaz tamaddun hamīnqadr āmūkht
Kah nahad dil bifasgh va rū bah fisād   Yā dahad tan bah nang va nām bah bād[56]

They learned only this art from Europe
And from civilisation only this they acquired
To give heart to immorality and face to corruption
Or to bring shame to their body or to lose name

---

[51] *Ibid.*
[52] In 1936, the Pahlavi state banned the wearing of the veil in public in Iran.
[53] "'Ifāf-Nāmah" [Book of Chastity], *Armaghān*, yr 15, no. 6 (Shahrīvar 1313 [August 1934]), 450.
[54] *Ibid.*   [55] *Ibid.*, 454.   [56] *Ibid.*

After accusing women of learning the art of "colourful dances" from the West and thus corrupting the nation, the poem then explored how cinema, novel and theatre, too, functioned to debase the society:

Va ān digar bīn kah tā chahā āvard   Sīm-i mā burd u sīnamā āvard
Dard āvard va burd darmān rā   Kufr parvard va kusht īmān rā[57]

And see what the other brought
Took away our silver (money), and brought cinema
Brought pain and detracted the antidote
Fostered blasphemy and killed faith

The space that cinema provided for the socialisation of men and women appears to have been specifically targeted in this poem:

Har kujā ka-ijtimā'i mard u zan Ast   Lājaram khāstah az ān fitn ast[58]

Wherever there is socialisation of Men and Women
Sedition is inevitably arisen

The poem further likened being "cinema-ish" (sīnamāyī), as in going to cinema gatherings, to being "demimondaine," like a woman who puts on "make-up" every night to seduce men other than her own husband.[59] On the other hand, the woman who "escapes the snare of ignorance" by not participating in such gatherings, the poet believed, would "never feel the desire for cinema," and would thus triumph in life for having refrained from "debasement" (pastī).[60]

As can be seen, objections to cinema took a more anti-imperialist and nationalist tone rather than a strictly religious attitude that opposed cinema on the basis of faith. In his 1934 book, *Āyīn*, Ahmad Kasravi (1890–1946), for example, criticised the institution of cinema as part and parcel of the hegemony of Western civilisation. In his treatises on what he considered as Europism (*Urūpāyīgarāyī*), i.e. being plagued by European (and in general "Western") modes of life, Kasravi stated that those who were plagued by the "West" contended that cinema, automobiles, theatre and other technologies and mores of European civilisation had to be imported from the West in order for the country to become civilised.[61] All the words of "commendation" that considered cinema as a device for the "goodness" (nikū-khūyī) and "awakening" (bīdārī) of people, and for which "academies were established" in Iran, Kasravi believed were "lies" and "exaggerations."[62] Believing film screenings to be futile (bīhūdah)

---

[57] *Ibid.*, 455.   [58] *Ibid.*, 456.   [59] *Ibid.*   [60] *Ibid.*, 457.
[61] Ahmad Kasravi, *Āyīn*, 23.   [62] *Ibid.*, 16.

and childish (kūdakānah), Kasravi felt that motion pictures made the "eyes weak" and "wasted" (tabāh) morale.[63] He further held "European and American" big companies that produced and distributed films to be responsible for the desolation of morality in Iran.[64]

Despite the criticisms that were aimed at the space and imagery that it fostered, cinema had become an indispensable part of Iranian everyday life by the 1930s. Nāzir Zādah Kirmānī's 1936 poem, entitled *Cinema and the Projection of Life* (*Sīnamā va Namāyish-i Zindigī*), alludes to the centrality of cinema within Iranian experience of everyday modernity. The poem touched upon the ways in which images on the cinema screen represented quotidian lives, like the actions one witnessed on a daily basis:

> This fine invention that you call cinema
> Illustrates [the Performances of] our Death and Life
> . . .
> In cinema, from an aperture are projected numerous images
> Onto the screen from which the image is quickly parted
> . . .
> The dream of life and the myth of being
> Like images in cinema, do not remain permanent for long
> . . .
> And do not think of this screen as permanent
> For whatever beginning it had, it will have an end
> . . .
> The world is a scene (as in a film) and in it people are diverse
> The actors, however, are all [to play by the script] of fate[65]

Symbolising Marx's famous words, "All that is solid melts into air," this poem clearly demonstrated the experience of modernity in Iran, as it exemplified the futural, fast-paced, sensationally felt and continuously changing ethos of lived experience.

2.3 Cosmo-National Cinema: The Emergence of a Persian-Language Film Industry

In the year 1930, among the literary masala of national progress, intellectual and technological advancement and moral refinement,

---

[63] *Ibid.*   [64] *Ibid.*
[65] Nāzir Zādah Kirmānī, "Sīnamā va Namāyish-i Zindigī" [Cinema and the Projection of Life], *Armaghān*, yr 17, no. 6 (Shahrīvar 1315 [August 1936]), 462–463. The above-mentioned lines are only a few stanzas of the poem.

a Persian-language cinema industry – what has generally been termed as a "national" (and at times "nationalist") cinema – emerged. But what constitutes a national cinema? Benedict Anderson defines "nation" as the mapping of an imagined community onto a geopolitical space with demarcated boundaries.[66] Although the inhabitants of this space are diverse and disunited, they are encouraged to consider themselves as members of a coherent community. Mass media play an integral role in creating such sentiments of nationhood. Cinema, as a medium of mass communication also plays an important part in reimagining this community as closely integrated. Many scholars of Iranian cinema consider the Persian-language cinema that emerged in the 1930s as a "national" cinema imbued with a nationalist mission, based on the argument that films that were produced during this era followed the nationalist agenda of the state, and aroused nationalist sentiments among the audiences. Branding cinematic activities of an era as nationalist, however, is limiting since such contentions "narrate the nation as just this finite, limited space, inhabited by a tightly coherent and unified community, closed off to other identities besides national identity."[67] In such historical arguments, the focus is on elements of films that are "patriotic" or "nationalist," and that fit closely with the modernisation projects that were implemented during the reign of Reza Shah (r. 1925–1941). Focusing on the transnational elements of the films of this era, on the other hand, reveals cinematic features that would arguably pose this cinema as a multinational or cosmopolitan enterprise. Higson argues that national films could operate on a transnational basis on two levels; the first is on "the level of production and the activities of filmmakers," and the second is "in terms of the distribution and reception of films."[68] Although the two aforementioned levels have some resonance in the case of the Iran of the 1930s, they are not necessarily as clearly defined as Higson has brought forth.

---

[66] Benedict Anderson, *Imagined Communities: Reflections on the Origin and Spread of Nationalism* (London: Verso, 1983).

[67] Andrew Higson, "The Limiting Imagination of National Cinema," in Mette Hjort and Scott Mackenzie (eds), *Cinema and Nation* (London: Routledge, 2000), 60.

[68] *Ibid.*, 61.

A great contradiction lies in the identification of the Persian-language cinema that emerged in the late 1920s and early 1930s as a "nationalist" cinema. While the Persian-language silent and talking films of the era embodied features that characterised the nation, or advocated nationalist sentiments, they were based on the cosmopolitan cinematic culture that preceded its emergence and continued to bear upon the shaping of this cosmo-national cinema. It is interesting to note here that similar to the first two decades of the twentieth century, some of the cinemas in the 1930s and 1940s were in fact owned by the diasporic communities of Iran. In Tehran, according to Jamal Umid (and echoed by Hamid Naficy), Māyāk Cinema (Sīnamā Dīdah-bān) was owned by Lidzeh (a Russian immigrant), Humā Cinema was co-owned by an Iraqi Arab, Georges Naim, and Salim Shāhānīyān, an Armenian-Iranian, Firdawsi Cinema was run by Haikaz Chāknāvāriān, another Armenian-Iranian, and Sitārah Cinema was run by Russian nationals.[69]

In 1930, the first Training Centre for Cinema Acting (Parvarishgāh-i Ārtīstī-yi Sīnamā) was established by a Russian-Armenian émigré, Ovanes Ohanians, or Ovanes Oganians (d. 1960), in Tehran. In the same year, with the acting of his first group of students, and the help of Khān Bābā Muʿtazidī (himself a filmmaker) as the cameraman, Ohanians directed the first silent feature film in Iran by the title of *Abi and Rabi* (*Ābī va Rābī*, 1930). The intertitles of this film are said to have been in two languages, Persian and Russian. There are no exact or detailed official reports in Persian on the life of Ohanians, but some reports indicate that he emigrated from Russia to Iran in 1929.[70] Ohanians, who had studied film in Russia, attempted to bring fruition to his studies by opening his own actor-training studio in Tehran. The activities of the training centre included a plethora of fields, namely music, acting, gymnastics, dance, acrobatics, filming and athletics – a smorgasbord of activities that to an extent resembled the curriculum of Russian film schools. Khān Bābā Muʿtazidī, the cameraman of the film, himself had acquired most of his film training outside the country. According to his memoirs, after receiving his diploma, Muʿtazidī moved to study at a college in Lausanne, Switzerland, and from there

---

[69] Jamal Umid, *Tārīkh-i Sīnamā-yi Īrān: 1279–1357* [*The History of Iranian Cinema: 1900–1979*] (Tehran: Rawzanah Publications, 1995), 110–111.
[70] *Ibid.*, 41.

to Paris.[71] Once in Paris, he befriended the son of the owner of
Gaumont Film Company, who then assisted him in finding a job there.
After two years of working for the company, when Mu'tazidī decided
to go back to Iran, the owner presented him with a "fully equipped
filming device, a projector for the screening of films, the special chem-
ical for the development of films, and a large amount of film stock."[72]
Khān Bābā Mu'tazidī used the equipment that he brought back with
him to Iran to shoot short family films, and later to film important
national events – discussed later in this chapter.

With the help of a fellow Russian émigré, Lidzeh, the owner of Māyāk
Cinema, Ohanians screened *Abi and Rabi* in 1930 in Tehran. The film,
according to Ohanians, cost around 5,500 Rial (currency of Iran) at the
time.[73] After the good reception of his first film, Ohanians continued
teaching and training more students at his cinematic institution. In
fact, by 1933, Ohanians was running the third term of his classes on
Istanbul Avenue, Tehran, as advertised in *Irān-i Bāstān* (Ancient Iran)
periodical. Changing the name of his institution to "Madrasah-'i Ārtīstī
va Mu'assasah-'i Sīnamā" (Artistic School and Cinema Institution),
Ohanians appointed a woman, Fakhruzzamān Jabbār Vazīrī, as the
Chief Head of the School, perhaps to solicit the registration of women.[74]
The advertisement allocated the morning hours, "10 to 12 in the morning," for women's registration and the afternoon hours, "5 to 7 in the
afternoon," for men's, perhaps to avoid the charges that many writers
attached to institutions that provided means for the mingling of different
sexes, or to make women and men more comfortable in the space of
this institution.[75] Ohanians also established the first Iranian film company, "Sté Persfilme Ltd" (generally known as Persefilme) in Tehran on
Shāh Avenue.[76]

[71] Part of Khān Bābā Mu'tazidī's autobiography is quoted in Hamīd Shu'ā'ī, *Nām-
āvarān-i Sīnamā dar Īrān: 'Abdulhussayn Sipantā [The Honourables of Cinema
in Iran: Abdolhossein Sepanta]* (Tehran: Herminko, 2535 [1976]), 12–16.
According to this book, the autobiography is based on a piece published in
Rastākhīz [newspaper], no. 403 (Shahrīvar 7, 2535 [August 29, 1976]), 23.
[72] Shu'ā'ī, *Nām-āvarān-i Sīnamā dar Īrān*, 13.
[73] Ovanes Ohanians, "Fīlm-i *Dukhtar-i Bulhavas*" [The Film, *The Capricious
Girl*], *Ittilā'āt*, yr 8, no. 2190 (Urdībihisht 29, 1313 [May 19, 1314]), 4.
[74] "Madrasah-'i Ārtīstī va Mu'assasah-'i Sīnamā" [Artistic School and Cinema
Institution], *Irān-i Bāstān*, no. 12 (Urdībihisht 2, 1312 [April 22, 1933]), 7.
[75] *Ibid.*
[76] Please note that here the spelling of "Persfilme" reflects the English spelling that
is used in the actual advertisement. When not quoting a specific text, I use the

Figure 2.2 An image of Café Pars on Lālahzār Avenue, where the actor of *Mr. Haji: the Cinema Actor* jumped from the third floor

Writing in *Irān-i Bāstān* in 1933, 'Atā al-lāh Shahābpūr reported on the cinematic activities of Ohanians without any mention of his name.[77] According to the article, an artistic institution, which accepted both "men and women" as students, was now in the process of shooting a film in which "Mr Safavi, an important artist," jumped from the upper level of Café Pars to the ground – a scene from Ohanians's second silent film, *Mr Haji, the Cinema Actor* (1933) (Figure 2.2).[78] The presence of such artists, in Shahābpūr's mind, facilitated the "progress" of cinema in Iran; upon watching such artistic scenes, Europeans would now realise that "cinema and the art of acting" in Iran could establish parity with European cinemas, so

common spelling of the studio, Persefilme. Naficy believes Persefilme Studio to have been established in 1930 (when Ohanians made *Abi and Rabi*), which would make sense if Ohanians's first film was produced under the auspices of this institution. On the other hand, as can be seen in the following paragraphs, a review of Ohanians's second film (*Mr Haji, the Cinema Actor*) in *Iran* newspaper considered Ohanians's film to be the *first* production of Persefilme; if we are to take this piece of information as evidence, then Ohanians's film studio was established some time after 1930. See Hamid Naficy, *A Social History of Iranian Cinema*, vol. 1: *The Artisanal Era, 1897–1941* (Durham, NC: Duke University Press, 2011), 210.

[77] 'Atā al-lāh Shahābpūr, "Sīnamā va Ārtīstī" [Cinema and Artistism], *Irān-i Bāstān*, no. 18 (Khurdād 11, 1312 [June 1, 1933]), 10.

[78] *Ibid.*

Europeans would no longer "know us based on unrealistic films that are shot according to old eastern books."[79] At the end of the article, the author recommended that in order for cinema to advance in Iran a number of factors needed to be improved: cinema magazines had to be published; the salary of artistic schools needed to increase; and filming companies had to be established that were equipped with new and complete filming gear.[80]

Aside from filmmaking and managing an acting school, Ohanisans had elaborate plans for the future of the art of filmmaking in Iran. A 1934 article in *Iran* newspaper commented on a proposal for a "cinema project" that "Monsieur Oganians" (Ohanians) had submitted to the publication. According to the article, Ohanians saw the creation of films in Iran to be necessary. Locally produced films that included beautiful sceneries and were cheap in production, Ohanians believed, would generate not only "monetary profit," but also "moral capital," especially since these films would be produced "under right conditions" and would be devoid of aspects that were "against morality."[81] Contending that with a budget of only 50,000 tomans the best Iranian film could be produced, Ohanians provided a table of expenses in his report that included the cost for items such as the salary of actors, directors and writers, as well as the expenditures for costumes and atelier.[82] Additionally, investing in a permanent filmmaking institution in Iran, he thought, would cost around 175,000 tomans, which would eventually create steady profits for local filmmakers and cinemas.[83] Ohanians also estimated the spending required for the establishment of a cinema acting school which would amount to around 17,000 tomans, and a theatre school which would require an investment of 15,000 tomans.[84] Some of the topics that Ohanians recommended for filmmaking in Iran included, "the life of Hakim Umar Khayyam," "the 1921 Coup d'état," "Tehran's daughter," "Firdawsi's life," "Rustam and Suhrab," "Shah Abbas," "Khusraw and Shirin," and stories relating to the time of Nadir Shah of Afshar.[85] Many of the themes and stories that Ohanians referred to in his proposal became the main plot of feature films that were produced in the years that followed – although not by Ohanians. In fact, despite his

---

[79] *Ibid.*   [80] *Ibid.*
[81] "Sīnamā-Tiātr: Purujah-'i Sīnamā va Ti'ātr" [Cinema-Theatre: Cinema and Theatre Project], *Īrān*, yr 18, no. 4366 (Urdībihisht 3, 1313 [April 23, 1934]), 3.
[82] *Ibid.*   [83] *Ibid.*   [84] *Ibid.*   [85] *Ibid.*

numerous attempts, Ohanians was unable to create any other films. He migrated to India in 1938, where he attempted to continue his cinematic career to no avail, and then returned to Iran in 1947, where he converted to Islam and took the name of Riza Muzhdah.[86] Despite his enthusiasm for and activities related to the creation of an Iranian *national* cinema, Ohanians's inactivity in terms of filmmaking makes one question if he was discriminated against as a non-native Iranian at a time when a nationalist discourse was overtaking cinematic practices in the country.

In a report in *Iran* periodical, 'Alī Daryābaygī, who had received his diploma in art and filmmaking from Germany, took issue with Ohanians's calculations, arguing that the amount of money required to invest in quality filmmaking equipment that could yield results similar to those of European films was quite high.[87] Ohanians's proposed project, according to the author, worked for the making of short actualités and educational films that were featured at the beginning of most screenings in Iran, but not for the making of historical feature films. Aside from the expensiveness of the gear, Iran did not have talented actors and directors; perhaps taking a jab at Ohanians, Daryābaygī stated that those filmmakers that were active in Iran only took an interest in "physical movements" and "changing the face of artists."[88] "The majority of people who claim to be directors in Iran," Daryābaygī continued, "are Armenian-speaking Iranians who cannot pronounce Persian words correctly"; then, how could one expect them to "point out the mistakes of the artists" and "coordinate actions with words?"[89] Persian-speaking men who also engaged in filmmaking, the author believed, were students of Armenian-speaking directors and did not have a comprehensive or theoretical knowledge about the art of filmmaking. The only aspect of Ohanians's proposal that was deemed important by the author was his proposition about the creation of an

---

[86] Naficy, *A Social History of Iranian Cinema*, vol. 1, 219. According to Naficy, and sources available at Cinema Museum in Tehran, Iran, upon his return to Iran, Ohanians engaged in the selling of hair-loss cures and opened a beauty shop in Tehran.

[87] "Purujah-'i Sīnamā va Tiātr" [Cinema and Theatre Project], *Īrān*, yr 18, no. 4396 [Khurdād 10, 1313 [May 31, 1934]), 3. It should be mentioned that Daryābaygī, who was involved in theatre and performative arts in Iran and Germany, became involved in filmmaking in the late 1940s. Chapter 4 will explore the first commercial film that he directed in 1948.

[88] "Purujah-'i Sīnamā va Tiātr," 3.   [89] *Ibid*.

artistic [or acting] school, however, even that was flawed; since the advent of talking films, according to him, there was no longer a need to establish one school for cinema and one for theatre, as both could now be combined.[90] Daryābaygī then proposed his own brief plan for the establishment of an artistic school in Iran. This school program consisted of three years of studies, where the first two years were dedicated to learning cinematic physical movements, make-up, the history of theatre and Iranian and international literature, and the third year to acting and filmmaking practices.[91] Notwithstanding its reception, Ohanians's projects and proposals created debates on Iranian cinema and filmmaking that stand as a testament to the dynamic cinematic culture that cosmopolitans continued to engender in the 1930s.

In the same year, 1934, *Irān-i Bāstān* periodical published an advertisement that announced the establishment of a "beneficial institution" called "Sté Persfilme Ltd." The newspaper announced that the institution had been established by "a number of educated, adept, and patriotic young people," who had obtained "new necessary film equipment to eliminate the need for foreign films."[92] The newspaper further praised the importance of the initiative for the benefit of the country in that films facilitated the "introduction of Iran to the outside world," prompted the "attraction of enthusiastic tourists," allowed for "special films to be delivered for the edification of social morale" and of course provided economic value by "introducing Iranian commodities to other countries."[93] With the "support and attention of the royal government of Iran," the newspaper announcement hoped that the

---

[90] *Ibid.*   [91] *Ibid.*

[92] "Ta'sīs-i Yik Mu'assisah-'i Mufīd-i Dīgar" [The Establishment of Another Beneficial Institution], *Īrān-i Bāstān*, no. 24 (Tīr 31, 1312 [July 22, 1933]), 8. There is a possibility that *Īrān-i Bāstān* publication is referring to one of the film companies founded by Ibrāhīm Murādī, i.e. Iran Film Company Ltd or Īrān Mahdūd, which was at times called Persfilme (for example, the screenplay for Murādī's *The Capricious* (1934) was signed under Persefilme, as discussed below.) It is also possible that *Īrān-i Bāstān*, an ultra-nationalist periodical, was referring to Ohanians's studio, but purposefully did not mention his name as the founder of the institution because of his origins as an Armenian, so as to not undermine "Iranian" nationalist sentiments. For example, when discussing the emergent cinematic activities in Iran, an *Īrān-i Bāstān* author, 'Atā al-lāh Shahābpūr, praised the performance of an Iranian artist who played in Ohanians's *Mr Haji, the Cinema Actor* (1934), but made no mention of the name of the film, the director or his training centre. See Shahābpūr, "Sīnamā va ārtīstī," *Īrān-i Bāstān*, no. 18, 10.

[93] "Ta'sīs-i Yik Mu'assisah-'i Mufīd," 8.

institution would be able to provide films that accommodated "our national morale and customs" and did away with foreign films that were imported by foreigners to promote "corruption in the society and empty the pockets of misfortunate people."[94] In a 1933 article, 'Atā al-lāh Shahābpūr of *Irān-i Bāstān* reported on cinematic activities of Persefilme company which, "similar to great international film companies," had undertaken the task of making newsreels and projecting them before feature films.[95] According to the author, the "daily" newsreel that he had watched was silent and it showcased two specific events.[96] The first part of the newsreel included scenes from the laying of the first bricks of "the new National Bank building" by Reza Shah and his reading of a speech; this section was then followed by scenes from the National Bank building in red, which "pleased the audience." The second part of the film included scenes from the "constitution celebration, reception halls, buildings, and gardens" where the celebration was taking place, as well as "Mr Dādgar, who was greeting the guests."[97] The film then showed, in "a blue context," night at the garden of the Iranian parliament. The film was accompanied by a "delightful" musical score, and it inspired "hope" for the bright future of cinema in Iran.[98] According to Shahābpūr, the film started with an intertitle in a font comparable with "the artistic writings of great world cinemas," which read, "Long Live His Majesty Pahlavi, the King of Iran," thus perhaps pointing to the ways in which filmmakers paid lip service to the government or showed patriotic sentiments, and how newspapers such as *Irān-i Bāstān* reproduced and circulated such attitudes.[99] The next intertitle then read what the author believed to be "the three words" that were at the top of the vocabulary of any Iranian: "God, Iran, the King."[100] Such patriotic gestures were reflected and mandated in film and cinema regulations of the time. For instance, according to Act 67 of the Code of Cinemas (1935), film screenings at grade one and grade two cinemas were required to be followed by the Iranian national anthem (Salām Irān) played either

---

[94] *Ibid.*
[95] 'Atā al-lāh ShahābPūr, "Sīnamā va ārtīstī: Rūznāmah-'i Pirsfilm" [Cinema and Artistism: Persefilme Newspaper], *Irān-i Bāstān*, no. 36 (Mihr 29, 1312 [October 21, 1933]), 9.
[96] *Ibid.*   [97] *Ibid.*   [98] *Ibid.*   [99] *Ibid.*   [100] *Ibid.*

through gramophone recordings or by a live orchestra.[101] These news-reels were shot and prepared by Khān Bābā Muʻtazidī.[102] Considering the collaboration of Ohanians and Khān Bābā Muʻtazidī in *Abi and Rabi* (1930), the studio to which the article alludes could be Ohanians's studio; alternatively, it could be referring to Ibrāhīm Murādī's Īrān Mahdūd or Persefilme Ltd studio. The establishment of such institutions and the publication of cinematic advertisements and reports in newspapers is suggestive of the increasing attempt on the part of practitioners and enthusiasts to localise the industry and develop a sovereign national cinema.

In the early 1930s, aside from Ohanians's Persefilme, other film companies had taken on the task of producing Persian-language-speaking motion pictures, namely the Imperial Film Company of Bombay (IFCB) in India. In 1933, IFCB produced its first Persian talking film, *The Lur Girl* (*Dukhtar-i Lur*, 1933). Fully shot in India, *The Lur Girl* was directed by Khan Bahadur Ardeshir Khan Irani (or Ardishīr Īrānī), an Indian of the Parsi community, also known as the Father of Talking Films in India. The film was based on a screenplay written by Abdol-hossein Sepanta (1907–1969), an Iranian poet and researcher, who had an avid interest in ancient Persian literature and history. In the late 1920s, Sepanta travelled to India to enrich his study of Zoroastrianism and ancient Persian culture.[103] While in India, Sepanta befriended Ardeshir Irani, and it was then that the seeds for the production of the first Persian-language talking film were planted.

The Lur Girl was advertised in *Īrān-i Bāstān* weekly two months before its first screening. The film was in fact advertised with the alternative title, *Iran of Yesterday and Iran of Today* (*Īrān-i Dīrūz va Īrān-i Imrūz*), as a production of a "Persian filming company," most likely referring to the Imperial Film Company of Bombay (Figure 2.3).[104] Furthermore, the announcement heralded the participation of "Iranian

---

[101] "Nizām-Nāmah-'i Sīnamāhā" [The Code of Cinemas], *Pāygāh-i Ittilāʻāt-i Qavānīn va Muqarrarāt-i Kishvar* [National Laws and Regulations Information Database] (1314 [1935]), accessed August 19, 2014, www.dastour.ir/brows/?lid=22666.

[102] Shuʻāʻī, *Nām-āvarān-i Sīnamā dar Īrān*, 14.

[103] See Umid, *Tārīkh-i Sīnamā-yi Īrān*, 62–63; and Naficy, *A Social History of Iranian Cinema*, vol. 1, 232.

[104] "*Dukhtar-i Lur* yā *Īrān-i Dīrūz va Īrān-i Imrūz*" [*The Lur Girl* or *Iran of Yesterday and Iran of Today*], *Īrān-i Bāstān*, no. 33 (Mihr 1, 1312 [September 22, 1933]), 11.

Figure 2.3 The newspaper advertisement for *The Lur Girl* (1933)

artists [i.e., actors]" in the film. The announcement invited people to "observe and compare the conditions of old Iran and the rapid advancement of Iran under the reign of the Just and Mighty Shah" (i.e. Reza Shah Pahlavi).[105] *The Lur Girl* was screened in both India and Iran in November 1933 and was a success in both countries.

"The street is full of people, people have rushed to Māyāk Cinema, and want to enter and buy tickets, but there is no way," Dīnyār Mazdīsnā wrote in a review of *The Lur Girl* in *Īrān-i Bāstān* on November 25, 1933.[106] "The theatre is suddenly darkened ... Khan Bahadur Ardeshir Irani gives a speech; how serene and [yet] how exciting. The audience gives a big round of applause."[107] According to another film review published in *Iran* newspaper, the film had several sections that were "worthy of attention" and made the production "on a par" with good films: "the subject of the film," "the setting," its "nice scenery," "precision in filming, and incarnation of the eastern spirit."[108] The part of the film that "depicted the progress of Iran in the last few years," hence its alternative title, *Iran of Yesterday and Iran of Today*, was met with enthusiastic applause of the audiences.[109] The *Iran* newspaper critic recommended that the institution must pay more attention to certain aspects in future productions, namely "the suitability of actors for their roles," "correction of accents," so that the actors spoke Farsi "naturally," "precision in the make-up" of actors, "rectification of the music of the film," as well as "the poses and movements of some of the actors."[110] Such diligent analysis of films perhaps points to how, in the 1930s, film critics had become professional in visually (and esthetically) examining films, and reveals the critics' envisioning of how Persian-language films (as part and parcel of a sovereign cinema) ought to be.

The film is about Gulnār, a Lur woman from the province of Khuzistan, who is abducted after the murder of her parents by Qulī Khan, the great Khan of Lur bandits. Gulnār, who works, dances and collects

---

[105] *Ibid.*
[106] "Dukhtar-i Lur" [The Lur Girl], *Īrān-i Bāstān*, no. 44 (Āzar 4, 1312 [November 25, 1933]), 2.
[107] *Ibid.*
[108] "Sīnamā – Tiātr: dar Sīnamā Māyāk, *Dukhtar-i Lur*" [Cinema – Theatre: In Cinema Mayak, The Lur Girl], *Īrān*, yr 17, no. 4250 (Āzar 1, 1312 [November 22, 1934]), 2.
[109] *Ibid.* [110] *Ibid.*

money in a teahouse owned by Qulī Khan, meets and falls in love with
Ja'far, a government official, who promises to take her to Tehran and
away from her abductors after he completes his mission. Qulī Khan,
however, sets out to kill Ja'far and the rest of the caravan with which
he travels. As a result of the attack, Ja'far is left severely wounded.
Gulnār finds Ja'far and dresses his wounds. She is, however, soon
found by members of the gang of bandits. Qulī Khan thus imprisons
both Ja'far and Gulnār. After a while, Qulī Khan asks Ja'far to work
with him as a bandit; he promises that, in return for his services, Ja'far
can have Gulnār. Ja'far, who sees the offer as a "betrayal" to his
country, refuses to band with Qulī Khan. Meanwhile, Gulnār promises
Qulī Khan that she can convince Ja'far to change his mind and to join
the bandit. Therefore, Gulnār gains access to Ja'far's dungeon, at
which point she sets him free and escapes with him. Withstanding
many hardships on the way, Ja'far and Gulnār leave Iran (of the Qajar
era) and sail on a ship to Bombay in search of a safe haven. After a
couple of years in Bombay, Ja'far suddenly receives some newspapers
from Iran, in which he reads about the advancements and changes that
have taken place there over the past few years (i.e. the Pahlavi era).
Believing that he can now be of service to his country, Ja'far, together
with Gulnār, decides to return to the new Iran. It was at this point that,
according to a film review, "patriots ... applauded, cheered, and
whistled out of joy," to an extent that one felt "the floor of the theatre
tremble" and as if the ceiling was "about to collapse."[111] Those who
had watched the film had become aware of "the nationalist (vatan-
parastānah) sentiments" of the producers and "the bright flame" that
was "burning in their hearts" because of "their love for the country."[112] Considering the success of *The Lur Girl* on its first screening,
the film critic of *Iran* newspaper encouraged the Indian institution to
produce more "Persian films with the same level of seriousness,"[113]
while the *Īrān-i Bāstān* film critic hoped that the "heroic and national
(vatanī) stories of *Shahnamah*[114] and the history of Iran"[115] would be

---

[111] "*Dukhtar-i Lur*," *Īrān-i Bāstān*, no. 44, 2.   [112] *Ibid.*
[113] "Sīnamā – Tiātr: dar Sīnamā Māyāk, *Dukhtar-i Lur*," 2.
[114] Shahnamah (Book of Kings) is an epic poem written by the Persian poet,
Firdawsi, from late tenth to early eleventh centuries AD. This long poem
recounts the mythical and to some extent historical past of Iran since the
beginning of the world to the Islamic conquest in late seventh century.
[115] "*Dukhtar-i Lur*," *Īrān-i Bāstān*, no. 44, 2.

filmed and screened by Imperial Film Company – an endeavour that was in fact undertaken by the same company in the years that followed. *The Lur Girl* involved numerous Iranian actors, including Sepanta who played the role of Jaʻfar, Suhrāb Pūrī and Rūhangīz Sāmī-Nijād, who played Gulnār and therefore gained the title of the first Iranian woman to have acted in a Persian-speaking film. The audio recording was executed by Bahram Irani, the "dialogues and poetry" (i.e. screenplay) were written by Abdolhossein Sepanta, and the "plot (hikāyat) and setting (manzarah)" was undertaken by Ardishir Khan Irani.[116] Hamid Naficy argues that the plot of *The Lur Girl*, that is, the story of the abduction and coercion of a naïve girl from a respected family into public performance (especially singing and dancing in cafés), was borrowed from Indian cinema.[117] As the following chapters will show, this plot became a template for many Iranian commercial films in the following decades.

The Lur Girl has received much attention as a "national/nationalist" film produced by Iranian natives. Abdolhossein Sepanta has been commonly identified and acclaimed as the "director" of the film, perhaps as part of a retrospective nationalist agenda to claim the film as an Iranian production, made by an Iranian director and based on a strictly patriotic storyline. This is in spite of Sepanta's name being absent in the original film advertisements of *The Lur Girl*.[118] The remaining copy of *The Lur Girl* includes a section at the beginning of the film which elucidates the temporal and spatial context of the film: "Before the jubilant Pahlavi era," when "regions in the south and west of Iran were under the influence of various tribes and nomads"; these statements were featured as a means to pay tribute to the government of the time.[119] This is especially supported by the fact that in the years that followed, the Iranian government endorsed Sepanta as the pivotal figure of the Iranian cinema industry, and commissioned him and the same Indian company to make other Persian-language films.

---

[116] This information is reflected in the credits section at the beginning of the film. See *Dukhtar-i Lur* [*The Lur Girl*], Youtube Video, directed by Ardishir Khan Irani (1934; Bombay, India: Imperial Film Company of Bombay).

[117] Naficy, *A Social History of Iranian Cinema*, vol. 1, 235.

[118] These are the movie announcements that the author has in possession, namely the announcements in the *Iran* and *Īrān-i Bāstān* newspapers.

[119] These statements are included at the beginning of the film, *Dukhtar-i Lur* [*The Lur Girl*].

Believing "the biggest propagandas both inside and outside [Iran] to be executed by film," *Irān-i Bāstān* periodical expressed delight in the launching of talking films in the Persian language.[120] Interestingly, the newspaper considered Imperial Film Company of Bombay to be "an Iranian institution" that was "run under the supervision and competence of Iranians."[121] This was in spite of the fact that Khan Bahadur Ardeshir Irani, the owner and manager of the institution and the director of *The Lur Girl*, was an Indian of Parsi religion (with ties to Zoroastrian ancient Persia). The article attributed Ardeshir Irani's interest in the making of Persian films such as *Dukhtar-i Lur* to his "mental and spiritual connection to the fundaments of Iranian patriotism."[122] While the article acknowledged the technical defects of the first few Persian films of the time, especially in comparison to "the greatness of European and American films," it encouraged the audience to "focus their attention with utmost interest and love" on such films.[123]

In 1933, the same year in which *The Lur Girl* was produced, Ohanians also wrote and directed his second feature film – and the first film produced in Iran that has an existing copy – *Mr Haji, the Cinema Actor* (*Hājī Āqā Āktur-i Sīnamā*, 1933). Praised by a film review in *Iran* newspaper as the first elaborate movie that had been "filmed in Tehran" and that included "the participation of Iranian actors," *Hājī Āqā*, the "first production" of Persefilme Company, was considered an "intimate" (khudimānī) film in its first screening on January 31, 1934.[124] The intertitles of the film were prepared in the three languages of "Farsi [i.e., Persian], French, and Russian," pointing to two languages, other than Persian, that were perhaps the most comprehensible by residents of Iran, again reflecting the social hybridity within which the film was produced and received.[125] According to the film critic, "music pieces" accompanied the film in such a way that they "corresponded" with the different parts of the plot; although the

---

[120] "Nukhustīn Fīlm-i Gūyā bah Zabān-i Fārsī" [First Talking Film in Persian], *Īrān-i Bāstān*, no. 17 (December 1935), 15.
[121] *Ibid.*   [122] *Ibid.*   [123] *Ibid.*
[124] "Sīnamā – Ti'ātr: dar Sīnamā Ruyāl, Hāj Āqā Āktur-i Sīnamā" [Cinema – Theatre: In Cinema Royal, *Mr Haj, the Cinema Actor*], *Īrān*, yr 18, no. 4309 (Bahman 16, 1312 [February 5, 1934]), 2.
[125] *Ibid.*

film was silent, the reviewer stated that *Hājī Āqā* was represented as "a talking film (fīlm-i Sidā-dār) and musical."[126]

In the film, *Hājī Āqā*, a traditional man with religious attributes,[127] has an unfavourable view toward cinema. Unbeknown to him, however, his daughter, in addition to his son-in-law, Parvīz, and servant, Pūrī, are all members of a cinema acting institution – one very similar to Ohanians's own training centre. The director of the institution, a worldly *fukulī* (faux-col wearer),[128] played by Ovanes Oganisans himself, is searching for an interesting topic for a film. Parvīz, a progressive and open-minded man who, unlike Hājī Āqā, wears European-styled suits – as opposed to Iranian traditional male outfits – suddenly comes up with the idea of filming Hājī Āqā surreptitiously, and later showing him the film to change Hājī Āqā's mind about cinema. To this end, Pūrī snatches Hājī Āqā's watch, which makes the subject furious enough to run after him. The director then shoots the chase, the spectacle of which involves numerous comic, carnivalesque (to borrow from Bakhtin) and surreal scenes. At the end of the film, the director projects the film for Hājī Āqā, who then, astonished by the spectacle and the familiarity[129] of the images, changes his mind about cinema; thus allowing his daughter and son-in-law to continue their activities at the institution. Ohanians's film drew on local everyday practices and goings-on in the making of a vernacular motion picture. *Mr Haji, the Cinema Actor* became the first Iranian film within a film that in its postmodern structure functioned to blur the lines of reified social divisions and multiply viewpoints. In depicting the dialogism between the old and new, conservative and open-minded ideologies, educated and uneducated, cosmopolitan and stagnant, modern faux-col-wearing

---

[126] *Ibid.* This was perhaps done as a competitive strategy, since *Hājī Āqā* was screened at the same time as when the Persian-language talking film, *The Lur Girl*, was featured in Iranian cinemas.

[127] The term "Haji" (hājī) implies that he has gone on a pilgrimage to Mecca, a religious ritual that is deemed mandatory for Muslims with financial capabilities.

[128] Faux-col is the French word for bow-tie. Faux-col-wearing (fukulī) was a title that was given to many cosmopolitans and intellectuals who wore a bow-tie or tie in Iran in the twentieth century; the term, used derogatively, would set apart these people as "Frankish," or those who had travelled to European countries and had thus acquired Western attributes, namely a "Western attire."

[129] The word "familiar" is used here to denote the unfamiliar experience of seeing oneself (as a familiar image) on the screen.

and locally dressed residents, the basic plot of the film clearly demonstrates the negotiations that defined the ethos of modernity in Iran.

Hājī Āqā also functioned to map the urbanisation of the city of Tehran in its modern depiction of a changing city with its shifting lifestyles. The film opens with a panoramic view of Tehran's Tūpkhānah Square, depicting the hustle and bustle of city life linked to the main plot of the film. One can say that the character of the director in the film, as the flaneur who devises the movement of the actors throughout the city, the character of the daughter who secretly disobeys her father, the character of the pickpocket who steals Hājī Āqā's watch and the character of the fiancé who is entangled in the plot combine to piece together the city of Tehran. In other words, through an assemblage of Iranian social categories (the flaneur, the dandy, the traditional man, the intellectual, the labourer and the modern woman), Ohanians tied together the fate of the characters to the cartography of Iranian urban modernity. Such characters and such a story would have been impossible if the filming had not taken place in a city; and perhaps they would not have been comprehended by the audience without access to the basic forms of perception and experience in an urban setting.

Like the social hybridity from which it drew in its making, the film, to borrow from Bakhtin, was a polyphonous construct like "an immense novel, multi-generic, multi-styled, mercilessly critical, soberly mocking, reflecting in all its fullness the heteroglossia and multiple voices of a given culture, people, and epoch."[130] Filmed by a Russian émigré, Georges Pavlov Potemkin, with its photography carried out by "Rembrandt," played by Iranian and Iranian-Armenian actors (Ohanians's daughter, Zema, also acted in the film as Hājī Āqā's younger daughter), based on everyday Iranian life, *Mr Haji, the Cinema Actor* was a modern cosmopolitan flick, one of an emergent cosmo-national cinema. Moreover, as Naficy contends, *Hājī Āqā* was indebted to Soviet Cinema, as the idea of filming the city and its everyday goings-on was reminiscent of Dziga Vertov's *The Man with a Movie Camera* (1929), and the melodramatic acting was evocative of Vsevolod Pudovkin's films.[131] Moreover, the editing of the film was informed

---

[130] Mikhail Bakhtin, "From the Prehistory of Novelistic Discourse," in Michael Holquist (ed.), *Dialogical Imagination: Four Essays* (Austin, TX: University of Texas Press, 1981), 60.

[131] Naficy, *A Social History of Iranian Cinema*, vol. 1, 216.

by the Soviet editing style, which constituted a series of independent images connected together to give force or meaning to a scene, rather than the content. Examples of Soviet montage include scenes that depict Hājī Āqā in the dentist's chair, and Hājī Āqā at the magician's performance where he sees what, he is told, is the ghost of her daughter performing an exotic dance on the stage. The erotic and overlapping cuts of Parvin's dance, juxtaposed with shots of musical performers, are particularly stimulating in this scene. The film's stunts, grotesque movements, comedic acts and the magician's tricks are also reminiscent of the tropes that were popular in early cinema productions in the West and gave the title of "cinema of attractions" to this body of work.

Hājī Āqā was made "without the necessary equipment"; some parts of the film were "extremely dark" and other parts "extremely bright," which made the poses and faces of the actors "unusual" and "unclear."[132] Such defects were due to the fact that the producer of the film did not have sufficient funds "to import new equipment for the filming and development of the film."[133] "Disregarding" its technical shortcomings, the *Iran* newspaper critic believed *Hājī Āqā* to be "a good film," especially since "no better production could be made" given the state of the equipment.[134] While praising the acting, the film critic identified the genre of the film as a "comedy" rather than a "drama," in contradiction to what had been advertised in announcements around the city,[135] thus pointing to the discernment of various genres in Iran by that time. The review further criticised the film's content and plot, arguing that the director could have chosen a more "beneficial" and "salient" topic that not only created a source of "recreation" and "entertainment" for the audiences, but also provided a "moral" lesson.[136] It was therefore the widely instilled tenet of Iranian modernity, "morality," which again surfaced, categorised cinema and shaped the film productions that came to follow.

By the early 1930s, in the northern province of Gilan, Ibrāhīm Murādī (1898–1976) had already been active in the field of cinema for a couple of years. In 1917, Ibrāhīm Murādī left Bandar Pahlavi/ Pahlavi Port (now known as Bandar Anzali) with his family for Russia, where he acquired the skills for still photography and purchased a

---

[132] "Sīnamā – Ti'ātr: dar Sīnamā Ruyāl, *Hāj Āqā Āktur-i Sīnamā*," 2. [133] *Ibid.*
[134] *Ibid.* [135] *Ibid.* [136] *Ibid.*

home cinematographic device with which he started to make amateur films.[137] Upon his return to Iran, Murādī established the Jahān-Namā film studio in 1929, and bought a camera from the German Zeiss (Ikon) Company.[138] In 1931, he then wrote the screenplay for his first film, *Brother's Revenge* (*Intiqām-i Barādar*), which was then shot and screened in Bandar Pahlavi – making it the second Persian-language film to have been showcased in Iran.[139] According to him, Murādī had already made many "documentaries," "actualités" and "short" films from 1926 to 1929, and from 1929 to 1933.[140] Shortly after the screening of *Mr Haji, the Cinema Actor* in 1933, Murādī projected his second film, *The Capricious* (*Bulhavas*, 1933) or *The Capricious Girl* (*Dukhtar-i Bulhavas*), in Tehran's cinemas.

In this film, Khusraw, a rich young man, and Surayyā fall in love and get married. Meanwhile, a shepherd from the same area, whom Surayyā loves like a brother, confesses his love for her and asks her for her hand. Surayyā, who has promised to marry Khusraw, refuses the shepherd's offer of marriage, as a result of which the shepherd leaves the country. Meanwhile, Khusraw has to leave the village to go to the city for a few days. In the city, he stays at his uncle's house, where his uncle's daughter, Nizhat, and a young man, Manūchihr, also reside. Nizhat is a capricious girl who wishes to marry a rich man, but is also interested in Manūchihr, her neighbour. Manūchihr, on the other hand, is in love with Nizhat. With the arrival of her handsome and rich cousin, however, Nizhat forgets about Manūchihr and attempts to attract Khusraw's attention. Eventually, Khusraw also falls head over heels for Nizhat and forgets about his love for Surayyā. The two lovers finally get married. In the years that follow, Khusraw sells many of his properties to pay for his wife's whimsical requests and unusual habits of spending money. Surayyā, who had waited for Khusraw's return for a long time, finally learns about the news of his marriage, and so

---

[137] Ibrāhīm Murādī, "Sah Nāmah bah Rūznāmah-'i Ittilā'āt" [Three Letters to Ittila'at Newspaper], in *Fīlm-Nāmah-'i Intiqām-i Barādar, Vazīfah, Dafīnah-'i Yazdgird-i Sivvum: Ibrāhīm Murādī* [*Screenplays of The Capricious, Brother's Revenge, Duty, Yazdgerd the Third's Casket: Ibrāhīm Murādī*] (Tehran: Farabi Cinema Foundation, 2000), 53.

[138] *Ibid.*

[139] Masud Mehrabi, "Darbārah-'i Ibrāhīm Murādī: Saratān-i 'Ishq" [About Ibrāhīm Murādī: Cancer of Love], in *Fīlm-Nāmah-'i Intiqām-i Barādar, Vazīfah, Dafīnah-'i Yazdgird-i Sivvum: Ibrāhīm Murādī*, 36.

[140] Murādī, "Sah Nāmah," 53.

travels to the city to confront him. Once at Khusraw's house, Nizhat and all the servants make fun of her simple appearance; to avoid embarrassment, Khusraw pretends not to know Surayyā at all. Surayyā then returns to the village and attempts to commit suicide by throwing herself in the water. A young man, however, who happens to be the suitor that Surayyā had rejected in the past, rescues her from the river. The young shepherd realises that Surayyā will try to commit suicide again, and in order to relieve her of her misery he attempts to go to the city to confront Khusraw. On the way to the city, he sees a woman on a horse that is unleashed, and so he runs to help her. The woman on the horse is Nizhat, Khusraw's wife. The shepherd reins in the horse, and Nizhat thanks him for his help. However, she secretly develops affection for the shepherd because of his bravery, and as such she takes him with her to the city, and lodges him in her house. Despite Nizhat's continuous advances, the shepherd remains loyal to Surayyā and rejects Nizhat every time. Eventually, the shepherd comes to learn about Nizhat's capricious personality, and the fact that Nizhat has secret meetings with Manūchihr. Disregarding his own feelings for Surayyā, the shepherd tells Khusraw about Surayyā's state of mind; Khusraw, however, is still in love with Nizhat. Once Nizhat sees her husband's rapidly declining wealth, she cuts relations with him altogether. Heartbreak, unkind treatment from his wife and the pressure of creditors eventually lead Khusraw to fall severely ill. Due to his bad financial situation, Khusraw decides to return to the village and reside in the small house that he still owns there. Nizhat refuses to accompany him and stays behind in the city. Upon his return, Surayyā – who had never forgotten her love for Khusraw – and the shepherd come to the aid of Khusraw, taking care of him in the last few days of his life. After Khusraw's death, Nizhat and Manūchihr marry each other in the city. However, Manūchihr loses all of Nizhat's money in gambling, and thus thereafter, they live a life full of hardship and adversity. With the insistence of the shepherd, Surayyā moves to another village and eventually marries the shepherd.[141]

---

[141] The screenplay for *The Capricious* [Bulhavas] is dated May 22, 1933, in Murādī's original notes: Ibrhaim Murādī, "*Bulhavas*: Pīs-i Sīnamā dar Shish Pardah-'i Mufassal" [The Capricious: Cinema Piece in Six Detailed Acts], in *Fīlm-Nāmah-'i Intiqām-i Barādar, Vazīfah, Dafīnah-'i Yazdgird-i Sivvum: Ibrāhīm Murādī*, 13–15.

Although Ibrāhīm Murādī had already established Jahān-Namā Film
Company, the screenplay for *The Capricious* was signed under the
name of a newly founded Persefilme Ltd (Shirkat-i Mahdūd-i Fīlm-i
Īrān) and the film production was also advertised on behalf of the same
company.[142] *Bulhavas* was premiered in Tehran in Māyāk Cinema on
May 12, 1934, and was received well by the President of the National
Assembly (Majlis-i Shawrāy-i Millī), the Minister of Education and a
number of other dignitaries.[143] In fact, Ibrāhīm Murādī was officially
acknowledged for his contribution to the advancement of cinema
technology in Iran, and thus received "a scientific medal" from the
Supreme Council of Education (Shurāy-i Ālī-yi Maʿārif) for his film,
"all of the actors and operatives" of which "were Iranian."[144] The
film's popular themes of morality and simplicity (illustrated in villagers' naïveté and loyalty), which resonated with discourses of morality
(especially as it concerned cinematic projections), were well received by
government officials and the public; these themes, too, became predominant themes in the commercial productions that ensued in the
following decades.

Upon the screening of the film in Tehran, Ohanians published a very
positive review in *Ittilāʿāt* newspaper. "I am so emotionally invested in
regard to the aforementioned film [i.e., *Bulhavas*] that I cannot keep
myself from writing the following lines," said Ohanians in his review;
he then summarised the reasons for his feelings as follows: "first,
anything that is related to filming in Iran is close to my heart, especially
since I have endured much in this path and have tried to provide my
service as much as possible," remarked Ohanians, indicating his
national aspiration for Iranian productions.[145] "Second, what greater
joy [to see] that Mr Quṭbī, Dihqān, Gurjī, and Āshtī, all of whom have
been my students and for whom I have so much love, have acted with
such natural talent and innate intelligence,"[146] and "third, that
this film has been made with no foreign (financial) help, and only with
the intellectual, financial, and potential strength (quvvat-i fikrī va
māddī va istiʿdādī) of the personnel of the young Iranian cinema."[147]

---

[142] Murādī, "*Bulhavas*: Pīs-i Sīnamā dar Shish Pardah-'i Mufassal," 15.
[143] Ohanians, "Fīlm-i Dukhtar-i Bulhavas," 4.
[144] "Iʿtāʾi Midāl va Nishān-i ʿIlmī" [Granting of Scientific Medal and Decoration],
      Ittilāʿāt, yr 8, no. 2194 (Khurdād 2, 1313 [May 23, 1934]), 3.
[145] Ohanians, "Fīlm-i *Dukhtar-i Bulhavas*," 4.   [146] *Ibid.*   [147] *Ibid.*

Such an endeavour, Ohanians believed, "proves in absolute terms" that Iranians, too, can participate in "European industries," and with their "natural endowment" succeed in the field.[148] Highlighting his hyphenated identity as an Armenian-Iranian, Ohanians clearly expressed his desire and hope for the establishment of a sovereign Iranian cinema industry. On the subject of the film, Ohanians considered the plot to be "ethical, beneficial, and worthy of seeing," with great "symbolic" scenes such as "the trampling of flowers, [and] the candle going out which signifies death."[149] The film, of course, had some shortcomings, such as "the lighting," which at times "was too dark" or "blurred faces."[150] According to him, the film cost 80,000 Rials, while his own film, *Hājī Āqā*, only cost around 15,000.[151] This third movie filmed in Iran, Ohanians contended, was "better than the second film" (i.e. *Hājī Āqā*), and the second film much better than "the first one."[152] Interestingly, there is no mention of *The Lur Girl* in Ohanians's review as an Iranian film production, perhaps indicating its position outside the "national" canon at a time when the discourses around a sovereign cinema and nationalism, alongside state nationalist projects, were at their height.

Iran newspaper also published a review in which it regarded *Bulhavas* as a "good" film, especially for its "social moralist" (akhlāqī ijtimā'ī) topic which left an impact on the "soul and thought" of the audience and would "yield beneficial results."[153] Other aspects of the film that the critic saw worthy of praise were its portrayal of Iran's best "landscapes," as well as the film's editing and "arrangement of scenes."[154] The author further commented on the performance of the actors who played the roles of Nizhat and Surayyā, who despite their "inexperience" and lack of training, performed "relatively well."[155] The critic then pointed out some of the film's minor issues such as the lighting in some of the scenes, which had also been noted by Ohanians, and the progression from one scene to another in certain parts of the film. For instance, the scenes that showed the trip "from Langarud to Tehran and from Tehran to Langarud" portrayed the trip as an "easy" one, with no changes in the scenes, in such a way that one did not even imagine the distance to be that from Tehran to Qulhak.[156] Reminding

---

[148] *Ibid.*   [149] *Ibid.*   [150] *Ibid.*   [151] *Ibid.*   [152] *Ibid.*
[153] "Sīnamā – Ti'ātr: dar Sīnamā Māyāk, *Bulhavas*" [Cinema–Theatre: in Mayak Cinema, *Bulhavas*], *Īrān*, yr 18, no. 4382 (Urdībihisht 25, 1313 [May 15, 1934]), 2.
[154] *Ibid.*   [155] *Ibid.*   [156] Qulhak is a region in the north of Tehran. *Ibid.*

the reader that "no matter in which period a film is made, it must portray the habits, mores, and common customs of its time," the critic took issue with the film's portrayal of Nizhat's means of recreation, namely, horse-riding, which was "common in Europe," but was extremely rare for "Iranian women, especially Muslims"; as such, the author believed that scenes such as this had, to some extent, "taken on a European colour."[157]

Early announcements for *The Capricious* in *Irān-i Bāstān* publication, in fact, regarded the film as "the first Iranian drama" with "professional Iranian actors."[158] Another Persefilme announcement in the same newspaper considered it to be "the only film" that has been directed by "an Iranian regisseur-operator," with the participation of "Iranian actors" and made "within Iran"; "the watching of it would bring joy to any nationalist (vatan-parast)."[159] Advertisements in *Iran* newspaper highlighted the film's depiction of "natural scenery, historical sites, and old buildings of Iran," as well as the "norms and customs of residents in the north" of Iran.[160] The indirect implication of such nationalist remarks was to discredit the considerable activities of non-native residents in a national industry. Such comments, however, did not stop extra-national films from being produced. *Noor Jehan* (1931) or *Nūr-i Jahān* was the second talking production of the Imperial Film Company of Bombay, by Ezra Mir, featuring "Miss Vimala & Nayampalli." The film was about the "Glory of the Moghul Court and Camp, Love Romance of a Mighty Emperor" according to the English poster of the film which was included as part of a Persian-language announcement for the movie in *Irān-i Bāstān*.[161] The poster promised to provide scenes of "caravans, cavalries, oriental glamour," in what promised to be an orientalist depiction of medieval India.[162] The Persian addition to the film announcement in *Irān-i Bāstān* described the plot of the "greatest historical film in India" to be about

[157] "Sīnamā – Ti'ātr: dar Sīnamā Māyāk, *Bulhavas*," 2.
[158] "Avvalīn Fīlm-i Dirām-i Īrānī" [The First Iranian Drama Film], *Irān-i Bāstān*, no. 40 (Ābān 8, 1312 [October 30, 1933]), 4.
[159] "Fīlm-i Dirām-i Īrānī (*Bulhavas*)" [Iranian Drama Film (*Bulhavas*)], *Irān-i Bāstān*, no. 43 [Ābān 27, 1312 (November 18, 1933)], 9.
[160] "Fīlm-i Dirām-i *Bulhavas* dar Sīnamā Māyāk" [Drama Film *Bulhavas* at Mayak Cinema], *Irān*, yr 18, no. 4377 (Urdībihisht 19, 1313 [May 9, 1934]), 4.
[161] "*Nūr-i Jahān*," *Irān-i Bāstān*, yr 2, no. 4 (Bahman 21, 1312 [February 10, 1934]), 9.
[162] *Ibid.*

"a queen of Iranian descent in the court of Akbar Shah of India."[163] *Nūr-i Jahān*, "a one hundred percent historical and oriental (sharqī) talking film, containing the secrets and wonders of the orient, Iran-India," based on newspaper announcements, was screened at Iran Cinema and Palace Cinema (pālās) in February 1934.[164] The announcement for the film in *Iran* newspaper (of February 1934), interestingly, attempted to appropriate the production as an Iranian one, by highlighting the subject of the film to be "Iranian" (muzū'i-i Irānī), and its "dance, song, and music" to be Eastern, with the participation of Iranian artists – again evoking aspirations for a sovereign national cinema.[165] This review, along with other film reviews of Persian-language films that were published in the *Iran* and *Īrān-i Bāstān* newspapers attest to the increasing professionalisation of film criticism, and express aspirations and visions for a sovereign cinema industry in Iran that was imbued with a vernacular colour rather than a European one.

The year 1934 embodied historical significance in Iran's historical narrative. The government decided to celebrate the millennium of Firdawsi (940–1020 CE), the Iranian epic poet, whose famous literary collection, *Shahnamah* (*The Book of Kings*), is considered to be a masterpiece in the Persian language. *Shahnamah* comprises mythical, and to some extent historical, poems that describe the history of a Persian Empire from the creation of time to the Islamic conquest of Persia. The celebration of such a long poem in the Persian language (rather than Arabic, which had been customary before the tenth century), and its subject of a "glorious" imperial past, proved to be an important and timely matter to a state that attempted to consolidate its royalty by looking to the past. Numerous dignitaries, scholars of literature and orientalist thinkers had been invited to the celebration to speak of the splendid work of Firdawsi and thus brilliance of a new monarchy that took its name from the ancient past. The event would be celebrated in cities such as Tehran, Mashhad, Tus and Isfahan, and lasted for almost a month. The celebrations included speeches, lectures, discussions, various plays, stunts and performances by primary school students and adults, as well as cinema screenings. Meanwhile,

---

[163] *Ibid.*
[164] "Sīnamā Īrān va Sīnamā Pālās" [Iran Cinema and Palace Cinema], *Īrān*, yr 18, no. 4321 (Isfand 7, 1312 [February 26, 1934]), 4.
[165] *Ibid.*

countries such as France, the Soviet Union, Britain, the United States, Germany, Egypt and Iraq held similar events in universities and other venues.[166] Having come to appreciate propagandistic and large-scale communication made possible through cinema, the Pahlavi government "undertook some measures to celebrate the millennium anniversary of Firdawsi's birth" by making "a film about the life and historical myths of this great man."[167] Since the Imperial Film Company of Bombay had already "endeavoured to make talking Persian films," the same company had been commissioned to produce this specific historical film.[168] The company included a number of "Iranian and Persian-speaking residents of Iran who had some experience in theatre" and in the making of its "feature film."[169] On September 27, *Iran* newspaper announced that the "news of the completion of the film" had been communicated and "the script of the film had been sent to the Office of Publications of the Ministry of Education," which then reviewed the scenario, made "certain remarks on a few defects," and sent it back to India. Because the "modification and adjustment" of the film took longer than expected, the film was directly sent to the province of Khurasan, in order to be screened at the Firdawsi millenary celebrations and the inauguration of the mausoleum that was erected in his honour, "in the presence of participants, among whom were some orientalists."[170] Based on "what had been heard," the film had "many benefits" and did not have "the defects of *The Lur Girl*"; overall, it was a film, according to the newspaper, that "could be displayed as a great Persian talking film in foreign countries."[171] Such statements reveal the Iranian elite's desire for cinematic contemporaneity with European countries, and the staging of Iran as an independent nation on a global level. The film was screened in the "Lion

---

[166] *Encyclopedia Iranica Online*, s.v. "Firdowsi, Abu'l -Qāsem iv. Millenary Celebration," accessed August 19, 2014, www.iranicaonline.org/articles/ ferdowsi-iv.

[167] "Sīnamā – Ti'ātr: Fīlm-i *Firdawsī*" [Cinema – Theatre: *Firdawsi* Film], *Īrān*, yr 18, no. 4494 (Mihr 5, 1313 [September 27, 1934]), 3.

[168] *Ibid.*   [169] *Ibid.*

[170] *Ibid.* It is perhaps interesting to note here that the nationalists of the time took advantage of the presence of orientalist scholars, as well as film plots that glorified ancient Iran, not to portray an exotic or stagnant image of the country (as had been done through orientalist international films), but to tap into popular nationalist sentiments by staging the nation as superior, sovereign and artistically advanced.

[171] "Sīnamā – Tiātr: Fīlm-i *Firdawsī*," 3.

and Sun Hall" in Mashhad (the capital of Khurāsān province) on October 14, 1934.[172] Aside from its projection at the millennium celebrations, the film was shown in various movie houses around Tehran, namely, Māyāk Cinema and Sun Cinema.[173] The quality of the finished project, however, is questionable; according to scholars such as Hamid Naficy, *Firdawsi* was not met with enthusiasm by the residents of Iran, perhaps because the "incoherence" of the film – due to its shortening to a 50-minute film – drove people away.[174] According to Naficy, although Sepanta played the part of the poet himself,[175] his name was not mentioned in the reports of the events of the millennium celebration in *Iran* newspaper. Instead, according to a report in *Iran*, "Mr Arbāb Kaykhusraw Nāmdār Marzbān, the sole representative of Imperial Film Company of Bombay," had travelled to Mashhad to "participate in the Firdawsi celebration, to film the events of the celebration, and screen the Firdawsi film."[176] In the opening ceremony of the Firdawsi millennium celebrations, based on another report in *Iran* newspaper, the representative of the film company and "the wife of Iskandar Khān (Farah Angīz Khānūm)," who had recently arrived in Iran from the United States, and a number of other people who had filming devices, "made elaborate films" of the celebration.[177] As such, through the millennium celebration of Firdawsi, a national symbol was staged on a global level, through the use of lectures and cinema screenings.

Interestingly, despite the success or failure of *Firdawsi*, the Imperial Film Company of Bombay still sought to "produce other Persian talking films."[178] Immediately after the making of *Firdawsi*, the company set out to "hire a number of men and women actors from

---

[172] "Akhbār-i Tiligrāfī-yi Dākhilah-'i Īrān: 22 Mihr 1313, Mashhad" [Telegraphed Domestic News of Iran: 14 October 1934, Mashhad], *Īrān*, yr 18, no. 4510 (Mihr 24, 1313 [October 14, 1934]), 1.

[173] "Nukhustīn Fīlm-i Gūyā," 15.

[174] Naficy, *A Social History of Iranian Cinema*, vol. 1, 241.   [175] *Ibid.*

[176] "Vurūd Barā-yi Shirkat dar Jashn-i Firdawsī" [Arriving to Participate in Firdawsi Celebrations], *Īrān*, yr 18, no. 4499 (Mihr 11, 1313 [October 3, 1934]), 2.

[177] H. R., "Marāsim-i Iftitāh-i Ārāmgāh-i Firdawsī" [The Opening Ceremony of Firdawsi Mausoleum], *Īrān*, yr 18, no. 4511 (Mihr 25, 1313 [October 17, 1934]), 1.

[178] "Sīnamā – Tiātr: Fīlm-i *Firdawsī*, Istikhdām-i Ārtīst Barā-yi Sīnamā" [Cinema – Theatre: *Firdawsi* Film, Hiring Actors for Cinema], *Īrān*, yr 18, no. 4494 (Mihr 5, 1313 [September 27, 1934]), 3.

Tehran" to perform in its next production.[179] This way, the company sought to account for the "defects" of its first Persian production, *The Lur Girl*, in which the accent of the actors was not quite right.[180] According to the advertisement, the accepted candidates would first "attain the required skills in India," and then act in the Persian talkies of the company.[181] A few days earlier, *Iran* newspaper had also advertised for "several men and women artists/actors," who were to be sent to India to act in Persian talking films.[182] The candidates were required to submit their "address" in addition to "two photos" to the Nūryānī Trade Firm, which appears to have been the management office of the Imperial Film Company of Bombay in Iran.[183] In a matter of days, the company had so many applicants that it published an announcement on October 2, 1934 containing the headline, "Actors (ārtīst) Sufficient," which asked people to refrain from sending applications for participation in the film.[184] The next Persian movie of the Imperial Film Company, *Shirin and Farhad*, was already underway in September 1934.

There is not much information available on *Shirin and Farhad*, but the tragic story of Khusraw and Shirin by Nizami Ganjavi (1141–1209) seems to have been a popular hit with filmmakers in India in the 1920s and 1930s. According to the *Encyclopaedia of Indian Cinema*, in 1926, Homi Master (d. 1949) made a silent film by the title *Shirin Farhad*, also known as *At the Altar of Love*, a variant drawn from the Persian story of Shirin and Khusraw by Nizami Ganjavi.[185] In 1929, Rama Shankar Choudhury (1903–1972), known for making historical films, directed a silent film entitled *Shirin Khush-rau* (1929), perhaps again based on the famous story of Ganjavi.[186] In 1931, J. J. Madan, of the Madan Theatres film company, produced a "big-budget musical," *Shirin Farhad*, which after Ardishīr Irani's and India's first talkie, *'Ālam Ārā* (1931), came to be the country's second talking motion picture.[187] The description of Madan's film, however,

---

179 *Ibid.*   180 *Ibid.*   181 *Ibid.*

182 "Chand Nafar Ārtīst-i Zan va Mard" [Several Numbers of Men and Women Actors], *Īrān*, yr 18, no. 4488 (Shahrīvar 29, 1313 [September 20, 1934]), 1.

183 *Ibid.*

184 "Ārtīst Kāfī Ast" [Actors Sufficient], *Ittilā'āt*, yr 9, no. 2303 (Mihr 10, 1314 [October 2, 1934]), 1.

185 Ashish Rajadhyaksha and Paul Willemen (eds), *Encyclopedia of Indian Cinema* (Oxford University Press, 1999), s.v. "Homi, Master."

186 *Ibid.*, s.v. "Choudhury, Rama Shankar."   187 *Ibid.*, s.v. "Madan Theatres."

is misleading in that it considers the film to be a narrative based on "a legend from the Shahnamah."[188] Although the tale of Khusraw and Shirin is touched upon in *Shahnamah*, with a focus on the battles of Khusraw, Nizami elaborates on the romantic encounter of Shirin, Khusraw and Farhad in his version. According to the filmography entry in *Encyclopaedia of Indian Cinema*, Shah Khusraw commissions the Persian sculptor, Farhad, to build a canal for a great reward. Meanwhile, Farhad falls in love with Queen Shirin. Shah Khusraw, who himself is in love with Shirin, agrees to let Farhad marry her provided he first single-handedly demolishes the Bīsutūn mountains.[189] Shirin and Farhad are "finally united in death as Farhad's tomb miraculously opens to accept Shirin."[190] The film apparently proved to be "a bigger hit" than the first Indian talkie, '*Ālam Ārā*. Furthermore, it recorded "sound and image separately," a technique that was later adopted to a great degree by filmmakers as it provided more "aesthetic flexibility."[191]

The film prepared by Abdolhossein Sepanta at the Imperial Film Company of Bombay, however, had a somewhat different plot: Shirin is upset over the fact that Khusraw has chosen another woman by the name of Shikar as his wife. The Roman Emperor invites Khusraw to participate in his son's wedding. In the absence of Khusraw, Shirin travels to Kirmanshah province with her handmaiden. During her trip, she comes to meet the sculptor, Farhad, in a tavern, where Farhad falls in love with Shirin. Meanwhile, a number of sculptors were invited to build a tunnel through Bisutūn Mountain to Khusraw's palace. While every professional sculptor in the court deems the task impossible, Farhad is convinced that because of his love for Shirin, he can overcome all obstacles. With his determination, Farhad starts the project, and sees Shirin a number of times. Khusraw, however, who sees Farhad as a love-rival, sends a woman to lie to Farhad that Shirin has died. Farhad loses his mind over the news and injures his hand severely, ultimately leading to his demise. Just before his death, however, Shirin appears at his deathbed.[192] Fakhruzzamān Jabbār Amīn Vazīrī, who for a while helped Ohanians with his Artistic School and

---

[188] *Ibid.*, s.v. "*Shirin Farhad.*"   [189] *Ibid.*, 254.   [190] *Ibid.*   [191] *Ibid.*

[192] See "*Shīrīn va Farhād*" [*Shirin and Farhad*] in Abbas Baharloo, *Fīlmshinākht-i Īrān: Fīlm-shināsī-yi Sīnamā-yi Īrān (1309–1357)* [*Iran's Filmoghraphy: Filmography of Iranian Cinema (1930–1979)*] (Tehran: Qatrah Publications, 2004), 31.

Cinema Institution, played the role of Shirin in the film. Nusratullāh Muhtasham (1919–1980),[193] who was a theatre actor (and director), played the role of Khusraw, Abdolhossein Sepanta acted as Farhad and Rūhangīz Sāmī Nijād, who had played the role of Gulnār in *The Lur Girl*, acted as Shikar, Khusraw's wife. Irān Daftarī played the role of Shirin's servant and sang some of the songs included in this semi-musical, the music for which was prepared by Nūrīyānī, a composer and violinist.[194]

The film, *Shirin and Farhad*, was for the first time screened in Iran by the alternative title of *Khusraw and Shirin*, on June 13, 1935, in both Māyāk Cinema and Sipah (Army) Cinema.[195] Film reviews and newspaper articles also used the name *Khusraw and Shirin* to refer to the production, perhaps because of the original title of Nizami Ganjavi's story. However, months later in late September, newspapers reverted to the original title, *Shirin and Farhad*, in their program announcements.[196] Considering it to be "the second Persian talkie," in an article in *Iran* Mīr-Hussayn Shabāhang did not have a favourable view toward the film. "I know," he declared, "few people who have seen the film and are not dismayed by the distastefulness (kaj-salīqigī) of the producers of this film."[197] Making a film, he remarked, "required a big budget, actors and actresses, sufficient knowledge, outstanding topics, taste, and a thousand other things," and so he wondered why Iranians were "adamant to undertake such a difficult task" while they lacked the necessary film devices.[198] Shabāhang was specifically worried about the quality of the film since it "converged

---

[193] It is noteworthy to mention here that Nusratullāh Muhtasham (who also played in *Firdawsi* and another Indian film by the name *Pia Pia* [My Man]) became a renowned stage actor in the 1940s and later a prominent cinema actor in the 1950s.

[194] "Āsār-i Sīnamāyī-yi 'Abdulhussayn Sipantā" [Cinematic Works of Abdolhossein Sepanta], *Farhang va Zindigī* [Culture and Life], yr 1975, no. 18, 37. This journal is published by the Publication of High Council of Culture and Art, at the Ministry of Culture and Art in Iran.

[195] "Purugrām-i Sīnamāhā-yi Imshab" [Tonight's Cinema Program], *Ittilā'āt*, yr 9, no. 2508 (Khurdād 22, 1314 [June 13, 1935]), 4.

[196] Sipāh Cinema used the original title, *Shirin and Farhad*, in its film announcement in *Ittilā'āt* newspaper on September 26, 1935. "Purugrām-i Sīnamāhā-yi Imshab" [Tonight's Cinema Program], *Ittilā'āt*, yr 9, no. 2596 (Mihr 3, 1314 [September 26, 1935]), 3.

[197] "Duvvumīn Fīlm-i Nātiq-i Fārsī" [The Second Persian Talking Film], *Īrān*, yr 19, no. 4714 (Tīr 5, 1314 [June 27, 1935]), 3.

[198] *Ibid.*

with the national history" of Iran, and the distribution of a "bad and disdainful" movie would dishonour the reputation of the country.[199] Rather than resembling an Iranian setting, the author believed, the façade of the buildings – with a few exceptions – corresponded to that of "Arab and Indian" buildings, while the indistinct "make-up" of the actors made it difficult to identify the "era and place" of the motion picture.[200] Shabāhang further blamed the script writer for making the characters unbelievable, making Shirin sing "when she cannot sing," and at times having the handmaid sing "in replacement of both Khusraw and Shirin."[201] Overall, the critic believed the production to have done a "disservice" (bī-lutfī) to the history of the Sassanian Empire (224–651 CE) and the love story of Farhad and Shirin. Shabāhang deemed it necessary for the authorities to "prevent the distribution of the film outside Iran."[202] Shabāhang's concern reveals, more clearly, the role of cinema in national propaganda by the 1930s.

Considering the fair success of Persian talking films at the Imperial Film Company of Bombay, Abdolhossein Sepanta endeavoured to direct yet another film in the ensuing months. *Black Eyes* (*Chashmhā-yi Sīyāh*, 1936) premiered in Tehran on June 2, 1936, at Iran Cinema, screened at 7.30 pm and 9.30 pm,[203] and then at Pārs Cinema on June 17 at the same show times.[204] *Black Eyes* was fully shot in India and produced by Krishna Film Company, which indicated that Indian production studios had realised the commercial potential of Persian-language films, both in India and in Iran. Written by Sepanta, himself, the plotline was based on a shared moment in the histories of Iran and India, which played to the national sentiments of both communities. The story revolved around the two characters of Humā and Humāyūn from Iran, who lived with an Indian Raja in medieval India. During this time, Nadir Shah (1688–1747) of Iran conquered Lahore, and thus the love story of Humā and Humāyūn was affected by the military and political goings-on of the time.[205]

---

[199] *Ibid.*   [200] *Ibid.*   [201] *Ibid.*   [202] *Ibid.*

[203] "Purugrām-i Sīnamāhā-yi Imshab" [Tonight's Cinema Program], *Ittilāʿāt*, yr 10, no. 2802 (Khurdād 12, 1315 [June 2, 1936]), 8.

[204] "Purugrām-i Sīnamāhā-yi Imshab" [Tonight's Cinema Program], *Ittilāʿāt*, yr 10, no. 2816 (Khurdād 27, 1315 [June 27, 1936]), 8.

[205] See "*Chashmhā-yi Sīyāh* (Fath-i Lāhūr bah Dast-i Nādir Shāh)" [*Black Eyes* (The Conquering of Lahore by Nadir Shah)] in Baharloo, *Fīlmshinākht-i Īrān: Fīlm-shināsī-yi Sīnamā-yi Īrān (1309–1357)*, 32.

On May 31, 1936, *Ittilā'āt* newspaper published an advertisement for Sepanta's next film, *Layli and Majnun (Laylī va Majnūn)*.[206] As "good news" for those interested in "the Art and Literature of Iran," the announcement heralded the coming of "an Iranian talkie film," a "masterpiece by East India Film Company of Calcutta," which was also fully shot and developed in India.[207] The film was praised for its national significance in that it depicted the tale of love between Layli and Majnun – popular in Middle Eastern and South Asian ancient literature – which was then adopted into a dramatic poem by the Iranian poet, Nizami Ganjavi. The "amazing decors" and "luxurious clothes" were highlighted in the announcement in a commercial attempt to bring attention to the high-budgeted production and attract the audience; the mentioning of the participation of "Iranian actors" was also a move to highlight the aspects of the film that made it "Iranian" and to play to the nationalist sentiments of the audience.[208] Moreover, the emphasis on "the beloved star" (Sitārah-'i Mahbūb), "Khānūm Fakhr Jabbār Vazīrī," alongside "regisseur and champion" (pahlivān), "Mr A. Sipanta," points to the beginning of the use of "cinema stars" in Persian-language films for commercial success by the mid-1930s.[209]

In *Layli and Majnun*, Qays and Layli fall in love with one another from a very early age when they both attend the same primary school (maktab). Layli's father, who had come to see Qays's affection toward his daughter throughout the years, disapproves of the relationship between the two and so he changes his daughter's *maktab*. Not seeing Layli, Qays becomes mad with love, for which he acquires the nickname, Majnun (possessed). A mystic in the tribe, to whom Qays had confided his love for Layli, advises him to reach the meaning of true esoteric love, that is, to keep his love alive, and to develop it to encompass the whole world. Majnun asks Layli's father for her hand, but since the father considers Qays as crazy and possessed by emotions, he refuses to allow them to wed. Instead, Layli's father marries Layli to another young man. Having received the news of Layli's marriage, Majnun flees the tribe and begins wandering the desert.

---

[206] "Mujdah bah Hizārān 'Alāqah-mandān Be-san'at va Adabīyāt-i Īrān" [Good News for Thousands of Interested People in the Art and Literature of Iran], *Ittilā'āt*, yr 10, no. 2800 (Khurdād 10, 1315 [May 31, 1936]), 1.
[207] *Ibid.*   [208] *Ibid.*   [209] *Ibid.*

Layli and Majnun marked the last Persian narrative film production in the 1930s. The corpus of films produced from 1930 to 1936 has been usually categorised as a nationalist cinema, mostly in part and parcel of its emergence in an era when the nationalist discourse of the elite and state came to imagine a fictional united nation. Films such as *Nūr-i Jahān, Shirin and Farhad* and *Layli and Majnun* point to the glorification of a national literary heritage, which was in fact a shared literary culture that linked Iran with its neighbours – namely, India and the Arab world. What we have here, therefore, is the formation of a "cosmo-national" cinema; national to the extent that it lends legitimacy to a shared historical era, a rich "glorious" past that would radiate the fictional peaceful, robust Persianate culture and literature against the backdrop of world wars and geopolitical strifes. What seemed to be at stake, for many writers and critics, was the "national customs" or mores which were dissipating in a cosmopolitan setting. Interestingly, it seems that language became the primary organising category for this industry which differentiated it from Hollywood and/or European cinemas, and also perhaps allowed for capitalising on the commercial value of a Persian-language cinema. On the other hand, this emergent cinema was cosmopolitan to the extent that it drew on the "weakening of communal," i.e. national or familial, boundaries; it was based on the creation of "institutions and means of communication outside communal and religious authority, in which individuals from diverse backgrounds and cultures" actively participated.[210] Of course, the praising of this cinema as national – as part and parcel of a nationalist culture in the 1930s – was, in the words of Susan Hayward, "in constant denial," since it was based on the principle of "representation" and "repression" of its cosmopolitan elements in a unifying nationalist rhetoric.[211]

The attempt to consolidate a national culture by the Pahlavi state meant the restriction and elimination of social pluralism in the 1930s – the reason why the names of Iranian-Armenians were not highlighted in film announcements and productions by an Indian company were distributed and co-opted as Iranian productions. In other words, the

---

[210] Sami Zubaida, "Cosmopolitanism and the Middle East," in Roel Meijer (ed.), *Cosmopolitanism, Identity and Authenticity in the Middle East* (Richmond: Curzon Press, 1999), 19.

[211] Susan Hayward, "Framing National Cinemas," in Mette Hjort and Scott Mackenzie (eds), *Cinema and Nation* (London: Routledge, 2000), 91.

standardisation of language, clothing and the culture by the Pahlavi state were concomitant with the standardisation of cinema and visual representations of the country. This meant the disappearance of diverse social practices and local traditions from the visual archive of Iranian cinema; as Chapter 4 will discuss, the "Film-Farsi" productions of the 1950s and onward, nevertheless, sought to screen such local nuances by focusing on the everyday lives of people in Iran.

There is no doubt that the popular national epics, history, poetry and figures which were featured in this national *literary* cinema – and highlighted in their grandeur and splendid settings and costumes – resonated with the modern nationalist discourse of the period. In line with Tavakoli-Targhi's discussion of competing narratives in the refashioning of national identity in the nineteenth century, the cinema of the 1930s also functioned to display contestations in the nationalist narrative. While, according to Tavakoli-Targhi, the official national discourse of the time could be regarded as a patriotic narrative, the cosmo-national cinema was shaped by and came to form a matriotic discourse of nationalism.[212] In films such as *The Lur Girl*, the character of Gulnār, for example, is arguably a gendered representation of *vatan* (nation). Gulnār, imagined as mother-nation, is a woman imprisoned by bandits (here interpreted as external and internal Others) and under the menace of "rape," in the unsafe times of "Iran of Yesterday," that is, before the onset of the Pahlavi Dynasty. Ja'far, the government official, the metaphorical son of mother-nation, saves Gulnār from the hands of the enemy, delivers her safely into the hands of the "Iran of Today" and fashions her into an urban and modernised woman – who plays "nationalist" songs on the piano and decorates her house with European-style sculptures. As such, Gulnār could be seen as the familiarisation of "mother-nation" in the modern public space that now embraced cinema.[213] Although not liberated, Gulnār's

---

[212] Tavakoli-Targhi's use of matriotic discourse of nationalism refers to counter-official narratives that imagined the nation as a "mother" (mādar-vatan) or a "woman" that is in need of rescue by its sons (the people of Iran). See Mohamad Tavakoli-targhi, "From Patriotism to Matriotism: A Tropological Study of Iranian Nationalism, 1870–1909," *International Journal of Middle Eastern Studies* 34(2) (2002): 217–238.

[213] It should be noted here that the image of Gulnār, however, does not easily fit into the notion of mother-nation as "a dying 6,000-year-old mother," thus perhaps addressing the multiple national identities in Iran of the 1930s. See Tavakoli-Targhi, "From Patriotism to Matriotism," 225.

confidence, ability to speak her mind and physical mobility (whether in her dance at the beginning of the film or in her activities), i.e. her capacity for individualised choice and action, could be understood in terms of agency, and new imaginations of mother-nation. The character of Hājī Āqā's daughter is also reminiscent of a self-willed, independent and cosmopolitan woman – traits that are manifested in her choice of clothing as an unveiled woman dressed in the latest fashion of the time, and in her signing up for acting in cinema despite her father's unfavourable view. Although not necessarily representing mother-Iran, the character of Hājī Āqā's daughter explored a new role for "brothers and sisters" of the nation in a modernising era. If, as Tavakoli-Targhi argues, the strengthening of mother-Iran in the early-twentieth-century national discourse was linked to the education of women,[214] these films could then be considered as part and parcel of this pedagogical project, especially since by the 1930s women enjoyed the prerogative to use the space of cinema alongside men.

* * *

The promotion of cinematic education both in official and unofficial discourses was enmeshed with a statist nationalist agenda in the 1930s. The institutionalisation of cinema and aspirations for cinematic sovereignty (expressed by critics and cosmopolitan cineastes) facilitated the formation of a Persian-language cinema and its propagation in Iran. The emergence of this cinema, as argued above, was very much entwined with the cosmopolitan society and culture of the region and could not be examined outside of such a paradigm. Thus, far from being a necessarily national (or even nationalist) cinema, the Persian-language cinema of the 1930s was in fact a cosmo-national cinema. While the productions of this cinema relied heavily on a cosmopolitan cinematic culture, international funding, figures and cinematic elements, the cultural offerings of this cinema were national as their content pertained to national (or Indo-Persian) history, heritage, myths and heroes.

One main preoccupation of the nationalist filmic narrative of the 1930s seems to have been the staging of Iran not in the orientalist depiction that had been widespread in the early twentieth century, but

[214] *Ibid.*, 233.

as a progressive country, contemporaneous with its European counter-parts. Mīr-Hussayn Shabāhang's concern about the quality of *Shirin and Farhad* and the distribution of the film outside Iran perhaps exposes this anxiety. From very early on, international cinemato-graphic companies embarked on recording narrative silent films based on biblical Persian stories and history, as well as newsreels based on Iranian political events. *Christian Martyrs*, a 1905 drama that included "realistic scenes" and was produced by Pathé Frères (Pathé Brothers), referred to the Persian Achaemenid King, Cyrus, who led an expedition to Babylon. The film is a loose adaptation of the Book of Daniel, about "the Hebrew Prophet," who is revered as a saint by Jews, Christians and Muslims.[215] In three acts, i.e. "Martyrs," "Daniel in the Lions' Den" and "The Feast of Belshazzar," the film attends to the character of Daniel who, according to the narrative published on Foundation Jérôme Seydoux-Pathé's website, is put in a lions' den, but is then miraculously freed from his shackles and caressed by the lions. The Persian King, Cyrus, who sees this miracle, calls the prophet and frees him from the prison. The next act depicts King Cyrus attacking the Babylonian palace at Belshazzar's feast, an event that makes him the King of Babylon.[216] *La Morte De Cambyse* (*The Death of Cambyses*, 1909) was another short fictional film that revolved around a fictional narrative.[217] Casting members of Comédie-Française performing troupe, the film depicts a fictional story based on another Achaemenid King, Cambyses, who expanded the Persian empire into Egypt.[218] D. W. Griffith's *The Fall of Babylon* (1919), which was a re-edited

---

[215] "*Martyrs Chrétiens* [*Christian Martyrs*]," Foundation Jérôme Seydoux-Pathé (Pathés Frères production), accessed April 5, 2016, http://filmographie .fondation-jeromeseydoux-pathe.com/5739-martyrs-chretiens.

[216] The film description explains that the events take place in "Rome," shortly after the reign of Emperor Nero. "Martyrs Chrétiens," accessed April 5, 2016, http:// filmographie.fondation-jeromeseydoux-pathe.com/5739-martyrs-chretiens.

[217] "*La Morte De Cambyse* [*The Death of Cambyses*]," Gaumont Fiction, 5:30, Gaumont Pathé Archives, accessed April 17, 2017, www.gaumontpathearchives .com/index.php?urlaction=doc&id_doc=308983&rang=6.

[218] Set in an elaborate background that is supposed to resemble Persian and Babylonian palaces, the film depicts King Cambyses, who accidentally kills the son of Amestris, the wife of Prexaspes, his loyal courtier, and the woman with whom he is in love. Amestris, who does not know that her son's death was accidental, vows to take revenge. As such, she lures the King into her quarters by seduction and pretence. Once in her residence, Amestris shows the lifeless body of her son to the king and then stabs him to death.

version of a sequence from Griffith's 1916 film, *Intolerance*, also dealt with the conquest of Babylon by the Achaemenid King Cyrus. The film, according to Naficy, was screened in Tehran in 1926 by an alternative title, *The Conquest of Babylon*, which aimed to glorify the Persian conquest of Babylon, despite the fact that the film's sentiments seemed to lay with the defeated.[219] In 1925, Merian C. Cooper, Ernest B. Schoedsnack and Marguerite Harrison, three Americans who had come to realise the economic and propagandist significance of cinema in reporting events, lifestyles and visual ethnography, travelled to the south-western parts of Iran to film *Grass: A Nation's Battle for Life*, the story of the "continuous struggle between the Baktyari and Nature for Grass."[220] The 71-minute feature film follows the Baba Ahmadi branch of the Bakhtiyari tribe in their semi-annual migratory journey up the Zāgrus mountains and across the treacherous Kārūn River in search of pasture. In the late 1920s, Soviet filmmakers, too, embarked upon making feature films based on Persian historical events. *Gilan Qizi* (*Gilan's Daughter*, 1928), depicting the struggles of the Jangali movement, was produced in Soviet Azerbaijan, while *Khaz-push* (1928), based on Iran's 1891–1892 Tobacco Protests, was made in Soviet Armenia by the Armenian filmmaker, Amo Bek-Nazarov (Hamo Beknazaryan).[221] Both films, informed by historical events in contemporary Iran, also attest to the transnational cinematic exchanges between Iran and neighbouring countries.

Aside from fictional and semi-documentary narratives, international cinematographers made newsreels and actualités of political events in Iran from the 1900s to 1930s, at a time when Iran was at the centre of political rivalry, especially between England, Russia and Germany. Newsreels and actualités shot by Pathé Frères, British Pathé and Gaumont Pathé attest to the centrality of Iran in international discussions, political debates and international wars; semi-documentaries and fictional films, on the other hand, were orientalist attempts at exoticising and ossifying Iran as a backward and stagnant country. While the international cinema made numerous attempts at picturing (and

---

[219] Naficy, *A Social History of Iranian Cinema*, vol. 1, 177–178.

[220] Merian C. Cooper, *Grass* (New York: Knickerbocker Press, 1925), xi.

[221] The author is currently working on an independent article that will attend specifically to fictional feature films, as well as newsreels and actualité films that were made by the international community on the topic of Iran or based on historical events in Iran.

representing) Iran and thus constituting the country as a zone of global political contestations or a backward oriental land, Iran made efforts to display its national heritage on the silver screen through productions that it deemed as "national" or Iranian. Most importantly, the national identity of these films was organised around their use of the Persian language. *The Lur Girl*, *Firdawsi* and *Shirin and Farhad* were some of the talking productions of this era that boasted the usage of the language in their depiction of a glorious Persianate heritage or a changing and modern Iran. Interestingly, as Chapter 4 will show, "the Persian language" became the signifying factor for a group of commercial films that was made from the 1950s to the 1970s, albeit now with a derogative connotation; the title of "Film-Farsi" (Persian-Films) was given to these popular films to separate them from the art house or alternative films of the period.

3 | Industrial Professionalisation
The Emergence of a "National" Commercial Cinema

The aspirations of filmmakers, critics, intellectuals and cinema enthusiasts for the creation of a sovereign cinema, as discussed in Chapter 2, were re-enacted in the form of a sustained commercial cinema industry that commenced its feature film productions in the late 1940s. After the production of the first few Persian-language films before World War II, Iranian feature film production came to a halt for almost a decade. The reasons for this drought have been attributed to many factors arising from the political and economic conditions of the time. Contrary to popular belief, the hiatus in film production did not mark a suspension of cinematic activities. The absence of feature film production created a vacuum that enabled the influx of international films to Iran, the making of documentary films, the establishment of alternative cinematic activities such as dubbing foreign language films, the bolstering of a consumerist culture linked to the circulation of local and global cinema and theatre stars, and the professionalisation of cosmopolitan actors and film critics, all of which laid the foundation for the establishment of a new industry. Toward the end of the 1940s, cinema and stage actors, critics and film directors who had engaged global cinema trends in one way or another participated in the production of the first post–World War II Persian-language commercial films.

In this chapter, I will first briefly explore some of the World War II international propagandist societies and films that intended to shape public opinion during a politically sensitive era. As I will demonstrate, the reactions of people to such propagandist offerings were not homogenous and/or favourable. The propaganda activities of the Allied cultural societies, the influx of international commercial films and their reception by the audiences made it clear to the Pahlavi government that it needed to boost Iran's cinematic presence on a global level. Meanwhile, the increasing number of international commercial films that were distributed in Iran and a lack of Iranian film production propelled some to start dubbing foreign language films to the Persian language in studios outside Iran, and later to establish studios within the country.

This era also witnessed the bolstering of an image culture that was highly informed by Hollywood, Indian and Arab (especially Egyptian) cinema cultures. The sustained commercial film enterprise that emerged in the late 1940s drew on this culture and recirculated its emergent post-war social prototypes, class- and/or gender-based typecasts, in its filmic offerings. The booming consumerist image culture of the 1940s was concomitant with the expansion of the industry, and the professionalisation of film critics, stage actors (many of whom entered the cinema enterprise) and dubbing and visionary film studios. The consolidation of post-war national commercial cinema, as I will demonstrate in this chapter, overlapped with the flourishing of the industry and technology, as well as the professionalisation of members of the industry, many of whom envisaged the crafting of a distinctive artistic Iranian cinema – one that could be distributed and displayed on an international level. In Chapter 4, then, I will deal with the "national" visual products of post-WWII and cinematic language offered by film critics and the nascent commercial film industry.

3.1 Cinema and Propaganda in Post-War Iran

In the 1930s and 1940s, Iranian movie theatres screened a large number and variety of international films – namely, Russian, British, German, American (Hollywood), French and Hindi films. In the 1930s, local cinemas were swamped with German UFA (Universum Film AG) films, some of which were commercial, and many of which had nationalist and propagandist subjects and were, according to the newspapers of the time, quite popular in the country. In the early 1940s, however, with the invasion of and occupation by the Allied forces, German films were banned from being screened. Instead, movie theatres showcased Russian, American and British newsreels from the battlefronts, and popular and educational films. At a time when the television had yet to be introduced to Iranian households and radios were uncommon, the public would swarm into cinemas to hear about the war and news from the front lines. Iranian movie theatres not only showed international newsreels, but also local and foreign documentaries about farming, public hygiene and national costumes. During this period, the Pahlavi state took many initiatives to enhance cinematic education and propaganda in Tehran and outside major cities. The following paragraphs will examine some governmental and international institutions that took actions to boost international cinematic exchanges, supervise national cinematic affairs and control international propagandist attempts.

After the invasion of the Allied forces in 1941, a Department of Theatres was established in Iran under the administration of an American, Nilla Cram Cook, who was made responsible for supervising and censoring film screenings and theatrical performances under the supervision of the Ministry of the State/Ministry of the Interior (Vizārat-i Dākhilah or Vizārat-i Kishvar).[1]

The Department of Theatres' responsibility to filter and supervise film screenings was shared with the Ministry of Work and Propaganda (Vizārat-i Kār va Tablīghāt), at least until the resignation of Nilla Cram Cook in 1946, therefore highlighting the significant role that cinema played as a propaganda tool in such a sensitive time in international history (Figure 3.1).[2] Attesting to this observation, in June 1942, the National Office of the Press and Propaganda (within the Ministry of Work and Propaganda) submitted a Code of Cinema Regulations (Āyīn-nāmah-'i Sīnamā-hā) to the Office of the Prime Minister for

---

[1] According to an article published by Nilla Cram Cook in 1949, she was approached by the Iranian Ministry of the State in 1942 to establish a Department of Theatres, to supervise film censorship and screenings, and to organise Iranian ballet and opera. Based on the same account, she resigned her post in 1946 to found a "Studio for the Revival of Classical Arts of Iran." See Nilla Cram Cook, "The Theatre and Ballet Arts of Iran," *Middle East Journal* 3(4) (1949): 406–407. According to Naficy, Cook also had a contract with the State Department and was responsible for the operation of the non-commercial Film Circuit in Iran for which the US embassy provided educational and documentary films. See Hamid Naficy, *A Social History of Iranian Cinema,* vol. 2: *The Industrializing Years, 1941–1978* (Durham, NC: Duke University Press, 2011), 433.

[2] There is no comprehensive and documented study of institutions responsible for the supervision and censorship of films in post-war Iran (from the early to late 1940s). The information mentioned above has been inferred from a series of secondary and primary sources that have been available to the author and may not reflect all the institutions that were involved in this endeavour. It is very probable, however, that while Nilla Cram Cook was the Head of the Department of Theatres, her department worked closely with the Ministry of Work and Propaganda (National Office of the Press/Publications and Propaganda) to grant screening permissions to international films.

Figure 3.1 Allied officers in front of Fārūs Publishing House on Lālahzār Avenue during or after the invasion of 1941

approval.[3] Ratified in 1943, this Code required all screenings to undergo a first approval by the National Police and the National Office of the Press and Propaganda – a policy that clearly identified cinematic offerings as political tools rather than strictly cultural and entertainment forms.[4]

Aside from measures to control film screenings, the government also took initiatives to disseminate state-sanctioned filmic offerings. In 1945, the Iranian government established the short-lived National Educational Film Circuit (NEFC), which exhibited educational films in various parts of Iran.[5] To forestall British and Russian propaganda,

[3] "Āyīn-nāmah-'i Pīshnahādī-yi Idārah-'i Kull-i Intishārāt va Tablīghāt rāji' bah Sīnamāhā: Sanad-i Shumārah 61" [The National Office of the Press and Propaganda's Recommended Code of Regulations in Regard to Cinemas: Document Number 61], in *Asnādī az Mūsīqī, Ti'ātr va Sīnamā dar Īrān (1300–1357)* [*Documents on Music, Theatre and Cinema in Iran (1921–1978)*] (Tehran: The Press and Publication Organisation of the Ministry of Culture and Islamic Guidance, 2000), vol. 1, 280–288.

[4] "Āyīn-nāmah-'i Pīshnahādī-yi Idārah-'i Kull-i Intishārāt va Tablīghāt rāji' bah Sīnamāhā: Document Number 61/2," 287.

[5] Hamidy Naficy, *A Social History of Iranian Cinema*, vol. 2, 4.

the circuit cooperated with the US Embassy and was headed by Nilla Cram Cook.[6] The activities of the NEFC were supervised by a committee of eight: three members of the committee were from the Ministry of Education who scheduled "programs for the schools," three were from the Ministry of Interior, which included Cook, "charged with complete technical responsibility for all educational and rural film circuits," her chief operator and her legal adviser, and three members were university professors who had "final responsibility for all Persian film scripts, documentaries, etc."[7] According to Naficy, the US Embassy in Tehran provided all the films projected by the circuit.[8] Working under the pretence of showcasing educational or non-theatrical films, the NEFC and "societies" for international cultural exchanges also functioned as conduits for the dissemination of national and international propaganda in Iran. After all, as Cook mentioned in one of her correspondences with the US Embassy, Iran was "the ideal springboard for Asia" when it came to the global Cold War power struggle.[9]

Cook was especially interested in assisting the Iranian government, rather than the US embassy, in confronting foreign, i.e. Russian and British, propaganda. In the year 1945, she specifically objected to the American proposition that a film circuit be established in Iran by the US Embassy to distribute American educational films and run automatic film strip projectors in "Teheran store windows and other display points" for the "projection of America."[10] According to her, Iranians would object to such measures on the grounds that Americans were dispersing propaganda; instead, she emphasised that the Iranians

---

[6] *Ibid.*, 4–5.
[7] Nilla Cram Cook to US Embassy (in Iran), January 14, 1945, "(Secret) Memorandum of Understanding: Department of State – O.W.I, October 1944"; Motion Pictures File No. 891.4061 (pp. 1–4); January–February 1945; National Archives Building, Washington, DC, 1. According to a note that accompanied these letters, Cook's letters were to be forwarded to the American Corporation of Radio.
[8] Naficy, *A Social History of Iranian Cinema*, vol. 2, 5.
[9] Nilla Cram Cook, from the Department of Theatres, to Harold; Motion Pictures File No. 891.4061; Note that accompanied the enclosed letters intended for the Radio Corporation of America; January–February 1945; National Archives Building, Washington, DC.
[10] Cook to US Embassy (in Iran), January 14, 1945, "Memorandum of Understanding," Motion Pictures File No. 891.4061, 2.

themselves "must incorporate the films into their educational systems."[11] According to her letter from January 14, 1945, Iran's Ministry of the Interior had taken the first step in this direction by issuing an order to provincial governments "to forbid the showcasing" of British and Russian documentary films, which did not carry a "censorship license," from the Department of Theatres, "up to now required only for commercial films."[12] Step by step, the government of Iran was scheming to "take the entire distribution of educational films into its own hands."[13] In her opinion, for the time being, the NEFC was a suitable institution for the containment of foreign propaganda, since the educational films of NEFC were to be prepared by the Department of Theatres and accepted by the NEFC committee for their suitability for the Iranian educational system. Cook suggested that her position in the Iranian government gave her "full power to choose the films for the Iranian National Educational Film Circuit."[14] In her letter to the US Embassy on the next day, January 15, 1945, Cook reasserted the validity of her opinion by affirming the success of the Iranian government's actions towards film censorship; on January 14, the Soviet agency had telephoned Cook to make arrangements for its films to be "censored," i.e. reviewed, by the department at Soviet Cinema Sitārah (Star Cinema). Cook, who pretended "not to be the censor," congratulated the Soviets on the "moral and innocent quality" of the films that they had sent to be reviewed.[15] The Soviet Agency, who were flattered by Cook's views against American gangster films, were quite pleased to have an American censor their films in place of a Persian.[16]

In addition to Cook's Department of Theatres, the Cultural Society of Iran and America also worked as a conduit for the distribution of American propagandist and educational visual offerings. Established

---

[11] *Ibid.*

[12] Cook to US Embassy (in Iran), January 14, 1945, "Memorandum of Understanding," Motion Pictures File No. 891.4061, 1. According to the letter, this order was in response to the efforts of the Soviet Union to force Cinema Mayak to distribute propaganda films on its provincial circuit. Cook mentions that such censorship measures would have been difficult to enforce in Tehran, especially in Soviet Cinema Sitārah, because of political reasons.

[13] *Ibid.*   [14] *Ibid.*, 3.

[15] Nilla Cram Cook to US Embassy (in Iran), January 15, 1945, "Memorandum of Understanding: Department of State – O.W.I, October 1944"; Motion Pictures File No. 891.4061; January–February 1945; National Archives Building, Washington, DC, 1.

[16] *Ibid.*

in 1925, the Cultural Society was closed down in 1927, but recommenced its activities in 1942, which included teaching English, and organising gatherings and conferences, film screenings, as well as concerts and art exhibitions. After the re-establishment of the Society, Americans, who felt that their allies were gaining an advantage in war propaganda, also intensified their presence in the cinematic political arena. In 1945, T. Cuyler Young, the Press Attaché of the American Embassy in Tehran, wrote to the American Secretary of State (Washington), drawing on an "October Memorandum of Understanding" between the Department of State (Division of Middle Eastern Affairs) and Office of War Information about the importance of speeding up the import of "non-theatrical films for Iran." Young felt that the newly established Department of Theatres headed by Nilla Cram Cook had not achieved its mission to furnish documentary films for educational purposes in the country – a notion that was specified in letters from the Governor of Mazandaran and some other provinces.[17] Young's letter is also interesting in that, similar to Cook's correspondences, it highlights the Iranian government's attempts to monopolise propaganda through film. In his letter to the American Secretary of State, Young mentioned that the National Educational Film Circuit, newly formed by the Pahlavi state, was designed to work only through the Iranian government's film circuits, since Iranians were "masters at obstructionism" when they wished to hinder what they regarded as "uncontrolled and unwanted foreign propaganda."[18] According to Young, the Iran–America Cultural Relations Society would be the first possible audience for the films of this circuit. Such instances point to the attempts of Allied forces to use "national" organisations such as the NEFC for filmic propaganda, and also highlight the anxieties and tensions that existed between and among international societies and national bodies to appropriate cultural media to sway public opinion.

---

[17] T. Cuyler Young, Press Attaché of the American Embassy in Tehran, to the Secretary of State, Division of Middle Eastern Affairs, March 1, 1945, "Declassified Memorandum of Understanding: Department of State – Office of War Information, October 1944, Motion Picture Program"; Motion Pictures File No. 891.4061/3–145 (pp. 1–2); January–February 1945; National Archives Building, Washington, DC.

[18] Young to the Secretary of State, March 1, 1945, "Memorandum of Understanding"; Motion Pictures File No. 891.4061, 2.

As early as 1949, the US Information Service in Iran had used mobile film units to screen American-produced newsreels and educational films in the country.[19] Soon after, however, they realised that locally produced educational newsreels would be of more interest to Iranian audiences. As a result, the US Information Agency in Iran made a contract with the Head of Syracuse University's Audiovisual Centre, Don Williams, to create an audiovisual centre in the Ministry of Education, create a team of film specialists (Syracuse Team) and train Iranian filmmakers to produce local documentaries about personal hygiene, agriculture and public sanitation, which were then distributed and shown in schools and villages across the country.[20] The Syracuse Team was perhaps commissioned to create and disseminate such educational documentaries as a means to hinder Soviet expansion in Iran.[21]

During this period, when Iranian feature film production was minimal, as both Issari and Naficy meticulously demonstrate in their seminal works, a lively documentary filmmaking industry flourished in the country.[22] This enterprise was especially supported and commissioned by the Pahlavi government. The activities of the Syracuse Team in Iran from 1951 to 1959 had given rise to a large number of documentary filmmakers who later joined the Fine Arts Administration and became part of the Ministry of Culture (and Art). Cutbacks in the US Information Agency's budget caused the Agency in Tehran to reduce its film productions in the early 1960s and then stop all together in 1964, leaving the market to the Ministry of Culture and Art.[23]

---

[19] See M. Ali Issari, *Cinema in Iran: 1900–1979* (London: The Scarecrow Press, 1989), 164–183. See also Naficy, *A Social History of Iranian Cinema*, vol. 2, 39.

[20] For a list of films produced by the Syracuse University team, and films produced by Iranian filmmakers under the supervision of Syracuse University advisers, see Issari, *Cinema in Iran*, 345–347.

[21] Naficy, *A Social History of Iranian Cinema*, vol. 2, 41.

[22] The topic of documentary filmmaking will not be discussed in this book. In his *Cinema in Iran*, Ali Issari lists American and Iranian documentary film productions by the US Information Service and Syracuse team in Iran. See Issari, *Cinema in Iran*, App. E and App. G. Hamid Naficy discusses the formation of an official statist documentary production in the waning years of World War II. For a comprehensive and detailed history of documentary filmmaking in Iran (statist and non-statist), see Hamid Naficy's chapter on "The Statist Documentary Cinema and Its Alternative," in Naficy, *A Social History of Iranian Cinema*, vol. 2, 49–145.

[23] Issari, *Cinema in Iran*, 183.

The Artish (Military) Film Studio, established in 1945, the Fine Arts Administration (and later Ministry of Culture and Art), National Iranian Television, established in 1966 (which in 1973 became National Iranian Radio and Television) and the Centre for the Intellectual Development of Children and Young Adults were among some of the governmental and semi-governmental institutions that produced and projected documentary and non-fiction films in Iran.[24] Characterising the style of these documentaries as "official," Naficy argues that the organisations that produced these films institutionalised documentary filmmaking in Iran.[25]

The Society of Iran–Russia Cultural Relations (Anjuman-i Ravābit-i Farhangī-yi Irān va Shawravī), was established in 1943 to enable – in theory – cultural exchanges between Iran and the Soviet Union. The Society, nevertheless, was also a conduit for the promotion of Russian propagandist cultural products in Iran and Soviet occupation of Iran after World War II. The society organised concerts, social gatherings, conferences, exhibitions and film screenings, and published a magazine called *Payām-i Naw* (New Message). By the 1940s, the All-Union Society for Cultural Relations with Foreign Countries (VOKS: Vsesoiuznoe Obshchestvo Kul'turnoi Sviazi s zagranitsei), which had been founded in 1925, had branches in some sixty countries, including Iran.[26] These branches and offices working under their jurisdiction were responsible for the circulation of information about Soviet films, the exchange of ideas and providing reports about foreign film organisations, among other tasks.[27] Sovkino, the company that was the chief importer and distributor of Soviet films in Iran, also provided the equipment and operators for film screenings managed by Soviets and pro-Soviet sympathisers.[28] According to Naficy, VOKS's director in Iran was a member of the Board of the Society of Iran–Russia Cultural Relations,[29] and perhaps ensured the cooperation of these societies. Other members of the Society's Board of Directors in Tehran of the mid-1940s were pro-Soviet advocates themselves.[30]

In terms of films, the Society would usually import educational films to be showcased in Iranian schools. The film exchanges between the two countries, however, were not always readily accepted by the

[24] See Naficy, *A Social History of Iranian Cinema*, vol. 2, 49–145. Some non-governmental organisations also created educational or propaganda films.
[25] *Ibid.*, 50.   [26] *Ibid.*, 17.   [27] *Ibid.*   [28] *Ibid.*, 19.   [29] *Ibid.*, 17.
[30] *Ibid.*, 18.

Iranian government and people. In October 1942, in response to a letter by the National Municipal Office (Idārah'i Kull-i Shahrbānī) and a report by the Department of Intelligence, Javād 'Āmirī (1891–1980), the Secretary of the State, asked the Prime Minister Qavām for a ban on a film made by the Soviet Union which was to be screened in Iran.[31] The film, *The Peasants* (*Dihqānān*, 1939), was an Azerbaijani talkie (2,900 metres) produced in Baku that had been examined in Tehran Cinema in the presence of four representatives from the Iranian Ministry of Culture, as well as four Soviet representatives. It depicted the struggle of peasants and proletariats against landlords in the Baku of 1919, and valorised communist values embodied in the revolt of peasants, assisted by the efforts of Lenin and Stalin.[32] Soviet representatives had refused to censor certain parts of the film as demanded by Iranian authorities, and were reportedly seeking to circumvent Iranian censorship by finding ways to screen films without having them examined by Iranian officials.[33] After a series of negotiations between the Soviet Embassy and the Iranian authorities, the latter had indicated that Soviet films were not to be shown in Iran unless they were examined and sanctioned by censorship authorities.[34] Cinematic relations between the two countries, however, were not always hostile. Another instance recorded in the 1943 correspondences between the Ministry of Foreign Affairs and the Prime Minister[35] points to a film entitled *Iran*, which was made in Iran by a Soviet cinematography institute (Mu'assisah-'i Fīlmbardārī-yi Shawravī) and which was to

---

[31] "Mukātibāt-i Vizāratkhānah-ha-yi Kishvar va Umūr-i Khārijah dar Khusūs-i Sānsūr-i Fīlmhā-yi Sākht-i Shawravī Hingām-i Namāyish dar Sīnamāhā-yi Īrān: Sanad-i Shumārah-'i 62" [Correspondences between Ministries of Interior/State and Foreign Affairs in Regard to the Censoring of Films Made by the Soviet Union for their Screening in Iranian Cinemas: Document Number 62], in *Asnādī az Mūsīqī, Ti'ātr va Sīnamā dar Īrān (1300–1357)*, vol. 1, 289–298. The original letter by Javād 'Āmirī is dated October 13, 1942.

[32] "Mukātibāt-i Vizāratkhānah-ha-yi Kishvar va Umūr-i Khārijah dar Khusūs-i Sānsūr-i Fīlmhā-yi Sākht-i Shawravī, Document Number 62/1," 290–291. The plot of *The Peasants* was apparently prepared in the form of intertitles in Persian and inserted at the beginning and end of the film, so that Persian-speaking audiences would comprehend it better.

[33] "Mukātibāt-i Vizāratkhānah-ha-yi Kishvar va Umūr-i Khārijah dar Khusūs-i Sānsūr-i Fīlmhā-yi Sākht-i Shawravī, Document Number 62/3," 292.

[34] Mukātibāt-i Vizāratkhānah-ha-yi Kishvar va Umūr-i Khārijah dar Khusūs-i Sānsūr-i Fīlmhā-yi Sākht-i Shawravī, Document Number 62/9," 298.

[35] The name of the Prime Minister was not mentioned in the correspondences, but he was likely Prime Minister Ahmad Qavām.

be brought to the country and screened for Mohammad Reza Shah.[36] According to the documents, the film "showed both the old and new Iran." It reportedly portrayed "the industrial progresses, factories, agricultural institutions and health facilities" established in the country, although at times in a biased fashion.[37] This instance is noteworthy in that it demonstrates the Iranian government's aspirations to portray itself on an equal footing with advanced countries and especially the Soviet Union when it came to national progress and industrial capabilities.[38] Iranian officials at the Iranian Embassy in Russia, however, disliked the "topic of Kurds" that was featured in *Iran*, since they were depicted in "their former state" of life (vaz'īyat-i sābiq), i.e. not modernised.[39] Regardless of the minor criticisms aimed at the film, *Iran* was thought to be "an expression of friendly relations" between the two countries; as such, the Ministry of Foreign Affairs asserted that the Iranian Embassy could organise a film gathering to appreciate the efforts of the film crew, under the condition that the film did not have "any vile parts."[40]

In 1942, the Cultural Society of Iran and England (Anjuman-i Farhangī-yi Īrān va Ingilīs) was established to organise and host cultural events and film screenings. Aside from the Society, the British Council in Iran also supplied and distributed projectors and educational and entertainment films – apparently in larger amounts than the US embassy, as the US government's policy limited the raw stock supply to its commercial film companies in the early post–World War II era.[41] Moreover, the Council would screen films in the oil-rich city of Ahvaz, namely, "the life of Bakhtiyari People living in Iran,"[42] "the evacuation

---

[36] "Tiligrāfī marbūt bah Fīlm-i Īrān Tahīyyah Shudah dar Mu'assisah-'i Fīlm-bardārī-yi Shawravī: Sanad-i Shumarah-'i 64" [Telegraphs in Regard to the Film, Iran, Produced at the Institute of Soviet Cinematography: Document Number 64], in *Asnādī az Mūsīqī, Ti'ātr va Sīnamā dar Īrān (1300–1357)*, vol. 1, 302–305.

[37] "Tiligrāfī Marbūt bah Fīlm-i Īrān Tahīyyah Shudah dar Mu'assisah-'i Fīlm-bardārī-yi Shawravī, Document Number 64/2," 303–304.

[38] These were aspirations that were also seen in the Persian-language films of the 1930s, as discussed in Chapter 2.

[39] "Tiligrāfī marbūt bah Fīlm-i Īrān Tahīyyah Shudah dar Mu'assisah-'i Fīlm-bardārī-yi Shawravī, Document Number 64/2," 304.

[40] *Ibid.*   [41] Naficy, *A Social History of Iranian Cinema*, vol. 2, 24–25.

[42] It is very probable that this is a reference to scenes from the film *Grass*, discussed in Chapter 2. Scenes from this film were also included in Ezra Mir's *In the Waters of Persian Gulf* (perhaps dating to the early 1940s).

of Paris by patriots" and other propagandist films.[43] In June 1945, according to a letter from Ibrāhīm Zand, Iran's Minister of War, to the Prime Minister, the British Vice-Consul in Tabriz had attempted to showcase a number of films first in Tabriz and then in the city of Mahābād through the use of mobile cinemas ("yik dastgāh kāmīyūn-i sīnamā").[44] The films screened in Mahābād, which included shots of the British Prime Minister, Winston Churchill, were first "met with obscene words from the audience," followed by the audience throwing stones and tearing apart the wires, as well as destroying the camera/projector.[45] It should be noted here that the hostility of the people of Tabriz and Mahābād to British propaganda films could be attributed to the political sentiments of the people in this region. In 1945 in (Iranian) Azerbaijan, a short-lived government was established with the help of the Soviet army by the name of the Azerbaijan Democratic Party (1945–1946), which had its capital in Tabriz; in Mahābād, likewise, the Republic of Mahābād (1945–1946) was founded with the help of the Soviets as a Kurdish self-governing state under the administration of Qāzī Muhammad. Both governments, which aimed to distance themselves from the Pahlavi state, were seen as threats by Western powers due to their dependence on Soviet supplies and forces. In the instance mentioned above, the British Vice-Consul had obtained permission from Qāzī Muhammad to screen the English film in Mahābād, but the incident reportedly took place minutes after Qāzī Muhammad had left the screening venue. The sentiments expressed by people of Mahābād in the movie theatre most likely arose from the hostility of the Kurdish people of Mahābād, most of whom sympathised with the Soviet cause, against the British forces and their cultural propaganda. In response to pressure from Western

---

[43] "Guzārish-i Shahrbānī-yi Kull-i Kishvar dar Khusūs-i Namāyish-i Fīlm-i Zindigānī-yi Bakhtīyārīhā-yi Sākin-i Īrān az Taraf-i Kunsūlgarī-yi Ingilīs dar Ahvāz: Sanad-i Shumarah-'i 69" [The Report of National Municipality in Regard to the Screening of the Life of Bakhtiyaris Living in Iran by the British Consul in Ahvaz: Document Number 69], in *Asnādī az Mūsīqī, Ti'ātr va Sīnamā dar Īrān (1300–1357)*, vol. 1, 321–322.

[44] Mahābād is located in the Iranian province of West Azerbaijan.

[45] "Guzārish-i Vizārat-i Jang dar Khusūs-i Namāyish-i Fīlm tavassut-i Mu'āvin-i Kunsūl-i Inglīs dar Tabrīz va Mahābād: Sanad-i Shumarah-'i 71" [The Report of the Ministry of War in Regard to a Screening by the British Vice-Consul in Tabriz and Mahabad: Document Number 71], in *Asnādī az Mūsīqī, Ti'ātr va Sīnamā dar Īrān (1300–1357)*, vol. 1, 334–335.

powers, the Soviet forces withdrew from the north-western provinces in 1946, which allowed for the Iranian government to assert its control there.

The cultural exchanges enabled through the international societies active in Iran, filmic exchanges that were prompted through the training of Iranian filmmakers by groups such as the Syracuse Team, and the general reception of newsreels, short non-fictions and documentaries, gave rise to cosmopolitan cinematic visions among its practitioners and arguably its receivers. While many of these educational films were distributed in rural areas and among farmers and villages, some of them were also featured in cinemas in urban centres to familiarise people of diverse backgrounds with the activities of various organisations and general technological or agricultural advancements. Some of the Iranian documentary filmmakers were trained outside Iran, and others involved in the production of non-fiction films were educated abroad. Although commissioned or funded by the Pahlavi state, cultural activities in the field of documentary filmmaking after World War II also attest to cosmopolitan exchanges and imaginaries that allowed many of the filmmakers to express themselves artistically and politically.

As the Allied forces continued their cinematic publicity, Iranian state officials and the religious establishment grew weary of their political agenda and began pressuring the government to limit their cinematic activities in Iran. In 1950, in response to widespread objections to foreign propaganda, a more comprehensive Code of Cinemas and Theatrical Institutions was issued by the Ministry of the State. According to this new Code, a central Commission of Theatres (Kumīsīyun-i Namāyish) was established under the supervision of the Ministry, the activities of which were very similar to the Department of Theatres. The Code reaffirmed that no film could be screened in Iran without prior approval from this Commission. According to the 1957 revision of this Code, the board of the Commission in Tehran included members from the Ministry of the State, Ministry of Culture, National Police, National Office of the Press and Radio and the Organisation of Intelligence and Security. From 1964 to 1965, film production and film revision came under the control of the Ministry of Culture and Arts and remained so until the 1979 revolution. As such, the post–World War II attempts of the Allied forces to publicise their activities on cinema screens and the importation of popular foreign language films did not go unnoticed by the government and, as we shall see, by cinema audiences. Despite the fact that cinematic affairs were under the control of governmental institutions, certain figures within the Iranian government and outside the above-mentioned institutions (namely Farah Pahlavi after her marriage to Mohammad Reza Pahlavi) enjoyed the prerogative to allow or ban the screening of certain films, depending on the content and its importance in terms of national interests.[46]

While the Allied forces withdrew their troops from Iran in 1946, international Cold War policies, Iran's oil reserves and its economic and industrial development thrusted the country into the throes of global politics in the years that followed. Iran's entanglement in national and international politics coincided with the increasing production of Iranian popular feature films in the 1950s, which then compelled film critics and social thinkers to demand state support for the development of a "national cinema." Some of the demands of the industry included the levying of taxes on Iranian films, efforts to promote national film offerings, preventing the screening of commercial, international motion pictures and encouraging the import of international art house and intellectual films – all of which allowed for the flourishing of a cosmopolitan national cinema in the decades that followed. In the following paragraphs, I will discuss how industrialists, film critics, cinema enthusiasts and writers laid the foundation for the establishment and thriving of a sustained mainstream national cinema in Iran.

3.2 Post–World War II Image Culture and Social Typecasts

In the late 1930s and 1940s, a number of of dubbing studios were established that translated the dialogues of Hollywood and other global commercial films into Persian, and re-recorded them with voice-overs by famous Iranian artists, most of whom already worked in radio and theatre. The production of Iranian (Persian language) films began again in the late 1940s, adding to the variety of films featured in movie houses across the country. Consequently, the number of cinema journals and publications that followed events

---

[46] Naficy, *A Social History of Iranian Cinema*, vol. 2, 70–71.

transpiring in Iranian and international cinema grew significantly from the 1950s to the 1970s.[47] Journals such as *Sitārah-'i Sīnamā* (*Cinema Star*), *Fīlm va Hunar* (*Film and Art*), *Nigīn* (*Jewel*), *Bāmshād*, *Sipīd va Sīyāh* (*White and Black*), *Payk-i Sīnamā* (Cinema Messenger), *Firdawsī* (*Firdawsi*) and *Tihrān Musavvar* (*Tehran Illustrated*) published numerous articles and posters that represented the latest screenings in international movie theatres, film reviews, news pieces and biographies of movie stars; these journals also featured the latest fashions from Hollywood, Indian, Egyptian, Mexican, French, Italian, Danish, German and Russian cinemas. Numerous articles were published on the technicalities of film production, as well as cinema-related gossip subjects ranging from the production of high-budgeted films to the merits that defined true actors and cinema audiences, to Iranian actors and directors who had travelled and studied abroad, to the international actors and directors who had visited Iran. Pictures of Iranian stars were published alongside internationally renowned actors – their hair and clothing styles remarkably resembling those of international stars. Such cinematic dynamism worked to stage Iranian cinema – and Iranian imaginary – as global participants in twentieth-century cinematic affairs. The interplay of national and international cultural forms, as displayed in such publications and discussed in the following chapters, was evocative of the cosmopolitan orientation of cinematic activities in Iran – a cinematic de-territorialisation and re-territorialisation that facilitated virtual and actual encounters between the local and global.

In the immediate post–World War II era, Tehran experienced a rapid growth in theatres and movie houses that featured a variety of international plays and films. Sipāh (Military) Cinema/Theatre (1929–1933), Āftāb (Sun) Theatre (1935–1938, later known as Firdawsi Cinema), Iran Cinema/Theatre (1925–1946, later known as Tehran Cinema), Pārs Theatre (1941–1980), Naw (New) Cinema (established in 1942), Farhang (Culture) Hall (1943–present), Sa'dī Theatre (1945–1953), Nikūyī Hall (1931–1938, later known as Humā Cinema in 1938), Shahrzād Theatre (1949–1979) and Gītī (Universe) Cinema/Theatre (1944–1955) were among the theatres that operated after the 1930s. Moreover, due to the commercial success of international

---

[47] For a full list of cinematic periodicals in Iran from the 1930s to the 1970s, see Table 7 in Naficy, *A Social History of Iranian Cinema*, vol. 2, 180–181.

films in the country, an increasing number of international film companies, including those from America, Mexico and Italy, started distributing their motion pictures in Iran. A report in *Sitārah-'i Sīnamā* in 1954, for example, reported that Lux Film Company, "the biggest film company of Italy," had decided to extend its activities to Iran, and had sent a representative to assess the possibility of establishing a branch in the country. According to the same article, Paramount Company was also planning to send its representative to the country within a month to sell its films.[48] Warner Brothers Studios and Metro Goldwyn Mayer were among other film companies that distributed their motion pictures in cinemas in Tehran. In the 1950s, the development of new cinematic technologies and government regulations impelled cinema owners to update and refurbish movie theatres around the country in order to meet government standards and target specific audiences.

According to a 1954 article in *Payk-i Sīnamā*, Tehran's Municipal Office had ordered the ranking of movie theatres in Tehran, and thus instructed theatres to refurbish their spaces.[49] Humā and Paramount cinemas, both of which engaged in the screening of "Iranian films,"[50] renovated their spaces in the summer of 1954 to also attract "clients of international films," pointing to the ways in which cinemas engaged in directing filmic taste as Iranian national cinema was still in its nascent phase.[51] According to the report, Humā (or Humāy) Cinema signed a contract with Paramount Pictures in 1954 to import the latter's 1952 and 1953 studio productions for screening.[52] After five

[48] "Namāyandigān-i Kārkhānah-hā-yi Fīlm-bardārī-yi Khārijī dar Īrān" [Representatives of International Film Companies in Iran], *Sitārah-'i Sīnamā*, yr 1, no. 21 (Bahman 1333 [January 1955]), 2.

[49] "Nazarī bah Vaz'-i Sīnamāhā-yi Tihrān: Sīnamā Humāy" [A Look at the Condition of Tehran's Cinemas: Humāy Cinema], *Payk-i Sīnamā*, yr 1, no. 9 (Āzar 6, 1333 [November 27, 1954]), 6.

[50] "Persian films" (Fīlm-i Fārsī) is the common title that film critics gave to Persian-language motion pictures, especially after World War II – films that were shot, produced and distributed in Iran. Here, again, the language of the films became a distinguishing feature of Iran's national cinema. Please note that this title is different from Fīlm-Fārsī (written as one word), a term that was used from the 1950s to the 1970s in a derogatory fashion to refer to popular films – a topic that will be discussed in detail in Chapter 4.

[51] "Sīnamāhā-yi Humā va Pārāmunt Qarārdādhā-yi Jadīdī Mun'aqid Kardah-and" [Huma and Paramount Cinema Have Made New Contracts], *Sitārah-'i Sīnamā*, yr 1, no. 27 (Isfand 11, 1333 [March 2, 1955]), 2.

[52] *Ibid.*, 2.

months of renovations, thanks to the manager of the theatre, "Monsieur Salmān," Humā Cinema now boasted "new chairs, [a new] hall, and [film] screen."[53] The cinema had previously had a contract with Warner Brothers Studio to show American films such as *Casablanca* (1942) and *Always in My Heart* (1942), but it restarted its activities in 1954 with the screening of the Persian film, *Agha Muhammad Khan of Qajar* (*Āghā Muhammad Khān-i Qājār*, 1954).[54] Sun Cinema (Sīnamā Khur-shīd), likewise, advertised the launch of its "beautiful and luxe theatre" that now featured popular Egyptian and Arabic language films, including *Love Taxi* (*Tāksī-yi 'Ishq*, 1954), starring Hudā Sultān and 'Abdu-l'azīz Mahmūd (an Iranian film with the same title was produced in Iran by Nusratullāh Vahdat in 1970, to which I will attend in Chapter 4). *Sitārah-'i Sīnamā* periodical published an editorial piece in 1956 which covered the booming topic of "New Cinemas, New Initiatives," inside and outside the country.[55] Seeing "a bright future ahead" for Iranian cinema, the editorial reported on the opening of two "big and A-Grade cinemas" in Tehran.[56] According to the article, "[o]ne of the factors in the development, advancement, and progress of cinema industry" was the proliferation of movie theatres, especially at a time when Iran did not have sufficient space and facilities for the recreation of the masses.[57]

Lālahzār, arguably one of "the best spots in Tehran"[58] in terms of entertainment, and its surrounding neighbourhood was now home to a large number of movie theatres and many more entertainment venues (Figure 3.2). The flourishing of dubbing studios and movie theatres, as well as popular periodicals, helped to further cultivate a popular culture that had its roots in the 1920s and 1930s. Similar to other countries in the region that had a thriving cinematic culture (Egypt and India, for example), the theatre boom coincided with a growing consumer culture that was dominated by and circulated in images. Tehran, like cosmopolitan Cairo, experienced the explosion of an image culture

---

[53] "Nazarī bah Vaz'-i Sīnamā-hā-yi Tihrān: Sīnamā Humāy," 6.
[54] See "Az Fardā Shab dar Sīnamā-hā-yi Humāy va Īrān: *Āghā Muhammad Khān-i Qājār*" [From Tomorrow Night at Humāy and Iran Cinemas: *Agha Muhammad Khan of Qajar*], *Payk-i Sīnamā*, no. 9 (Āzar 6, 1333 [November 27, 1954]).
[55] "Sīnamā-hā-yi Jadīd. Ibtikārāt-i Tāzah" [New Cinemas. New Initiatives], *Sitārah-'i Sīnamā*, yr 3, no. 82 (Mihr 15, 1335 [October 7, 1956]), 2.
[56] *Ibid.*, 2.   [57] *Ibid.*, 2.
[58] "Mujdah bah Dūst-dārān-i Sīnamā" [Good News for Cinema Enthusiasts], *Umīd*, yr 3, no. 68 (Khurdād 1, 1324 [May 22, 1945], 7.

Figure 3.2 An Image of Lālahzār Avenue in the 1940s

that increasingly infiltrated Iranian daily life. Commodities were commercialised and fetishised through the use of images of what many deemed as Hollywood lookalikes. New lifestyles and novel everyday practices that were at times in conflict with traditional ways of life were further advertised through television, periodicals and posters. Films and filmic images in Egypt, Joel Gordon argues, penetrated Egyptian life throughout the twentieth century, both culturally and intellectually.[59] He argues that "Hollywood set fashion trends" in Egypt, "clothing, hairstyle" and "make-up" prototypes of the American film industry, further engendered images of glamour and glitz. Iranian magazines, similar to Egyptian periodicals, featured pictures of international stars such as, Marlene Dietrich, Rita Hayworth, Cary Grant, Bob Hope, Loretta Young, Maria Montez, Humphrey Bogart, Gary Cooper and Raj Kapoor, while their gossip columns discussed the latest hairstyles, hobbies and lifestyles of these artists. With their emergence in the late 1940s and increase in number in the 1950s, Iranian film posters and the stars of Persian-language films also began

---

[59] Joel Gordon, *Revolutionary Melodrama: Popular Film and Civic Identity in Nasser's Egypt* (Chicago, IL: Middle East Documentation Centre, on behalf of University of Chicago, 2002), 3.

to be featured and praised in film periodicals. The public's fascination with the growing image culture was accompanied by the popularisation of certain social stereotypes that had emerged with the urbanisation of Tehran in the early twentieth century, but which gained prominence after World War II.

As attempts were made in early post–World War II to solidify national sovereignty after it had been compromised in 1941 with the invasion of the Allied forces, social and cultural critics engaged in reimagining and disseminating new notions of "Iranianness." These gender- and class-based notions, which often discerned between categories of urban residents who were morally fit and/or unfit for a futural Iran, were rearticulated and disseminated in works of literature and in the popular press. In these times of social and political chaos, dividing and classifying urbanites into preconceived typecasts made it easier to make sense of the conflicted situation. Social stereotypes had become more visible in the early post–World War II era, as they were increasingly circulated and regenerated in the image culture of popular magazines. The weekly journal of *Sabā* highlighted some of the Iranian social categories that were commonly spotted in various neighbourhoods of Tehran, further crystallising them into the society's popular imagination. With the emergence of a sustained commercial film industry, cinema, too, became increasingly complicit in this affair as many of these social typecasts were circulated and reconfigured in the popular films of the Iranian cinema industry – a topic that will be further elaborated in Chapter 4.

"The Iranian Female Typewriter" typecast exemplified one of these categories: "Laughter on her lips, a face in the shape of a moon, a stature like cedar . . ." an article authored by "Bahman" described how the Lālahzār youth and bazaar employees imagined a typical typewriter woman in the 1940s – an image that was constructed through a male gaze; the social reality of this category, Bahman argued, was far from this imagined picture.[60] Characterised in reality as a woman in her 20s, married or divorced, educated only to the sixth grade, lacking skills of fast typing in comparison to her Frankish (European) counterpart, Bahman's female typewriter was portrayed as a woman jealous of

---

[60] Bahman, "'Ishq va Zindigī-yi yik Khānum-i Māshīn-nivīs-i Īrānī" [Love and Life of an Iranian Female Type-Writer], *Sabā*, yr 7, no. 2 (Murdād 20, 1327 [August 11, 1948]), 8.

her female colleagues and desperately in search of a husband – which made her eager to get close to her male colleagues.[61] Although weighing only "42 kilograms," she was deemed not only physically unfit, but also socially frail. "After August 1941,"[62] the family of the "type-writeress" had descended to a social stratum below the middle class, into what the author termed "the third [working] class." The "image" that her family conveyed was still that of a middle-class category, as this typecast pretended not to see the reality of life – the fact that "national democracy" had steered the family "towards poverty and destitution."[63] "The female typewriter" was clearly a victim of the social and political circumstances of the period, but one that was also responsible for her own misfortunes.

"The Average Lālahzāri Woman," another social category of postwar Iranian women typified in *Sabā*, strolled the streets of Lālahzār and Islāmbul (Istanbul) in Tehran around 10 to 11 am in the morning, hung out at Tajrīsh Bridge (a popular site of sociability) on Friday afternoons and spent her nights gambling or dancing in soirée gatherings.[64] What was most important to the Lālahzāri woman was to attend important parties, dressed in the latest fashion – albeit bought with someone else's money. If not to Europe (and "these days to America"), she had at least travelled to "Beirut, Palestine, or Turkey."[65] Many would consider her to be of an upper social class from Tehran or another province, but, in reality, she came from various social and economic strata. Regardless, she was rich as she had inherited a fortune that her husband or father had acquired through financial embezzlement; a fortune that this "beautiful lady" invested on her appearance to sell herself visually.[66] The Lālahzāri woman was a "black-hearted" beauty who participated in various societies and engaged in acts of lust, love and adventure.[67]

The "Average Gigolo of Lālahzār," like the Lālahzāri woman, was described as a transnationalist. Defined as "a dancer" and "a male prostitute" in "Frankish" dictionaries, the author pointed out that in

[61] *Ibid.*
[62] 1941 is the year that the Allied forces occupied Iran and forced Reza Shah to abdicate the throne in favour of his son, Mohammad Reza Shah.
[63] Bahman, "'Ishq va Zindigī," 8.
[64] Bahman, "'Ishq va Zindigī-yi yik Khānum-i Mutivassit-i Lālahzārī" [Love and Life of an Average Lālahzāri Woman], *Sabā*, yr 7, no. 3 (Murdād 27, 1327 [August 18, 1948]), 14.
[65] *Ibid.*   [66] *Ibid.*   [67] *Ibid.*

Iran the title of gigolo was given to "a chic, well-dressed, and loafer young man" who hung about Lālahzār Avenue, and whose sole vocation was "to attend to his [look] and clothing."[68] Spotted in the same neighbourhood, he complemented the average Lālahzāri woman. An absolute materialist who only cared about the image he presented, he filled the shoulders of his coats with cotton balls in order to appear broad-shouldered.[69] His hobbies included skiing, hanging out in cafés (especially "*Café Fard* at the beginning of Tajrīsh Bridge"), Armenian clubs, Lālahzār Avenue, Crystal Cinema or in Armenian diners. In the summer, he went dancing or fishing with his female friends, although his timid personality prevented him from swimming in the lake's cold water.[70] His talents comprised being a charlatan and a poker-player, dancing, walking gigolo-ish and deceiving women who had been picked up and deceived far too many times and knew the drill all too well.[71] Although the gigolo flirted with young women, he usually ended up with paid pleasures (i.e. prostitutes), that is, until the day he finally settled down with an average woman and discarded his old Lālahzār habits.

Another social category, according to Bahman, was "the Average Haji of Bazaar."[72] The Haji was cast as a medium-height, tanned and slightly overweight man with a number-4-shaved beard.[73] He would not wear a tie, but his shirt collar was always clean. He was clever, "his eyes curious" and his ears heard more than one expected, traits that had helped him secure his business and fortune in the bazaar. At the age of 45, he usually had a wife and five to six children.[74] The Haji's love life, however, was not the kind that one would find in poems and love stories. He might have fallen in love at a young age, but it was to no avail, since unbeknown to him, his mother had already

---

[68] "'Ishq va Zindigī-yi yik Jīgulu-yi Mutivassit-i Lālahzārī" [Love and Life of an Average Lālahzāri Gigolo], *Sabā*, yr 7, no. 5 (Shahrīvar 10, 1327 [September 1, 1948]), 9.

[69] *Ibid.*　　[70] *Ibid.*　　[71] *Ibid.*

[72] The term "Haji" or "Hājī" is usually attributed to Muslims who have made the holy pilgrimage to Mecca; the Haji usually has the financial resources to make this expensive pilgrimage. In colloquial Persian, Haji might also be used to refer to affluent, middle-aged and elderly people who own shops in the bazaar.

[73] Bahman, "'Ishq va Zindigī-yi yik Hājī Āqā-yi Mutivassit-i Bāzārī" [Love and Life of an Average Haji of Bazaar], *Sabā*, yr 7, no. 6 (Shahrīvar 17, 1327 [September 8, 1948]), 8.

[74] *Ibid.*

arranged his marriage – a marriage that at times resulted in long-lasting love. The Haji, sometimes, would take a new wife, at which point he would divide his love, resources and life and spend one night with the first wife and another with the second.[75] If you visited his shop, you would hear him complain about the "market downturn," the "oppression of the state officials" and the complicated regulations of the government; he abstained from socialising with corrupt government officials and deemed them unrespectable.[76] The Haji's true and "indivisible" love was his love for life, business and reputation at the bazaar.[77] It was this love that had made the Haji faithful to the nation; being one of the most moral (sālim-tarīn) members of Iran, he would lose love and life over his "country and religion."[78] The appeal of "the Average Haji of Bazaar" was perhaps informed by the role that bazaaris had historically played in revolts and social movements in modern Iran, including the Constitutional Revolution of 1906 to 1911. In fact, the representation of the Haji character in cinema culture can be traced back to the Haji in *Mr Haji, the Cinema Actor* (1934). Naficy draws a link between the Haji of this film and the Haji that appeared in literary works such as Sadeq Hedayat's 1945 *Hājī Āqā* (Mr Haji) – although this time transformed into a "filthy, lecherous, greedy, polygamous" and misogynistic Haji.[79] The character of the Haji makes numerous appearances in popular films from the 1950s to the 1970s.

"The Average Iranian Politic-schemer (sīyāsat-bāz)" appeared as a new phenomenon after the "horrific storm" of August 1941 (i.e. the Allied invasion of Iran). The "Politic-schemer," who had multiplied in number "like a poisonous mushroom," vied for the position of a Minister or a Member of Parliament despite being unqualified for the job.[80] The Politic-schemer was described as an "illiterate" (khar-savād) "Cadillac-owner" (kādīlāk-savār) who had no opinion of his own and loved to make speeches to express himself, albeit needlessly.[81] Over the age of 40, the Politic-schemer could be found everywhere; one could find him at celebrations, official and semi-official gatherings, soirées

[75] *Ibid.*   [76] *Ibid.*   [77] *Ibid.*   [78] *Ibid.*

[79] Naficy, *A Social History of Iranian Cinema*, vol. 1, 213.

[80] Bahman, "'Ishq va Zindigī-yi yik Sīyāsat-bāz-i Mutivassit-i Īrānī" [Love and Life of an Average Iranian Political-schemer], *Sabā*, yr 7, no. 7 (Shahrīvar 24, 1327 [September 15, 1948]), 8.

[81] *Ibid.*

and gambling parties in the capital.[82] While he could be from one of a number of disparate social backgrounds, he generally wore a black coat, striped pants and a tie that was usually crooked because he had had too much whiskey or gin to drink at parties.[83] Having established a reputation for himself, he married daughters of people from higher social strata.[84] A conformist, he would become "civilised" and "religious" after marriage, albeit in appearance only; his wife would engage in learning the new dances of "step" and "swing" with a certain "Monsieur" (i.e. non-Iranian), while his children would travel to Europe. He endorsed literature and the arts, launching a newspaper or journal, only to gain a reputation.[85]

Aside from the typecasts that were delineated by *Sabā* periodical, other socio-cultural tropes such as *Lūtīs*, *Jāhils*, naïve peasants, modern businessmen/gangsters, bourgeois women, suffering mothers and deceived women were increasingly deliberated and (re)configured in literature, and later cinematic images. These typecasts, imagined in periodicals, novels and short stories, were formulated in response to the new social relations of post 1941, and came to be reincarnated in Iranian commercial films. At times, these social prototypes were re-casted into mixed and hybrid film characters based on the socio-political context of the time. The Average Haji of the Bazaar of the early 1940s, for example, was not necessarily always portrayed as the honest man of the nation in the 1950s and 1960s, but also as a mischievous, selfish businessman; although, in the common moral twists of films, the Haji learned a lesson from his dishonest actions and returned to his honest traditional roots. The use and development of these social categories exhibited in commercial films from the mid-1950s to the late 1970s will be discussed in more length in Chapter 4.

3.3 Cinema and Westoxication: Reactions to Cinema in a Time of Political Chaos

The popular manifestation of social categories that reinforced Tehran's bolstering image culture was only one side of the picture. The consolidation of the Pahlavi dynasty in the interwar period accompanied competing ideological, political and religious debates from various

---

[82] *Ibid.*   [83] *Ibid.*   [84] *Ibid.*, 18.   [85] *Ibid.*, 8.

sectors of the society. On the other hand, the forced unveiling of women in 1936 and the invasion of the Allied forces in 1941 played a critical role in arousing feelings of distrust and contempt among the Iranian religious as well as secular communities, and contributed to the fermentation of political and ideological sentiments against the government. Cinema and the image culture upon which it increasingly drew and contributed toward proved to be a visible target for protestations and social complaints. Widespread denunciations against cinema based on charges of Europeanism (urūpāyī-garāyī) and Westoxication (gharbzadigī) became prominent in the mid-1930s and soared in the 1940s and early 1950s in the early stages of the Cold War. During this period, social and cultural elites resorted to contesting the space of cinema and films that it showcased onscreen as a means to engage in a political struggle against European (or Western) imperialism.

The popularisation of international cinema stars and the promotion of a consumer image culture that closely followed and promoted the latest international fashion trends and entertainment enterprises were not viewed favourably by both religious and secular elites, who either encouraged the blossoming of a high art or opted for a more pious lifestyle. Considered as visual embodiments of a decadent Western culture, American Hollywood films came under heavy attack from Iranian scholars and cultural elites. As early as 1934, 'Alī Akbar Hakamīzādah associated the "moral corruption of the youth" (fisād-i akhlāghī-yi javānān), the "impurity" and "unveiling of women" to the youths' imitation of cinema, novels and gramophone.[86] Egyptian and Indian films that were considered as blind imitations of Hollywood and promoters of nudity and licentious acts, also endured hefty criticism. The intermingling of youth in the actual space of movie theatres – which was now common – and their potential sexual arousal through scenes of nudity and song-and-dance forms proved to be a grave concern. Movie theatre spaces were perceived to foster "spatial corruption" and images to cultivate "incurable personal and social ailments."[87] Such concerns and criticisms increased dramatically after the early 1940s.

[86] 'Alī Akbar Hakamīzādah, "Tablīghāt" [Propaganda], *Humāyūn*, yr 1, no. 7 (Farvardīn 1314 [March 1934]), 31–32.
[87] Sīraj Ansārī, "Dar Pīrāmūn-i Islām va Susīyālīzm" [On Islam and Socialism], *Āyīn-i Islām*, no. 163 (Khurdad 22, 1326 [June 13, 1947]), 14.

In 1946, Nuṣratullāh Nūryānī, the editor-in-chief of the Islamic magazine, *Āyīn-i Islām* (Islamic Faith), considered the presence of cinema in Iran to be "destructive and perverting," since it taught the youth Western values and ways of life.[88] The passing of time in movie theatres – instead of other sites of sociability, such as mosques and religious gatherings – was believed to "shape the thoughts and beliefs" of the youth, for their interaction with other societies through cinematic image and space encouraged them to "imitate the fashion and make-up trends" of those societies.[89] In an article in *Parcham-i Islām* (Flag of Islam) publication in 1946, Manūchihr Aʻlāyī likewise remarked that the aspects of "dancing, singing and revelry" portrayed on screen aroused "lustful desires" and destroyed "the foundations of religion and spirituality" that had made Iranians "depend on what is sacred" for centuries.[90] Aʻlāyī believed that since the first introduction of "films and cinema" into the "land of Islam," "business operators" and "cunning politicians" had purposefully imported films that encouraged "lust and debauchery" among the people of Iran to "destroy the moral foundation" of that society.[91] He found it very "unfortunate" that the national financial capital of Iran was going "into the pockets of foreigners" through Iranian consumption of foreign films and the "blind imitation" of cinema stars.[92] In a patriarchal commentary, an article in *Āyīn-i Islām* specifically criticised women in 1948 who not only put on make-up, but took their "10-year-old daughter and son" to the cinema, and from that age exposed them to "scenes of kissing, smooching, and love-making," stimulated "the lustful instincts" of innocent children, and thus "push[ed] them down the abyss of prostitution."[93] While reprimanding women for conceiving cinema as "an entertaining and recreational" medium,

---

[88] Nuṣratullāh Nūryānī, "Sīnamā va Andīshah-hā-yi Mardum" [Cinema and Public Opinion], *Āyīn-i Islām* (Isfand 23, 1325 [March 14, 1946]), 12.

[89] Mahdī Vazīrnīyā, "Sīnamā va Asarāt-i Ān dar Javānān-i Īrānī" [Cinema and Its Effects on the Iranian Youth], *Maktab-i Mām*, no. 11 (Bahman 1348 [February 1969]), 18.

[90] Manūchihr Aʻlāyī, "Sīnamā yā Buzurgtarīn ʻĀmil-i Fisād-i Akhlāgh" [Cinema or the Most Significant Cause of the Corruption (of the Youth)], *Parcham-i Islām*, yr 1 (Urdībihisht 20, 1325 [May 10, 1946]), 4.

[91] *Ibid.*, 1. [92] *Ibid.*, 5.

[93] Hassan Nīkkhū, "Aksarīyyat-i Mardum dar īn Kishvar Vazīfah-'i Khudishān rā Anjām Nimīdahand" [The Majority of People in this Country Do Not Perform Their Responsibilities], *Āyīn-i Islām*, no. 220 (or alternatively, no. 21) (Day 3, 1327 [December 24, 1948]), 19.

the author also expressed his objection to having acquired cinema "from European civilisation."[94]

For some, protestations against governmental incompetence and political circumstances of the time were sublimated in reactionary stances against cinema. Expressing his concerns about the dangers associated with "imitation" in 1947, Vā'izī Tabrīzī, an Islamic thinker, questioned how one could "look forward to a bright future?" when Iran's contemporary "literary and cultural" ethos "stemmed from the nonsensical and exaggerations of European deceiving novelists," or that the roots of Iranian "moral guidelines were now supplied by the viewing of erotic and animal-instinct-stimulating films."[95] In a 1948 article in *Parcham-i Islām*, Vā'izī Tabrīzī found it disturbing that "instead of religious orations, instructive sermons and useful lectures," the government promoted corruption through "cinema, theatre, dance, swimming [and a preoccupation with] appearances."[96] The "imitation" of the behaviours, fashion and lifestyles of "Western" societies facilitated through international film spectatorship, and their promotion by cultural magazines was deemed responsible for what social critics professed to be a form of national "moral pollution" (fisād-i akhlāqī).

Charges aimed at the Iranian "imitation" of unfamiliar customs through cultural products also evoked disapproving reactions from more secular critics. "Do books, newspapers, images, and fashion, have any impact on the committing of crimes?" asked Shamsuddīn Amīr-'Alāyī in 1942; "affirmative," he responded, "one could not deny the obvious impact that publications and the watching of scenes on cinema screens, theatre stages, etc. have on the public."[97] In an article entitled "The Impact of Publications, Cinematic and Theatrical Literature and Fashion on Committing Crimes," he elaborated on the ways in which "the sense of imitation (hiss-i taqlīd)," especially acquired through film spectatorship, had corrupted the

---

[94] *Ibid.*
[95] Majīd Vā'izī Tabrīzī, "Tamaddun-i Imrūzī, Giriftārīhā-yi Īrānīyān, Chārah-'i Munhasir bah Fard" [Today's Civilisation, the Troubles of Iranians, One-of-a-Kind Solution], *Āyīn-i Islām*, no. 182 (Ābān 22, 1326 [November 14, 1947]), 16.
[96] M. Vā'izī- Tabrīzī, "Dastūrāt'-i Akhlāqī-yi Islāmī" [The Ethical Guidelines of Islam], *Parcham-i Islām*, yr 3, no. 1 (Farvardīn 12, 1327 [April 1, 1948]), 2.
[97] Shamsuddīn Amīr-'Alāyī, "Āsār-i Matbū'āt va Adabīyyāt-i Sīnamā va Tiātr va Mud dar Irtikāb-i Jināyāt" [The Impact of Publications and Cinema Literature and Theatre and Fashion in the Committing of Crimes], *Majmū'ah-'i Huqūqī*, yr 6, no. 4 (Tīr 31, 1321 [July 22, 1942]), 139.

youth and prompted the masses – rather than tutored and knowing people – to commit crimes.[98]

Khalq rā taqlīdishān bar bād dād   Ay daw sad la'nat bar īn taqlīd bād[99]

People are gone adrift because of their imitation
Damnation be cast upon this imitation

With the dubbing of foreign language films into the Persian language, a practice that became popular in the 1940s and 1950s, the risk of imitating "foreign" lifestyles increased; unfamiliar codes and non-traditional mores depicted in international films were now accessible to a large number of spectators, who were previously incapable of fully internalising the films' content due to the language barrier. In the early 1940s, Ismā'īl Kūshān, later a film director, commenced dubbing French films into Persian in Istanbul, where some professional dubbing studios had developed, and started to screen them in Iran in the mid-1940s. In Turkey, Kūshān dubbed the French film, *Premier Rendez-Vous* (1941), into Persian and showcased it under the title *The Runaway Girl* (*Dukhtar-i Farārī*); he then dubbed the second foreign language film, *La Gitanilla* (1940), into Persian under the title, *The Gypsy Girl* (*Dukhtar-i Kawlī*).[100] Following Kūshān's first attempts, dubbing became a fashionable trend inside and outside Iran, and a stepping stone for some to enter filmmaking operations in the late 1940s. According to a 1954 *Payk-i Sīnamā* article by Siamak Pourzand, a film critic, Studio Shahrzād had first started its operations as an extensive dubbing studio, but then began to produce Persian films as early as 1950.[101] In Italy, Dāyūsh Studio had also been successful in dubbing Italian films into Persian; *Le Meravigliose Avventure di Guerri Meschino* (The Wonderful Adventures of Guerrin Meschino, 1952) was the studio's first Italian film to be dubbed into its Persian version, *Sarguzasht-i Firaydūn-i Bīnavā* (*The Adventures of Miserable Firaydun*).[102] In 1955, a column in *Intellectual* (*Rushanfikr*) weekly periodical, "A Look at Weekly Films," reported on the studio's second attempt at dubbing: *Il Lupo della Sila* (*Lure of the Sila*, 1949), or *The Wolf of the Farm* (*Gurg-i Mazra'ah*) in Persian, was

---

[98] *Ibid.*, 139–146.   [99] *Ibid.*, 144.
[100] Naficy, *A Social History of Iranian Cinema*, vol. 2, 251.
[101] Pourzand, "Dar Atrāf-i Istūdīyaw-hā-yi Īrānī: Istūdīyaw Shahrzād" [Around Iranian Studios: Studio Shahrzad], *Payk-i Sīnamā*, yr 1, no. 10 (Āzar 20, 1333 [December 11, 1954]), 6.
[102] Naficy, *A Social History of Iranian Cinema*, vol. 2, 253.

dubbed under the supervision of Alex Aqābābīyān.[103] As demonstrated in the examples above, dubbing studios regularly changed the title of films and chose Iranian names for film characters in their dubbed offerings. For example, in *The Wolf of the Farm*, Vittorio Gassman played the role of Mahmūd and Amadeo Nazzārī played 'Alī, the father of Jacques Sernas, named Manūchihr in the film. The replacement of names and titles gave a much more familiar feel to the films and made them more popular among the Iranian public. The female star of the film, Silvana Mangano, was also noted for her "Eastern beauty" and her "plump bust and voluptuous body."[104] Such Iranianisation of foreign language films boosted movie theatre revenues, allowed a larger number of audience members to comprehend film plots, and therefore increased what the critics believed were the "dangers" associated with film spectatorship.

Aside from being criticised for making "foreign" customs more accessible to the public, dubbing also faced criticism for the immoral language that it promoted in its translations. In 1969, Tājī Ahmadī, one of the prominent figures of Iranian theatre who had entered the field of dubbing "after theatre was commercialised," spoke about her frustration with the "instability" of the industry, and her feeling that there "no longer was any belief" in the work.[105] The use of "sexual innuendos," "swear words" and "vulgar songs" in the Persian translation of international films was deemed unnecessary and "shameful."[106] Ahmadī, in fact, mentioned that many people in the dubbing industry had, similar to her, left dubbing for commercial cinema and instead started dubbing for television programs, which was administered or controlled more carefully and "had a better environment."[107]

3.4 Professionalisation and the Emergence of a "National" Commercial Film Industry

"If you want to prohibit the [import] of dubbed films, you only have one solution ahead; enhance the artistic and technical values of your

---

[103] Bahrām, "Nazarī bi-fīlmhā-yi Haftah, Sīnamā Mitrupul: *Gurg-i Mazra'ah*" [A Look at Weekly Films, Metropol Cinema: *The Wolf of the Farm*], *Rushanfikr*, yr 1, no. 29 (Bahman 8, 1332 [January 28, 1954]), 9.
[104] *Ibid.*
[105] "Iftizāh-i Dūblah-'i Fīlm-hā" [Terrible Dubbing of Films], *Firdawsi*, no. 929 (Shahrīvar 31, 1348 [September 22, 1969]), 43.
[106] *Ibid.*   [107] *Ibid.*

film industry, then you will see how people will welcome it," wrote
Hūshang Kāvūsī, a film director and critic, in 1954, paraphrasing a
friend whom he believed knew cinema "from an international point
of view."[108] From very early on, critics and experts envisaged a
cinematic horizon of expectation for "the art of cinema" in Iran that
made it "on a par with that of international" cinemas, so that Iranian
films could be distributed outside national borders.[109] It was amid
a plethora of contentious reactions that the Iranian cinema industry,
after having founded a somewhat strong industrial establishment,
commenced to make films again. After allocating a few years
solely to the creation of dubbing institutions, TV productions and
documentary/newsreel-making in the 1940s, a few filmmakers once
again began fiction or narrative feature-film production. The cinematic activities starting in the late 1940s gave way to the blooming of
a sustained commercial cinema that was increasingly produced or
directed by Iranians (of various ethnic, religious and ideological
backgrounds), and that involved mainly Iranian actors and actresses.
Being sensitive to the terminology used by historical practitioners of
the field, I adopt the term "national" (millī) for this industry as it was
used by film critics at the time based on the notion that films were
mainly produced and financed within Iran (in contrast to the majority
of films made before them).[110] This "national" cinema, in the opinion
of critics, had to distinguish itself, visually and in narrative, from its
regional (i.e. Middle Eastern cinemas) and international (i.e. Hollywood) competitors. Following the discussions surrounding cinematic
independence which had started to take shape during the Qajar era
and became more pronounced during the 1930s, Iranian cinematic
sovereignty was now embodied in this national popular industry.

---

[108] Hūshang Kāvūsī, "Fīlm-i Fārsī, Fīlm-i Dūblah-'i Fārsī" [Persian Film, Persian-
Dubbed Film], *Payk-i Sīnamā*, no. 10 (Āzar 20, 1333 [December 11, 1954]), 21.

[109] Bihzād Vusūq, "Sīnamā dar Kirmānshāh" [Sīnamā dar Kirmanshāh], *Nijāt*, yr
1, no. 3 (Khurdād 18, 1333 [June 8, 1954]), 23.

[110] It should be mentioned that the economic base of the majority of commercial
film productions from the late 1940s to 1970s was in Iran. Most studios
involved in commercial film productions were privately and independently
financed. Starting in the 1960s, some studios began producing collaborative
projects with Egyptian, Turkish, French and American film studios. Naficy
considers the production of commercial films to have been in a "hybrid
productional mode" combining artisanal and industrial practices. See Naficy,
A Social History of Iranian Cinema, vol. 2, 147.

This post-war enterprise was arguably borne out of the cosmo-national cinema of the 1930s, especially since some themes (and characters) included in the films of the 1930s now reappeared in this industry. As discussed in the following paragraphs and in more length in Chapter 4, the concern of many critics of this era (in line with their predecessors in the 1930s) was to create a Persian-language cinema that was founded on Iranian sensibilities, ethics, practices and history, and that would be comprehended by the Iranian audience – a cinema that could be staged on an international level as a true representative of the nation, and that would be a source of revenue for the country.

The consolidation of national cinema entailed the professionalisation of the industry. The mushrooming of studios, directors, film critics and actors collimated the official legitimisation of the industry and the establishment of visual, technical and literary standards, as well as bodies that oversaw, critiqued and shaped the application of such standards in the Iranian cinematic enterprise. In other words, a two-decades-long engagement in cinematic activities engendered a "formal knowledge" of cinema, an "elite knowledge" that was not part of everyday understanding – a kind of expertise that is acquired through higher education or training in institutions; organisations that are "the major source of the transformation of the source and the role of agents of formal knowledge."[111] In terms of critical film analysis, for example, Iranian critics had already gained adequate experience in examining and writing film reviews for over two decades since the 1930s when Iranian newspapers started reporting on the first Persian-language film productions, and an abundant number of German (UFA), Hollywood, Soviet and French films. Although the authors of the first film critiques were few in number, one might argue that their style of writing and professional knowledge supplied a form of worldly critical imagination for subsequent generations.

Eliot Friedson considers the carriers of formal knowledge to be professionals. Iranian critics' proclamations and comments regarding the establishment of an Iranian cinema on a par with global standards are very much aligned with the root of the word "profession": to profess

---

[111] Eliot Freidson, *Professional Powers: A Study of the Institutionalization of Formal Knowledge* (University of Chicago Press, 1986), 4–15.

as a "declaration" or "expression of intention or purpose."[112] Friedson considers "profession" to be a "changing historic concept"[113] in nations that have been influenced by Anglo-American institutions as a result of contact with Europe and America via commercial and ideological exchanges enforced through imperialist interactions, especially conducted through cinema and propaganda. Following Friedson, then, one could argue that the cinema industry in Iran was much informed by the professionalisation of the enterprise modelled by the Anglo-American institutions, as well as Indian and Egyptian establishments, albeit shaped according to Iranian conditions. At a time when cinema was privatised, the Iranian middle class acquired the funds to buy international films and film projection equipment, establish dubbing and film studios, produce films, inaugurate acting institutions, attend acting training centres and obtain the cinematic formal knowledge to review, criticise and thus shape the making and viewing of films. In other words, the screening of international films, mainstream and artistic, throughout the 1940s and 1950s (in fact over forty years of international film projection) trained a generation of commercial film directors and critics who were influential in the establishment of an independent popular film industry and supported the birth of an artistically superior cinema that was to emerge in the late 1950s.

One key aspect that contributed to the consolidation and professionalisation of the national motion picture industry was the creation of film studios. Iranian popular cinema did not follow the studio system of Hollywood. This industry was dominated by independent producers (sometimes more than one) who established studios that financed films of certain genres. In the 1960s, with the increasing success of popular films, more independent producers began to make their own films using the facilities of various film studios.[114] At times, individual and more successful directors founded their own studios and made films. The establishment and transformations of studios in Iran is an understudied topic that is worthy of scholarly attention, but one that is outside the scope of the present project. The first feature films made in the late 1940s and early 1950s were mostly produced by Mitra Studio and Pars Studio, but, in the mid-1950s,

---

[112] *Ibid.*, 21. [113] *Ibid.*, 32.
[114] M. Ali Issari, *Cinema in Iran: 1900–1979* (London: The Scarecrow Press, 1989), 155–156.

film studios grew in number. Most of these studios were private enterprises and financed by the commercial revenue of film productions – one of the reasons that prompted the inclusion of song-and-dance numbers in motion pictures to ensure commercial success. Pars Film Studio, one of the pioneering and major studios of the time, embarked on creating a number of historical productions. Diana Film Studio also produced historical and epic films, while Mīsāqīyah Studio was involved in the making of high-budget films with extravagant sets in the 1950s.

The productions of this national industry required commercial elements that ensured its profitability – some of the commercial success of this enterprise could be attributed to its stars. Starting in the early 1950s, when the number of Persian film productions was growing rapidly,[115] the number of film studios increased concurrently. Despite the drought of commercial film productions in the previous decade, Iranian theatre had been very active in staging theatrical productions. With the recommencement of filmmaking, many stage actors became involved in cinema in the 1940s and 1950s. Mahīn Dayhīm (1925–2001), Farah Panāhi, Zhālah (Shawkat 'Alaw, b. 1927), Murīn and Sūdābah were among such actors who became stars of the early Iranian commercial cinema. Filmmakers and publications were quick to understand the commercial value attached to the star system associated with Hollywood cinema. In order to maximise revenues in an industry dominated by independent producers, the actors and actresses who appeared most frequently in magazine gossip columns were often approached and selected in order to (re)generate hype and publicity.

A comparative survey of cultural products in the region, namely Indian cinema, also suggests the formation of a star system that went hand in hand with the commercialisation of the industry – one that did not necessarily follow the studio-based star system of Hollywood either. Prasad argues that in the India of the 1950s, the ideological contradictions of the Nehruvian ruling bloc were not only embodied

---

[115] I call the film productions of this era "Persian film" (and note that it is not hyphenated) for two reasons: (1) this was the title given to Iranian film productions of the time by film publications and critics, due to the language used in the films; and (2) it seems to be an appropriate term in retrospect, considering that "Persian" was the ethnic language dominant in the films of that time.

in the narrative strategies of Bombay films, but they also structured its star system.[116] Prasad contends that the Bombay star system, manifested in the image of glamorous, noble, aristocratic upper-caste appearance of the star, drew on and replicated an overarching feudal ideology; in other words, the star was a god. However, Iranian stars (at least until the mid-1960s) had a different iconic significance than the Indian stars of Bombay cinema. The star system in Iran seems to have focused on the moral, "human" and "Iranian" qualities of the stars, advertised and promoted through magazine articles. Iranian stars were praised for their intellect, modesty, talents and, of course, beauty – the latter of which was at times likened to that of the Hollywood, French and Italian stars. For instance, Zhālah (Shawkat 'Olov), the main actor in the *Bride of the Tigris* ('Arūs-i Dijlah, 1954), was likened in terms of appearance to the Dominican actress, Maria Montez, who had gained much fame in Hollywood in the 1940s.[117] To cite another example, Muhsin Mahdavī (b. 1925) was commended as a "talented actor," "competent writer" and "master of painting" in an article in *Payk-i Sīnamā* magazine.[118] Having studied composition at the Rome Conservatory of Music and graduating with a Bachelor of Arts degree in Literature in London, Mahdavī created a number of theatrical pieces for London Radio's Persian program.[119] After travelling to Egypt, Turkey, Lebanon and Iraq, Mahdavī returned to Iran and eventually started working for Pars Film Studio as the principal actor in *Tehran Nights* (*Shabhā-yi Tihrān*, 1953).[120] Having praised him for his modesty and extensive knowledge in literature, the article addressed Mahdavī's religious beliefs and his weekly trips to the 'Abdul'azīm Shrine.[121] As a worldly actor who valued Iranian moral ethics, Mahdavī's vernacular cosmopolitan outlook was admired and encouraged by the

---

[116] M. Madhava Prasad, "The State and Culture: Hindi Cinema in the Passive Revolution" (PhD diss., University of Pittsburgh, 1994), 131–137. Quoted in Ajanta Sircar, *Framing the Nation: Languages of "Modernity" in India* (Calcutta: Seagull Books, 2011), 110.

[117] Such direct comparisons to American and European stars perhaps explain the reasons as to why the Iranian elite reprimanded Persian-language films for "imitating" foreign films.

[118] Siamak Pourzand, "Hunarpīshah-hā-yi Īrānī rā Bishināsīd: Mahdavī" [Get to Know Iranian Actors: Mahdavi], *Payk-i Sīnamā*, yr 1, no. 9 (Āzar 6, 1333 [November 27, 1954]), 11.

[119] *Ibid.*   [120] *Ibid.*   [121] *Ibid.*, 23.

magazine – attributes that arguably deemed him worthy of "national" cinema. These actors, in a way, portrayed the ideal notions of Iranianness on screen, an identity which had entered a period of moral crisis in the modern period.

The professionalisation of the industry also meant a more critical examination of Iranian film productions, which could account for the growth in publications and articles that addressed cinema events and Iranian films. As demonstrated above, new pages and columns were dedicated to local film events. *Nijāt* (Salvation) magazine's "The Magnifying Glass of Cinema" column is one example. Reporting on the latest cinema news, the column was published on the second page of the magazine, the first page constituting the cover page of the issue.[122] M. Kunjkāv reported on the latest news of famous Iranian actors, the dubbing of renowned international movies into Persian, the installation of new technologies such as cinemascope in Tehran cinemas and the production of high-budget Persian films such as *Bride of the Tigris*.[123] Iranian actors and actresses, many of whom had already been successful in theatre, were now entering the cinema scene and were being featured in cinema publications for their roles on an unprecedented level. Murīn, who was not a "native Persian speaker," but spoke Persian, "French, English . . . Russian and Turkish" fluently, was praised for her past as one of the "most-experienced stage actors" and for her future as "one of the hopes of the national cinema."[124] Having married Mansūr Matīn, another Iranian theatre star who had been trained by the famous "Maestro" 'Abdulhussayn Nūshīn's theatrical ensemble, the two had abstained from the stage ever since "Iranian theatre had deviated from the right path of art" and both had started to act in films in 1952 (Figure 3.3).[125] The idea of deviation from the "right path" of art, an art form that pivoted around critics' sense of public morale and Iranianness, therefore, was not only limited to cinema, but also to the performing arts.

---

[122] M. Kunjkāv, "Zarrah-bīn-i Sīnamā" [The Magnifying Glass of Cinema], *Nijāt*, no. 7 (Ābān 8, 1333 [October 30, 1954]), 2.
[123] *Ibid.*
[124] Siamak Pourzand, "Hunarpīshah-hā-yi Īrānī rā Bishināsīd: Murīn" [Get to Know Iranian Actors: Murin], *Nijāt*, no. 7 (Ābān 8, 1333 [October 30, 1954]), 9.
[125] *Ibid.*

موريّن

هنرپیشه هنرمندی که هنوز از او فیلمی نمایش نداده‌اند

از : سیامک نورزند

هنرپیشه‌های ایرانی را بشناسید

موریّن، متین و مهرگان

شماره ۷

بقیه درصفحه ۱۹

صفحه ۹

Figure 3.3 An image of a 1954 newspaper article about Iranian actress, Murīn

3.5 The Shaping of a Cinematic Visionary

Film critics and enthusiasts, similar to other social and cultural critics, did not promote the obliteration of cinema; instead, they believed in the flourishing of a cinema culture that celebrated noteworthy foreign language films, drew on the experiences of international filmmakers and crafted a national cinema that was representative of such cosmopolitan outlooks. More than ever before, film critics now took part in film analysis and review, especially art films from the French New Wave and Italian Neorealism movements, and published their views in popular publications. Film periodicals became increasingly engaged in directing the taste of audiences toward their own cultural preferences, namely, toward more artistic and philosophical film offerings. Hūshang Kāvūsī, a film critic, filmmaker and writer, better known as Dr Hūshang Kāvūsī, was one of the prominent names that would appear frequently in periodicals such as *Rushanfikr*, *Firdawsi* and later *Nigīn*, offering filmic perspectives and directives that were temporally protentional.[126] Having studied film at the *Institut des Hautes Etudes Cinématographiques* in Paris in the 1940s, Kāvūsī was an elitist cosmopolitan who envisioned a future for Iran's cinema that situated it on a par with international cinemas, or as artistically and thematically superior to the commercial Hollywood movies showcased in the country. Commenting on "great films" of international cinemas (mainly French, Italian and American festival films) in *Rushanfikr*, he praised motion pictures that "immersed" the audience and "engaged" the spectator in the events of the plot; he therefore urged

---

[126] I am borrowing the concept of "protentional" from Husserl's phenomenology of temporality, although with a non-phenomenological twist. In his conception of temporal perception, Husserl designates a threefold notion of temporality to describe how we perceive duration: primary sensation, retention and protention. Primary sensations of time, according to Husserl, remain in the consciousness briefly in a "running-off" mode, while one is constantly confronted with new primary sensations. Husserl calls the ability to retain the immediate past sensations in consciousness "retention." Thus, retention enables us to keep the "present" in our consciousness. Protention, then, is the act of anticipating, or protending, the immediate future's sensation (like hearing a symphony, where one hears and retains the preceding note, and thus one hears the next note as different from the previous one). Neil Deroo argues that protention, however, is not phenomenologically identifiable. While retention deals with the past, protention deals with the future with a passive directness. This passive intentionality allows for a constant gesture toward the future in an essentially open manner. See Neal Deroo, "The Future Matters: Protention as More than Inverse Retention" *Bulletin d'analyse phénoménologique* 4(7) (2008): 1–18. In this instance, I use protentional perspective to denote a perspective that looks into the future and envisions the crafting of an arthouse or intellectual cinema.

his fellow Iranian directors to learn and follow such rules in their filmmaking.[127] In his review of Henri-Georges Clouzot's *Le Salaire de Peur* (*The Wages of Fear*, 1953), Kāvūsī especially encouraged film-importing companies to discard their presupposition that "French and Italian films do not work well in Iran," and to import such films because he was sure that they would be proven wrong about the taste of the Iranian audience.[128] Disappointed with the technical and thematic shortcomings of the Persian film industry, Kāvūsī was one of the critics who believed that the projection of dubbed foreign films was more worthwhile than the screening of puny Persian talkie films that had branched out like "weeds," spoiling the "garden" of Iranian cinema and preventing the blossoming and growth of "flowers."[129] Kāvūsī's desire for the projection of prominent international films in Iran was also echoed by many other critics, film analysts and intellectuals. An article in *Cinema* (*Sīnamā*) journal, for example, lamented that valuable films by Orson Welles had been stored in "the warehouse of film-importing cinema studios" rather than being screened in the country, to avoid the risk of "experiencing a lack of commercial success."[130] The commercial value and success of films that were of importance to cinema owners and film-importing companies during the 1940s and 1950s were viewed as deplorable by many critics.

As can be observed in Kāvūsī's remarks, objections were not aimed at international films alone. Critics, who sought to craft an arthouse cinema as a "national cinema," also targeted Iranian (Persian-language) motion pictures that had started to emerge in large numbers by the mid-1950s. Tughrul Afshār, one of the prominent post-war film critics who started his career at a very young age and lost his life when he was only 23 years of age, became the publisher and chief-editor of *Nijāt* magazine in the early 1950s. In a 1954 editorial piece entitled "The Struggle that We Continue," Afshār specifically aimed his words at those filmmakers who, in their "first steps," led the art of cinema toward the "sinkhole of collapse and corruption."[131] Afshār was

---

[127] Hūshang Kāvūsī, "Yik Fīlm-i Buzurg: *Muzd-i Tars*" [A Great Film: *The Wages of Fear*], *Rushanfikr*, yr 1, no. 13 (Mihr 2, 1332 [September 24, 1953]), 10.

[128] *Ibid.*, 15.   [129] *Ibid.*, 21.

[130] "Ursun Vilz" [Orson Welles], *Sīnamā*, Round 2, no. 1 (Mihr 20, 1333 [October 12, 1954]), 18.

[131] Tughrul Afshār, "Mubārizah-yī kah mā Dunbāl Mīkunīm" [The Struggle That We Continue], *Nijāt*, yr 1, no. 3 (Khurdād 18, 1333 [June 8, 1954]), 2.

concerned that cinema had turned into such a commercial commodity that "talented girls and boys from good families" would not be willing to step foot in that enterprise.[132] According to Afshār, despite its popular material, *Nijāt* magazine "elucidated the wrong path that Iranian cinema and [its] merchants followed" and attempted to show the "true art of cinema."[133] The author described his "great dream" to be the development and progress of filming and cinema in "solely artistic" forms.[134] Likewise, in 1953, an article in the monthly journal of *Shīvah* (The Way) lamented Iranian cinema which had not been "able to open a space for itself as an art form."[135] Quoting Lenin, that "of all the arts, for us cinema is the most important," the author added, "until a few years ago ... Iran did not have a national cinema, and ever since this national cinema has been created, the only thing that it does not constitute, is art itself."[136]

At times, Afshār took issue with international popular films that shaped Iranian visual taste and future filmmaking. In a biweekly review of films, for example, he disapproved of Arabic-language films featured in Iranian cinemas. Sarcastically listing made-up film titles such as "love and blood," "I fell in love with my mother," "I love my father," "love and flower," and "love and tears," which resembled the titles of many popular Egyptian films, Afshār did not see the futile and popular topic of "love or youthfulness" as playing a critical role in the flourishing of an artistic palette.[137] Afshār's critique was especially aimed at the Arabic musical, *Love Taxi* (1954) by Nīyāzī Mustafā, featured at Sun Cinema as the theatre's first film screening on its opening night after renovations.[138] The Egyptian film tells the story of a wealthy woman who takes a ride in a taxi, falls in love with the poor driver and consequently asks him to marry her. The taxi driver, who has also fallen in love with the woman, refuses, as he is ashamed of their disparate social backgrounds. To win his love, the woman disguises herself as a poor singer in a nightclub. The taxi driver

---

[132] *Ibid.*   [133] *Ibid.*   [134] *Ibid.*

[135] Īraj, "Bahs-i Mukhtasarī Darbārah-'i Hunar-i Sīnamā: Sīnamā-yi Millī-yi Īrān va Navāqis-i Ān," *Shīvah*, yr 1, no. 3 (Tir 1332 [June–July 1953]), 59.

[136] *Ibid.*

[137] Tughrul Afshār, "Intiqādī bar Fīlmhā-yi Daw Haftah-'i Akhīr" [A Critique of Films from the Last Two Weeks], *Payk-i Sīnamā*, yr 1, no. 10 (Āzar 20, 1333 [December 11, 1954]), 25.

[138] *Ibid.*

Figure 3.4 An image of *Nijāt*'s column, "A Critique of Films from the Last Two Weeks"

eventually falls in love with the singer before discovering that she is the same woman with whom he had initially fallen in love. With the help of friends, the two marry and live happily ever after.

Afshār accused national filmic productions and especially film studios for demoting the audience's cinematic taste. In fact, his biweekly column in *Nijāt*, "A Critique of Films from the Last Two Weeks," focused on early Persian film productions from the late 1940s and early 1950s (which will be discussed in length in Chapter 4). The graphic design of the title of the column was symbolically significant, in that the word "films" was crossed out with a paint brush stroke, as if to strike out films that were being produced during that era, both symbolically and physically (Figure 3.4).[139] Afshār blamed the frail state of filmmaking in Iran on the rapidly growing number of studios and producers of Persian films.[140] Instead, he suggested that studios in Iran should be limited in number but better financed; He further urged "small producers" who were not necessarily in the film business to avoid making films.[141] Aside from film reviews and critiques, Afshār attempted to publish numerous articles that elaborated the technical aspects of filmmaking, namely the art of camera work, montage and casting. These articles were not simple translations of pieces published in international journals, but were written by Iranians who were

---

[139] *Ibid.*

[140] Tughrul Afshār, "Intiqādī bar Fīlmhā-yi Duw Haftah-'i Akhīr" [A Critique of Films from the Last Two Weeks], *Nijāt*, yr 1, no. 3 (Khurdād 18, 1333 [June 8, 1954]), 24.

[141] *Ibid.*, 25.

familiar with the craft of cinematography. "Familiarise Yourself with Filmmaking" (Bā Fīlm-bardārī Āshnā Shavīd), was an example of a journal column in *Nijāt* that not only attempted to introduce readers to various filmmaking techniques but also brought examples from the Iranian industry and discussed shortcomings of "Persian-language films," to engender serious changes within the industry.[142]

In addition to a number of critics who were unhappy about the state of Persian-language film productions, some actors were also discontent with the conditions and their roles as stars in the motion pictures of the period. As early as 1954, Nāhīd Sarfarāz, who had been an active radio, theatre and cinema figure, allegedly withdrew from the Iranian artistic world. According to an article, having "bitter memories" from her involvement in the industry, the star of *White Glove* (*Dastkish-i Sifīd*, 1951) and *Familiar Face* (*Chihrah-'i Āshnā*, 1953) did not intend to "pollute" herself by engaging with the new cinema, nor to sell her art for money.[143] Expressing a more socialist tone in pursuit of a "literary combat" (mubārizah-'i qalamī), *Payk-i Sīnamā* magazine called Sarfarāz a "combatant artist" and asked her to join the magazine's collective fight to illustrate art comprehension and appreciation to those who seek it.[144] Believing that "art in Iran had lost its real meaning," Sarfarāz stated that it was sensible for families "to prevent their children from entering artistic careers."[145] Sarfarāz was especially disappointed that some people in the industry had "foul and perverted ideas" about radio, cinema and theatre artists. Feeling that she had been commodified as a female artist, she believed that it was more "noble" to "suffer and yet distance" oneself from the art realm than to jeopardise one's reputation. In fact, the commercialisation of the industry and filmmakers' concern with profitability seem to have been condemned by prominent theatre and radio stars who had entered the world of cinema. Despite these charges, the profitability of Persian films suggested their widespread popularity and thus their general

[142] T. Gīlānī, "Bā Fīlm-bardārī Āshnā Shavīd" [Familiarise Yourself with Filmmaking], *Nijāt*, yr 1, no. 3 (Khurdād 18, 1333 [June 8, 1954]), 7.

[143] "Nāhīd Sarfarāz: "Hunarmandī kah az 'Ālam-i Hunarī-yi Tihrān Kinārah-gīrī kard" [Nāhīd Sarfarāz: The Artist Who Rejected the Artistic Realm of Tehran], *Payk-i Sīnamā*, yr 1, no. 9 (Āzar 6, 1333 [November 27, 1954]), 7.

[144] *Ibid.*

[145] Nāhīd Sarfarāz, "Sarguzasht-i yik Hayāt-i Hunarī bah Qalam-i Nāhīd Sarfarāz" [The Fate of an Artistic Life Written by Nāhīd Sarfarāz], *Payk-i Sīnamā*, yr 1, no. 10 (Āzar 20, 1333 [December 11, 1954]), 17.

acceptance by the masses. Predicting that "perhaps in a couple of years, a change might take place in [the] Iranian art" scene, Sarfarāz had seen it worthy to speak out in *Payk-i Sīnamā* magazine against "mindless and degenerate people" in the industry.[146] The future success of Iranian cinema, to which Sarfarāz wanted to contribute, was in her opinion contingent upon the collaboration of "the government, people, and artists."[147]

In *Payk-i Sīnamā* periodical's column, "The Magnifying Glass of Cinema," the author recapped some of the responsibilities of "the Commission of Theatres" and "the censors," who ultimately determined the fate of films and theatrical plays at the time.[148] The article reminded readers and censorship officers that "people who have specialisation and adequate information in affairs of cinema and art" must be employed in such positions so that critical sections of a film are not censored due to insufficient knowledge.[149] Rather than futile and irrelevant, the responsibilities of censors were deemed as "sensitive" and "momentous" by critics, who suggested that many industry professionals were in fact not against the institution of censorship, but rather opposed to its incorrect application.[150]

In addition to national and international motion pictures, film periodicals also faced reprimands. The most common type of news reports featured by Iranian cinema magazines, according to M. Kunjkāv, another film critic, related to "biography of foreign cinema artists, global cinema news, marriage, divorce, or some other aspect of artists' lives."[151] Taking issue with cinema journal editors for only publishing superficial topics, the author remarked that journals' most common justification for the circulation of such futile pieces was that "*people demand such material.*"[152] Reminding journals of their significant role as "the fourth pillar of the [Iranian] constitution," Kunjkāv urged magazines to stop publishing exaggerations, lies and vain articles about cinema stars.[153] Considering the work of such magazines as "a betrayal to society," the author chastised the commodification of

---

[146] *Ibid.*   [147] *Ibid.*, 19.
[148] "Zarrah-bīn-i Sīnamā" [The Magnifying Glass of Cinema], *Payk-i Sīnamā*, yr 1, no. 9 (Āzar 6, 1333 [November 27, 1954]), 2.
[149] *Ibid.*   [150] *Ibid.*
[151] M. Kunjkāv, "Nazarī bah Matbūʿāt" [A Look at Publications], *Sīnamā*, Round 2, no. 1 (Mihr 20, 1333 [October 12, 1954]), 15.
[152] *Ibid* (emphasis added).   [153] *Ibid.*

cinema stars as the means to play to the superficial pleasures of the masses, and thus criticised the commercialisation of the arts and literature.[154]

In addition to magazines that promoted the art of filmmaking in Iran, some publications also became critical of certain international cinematic productions that disseminated orientalist depictions of "the East." In a short 1953 review of the film, *The Golden Horde* (1951) by George Sherman (1908–1991), described as "What American Producers Call an Eastern! Film," an article in *Rushanfikr* deemed the film to be "tawdry and meaningless, with gaudy decor, and a mediocre cinematic and hollow love story."[155] Aside from attacking the weak cast and uncreative filmmaking, the author specifically took issue with the film's plot as it was "not clear according to which historical source" the screenwriter had based his plot, since such events had "never been mentioned in history."[156] Such reading of orientalist films is reminiscent of film reviews in the late 1920s and early 1930s, and perhaps points to a continuation in and professionalisation of film criticism and the industry.

Although cinema magazines were inundated with images of and stories about movie stars (both international and national), such commentaries compel us to study the reception of popular arts in Iran in the context of its multifaceted contingencies, contradictions and conflicts. While some directors appropriated the latest fashion trends set by Hollywood and Arab stars in their national visual offerings, others distanced themselves from such consumerist sensibilities and envisaged alternative cultural trends. Most of these critics were people who had been educated outside Iran, or thinkers and writers who were well aware of international cinematic movements and connected cinema to broader trends in the social, intellectual and political history of the Cold War period. Remarks made by Afshār, Kāvūsī and other critics not only reveal the kinds of contestations and debates that drove

---

[154] *Ibid.*, 18.
[155] *The Golden Horde* (1951) is a film about Genghis Khan's notorious army and the Mongol invasion of Samarqand, which had been part of Iran at some points during its history.
[156] "Sīnamā-hā-yi Īrān va Alburz: *Sipāh-i Talā-yi Changīz Khān*" [Iran and Alburz Cinemas: *Genghis khan's Golden Horde*], *Rushanfikr*, yr 1, no. 28 (Bahman 1, 1332 [January 21, 1954]), 9.

the industry, but also expose the multifaceted cosmopolitan visions that shaped the film enterprise in Iran.

Cinematic visionaries and reaction to cinematic offerings varied. While some intellectual cosmopolitans envisioned an artistic and philosophical film spectatorship and national cinema that was informed by modes of realism popular in European cinemas, others engaged with international popular films in the creation of their Iranian visual offerings. Film critics not only continued to report on and review national and international motion pictures for the Iranian audience, they had the informed opinion, access to local and global publications, and the space to provide more critical views on the conditions and direction of Iranian cinema. As the following chapters will demonstrate, cosmopolitan film critics, enthusiasts and cultural thinkers crafted a loose but professional film critique movement, a cinematic visionary in the early 1950s, that came to bear upon the course of Iranian filmmaking in the years that followed. Chapters 4 and 5 will further discuss how the visions and prognosis of members of this cosmopolitan movement facilitated various trends in filmmaking in the period before the 1979 revolution.

3.6 The Question of Taxes on National Films

In order to craft a desirable national cinema that was worthy of a "progressive" Iran and one that combatted the importation of international films, many critics and state officials called for a stricter control over film importations. In February 1955, the Ministry of Culture issued a letter to the office of the Prime Minister concerning imported "films that were contrary to chastity and public morality."[157] The letter addressed the Prime Minister to ask the Ministry of the State and the National Police to prevent film companies from importing "harmful films," especially since "theatre and cinema have a strong influence on the morality of people from different countries" and are

---

[157] "Darkhāst-i Vizārat-i Farhang az Nukhust Vazīrī Mabnī bar Tajdīd-i Nazar dar Āyīn-nāmah-hā va Mugharrarāt-i Namāyishī bah Manzūr-i Julugīrī az Vāridāt-i Fīlmhā-yi Khalāf-i 'Iffat va Akhlāgh-i 'Umūmī: Sanad-i Shumārah 117" [A Request by the Ministry of Culture to the Prime Minister Concerning the Codes and Regulations of Theatres to Prevent the Importation of Unchaste and Publicly Immoral Films into the Country: Document Number 117], in *Asnādī az Mūsīqī, Ti'ātr va Sīnamā dar Īrān (1300–1357)*, vol. 2, 574–576.

"considered as one of the most significant agents of pedagogy."[158] Films with subjects relating to mischief, theft, intimidation, murder, looting and chasing of women were deemed as inappropriate for the edification of the public. A number of films, the letter stated, "portrayed half-naked women and lustful dances which pushed the youth towards decadence," while it was "obvious that in an Islamic country," the projection of such films was "against chastity and public morality."[159] In response to this official inquiry, the Head of the National Police (Ra'īs-i Shahrbānī-yi Kull-i Kishvar), 'Alavī Muqaddam, wrote a letter in which he agreed with the Ministry of Culture's criticisms, and reportedly ordered the National Police representative in the Commission of Theatres to address the concerns of the Ministry in terms of film selection.[160] Muqaddam further recommended the Commission to approve and promote films that had "subjects relating to patriotism and dedication to the Shah, homeland and fellow country people," especially since films could be used as "effective media for propaganda."[161]

As mentioned above, during the reign of Reza Pahlavi, the examination of films and issuance of permits for film screenings were under the central control of the Ministry of the State (Vizārat-i Kishvar) and its sub-departments – a fact that perhaps points to two issues: first, the lack of a defined institutional infrastructure; and second, the importance of film and political propaganda during the first Pahlavi era, especially before and during World War II.[162] In line with the debates of the 1930s, the issue of film and education loomed large once again in the 1950s and early 1960s. In 1957, for example, an article in *Film and Life*

---

[158] "Darkhāst-i Vizārat-i Farhang az Nukhust Vazīrī Mabnī bar Tajdīd-i Nazar dar Āyīn-nāmah-hā," Document Number 117, 574–575.

[159] *Ibid.*, 575. This quotation by a state official is interesting in that it shows that concerns surrounding chastity and morality (based on religious sentiments) are not necessarily limited to a post-revolutionary cinema; such topics were also discussed and debated widely in pre-revolutionary era.

[160] "Darkhāst-i Vizārat-i Farhang az Nukhust Vazīrī Mabnī bar Tajdīd-i Nazar dar Āyīn-nāmah-hā," Document Number 117/2, 578.

[161] *Ibid.*

[162] 'Alī Asghar Kishānī has published a comprehensive chapter on the establishment of the Ministry of Culture and the Arts with the help of Islamic Republic of Iran Documentation Centre. See 'Alī Asghar Kishānī, *Farāyand-i Taʿāmul-i Sīnamā-yi Īrān va Hukūmat-i Pahlavī [The Processes of Interaction of Iranian Cinema and Pahlavi Regime]* (Tehran: Islamic Republic Documentation Centre Publications, 2007), 262–281.

(*Fīlm va Zindigī*) magazine concentrated on the benefits of "educational films."[163] The author believed entertaining and narrative films that were made by "national and sovereign studios" of the time were involved in "the task of training and education"; nevertheless, since these films were popular they could not be deemed as "educational."[164] In 1953, an article in *Mihr* magazine considered "radio, cinema, and newspapers" as three "important," "essential" and "prevalent" media that can be used for education and the "awakening of people."[165] In the same year, "with the help of American technical experts," the Ministry of Culture had prepared some films for the purpose of teaching "history and geography" to students, similar to other "advanced countries."[166] Audio-visual education, the article claimed, was not only "beneficial," but "necessary," since it elucidated course topics, provided a more practical aspect to the studies and nurtured creativity.[167] Thus, despite the negative criticisms that were aimed at cinema's "Westoxicated" imagery, and the "cheap" and "degenerative" Iranian film productions, cinema was still respected by some as a disciplinary tool that could be further harnessed for the benefit of the masses.

An essay published in the *Centre of Commerce Newspaper* (*Nāmah-'i Utāq-i Bāzargānī*), in 1959, conceptualised cinema as the most significant "social art of the twentieth century."[168] Still regarding it as "the school of society," the essay promoted the sponsorship and promotion of cinema by the state, as long as beneficial and useful films were screened. For a cheap price, the author stated, cinema entertained the audiences and prevented them from engaging in malefic forms of recreation.[169] Remarking that cinema had received much support in American and European countries, the author urged the Iranian government to realise the importance of cinema now more than ever, and to invest more money

---

163 "Fīlmhā-yi Farhangī" [Educational Films], *Fīlm va Zindigī*, no. 2 (Pāyīz 1336 [Fall 1957]), 15.
164 *Ibid.*
165 "Rādīyaw, Sīnamā, Rūznāmah" [Radio, Cinema, Newspaper], *Mihr*, yr 9, no. 93 (Farvardīn va Urdībihisht 1332 [March and April 1953]), 17.
166 "Fīlmhā-yi Āmūzishī" [Instructional Films], *Āmūzish va Parvarish (Ta'līm va Tarbīyat)* [Instruction and Training (Education and Pedagogy)], yr 26, no. 8 (Murdād 1332 [July 1953]), 463.
167 *Ibid.*
168 "Film va Sīnamā dar Īrān va Khārij" [Film and Cinema in Iran and Outside], *Nāmah-'i Utāq-i Bāzargānī* [Centre of Commerce Newspaper], no. 76 (Day 1337 [January 1959]), 32.
169 *Ibid.*, 31.

in supporting this "art and vehicle for positive recreation."[170] Aside from being an educating and entertaining medium, cinema was also deemed to be a source of income for the country. Aside from creating a significant amount of revenue through the international exportation and distribution of national films, the article believed the production of films in advanced countries to be a great source of national income – especially since those governments levied high taxes on cinema stars and production companies who made a considerable amount of money through their artistic work.[171] "If one considers the large sums of money that [Iranian] cinemas pay to the municipal office for the films that they show" in Iran, then "one can just imagine how much revenue film-producing countries" create.[172] "Cinema taxes" imposed on Iranian films had "increased so much" by the late 1950s that they had led to the "constant complaining of cinema owners." The article encouraged the lowering of taxes in order to promote a "national cinema" which could export its cultural productions internationally – a cinema that would in turn create national revenue for the country.

It was perhaps the plentiful debates, discussions, tensions, dialogues and criticisms conducted through cinematic public spheres that prompted certain laws pertaining to cinemas to change and some film institutions to form in this period. For instance, in a 1954 letter to the Prime Minister, the Industrial Deputy of the Ministry of National Economy, Ḥabīb Nafīcī (Naficy), complained about the high taxes imposed by Tehran Municipality on Iranian films that, in his opinion, had led to the recession of the work of the national industry, which was held together by "tasteful Iranian youth."[173] The author believed that, with the cutting of taxes on Iranian films, the industry would grow faster. Not only would the development of the industry create more jobs for the youth, artists and technicians, but it would prevent the Iranian currency from exiting the country; the exportation and screening of Iranian films outside Iran, the author believed, would bring more money into the country and thus help the economy.[174]

---

[170] *Ibid.*   [171] *Ibid.*, 32.   [172] *Ibid.*, 33.

[173] "Pīshnahād-i Ḥabīb Nafīsī mabnī bar Kāhish-i ʿAvāriz-i Fīlmhā-yi Īrānī: Sanad-i Shumārah-'i 119" [The Recommendation of Habib Naficy Concerning Tax Cuts for Iranian Films: Document Number 119], in *Asnādī az Mūsīqī, Tiʾātr va Sīnamā dar Īrān (1300–1357)*, vol. 2, 584–585.

[174] *Ibid.*, 584.

In 1956, *Sitārah-'i Sīnamā* also published a number of articles –
addressing the Ministry of the State and Municipality – that objected
to the high taxes on Iranian films and imported foreign films.[175]
One article deemed it "necessary" for the authorities to reduce the
40 per cent tax levied on Iranian films, and to also cut down the high
taxes inflicted on foreign films.[176] Such high taxes levied on imported
films, the article contended, prompted the flow of "deplorable" commercial foreign titles to Iranian movie theatres, and halted the importation of "excellent and interesting" films that – while pivotal to the
history of cinema – were believed to have "limited audiences."[177]
Expressing the general opinion that state-funding "restrictions only
applied to the works of art," and not commercial films, the same article
objected to the government's neglectful attitude toward the state of the
arts in the country.[178] In fact, the taxes on Iranian films were only
15 per cent until 1954, when a newly formed commission (Commission of Theatres) in Tehran municipality – which believed Iranian films
to have "profited immensely" and the City Hall to "require more
budget" – raised the taxes on Iranian films to 40 per cent.[179] As such,
following the tax increase in 1954, many cinema periodicals expressed
their concerns over the problems arising from high taxes enforced on
Persian film studios.

In line with the nationalist agenda of the state and visions of the
people in the industry, the state implemented some measures that would
not only promote national cinema, but aimed to advertise a civilised,
industrialised and glorious Iran to a global audience. The 1954 decree
by the government, for example, necessitated the screening of two
Persian films in Iranian movie theatres, at a time when Iranian film
production had not yet fully consolidated. Critics such as Kāvūsī took
issue with the decree. "For those who see a horizon beyond the tip of
their nose," Kāvūsī stated, this official decision seemed "ridiculous";[180]
if Persian films were good enough to watch, he believed, then "there

[175] "Taqlīl-i 'Avāriz-i Fīlmhā-yi Fārsī Muvāzī Bā Taqlīl-i 'Avāriz-i Fīlmhā-yi Khārijī
Bāyad Sūrat Bigīrad" [The Tax Reduction on Iranian Films Must Be
Implemented Parallel to the Tax Reduction on Foreign Films], *Sitārah-'i
Sīnamā*, yr 3, no. 79 (Shahrīvar 25, 1335 [September 16, 1956]), 2.
[176] *Ibid.*   [177] *Ibid.*   [178] *Ibid.*
[179] "Rāji' bah 'Avāriz-i Fīlmhā-yi Fārsī Chah Nazarī Dārīd?" [What Do You Think
about the Taxes on Persian Films?], *Payk-i Sīnamāyī-yi Nijāt*, no. 7 (Ābān 8,
1333 [October 30, 1954]), 20.
[180] Kāvūsī, "Fīlm-i Fārsī, Fīlm-i Dūblah-'i Fārsī," 21.

was no need for their imposition" in cinema programs.[181] The best
solution to "eliminate dubbed films," Kāvūsī exclaimed, was to enhance
the technical and artistic quality of national films.[182] Later on, with the
creation and efficient operation of cinema clubs and semi-governmental
institutions, more Iranian films would be commissioned by the state.[183]
Filmmakers and critics such as Farrokh Ghaffari established the
National Film Centre in 1949, where critically acclaimed international
films would be screened until 1951, when Ghaffari left for France.[184]
With the help of the government-run Fine Arts Administration,
Ghaffari revived the National Film Centre again in 1959, and screened
foreign language and Iranian films.[185] As Chapter 5 will demonstrate,
starting in the mid-1960s, a number of governmental and semi-
governmental institutions such as the Ministry of Culture and Arts
and the Centre for the Intellectual Development of Children and Young
Adults were established in Iran which promoted Iran's "national"
cinema, and especially the alternative cinematic movement.

In spite of cinema regulations, code revisions, commissions and
film review departments, there were still never-ending criticisms aimed
at the inefficiency of such apparatuses for failing to prevent the
screening of films that were deemed as "immoral," and for censoring
and preventing films that critics claimed as "worthy," "moral" and
"significant" in the history of cinema. Despite the ways in which
such state apparatuses aimed (and functioned) to intervene in the
processes of producing and circulating meaning in films,[186] Iranian
directors found ways to circumvent certain restrictions, while Iranian

---

[181] *Ibid.*   [182] *Ibid.*
[183] In the 1960s and 1970s, for example, the General Office of National Cinematic
Administration had commissioned the production of a number of films to
promote the cultural and national history of Iran. By 1969, *The Shah Mosque
of Isfahan* by Khusraw Sīnāyī and *The Jāmiʿ Mosque of Isfahan* by Manūchihr
Tayyāb were already in production, while *Mahābād* by Sohrab Shahid Sales
was ready for screening, according to an article in *Firdawsi* magazine. See
"Khabarhā-yi Tāzah az Sīnamā-yi Īrān" [News from Iran's Cinema], *Firdawsi*,
no. 919 (Tīr 23, 1348 [July 14, 1969]), page number not available.
[184] Naficy, *A Social History of Iranian Cinema*, vol. 2, 182.   [185] *Ibid.*, 183.
[186] For a comprehensive discussion of censorship and films that had been either
banned or modified by the Commission of Theatres in the 1950s and the
Ministry of Arts and Culture in the 1960s and 1970s, see Jamal Umid, *Tārīkh-i
Sīnamā-yi Īrān: 1279–1357* [*The History of Iranian Cinema: 1900–1979*]
(Tehran: Rawzanah Publications, 1995), 871–891.

audiences received and negotiated multiple meanings enabled through their socio-historical contexts.

After having moved from one ministry to another in the 1940s and 1950s, in the mid-1960s, the administration and control of film production and review was finally passed to the Office of Supervision and Theatres (Idārah-'i Kull-i Nizārat va Namāyish) of the Ministry of Culture and Arts.[187] Over the next decades, according to 'Alī Asghar Kishānī, with the establishment of a solidified infrastructure for cinema-related activities, the government budget allocated to the Ministry of Culture and the Arts for artistic creations increased in comparison to the previous decades. This increased revenue, as Chapter 5 will show, helped the new cinematic movement to gain strength in the 1960s.[188]

***

By the late 1950s, cinema in Iran had come a long way since the end of World War II. Despite the decade-long hiatus in feature-film production from the late 1930s to late 1940s, cinematic activities did not halt. In fact, the cinematic dynamism of the 1940s and 1950s provided the momentum for the establishment of a sustained Iranian commercial film industry. Post-war national and international propagandist documentary and newsreel screenings, the influx of foreign-language motion pictures, the establishment of dubbing studios and film studios,

---

[187] The practice of reviewing scenarios or motion pictures before public screenings and censoring films, according to Dilek Kaya Mutlu, was also common in Turkey. Film censors, called "controllers," attempted to inscribe the state in Turkish filmmaking "to ensure films conformed to its political and cultural agenda." Film with bad qualities or technical defects, or films that had racy topics or scenes of sexuality, were allegedly banned from presentation and censored through such commissions. The Central Film Control Commission, according to Kaya Mutlu, was responsible for the examination of domestic films and the re-examination of foreign films that were rejected by two other controlling commissions in Istanbul and Ankara. In the context of Iran, many critics and social intelligentsia in the 1940s took issue with the office of censorship (Department of Theatres), then headed by Nilla Cram Cook, and with the Ministry of Work and Propaganda in the early 1950s for failing to stop the screening of "cheap," "immoral" and "corruptive" films. See Dilek Kaya Mutlu, "Film Censorship during the Golden Era of Turkish Cinema," in Daniel Biltereyst and Roel Vande Winkel (eds), *Silencing Cinema: Film Censorship around the World*, (New York: Palgrave Macmillan, 2013), 131.

[188] Kishānī, *Farāyand-i Ta'āmul-i Sīnamā*, 265.

the flourishing of dubbed films, the professionalisation of the people in the industry and craft, and governmental programs all engendered a fertile ground for the basis of a national film industry.

While Iranian cinema screens were used as propagandist sites for competing international forces to win public opinion in the 1940s, a group of film critics, stage actors/actresses, film enthusiasts, producers, dubbing studio owners and artists, who engaged with global cinematic affairs, were busy laying the foundation for this cinema. After the first film studios started operating in the late 1940s, many pursued an investment in the enterprise to gain economic profits, which facilitated the fast commercialisation of the industry and the flourishing of an image consumer culture. The propagation of the images of cinema stars and singers in film journals and movie posters, the inclusion of song-and-dance numbers in national motion pictures, the commercial (low) quality techniques used in filmmaking and hotchpotch mixed genres of films prompted various reactions from the religious and secular social and cultural critics. The cinematic visionary that such reactions engendered, as Chapters 4 and 5 will show, prognosed a direction for the future of national cinema that leaned toward an arthouse cinema.

As Chapter 4 elaborates, apart from a number of historical films that were based on Persian epic poems and folktales in the 1950s, the themes and stories of commercial films mostly concerned the contemporary lives of the masses in urban and rural areas. One of the most prominent narratives of these films was the migration of people from rural areas to urban centres, especially Tehran. The urbanisation of cities, the rapid population growth and the social issues that came with it (i.e. poverty, traffic congestion, pickpocketing and a general disappearance of traditions, rituals and social values and the changing dynamic of families) were featured prominently in these films. Made for commercial profit, the films of this era drew on commercially successful Hollywood, Indian and Egyptian films in themes, titles, characters and settings, rebranded such elements and created motion pictures that spoke to the sensibility of the masses. Many, if not all, of these commercial films included song-and-dance numbers, sometimes as the means to express certain monologues and messages, and sometimes to exploit the sensationalism of seductive dances or steamy scenes. The music and lyrics used in some films were sometimes employed to convey emotions and to narrate everyday circumstances that were borne out of the socio-political currents of the time. Similar to how Gokulsing and Dissanayake have described Indian popular cinema, Iranian commercial film was arguably a narrative of "cultural change";[189] a playful "expression of anxieties" over new social roles.[190] Chapter 4 demonstrates the transformations within commercial cinema by attending to some of the above-mentioned themes, and shows how these films express narratives of cultural change.

[189] K. Moti Gokulsing and Wimal Dissanayake, *Indian Popular Cinema: A Narrative of Cultural Change* (London: Trentham Books, 1998), 21.

[190] Miriam Bratu Hansen, "The Mass Production of the Senses: Classical Cinema as Vernacular Modernism," *Modernism/Modernity* 6(2) (1999): 70, 71.

4 | "Film-Farsi"
Everyday Constituencies of a Cosmopolitan Popular Cinema

The Iranian popular film industry that emerged in the late 1940s and boomed in the 1950s has been almost fully dismissed in both pre-revolutionary and post-revolutionary literature on Iranian cinema. Viewed as "immoral," "vulgar" and "imitative" of Hollywood, Indian and Egyptian films, the national products of this industry came under heavy criticism in the 1950s, and eventually came to be derogatively categorised as "Film-Farsi" or "Persian-Films."[1] In the nationalist cinematic discourse that called for a serious, philosophical or art-house cinema that was befitting of a futural Iran, there was no place for hotchpotch "Film-Farsi" productions. In the post-revolutionary literature, "Film-Farsi" is also regarded as a debased, cheap and obscene industry, and remains maligned in official and most unofficial milieus. In a move to distance the "moral" cinema of post-revolutionary Iran from that of its predecessor, "Film-Farsi" cinema has been almost fully overlooked, if not incriminated.[2] This chapter will aim to discuss in detail the often-unnoticed aspects of this industry, namely, its internal conflicts, social implications, cosmopolitan aspirations and general reception.

By examining discourses surrounding "Film-Farsi" in newspapers and film journals that covered the emergence and development of this enterprise, I articulate Iranian national imaginings in the second Pahlavi era (1941–1979). I argue that in addition to the diversity

---

[1] The concept of "Persian-Film" or "Film-Farsi" (as one compound word) is not to be confused with "Persian Film" (as two separate words), which was a common title given to Persian-language films of the Iranian cinema industry. The concept will be discussed in more length in the following paragraphs.

[2] Pedram Partovi has recently published a book on Iran's pre-revolutionary popular cinema, where he examines notions that signalled the nation in "Film-Farsi" films. At the time of the publication of this book, this is the only book, to the author's knowledge, that specifically attends to this popular cinema before the revolution. See Pedram Partovi, *Popular Iranian Cinema before the Revolution: Family and Nation in FīlmFārsī* (New York: Routledge, 2017).

of people involved in the industry, many films engaged with the content of international popular films in a haphazard, hotchpotch manner. Such assortment of characters, elements, visual motifs and genres that were informed by international films created a cinema viewed by critics as not necessarily "Iranian." With the increased production and projection of films which were considered as "merely entertaining," "inartistic" and "debased," Iran's popular cinema came under attack by both the religious establishment and secular critics who perceived the cosmopolitanism of local film productions as attempts at "imitation," and thus a means to "Westernisation"; attributes that are, to this day, attached to pre-revolutionary commercial films. Nevertheless, globally informed, popular motion pictures were strongly rooted in Iranian lived experience and local circumstances – albeit in excessive and exaggerating modes. While engaging with the commercial elements of Hollywood, European, Egyptian and Indian motion pictures, the films of the "Film-Farsi" industry laid the ground for a multi-layered Iranian national imagining. In this chapter, I examine several films from this cinematic category to highlight the ways in which they evoked an everyday moral substance that was based in the Iranian vernacular traditions, but that drew from the esthetic and narrative vocabulary of international commercial films – cinematic visions with which the Iranian audience was already well familiar. In other words, while conversant with global popular films, the "Film-Farsi" industry simultaneously played out and shaped everyday religiosity and socio-cultural concerns of its time. The cinematic offerings of this industry informed and supplied by a well-developed and trendy image culture, were popular and readily consumed by the masses (Figure 4.1).

With the development of "urban-industrial technology" and a shift to "mass consumption," as Miriam Hansen argues, "new modes of organising vision and sensory perception" and "a changing fabric of everyday life, sociability and leisure" also emerge.[3] Following Hansen, the post–World War II Iranian filmic productions can be considered as "cultural practices" that "articulated and mediated the experience of modernity," especially manifested in the "mass-produced and

---

[3] Miriam Bratu Hansen, "The Mass Production of the Senses: Classical Cinema as Vernacular Modernism," *Modernism/Modernity* 6(2) (1999): 59.

Figure 4.1 Iran's image culture: Iranian actresses looking like Hollywood actresses? Photo by Mondadori Portfolio / Getty Images.

mass-consumed" phenomena of "fashion, design" and "advertising" – phenomena that were common and popular in Iran by the 1950s.[4] In this chapter, I study commercial films as products of "vernacular" modernism, as the vernacular, according to Hansen, "combines the dimension of the quotidian, of everyday usage, with connotations of discourse, idiom, and dialect, with circulation, promiscuity, and translatability."[5] "Film-Farsi," as I will demonstrate, played a part in enacting and facilitating the contestations of Iranian modernity by registering, responding to and working through the conflicts between tradition/modernity, low/high culture, official/unofficial, rural/urban and other societal transformations in a rapidly changing Iran. It was from within the discourses surrounding "Film-Farsi" and through the critics' horizon of expectation that an alternative cinematic trend emerged in the late 1950s and early 1960s. For the most part, the periodicity of this alternative cinema overlapped with that of the popular cinema, therefore blurring the preconceived lines between the commercial and alternative cinemas before the revolution. As such, readers will notice a commonality between the current chapter and Chapter 5, especially in film titles,

[4] *Ibid.*   [5] *Ibid.*, 60.

critiques and narratives. Chapter 5 will then attend to the alternative movement that bore a revolutionary esthetic in cinema before the actual political revolution of 1979.

4.1 The First Stones: The First Post–World War II Fiction Films and Their Reception

The first Iranian film screened in 1948, *Tūfān-i Zindigī* (*The Storm of Life*), was, according to Fakhrī Nāzimī, "a film with Iranian taste, made by Iranians" and with the use of "Iranian actors"; however, it was also a film that did not effectively draw upon "thirty years of experience of foreign [film] specialists who had made efforts" in advancing the art of filmmaking.[6] Although *Tūfān-i Zindigī* – produced by Ismāʿīl Kūshān and directed by ʿAlī Daryābaygī – was a manifestation of Iranian aspirations for cinematic sovereignty and the establishment of a particularly "Iranian cinema," its form was not necessarily favoured by cosmopolitan film critics and intelligentsia. This is interesting considering that Daryābaygī had studied theatre in Germany, while Kūshān had also finished his studies in Germany and had been involved in dubbing and other film projects outside Iran. Many Iranian films made in the coming years were likewise met with skepticism, criticism and, at times, exhortation. Amid a bolstering of nationalist sentiments when attempts were made at reimagining a post–World War II (and post-Mosaddeq) Iran, the flourishing of a national cinema was deemed imperative. As such, the industry's unfolding as an "immoral" and/or "entertaining" one was seen as a disappointment to many cineastes who awaited the crafting of an arthouse cinema.

In a report on the second Persian film to have been produced in the late 1940s, an article in *Sabā* specifically praised Ismāʿīl Kūshān, the producer and cinematographer of the film,[7] for having taken into

---

[6] Fakhrī Nāzimī, "*Tūfān-i Zindigī*" [*The Storm of Life*], *Jahān-i Naw*, yr 3, no. 5 (Khurdād 1327 [May 1948]).

[7] In an interview with Jamal Umid, Kūshān mentions that a German man by the name of Heinrich (he could not recall his last name) assisted him with the film's cinematography. Heinrich, according to Kūshān, had been a political prisoner in Russia. After having being released after the war, he attempted to return to Germany via Iran. See endnote 12 in Jamal Umid, *Tārīkh-i Sīnamā-yi Īrān, 1279–1357* [*History of Iranian Cinema, 1900–1979*] (Tehran: Ruwzanah, 1995), 205.

account the criticisms aimed at the first Persian film produced by him, and yet ignoring the empty negative commentary of the critics.[8] Having worked for three whole months on *Emir's Prisoner* (*Zindānī-yi Amīr*, 1948), in an interview Kūshān claimed to have been happy with the result: "the scenes were bright, the voice-over was clear and in sync with the movement of lips, and the acting of performers, although not perfect, was good enough."[9] The film equipment used was all new (and imported) and different from that used for *The Storm of Life*. With a budget of about 650,000 rials, this 90-minute film production used 20,000 metres of film stock, of which only 3,000 metres were screened. The film was directed by K. Kīyāyī, while Kūshān acted as the producer and screenwriter. The story of the film was claimed to have been based on "Iranian history," blended with a sensational love story and a few exciting war scenes. The story drew on nationalist narratives and racist anti-Arab accounts that had become increasingly prevalent in the writings of nationalists since the early twentieth century. According to *Sabā*'s article, the story of the film was about an Iraqi Arab tyrant who attacks Iran, arrests the Emir of Iranian Kurds, and imprisons the daughter of the Emir and takes her into his haram by force. The fiancé of Emir's daughter, however, finds a dissatisfied vizier in the royal household and schemes against the tyrant. Dressed as a sorcerer, the fiancé finds a way into the palace where his lover is held captive, kills the tyrant with the help of a small recruited army, frees the Emir from imprisonment and then marries his daughter.[10] The film was screened at Rex Cinema and Humāy Cinema in Tehran. The music of the film was prepared by Ismāʿīl Mihrtāsh (1904–1980). The film reportedly also included many interesting scenes of Kurdish folk dance and songs.

Prior to the screening of *Emir's Prisoner*, a 15-minute newsreel was showcased that was made by News Film (Khabar Fīlm) under the supervision of the "*Sabā* Office," and which was produced by Kūshān Filming Institution (Sāzimān-i Fīlmbardārī-yi Kūshān). Displaying the extant statist nationalist rhetoric, the newsreel depicted Mohammad Reza Shah's trip to Isfahan and the inauguration of the construction of Kūhrang Tunnel. The *Sabā* article further heralded that News Film planned to make more short films about important events in Iran, to

---

[8] "Duvvumīn Fīlm-i Fārsī: *Zindānī-yi Amīr*" [Second Persian Film: *The Emir's Prisoner*], *Sabā*, yr 7, no. 12 (Mihr 28, 1327 [October 20, 1948]), 16.
[9] *Ibid.*   [10] *Ibid.*

"make all Iranians aware of the events in the country" and "to introduce our beloved Iran to the world."[11] As film institutions continued to develop in the country, Iranian newsreels increased in number and replaced those of international origin, contributing to nationalist sentiments channelled by the young Pahlavi government. Arguably, such newsreels and documentaries featured before commercial Persian motion pictures sought to convey to the masses an image of a young, strong-willed and progressive Shah representing a new country on a path toward advancement. Such moving images in cinema accompanied textual and visual illustrations in magazines that depicted the Shah on visits to various industrial projects or delivering speeches at different events across the country.[12]

Kūshān's interest in cinema went beyond his attempts at filmmaking for domestic audiences. Describing cinema as "a manifestation of contemporary world civilisation," Kūshān expressed his cosmopolitan outlook by conveying his desire for Iranian cinema to go global; he remarked that "all the artists who want to introduce Iranian art and culture to the world" must "gather" and "with the help of one another develop this apparatus."[13] Cinema, he added with a patriotic tone, "does not belong to me alone, but rather to Iran and Iranian people."[14] Conceptualising cinema as a space for the "gathering of Iranian artists," as well as a "device through which artists could stage their art to Iran and the world," Kūshān attested to the compatibility of nationalism and cosmopolitanism, while projecting a path for the future cinema.[15]

Another historical film produced in the early 1950s was *Agha Muhammad Khan of Qajar* (*Āghā Muhammad Khān-i Qājār*, 1954), which was advertised as the "first Iranian historical film" with an "excellent and unprecedented set design" in a film poster published in *Payk-i Sīnamā* (*Cinema Messenger*) periodical (Figure 4.2).[16]

---

[11] *Ibid.*
[12] See, e.g., the cover page of *Sabā*, yr 5, no. 11 (Khurdād 20, 1326 [June 11, 1947]), or the cover page for *Sabā*, yr 5, no. 17 (Tīr 31, 1326 [July 23, 1947]).
[13] "Duvvumīn Fīlm-i Fārsī," 16.   [14] *Ibid.*
[15] *Ibid.* Starting in the late 1950s and early 1960s, an ever-increasing number of Iranian films found their way to international movie theatres and film festivals. Chapter 5 examines some of these films.
[16] "*Āghā Muhammad Khān-i Qājār*: az Fardā Shab dar Sīnamāhā-yi Humāy va Īrān" [*Agha Muhammad Khan of Qajar*: From Tomorrow Night at Cinema Humāy and Iran], *Payk-i Sīnamā*, yr 1, no. 9 (Āzar 6, 1333 [November 27, 1954]), Announcement 38.

Figure 4.2 Poster for *Agha Muhammad Khan of Qajar* (1954)

Starring prominent stage actors such as Nusratullāh Muhtasham, Zhālah, Murīn, Matīn and Taslīmī, the film reportedly included images from "wars in the Caucasus," "events and conspiracy plots during the Qajar era," "Eastern dances" and "scenes from the Harem of Agha Muhmmad Khan of Qajar."[17] In 1955, Hūshang Ghadīmī, a film critic, considered *Agha Muhammad Khan of Qajar* as "one of the best Persian films produced, if not the best."[18] According to Tughrul Afshār, however, the film was not historically accurate, since it depicted Qajar women as tall and slender and showcased European fashion and modern gestures, while the actual women of Qajar harems were plump and large with distinctive unibrows.[19] The author agreed with other critics that Nusratullāh Muhtasham, the stage actor who had directed the film and played the role of Muhammad Khan, was a competent actor. Although still not convinced that Muhtasham was a "cinema actor," Afshār regarded Muhtasham to have been one of the best to have appeared on cinema screens up until that date. The creators of the film had used the Qajar Gulistan Palace for the setting, albeit embellished with decor and costumes that were not executed in the best possible fashion.[20] Despite the technical weaknesses of the film, especially in terms of sound recording, Afshār still considered *Agha Muhammad Khan* as a film superior to other productions of the same year, namely, *Nughl-'Alī* (1954) and *The Millionaires* (*Mīlyūnirhā*, 1954), which were deemed as strictly commercial and "worthless."[21] *The Bride of Tigris* (*'Arūs-i Dijlah*) was yet another historical production from 1954 which, according to its published film poster in *Payk-i Sīnamā*, cost over 250,000 tumans (an expensive production for its time) and took more than two years to finish.[22] Also including scenes of "Eastern dances" and the "most famous Iranian actors," Zhālah, Murīn, Rakhshānī and Matīn, the film attended to events from the time of the Abbasid Caliph, Harun al-Rashid and his vizier, Ja'far Barmaki from the influential Barmaki family, who was beheaded for unclear reasons.[23]

[17] *Ibid.*

[18] Hūshang Ghadīmī, "Intiqād-i Fīlmhā-yi Haftah: *Āghā Muhammad Khān-i Qājār*" [A Critique of This Week's Films: *Agha Muhammad Khan of Qajar*], *Sitārah-'i Sīnamā*, no. 21 (Bahman 1333 [January 1955]), 17.

[19] Tughrul Afshār, "Intiqādī bar Fīlmhā-yi Daw Haftah-'i Akhīr" [A Critique of Films from the Last Two Weeks], *Payk-i Sīnamā*, yr 1, no. 10 (Āzar 20, 1333 [December 11, 1954]), 24.

[20] *Ibid.*   [21] *Ibid.*, 25.

[22] "*'Arūs-i Dijlah*: Buzurgtarīn va Mujallaltarīn Fīlm-i Tārīkhī-yi Fārsī" [*The Bride of Tigris*: The Biggest and Most Extravagant Historical Persian Film], *Payk-i Sīnamā*, yr 1, no. 9 (Āzar 6, 1333 [November 27, 1954]).

[23] *Ibid.*

A Girl from Shiraz (Dukhtarī az Shīrāz, 1953) by Samuel
Khāchīkīyān – which in the "first two weeks of its screening was well
received by a hundred thousand people in the capital" – was lauded by
publications in Tehran as "one of the best Persian films" to have
been screened.[24] The Last Night (Ākharīn Shab, 1955), by Hussayn
Dānishvar, was likewise praised as a "real drama-thriller" by the film
magazine Sitārah-'i Sīnamā (Cinema Star).[25] The story of The Bandit
(Rāhzan, 1955), by Sīyāmak Yāsimī, was praised as "an entirely indigenous tale," where "the real life of nomads and customs and
mores ... love, chivalry, and hospitality of Kurds," were depicted in
a "very exciting" narrative.[26] In fact, according to Sitārah-'i Sīnamā,
these scenarios and motion pictures were successful "not only inside
Iran but also outside."[27]

Hansen considers classical Hollywood (from 1917 to 1960) as
"the very symbol of contemporaneity, the present, modern times," as
a cultural practice "on a par with the experience of modernity" that
held an appeal for the intellectuals of the United States and other
modernising countries, as well as emerging mass publics.[28] Following
Hansen, Hollywood's modernity and "appropriative flexibility"[29] was
significant "in mediating competing cultural discourses on modernity
and modernisation" in other parts of the world too; as it "articulated,
multiplied, and globalised a particular historical experience,"[30] it
spoke to culturally and ethnically diverse audiences outside its original
home. For the same reasons, Hollywood's genres and concern
with external appearance and the sensual were easily dissolved and
integrated into Iranian generic traditions. In fact, some critics and
filmmakers unabashedly encouraged the inclusion of scenes that were
compatible with the popular tropes of Hollywood and other international mainstream films, as long as they were appropriately used.
The Falcon of Tus (Shāhīn-i Tūs, 1954), a historical drama, for
example, was meant to include scenes of "fighting and horseback

---

[24] "Dukhtarī az Shīrāz" [A Girl from Shiraz], Sitārah-'i Sīnamā, yr 1, no. 7
(Tīr 2, 1333 [June 23, 1954]), 7.
[25] "Yik Dirām-i Muhayyij-i Vāqaʻī: Ākharin Shab" [A Real Drama-Thriller:
The Last Night], Sitārah-'i Sīnamā, no. 20 (Day 1333 [January 1955]), 9.
[26] "Rāhzan" [The Bandit], Sitārah-'i Sīnamā, no. 21 (Bahman 1333 [January
1955]), 12.
[27] Ibid.   [28] Hansen, "The Mass Production of the Senses," 65.   [29] Ibid.
[30] Ibid., 69.

riding similar to American [western] films," but had encountered many problems, as the artists did not know how to ride horses and there were insufficient resources for the production of such a film.[31] The seriousness of the situation was such that when one of the actors, Jamshīd Mihrdād, fell off a horse during production, he refused to get back on to continue filming. In a report on the The Port Thief (Duzd-i Bandar, 1955), a ten-month-long production by Studio Shahrzād which was classified as a detective-drama, Pourzand remarked that some sections of the film resembled scenes from the American film, Black Jack or The Ghost Ship (1952), screened at Crystal Cinema a few years back. The scenes were so comparable that he believed an "Eastern" Black Jack had been produced in Iran.[32] Such similarities – noted by critics – indicate to what extent Persian productions (scenes, characters and cinematic style and language) were visually and categorically informed by international films showcased in movie theatres in Iran.[33] To make the production more convincing, the film had casted a boxing crew for its fight scenes; Mubārakīyān, "the black boxer from Abadan," as well as Javād Tarkpūr, the "former boxing champion of Tehran," were among the actors in this film.[34] Introducing such "new" and real elements in the film, Pourzand predicted that The Port Thief would be "a fresh film in its own genre" in the spring of 1955.[35]

Despite the initial appraisals of Persian-language and especially historical films, it did not take long for critics and reporters to attack popular films for what they perceived as their "repetitive" themes and "degenerative" narratives. In a column entitled "A Critique of Films from the Last Two Weeks," Tughrul Afshār provided a detailed and mainly negative review of A Girl from Shiraz, produced by Dīyānā (Diana) Film Studio.[36] Highlighting both the positive and the negative aspects of the film, Afshār remarked that A Girl from Shiraz demonstrated the same "decay" (pūsīdigī) and "degeneration" (ibtizāl) as

---

[31] "Zarrah-bīn-i Sīnamā" [The Magnifying Glass of Cinema], Payk-i Sīnamā, yr 1, no. 9 (Āzar 6, 1333 [November 27, 1954]), 2.

[32] Pourzand, "Dar Atrāf-i Istūdīyaw-hā-yi Īrānī: Istūdīyaw Shahrzād" [Around Iranian Studios: Shahrzad Studio], Payk-i Sīnamā, yr 1, no. 10 (Āzar 20, 1333 [December 11, 1954]), 23.

[33] Ibid.   [34] Ibid.   [35] Ibid.

[36] Tughrul Afshār, "Intiqādī bar Fīlmhā-yi Daw Haftah-'i Akhīr" [A Critique of Films from the Last Two Weeks], Nijāt, yr 1, no. 3 (Khurdād 18, 1333 [June 8, 1954]), 24. A Girl from Shiraz was directed by Samuel Khāchīkīyān.

other Persian films.[37] The film starts with a flashback where 'Āyishah (Aisha), a girl from Shiraz who has just lost her child due to poverty, tells the story of her misfortunes to a young man called Sīrūs. When a young adult, she is introduced to a young man, Afshār – a conniving man who marries 'Āyishah only to arouse the jealousy of his true love, Munīr, who lives next door. Once he attracts Munīr's attention and affection, Afshār stops caring for 'Āyishah. Munīr plots to dispose of her rival; she accuses 'Āyishah of poisoning Afshār and throws her into jail. Upon her release, 'Āyishah, who has given birth to Afshār's child in prison, becomes an aimless drifter on the streets, and, is forced into prostitution and cabaret singing until she meets Sīrūs.[38] In a series of events, Munīr marries Afshār, then kills her husband as she courts other lovers, and is finally murdered herself. Before her demise, however, Munīr becomes convicted as a criminal, and therefore her charges against 'Āyishah are dropped. From then on, 'Āyishah begins a new life with Sīrūs, the man whom she now loves.[39]

The critic considered some aspects of *A Girl from Shiraz* to have been "unnatural"; for example, "prostitutes" and "debased people" who live under terrible conditions were depicted as "beautiful"; fallen women were obliged to work as "singers" in cabaret venues, as if "the art of singing" was reserved for the corrupt "entertainment" (mutribī) industry. In his commentary, the reviewer reproduced the binaries between low art and high art that had been at the centre of debates on Iranian modernity since the turn of the twentieth century; cabaret venues – as spaces where women moved their bodies in song-and-dance numbers – were envisioned as seditious forms and were therefore thought of as a threat to the progressive and moral image of the nation; minstrel singing, on the other hand, as the unofficial lowbrow culture, was linked to corruption and inferior entertainment forms that had no artistic merit.[40] Moreover, Afshār took issue with the film's

---

[37] *Ibid.*
[38] The theme of "deceived girl" becomes a popular theme among commercial films from the 1950s to the 1960s.
[39] Afshār, "Intiqādī bar Fīlm-hā," 24.
[40] For more information on the creation of dominant categories of "high" or "modern" art and "inferior" cultural realms in modern Iran, see Ida Meftahi, *Gender and Dance in Modern Iran: Biopolitics on Stage* (Abingdon: Routledge, 2016). Meftahi investigates the discourses surrounding the public dancing body from the early twentieth century to the post-revolutionary era to examine the ways in which certain cultural realms were "othered" and marginalised in

attention to the topic of "personal revenge," which in a "progressive world," like that of Iran, was a ridiculous and unworthy topic.[41] From a social perspective, the author believed that the film had tried to convey a moral lesson by relying on the notion that "a corrupt environment is to blame" for prostitution and corruption in Iranian society – albeit to no avail. Afshār was convinced that the film was very far from the "ordinary and real life" of Iranians in its unrealistic and romantic depiction of events.[42] Such comments may direct us to the ways in which some popular films functioned to criticise the ruling government and its incompetence in establishing a moral and just order in the country. They also point to the ways in which cosmopolitan critics attempted to promote a national cinema that depicted everydayness in a social realistic cinematic language – a cinematic form that, as Chapter 5 demonstrates, emerged in the late 1950s and consolidated into a movement in the 1960s. Regardless of the film's shortcomings, the technical aspects such as camera work and montage were, in the eyes of the critic, a major improvement compared to previous Persian films, and the acting of Farah Panāhi and Mahīn Dayhīm were worthy of attention.[43]

Sitārah-'i Sīnamā publication, on the other hand, publicised *A Girl from Shiraz* as "one of the best Persian films" to have been showcased in Iran.[44] Far from being homogenous, the discourse in Iranian film publications was quite contentious and multi-layered. While certain authors and critics downplayed Persian film offerings, others lauded them as "national productions" worthy of special attention and support. In a negative review of the film *Taqdīr Chinīn Būd* (*Destiny Was Such*, 1954), directed by Tirū-Āl Gīlānī and produced by Kāvah Studio, Afshār remarked that film critics and cinephiles were "against the making of such moving reels," since "from an artistic point of view," such film productions worsened the status of the enterprise

comparison to those that were deemed as "modern" and publicly staged as "national." For a discussion of lowbrow music forms such as motrebi which declined with modernity and the booming of highbrow forms of music known as "modern," see G. J. Breyley and Sasan Fatemi (eds), *Iranian Music and Popular Entertainment: From Motrebi to Losangelesi and Beyond* (Abingdon: Routledge, 2016).

[41] Afshār, "Intiqādī bar Fīlmhā," 24.   [42] *Ibid.*   [43] *Ibid.*, 25.
[44] "*Dukhtarī az Shīrāz*" [*A Girl from Shiraz*], *Sitārah-'i Sīnamā*, yr 1, no. 7 (Tīr 2, 1333 [June 23, 1954]), 7.

in Iran.[45] On the other hand, conveying a more positive attitude toward some other national film productions, a review of Samuel Khāchīkīyān's *The Crossroads of Incidents* (*Chahār Rāh-i Havādis*, 1955) stated that even though the film was devoid of the features of a good film, its production was "a promise for the advancement of our national cinema," and to foster encouragement, one *had* "to watch this Persian film."[46]

As demonstrated above, film critics' aim of endorsing the art of cinema not only depended on their promotion of what they deemed as an "appropriate" or "realist" Iranian cinema, but frequently involved demeaning the extant popular Persian film productions. *Payk-i Sīnamā* magazine, for example, was critical of the municipal order that obliged Cinemas Rex and Iran to show "Persian films" such as *Agha Muhammad Khan of Qajar* as part of their mandatory program to "showcase two Persian films per year."[47] Speaking sarcastically about Iran Cinema's program to screen *Agha Muhammad Khan of Qajar* after the American musical, *An American in Paris* (1951), the magazine reported that the cinema hall had been so empty during the third screening on the first night that the dark movie theatre had become "the retreat of lovers."[48]

Many film critics had become weary of the circumstances of Iranian cinema. In a report entitled "A Commentary on the Artistic-Cinematic Environment of Tehran," the editorial board of *Payk-i Sīnamā* magazine bemoaned that "telling the truth" no longer had real value in the present conditions.[49] The guild, according to the report, had become a gossip industry where people would belittle one another for their films and their views on various cultural productions. Studio owners would make films that they considered to be "the best of the best," and if anyone made any criticisms, they would dismiss these as "personal bias" or brush aside the critics as "foreign-worshippers."[50] The report

---

[45] Afshār, "Intiqādī bar Fīlmhā," 25.
[46] A. M., "*Chahār Rāh-i Havādis*" [*The Crossroad of Incidents*], *Sitārah-'i Sīnamā*, yr 2, no. 29 (Farvardin 23, 1334 [April 13, 1955]).
[47] "Zarrah-bīn-i Sīnamā" [The Magnifying Glass of Cinema], *Payk-i Sīnamā*, yr 1, no. 10 (Āzar 20, 1333 [December 11, 1954]), 2.
[48] *Ibid.*
[49] Editorial Board, "Nazarī bah Muhīt-i Hunarī Sīnamāyī-yi Tihrān" [A Commentary on the Artistic-Cinematic Environment of Tehran], *Payk-i Sīnamā*, yr 1, no. 10 (Āzar 20, 1333 [December 11, 1954]), 5.
[50] *Ibid.*

believed that the work of these studios lacked "purpose and methodology," and their only defence mechanism was "vilification."[51] Studios such as Shahrzād Studio, which was established in 1948 and had produced two films "without much commotion," *Innocent Convict* (*Mahkūm-i Bī-gunāh*, 1953) and *The Port Thief* (*Duzd-i Bandar*, 1954), were approved by the critics at *Payk-i Sīnamā*. Shahrzād Studio, according to *Payk-i Sīnamā*, was run by "a number of young people" who made films that, unlike their predecessors, were not "worthless and ridiculous commodities."[52] Such observations and commentaries demonstrate the ways in which elitist cosmopolitan film critics worked to direct the course of the national cinema.

4.2 "Film-Farsi" or "Faux" Persian-Language Films

What were commonly known as "Persian films" from the late 1940s to the early 1950s eventually came to be stereotyped as "Moving Reels" (navār-i mutiharrik) – a title that aimed to highlight the emptiness and triviality of the films' content by emphasising the rapid movement of the reel.[53] Soon after, however, the popular film industry came to be derogatively categorised as "Film-Farsi" (Persian-Film). Dr Hūshang Kāvūsī was the first person to designate Persian-language films as "Film-Farsi" in 1953.[54] Linking the two words "Persian" and "Film" in the hyphenated concept of "Film-Farsi" (Persian-Film), Kāvūsī attempted to draw attention to the one-sided nature of Persian films. According to him, the only indicator of these films' Iranianness was the Persian language used in its dialogues; other aspects of the film were believed to be imitations of international Grade B and C films. Being sensitive to how historical actors regarded commercial films, in this chapter I use the hyphenated construct "Film-Farsi" within quotation marks to denote my adoption of the Persian terminology (as one word)

---

[51] *Ibid.*
[52] Siamak Pourzand, "Dar Atrāf-i Istūdīyaw-hā-yi Īrānī: Istūdīyaw Shahrzād" [Around Iranian Studios: Shahrzad Studio], *Payk-i Sīnamā*, yr 1, no. 10 (Āzar 20, 1333 [December 11, 1954]), 6.
[53] Samuel Khāchīkīyān (Samuel Khachikiyan), "Chigūnah Mītavān Navāqis-i Fīlmhā-yi Fārsī rā Rafʿ Kard?" [How Can the Flaws of Persian Films Be Rectified?], *Sitārah-ʾi Sīnamā*, no. 24 (Day 22, 1333 [January 12, 1955]) 14.
[54] Hamid Naficy, *A Social History of Iranian Cinema*, vol. 2: *The Industrializing Years, 1941–1978* (Durham, NC: Duke University Press, 2011), 149.

used by the practitioners. In other cases, I will refer to commercial films as Persian-language films or Persian films (as separate words).

Reiterating his views on the commercial industry in an article in *Firdawsi* periodical in 1955, Kāvūsī remarked that it had been "almost seven years" since the *"business"* of "Film-Farsi" had begun in Iran; an industry with films that were "unfortunately" of no "cinematic value in absolute form."[55] Highlighting cinema only as an art form, devoid of entertaining qualities, Kāvūsī blamed the government and its affiliated institutions for not paying enough attention to the art of cinema. He believed that if "Film-Farsi" freed itself from its "current puniness," then "people would welcome it" and "would not allow this national art to vanish."[56] On the other hand, entertaining a nuanced view in 1954, Samuel Khāchīkīyān, a film director and critic, both praised and criticised the state of Persian films.[57] Expressing his awareness of commercial films' shortcomings in terms of technical and artistic aspects, Khāchīkīyān believed many factors, including "studio owners, directors ... actors ... unfavourable circumstances ... film critics, the government and audiences," to be involved in the failure or success of a film.[58]

Identifying "Film-Farsis" as "faux films" in 1969, Kāvūsī specifically likened the commercial enterprise of Iranian cinema industry to the trade of fake saffron, lemon juice and jam, which were illegally sold in Iranian bazaars in the presence of "health officials and the authorities of public health," who acted as mere "spectators" to such economic exchanges.[59] Kāvūsī regarded the filmmakers of this mainstream industry and the cinema owners who showcased their films, as well as the national television which featured film announcements to be no less than "merchants" (tājir), thus denoting the commercial quality of the productions of the time.[60] "Newspapers and magazines" were likewise "merchants" in that "they would write well" about films that were "bad," and at times when they thought it necessary, they would "write unfavourably about films that [were] good."[61] In a 1969 article

---

[55] Hūshang Kāvūsī, "Fīlm-Fārsī bah Kujā Mīravad?" [Where Is Film-Farsi Going?] *Ferdawsī*, no. 144 (Tīr 8, 1333 [June 29, 1954]).
[56] *Ibid.*   [57] Khāchīkīyān, "Chigūnah Mītavān," 14.   [58] *Ibid.*
[59] Hūshang Kāvūsī, "Guftah-hā va Nāguftah-hā: Man Tājiram, Taw Tājirī, Ūw Tājir ast" [The Said and Unsaid: I Am a Trader, You Are a Trader, He/She Is a Trader], *Nigīn*, no. 55 (Āzar 1348 [November 1969]), 5.
[60] *Ibid.*   [61] *Ibid.*

entitled "The Friday Bazaar of Film-Farsi," Farhang Farahī also characterised "Film-Farsi" as "ridiculous moving pictures" that had "hindered the progress of the national cinema industry."[62]

Protests against popular cinema and its "imitation" of international commercial films continued into the late 1960s and 1970s. Such cultural criticisms were not conveyed by critics alone and were not limited to cinema either. By the 1960s, theatre was also deemed as inane and absurd for its "imitative" qualities. In 1968, Mahīn Uskūyī, a stage actress, remarked that "a number of imitators" imposed themselves upon the Iranian society in the form of "a confused and aimless theatre prevalent in the degenerate and ill society of the West."[63] Uskūyī held that a form of "transformation" and "revolution" was essential for the Iranian theatre to survive.[64] While some theatrical pieces were considered as imitative, the theatrical performances of Bījan Mufīd, especially his prominent play, *The City of Tales* (*Shahr-i Qissah*), were regarded highly among the critics and intelligentsia. Considered as "the most important representative of modern Iranian theatre," Bījan Mufīd was described as "the Iranian Bertolt Brecht."[65] According to an article in *Firdawsi* magazine, Mufīd grew up in "the street" in the "southern parts of the city," which explained why he "liked the street, its rhythm, and pulse." Mufīd's *The City of Tales*, the article contended, could be conveniently considered as a "musical." However, according to the observations of a German critic, Heinz Ludwig Schneiders, his play had more in common with Brecht's socially committed theatre. Its narrative style, similar to the "naqqālī" style of traditional coffee houses in Iran, did not follow any European models, and yet it placed a "mirror in front of time and humans" to critique those who opposed and resisted "change" and "innovation" based on religious, social and political proclivities.[66] Critics believed that, unlike other theatrical plays and commercial films of the period, *The City of Tales* drew on Persian traditions of storytelling that were withering

---

[62] Farhang Farahī, "Jum'ah Bāzār-i Sīnamā-yi Fīlm-Fārsī" [The Friday Bazaar of Film-Farsi], *Nigīn*, no. 44 (Day 30, 1347 [January 20, 1969]), 25–26.

[63] "Mā Ti'ātr-i Vāqi'ī Nadārīm" [We Do Not Have a Real Theatre], an interview with Mahīn Uskūyī, *Firdawsī*, no. 872 (Murdād 21, 1347 [August 12, 1968]), 18.

[64] *Ibid.*

[65] "Yik Birtult Birisht-i Īrānī" [An Iranian Bertolt Brecht], *Firdawsī*, no. 891 (Day 2, 1347 [December 23, 1968]), page number not available.

[66] *Ibid.*

away, and yet engaged with international models in a sophisticated and explicitly socio-politically conscious manner. Na'lbandīyān, a playwright, was likewise praised as "an intellectual artist" by *Firdawsi* magazine for his "global (jahānī) play," "another 'Becket' of the Mythical East," which was "truly global" in that it engaged salient figures such as "Sartre," "Shakespeare," "Brecht," "Camus," "Forough Farrukhzad,"[67] "Ubayd Zakani" and others.[68] In theatre too, therefore, criticisms were made against commercial and entertaining performances. Such assertions indicate that critics deemed socially committed productions that attended to what they considered as Iranian traditions in realist or innovative forms to be worthwhile cultural enterprises.

Distancing itself from publications such as *Sitārah-'i Sīnamā*, which explored a plethora of Persian films and international commercial motion pictures, *Firdawsi* represented itself as an intellectual magazine and mostly attended to international arthouse films, or alternatively to denigrating Persian film productions. In a 1968 article, the magazine charged Persian films with having made "copies of American films" and having marketed them as "national (vatanī) productions."[69] The author complained that Persian films made use of scenes that were predominant in "foreign" motion pictures, namely "platonic love" and "sexual scenes" that involved both Iranian and non-Iranian actors, such as Bihrūz Vusūghī and "Marina." In films such as *Stranger Come* (*Bīgānah Bīyā*, 1968), where the use of Iranian female characters (i.e. Pūrī Banāyī) in sexually explicit scenes was deemed inappropriate, the author argued that non-Iranian female actors (such as Marina) were cast to allow for a better "imitation" of European New Wave films.[70] Interestingly, such declarations underscore the integration of various aspects of international mainstream films in national commercial productions that were popular among the masses. In another article, nevertheless, *Firdawsi* expressed approval of local young actors such as Farrukh Sājidī, who had "studied acting in Europe" and

---

[67] Furugh Farrukhzad was a prominent Iranian filmmaker and poet.
[68] "'Bikit-i' Dīgarī az Sharq-i Afsānah-'ī" [Another "Becket" from the Mythical East], *Firdawsī*, no. 891 (Day 2, 1347 [December 23, 1968]), page number not available.
[69] Al'ām, "Bakhsh: Khudā Quvvat" [Section: May God Give You Strength], *Firdawsī*, no. 866 (Tīr 10, 1347 [July 1, 1968]), 8.
[70] *Ibid.*

"kept himself away from the degeneracy of Persian cinema."[71] The report stated that it was "much better" for an actor to play "in a few films" rather than a large volume of Persian-language films that were "distorted adoptions" of C- and D-grade Turkish and Arab motion pictures.[72] The competing discourses of periodicals such as *Sitārah-'i Sīnamā* and *Firdawsi* are particularly noteworthy as they embody the same debates that "othered" lowbrow cultural products in the realms of dance, music and cinema for being "imitative," "Westernised" or "entertaining" in order to bring to the foreground a highbrow "national" culture (or cinema in this instance) that was also – ironically – in conversation with European films, particularly critically acclaimed and politically conscious productions.

Regarding it as a "disgrace," an article in *Firdawsi* accused "Film-Farsi" cinema of depicting Tehran's streets as "the unsafest roads" in the world (Figure 4.3).[73] Showing scenes of "murder, crime, betrayal ... grand thefts, street shootings, and horrifying police chases in Tehran," Persian-language films had made a monster out of Tehran, similar to the city of "Chicago during its gangster era."[74] Such scenes were arguably objectionable as they perhaps deterred international tourists from visiting Tehran – especially since tourism had become quite popular in Iran in the late 1960s and 1970s. The author criticised film producers for lying to the public about the advancement of this "national product." What some critics called "improvement" in Iran's cinema industry, the article stressed, was in fact a result of the activities of some actors who depended on their connections and cheek-to-cheek pictures with unknown international actors.[75] Strongly critical of the industry, the author believed Persian films to be "full of [technical] defects" and to have "putrid and banal subjects" which had been "stolen" from "Turkish, Indian, American and Italian junk films."[76] The "art" of the industry, the author mentioned sarcastically, was evocative of the famous expression, "a penny from you, a dance from us" ('abbāsī az shumā, raqqāsī az mā) – an idiom that associated

---

[71] "Yik Chihrah dar Sīnamā-yi Javān" [A Face of the Young Cinema], *Firdawsī*, no. 891 (Day 2, 1347 [December 23, 1968]), page number is not available.
[72] *Ibid.*
[73] '. P., "Īn-ham Pīshraft-i Fīlm-i Fārsī?!" [Such an Improvement for Persian Film?!], *Firdawsī*, no. 873 (Murdād 28, 1347 [August 19, 1968]), page number not available.
[74] *Ibid.*   [75] *Ibid.*   [76] *Ibid.*

Figure 4.3 *Firdawsi* magazine's article on "Film-Farsi" films in 1968

commercial films with minstrel and troubadour performances. Conceiving the whole enterprise as an unnecessary body organ such as the appendix, the author believed that "merchants" of the industry had no right to demand exemption from governmental taxes.[77] Since popular films and the arthouse productions that slowly began to emerge by the late 1950s were both in dialogue with global cinematic productions the main point of concern for critics seemed to relate to the ways in which everyday reality and Iranian customs were depicted in films.

Critics' expressions against the screening of "degenerative" films did not go unnoticed by the government. In 1969, the Theatrical Arts Council (Shawrā-yi Hunar-hā-yi Namāyishī) banned the screening of a number of films from Italy, the United States and India.[78] The films were banned for being "vulgar, teaching immorality, violating human emotions, and being devoid of positive and beneficial aspects."[79] At this time, two main organisations, the Commission of Review and Theatrical Arts Council (under the supervision of the Ministry of Culture and Art) and the Representatives of Home and School Associations (Namāyandigān-i Anjuman-hā-yi Khānah va Madrasah), were responsible for the overview of films and the provision of screening permissions. Despite the activities of such institutions in controlling cultural flow in Iran, cinema was already the locus of social, cultural and political debates.

4.3 "Film-Farsi": Negotiating Modernity and Modernisation

For the reasons mentioned above, pre-revolutionary commercial films have rarely received scholarly attention and analysis in pre- and post-revolutionary eras as they do not readily lend themselves to sophisticated debates. Many religious figures, film critics and secular social thinkers believed the creators of commercial films to follow solely the logic of the market, and thus to include scenes of dancing, revelry and fighting for the sake of profitability. However, the response of the masses as consumers of cinema shed light on these films as popular constructs that were socially conscious and fulfilled consumer desires. As the following paragraphs show, these productions were informed

---

[77] *Ibid.*
[78] "Tawqīfī-hā" [The Prohibited (Films)], *Firdawsī*, no. 919 (Tīr 23, 1348 [July 14, 1969]), page number not available.
[79] *Ibid.*

by the social reality of Iranians and drew on ancient Persian and Islamic values in hyperbolised, grotesque and entertaining cinematic forms.[80] Films of the commercial industry were most often critical cinematic offerings that explored social problems experienced in the lived experiences of Iranians, albeit in entertaining cinematic forms. For a more fruitful analysis, this section divides commercial films of the 1950s to the 1970s into three broad thematic categories that highlight some of the major national debates, concerns and commercial interests of the filmmakers of the era. Exploring a number of films in each category, the following paragraphs explore how popular films – while borrowing from international cinemas' esthetic and narrative language, and including international figures in their plots – registered, reflected upon and negotiated competing discourses of modernity and tensions related to modernisation.

Similar to many other popular cinemas, Iranian commercial cinema included an assortment of genres in its making based on the sensibilities and popular taste of the audience, thus creating hybrid genres that could not necessarily fit into universally recognised and firmly delineated categories. Naficy addresses two distinctive genres in popular film productions: the "stew-pot" and the "tough-guy."[81] The "tough-guy" category, Naficy contends, was modelled after Majīd Muhsinī's *The Chivalrous Villain* (*Lāt-i Javānmard*, 1958), and the "stew-pot" genre was solidified through Sīyāmak Yāsamī's *Qarun's Treasure* (*Ganj-i Qārūn*, 1965).[82] One could argue that Iranian popular cinema did not have "pure genres," but instead blended a romantic genre based on a love story with other genres such as comedy, musical or crime. Rather than dealing with commercial films within specific genres, in the following paragraphs I draw on prevalent social themes that were popular from the late 1950s to the late 1970s. Before exploring these over-encompassing themes, a short examination of Indian popular cinema can perhaps help us better conceptualise the emerging trends in Iranian cinema.

In India, up until the 1940s, cinema was dominated by "mythological," "costume film or 'historical,'" devotional and social themes;

---

[80] For more information on the integration of the nation or "Persian values" in commercial productions, see Partovi, *Popular Iranian Cinema before the Revolution*.
[81] Naficy, *A Social History of Iranian Cinema*, vol. 2, 154.
[82] *Ibid.* Naficy's translations.

films that were primarily concerned with issues of social reform and critique, as well as giving expression to anxieties about national cultural identity.[83] Interestingly, as discussed in Chapter 2, many of these themes were also tackled in the Persian-language productions of the interwar period, especially in attempts to solidify a national culture by highlighting a Persian(ate) heritage – albeit using cosmopolitan figures, themes and settings. In post–World War II Indian commercial cinema, Prassad argues that genre distinctions appeared to hold less value in contrast to Hollywood mass productions, in part due to the absence of the "industrial production logic" prevalent in Hollywood's classical era. Genre-mixing, Prassad contends, may be shown to bear ideological significance, "by means of assemblage rather than invention."[84] The emergence of new-found genres such as the "social" film, itself a hybrid genre – which became the defining feature of Indian mainstream cinema – coincided with social processes and political circumstances, such as post-war uncertainties and political mobilisation following independence. The generic distinctions of Iranian cinema arguably resemble the models of Indian cinema. The popular uprising of 1951 in support of the nationalisation of oil by Prime Minister Mosaddeq (1951–1953), the subsequent international boycott of Iranian oil and the 1953 coup d'état designed and led by the CIA and British MI6 gave way to increased post-war political tensions and social conflicts, which made appearances in films. Themes of victimhood, loss and poverty, especially expressed through the female body, were some of the common tropes of the popular films of this era. In its hybrid genre, Iranian popular film industry, which was for the most part privately owned, drew from the religious culture of mythological and historical films (especially in engendering the distinctive Iranian characteristics of its heroes and mythical figures), drama, American film noir and social prototypes that particularly manifested the contradictions and conflicts in Iranian society of the post-Mosaddeq era.[85]

---

[83] Prassad, "Genre Mixing," 71.   [84] *Ibid.*

[85] I do not mean that none of the films of this era followed generic models or that they could not be categorised according to specific or recognised genres. In fact, one could point to a number of films in the late 1940s and early 1950s that closely followed models of thriller and crime genres. Nevertheless, in this chapter, I am more interested to see how films tapped into Iranian everyday lives in their different accents and forms. Focusing on social themes, rather than genres, would allow for a better understanding of the representation of such lived experiences in films.

Around the mid twentieth century, Iran witnessed a large influx of people from rural areas into urban centres, especially Tehran, which had become a metropolitan site of political importance. With the overpopulation of cities and insufficient urban infrastructure and facilities, new social and cultural problems arose that also became the concern of many films of this period. As the national revenue from the country's industrialisation and oil resources grew and gave way to rapid and sustained processes of urbanisation and social reform, cities became increasingly perceived as dystopic metropolises where class conflicts, cultural differences and political concerns grew swiftly; as such, more films focused on the struggles of everyday Iranians on the street and their means of acclimatisation (or lack thereof) to the rapid processes of change. The films discussed below are only a few examples compared to the large number of feature-film productions that revolved around social themes. They may, however, be studied to probe the social conventions that were employed by directors and film critics based on a cultural consensus. Almost all popular films (especially the large number that tapped into the comedy genre), except for historical films, drew on the post-war social categories discussed in Chapter 3 to tackle social tensions and competing definitions of Iranianness. The contingency of Iranian modernity was depicted, often in exaggerated and stereotypical manners, in the conflicts of tradition/ modernity, low/high culture, official/unofficial, rural/urban and other societal transformations in a rapidly changing Iran. This cinema that emerged out of a post-war and post-Mosaddeq era was increasingly preoccupied with the theme of the "social" which, like Indian cinema, was a hybrid genre. The general themes of the films discussed in the following paragraphs can be described in three broad and at times overlapping categories: "historical films," "rural-urban films" and "social-urban films."

4.3.1 Historical films

Historical films attended to past events and/or myths from the Persianate world that aimed to portray a prosperous ancient culture and society. From the late 1940s to the 1970s, Iranian commercial cinema produced only a few historical films, some of which have already been mentioned above. Although the production of "historical" films was deemed favourable by critics and especially nationalists beginning in the 1930s, it seems that the high cost of the décor and mise-en-scène of such films and the difficulty faced in competing with high-budget international historical productions prevented most filmmakers from engaging in such endeavours. Many of the "historical" films made during this period were based on stories from *Shahnamah* (Firdawsi's *Book of Kings*) and Iranian pre-Islamic mythical legends and (post-Islamic) dynastic figures and national heroes – all glorifying an Iranian past, Persianate heritage and tales that once were – a past projected onto the future.

In its column, "The Magnifying Glass of Cinema," *Payk-i Sīnamā* heralded the launch of the historical production *Nadir the Conqueror of Asia* (*Nādir, Fātih-i Āsīyā*) in 1954, based on the historical events during the time of Nadir Shah of Afshār, variations of which had been staged in Iranian theatres in the early twentieth century as collaborative projects of cosmopolitan Iranians and diasporic communities.[86] The report specifically quoted Nusratullāh Muhtasham (1919–1980), the actor and director of the film and Head of the Commission of Theatres at that time, who planned to be astute in the making of the film so that it could be "projected in advanced countries of the world" – a task that the magazine especially esteemed since it could "supply the world with a live history" of Iran.[87] Muhtasham was a talented and successful stage actor, who was also involved in radio and dubbing projects. Prior to World War II, Muhtasham had acted in Sepanta's cosmo-national movie, *Firdawsi* (1934).

The Falcon of Tus and *Agha Muhammad Khan of Qajar*, as discussed above, were two other historical films that were produced during the early years of Persian-language cinema's re-emergence. Although the film critic, Qadīmī, had an overall favourable view toward *Agha Muhammad Khan of Qajar*, he believed the mise-en-scène of the film to be more theatrical in setting than cinematic; however, "the acting of the actors" was believed to have compensated for the film's technical shortcomings.[88] In his column, "A Critique of Films from the Last Two Weeks," Afshār considered *Agha*

---

[86] This film was never completed and released.

[87] "Zarrah-bīn-i Sīnamā" [The Magnifying Glass of Cinema], *Payk-i Sīnamā*, yr 1, no. 9 (Āzar 6, 1333 [November 27, 1954]), 2.

[88] Hūshang Qadīmī, "Intiqād-i Fīlmhā-yi Haftah: *Āghā Muhammad Khān-i Qājār*" [A Critique of This Week's Films: *Agha Muhammad Khan of Qajar*], *Sitārah-'i Sīnamā*, no. 21 (Bahman 1333 [January 1955]), 17.

Muhammad to be the kind of film that could be visually and technically "decomposed and analysed," since its production had cost its
producers much money and effort.[89] From a historical point of view,
however, Afshār considered *Agha Mohammad* to contradict historical
narratives and records, particularly in terms of the Khan's assassins
and the manner in which he was murdered according to the author, the
film had portrayed an image of the Qajar dynasty which was much
better than the reality – an issue that Afshār disapproved of.[90] Regardless of its subject, *Agha Muhammad Khan of Qajar* was a historical
film with a significant historical archive in that it "used real scenes
from the inside of Gulistan palace."[91]

One of the most successful historical films of the 1950s was
Amīr-Arsalān (or *Amīr-Arsalān-i Nāmdār*, 1955), produced by the
cosmopolitan director and producer, Ismā'īl Kūshān, and directed by
Shāpūr Yāsamī.[92] The movie was based on the Persian epic of Amīr
Arsalān, about the Anatolian prince whose father, Malikshāh, had
been dethroned by the Roman King Patras. The movie mainly focused
on Arsalān's love story and portrayed his successful military cam-
paigns to the Roman lands (Constantinople), and included exciting
scenes of sorcery and a happy ending. Although the film was not well
received by film critics, it was very successful at the box office.[93] *Yūsuf
and Zulaykhā* (1956), directed by Sīyāmak Yāsamī, which drew
from the biblical and Quranic story of Joseph and Potiphar's wife,
Zulaykhā, was another film of the historical genre. The film was not
very successful at the box office.[94] *Rustam and Suhrāb* (1957), directed
by Shāhrukh Rafī', was based on Firdawsi's *Shahnamah*. Adopting the
famous story of Iran's historical and mythical hero, Rustam, and
his son, Suhrāb, the film was an expensive production in that it
included the construction of a "fake dragon," an elaborate décor and
maquettes, and featured a large number of swords, spears and shields,
as well as historical costumes.[95] The film, however, was not

[89] Tughrul Afshār, "Intiqādī bar Fīlmhā-yi Daw Haftah-'i Akhīr" [A Critique of
Films from the Last Two Weeks], *Payk-i Sīnamā*, yr 1, no. 10 (Āzar 20,
1333 [December 11, 1954]), 24.
[90] *Ibid.*   [91] *Ibid.*, 25.
[92] According to Umid, the movie was partially directed by Ismā'īl Kūshān and
Kasmāyī. See Umid, *Tārīkh-i Sīnamā-yi Īrān*, 265–266.
[93] See *ibid.*, 265–266.   [94] *Ibid.*, 282.
[95] Ahmad Maghāzah-yī, "*Rustam va Suhrāb*," *Sitārah-'i Sīnamā*, yr 4, no. 101
(Bahman 28, 1335 [February 17, 1957]).

commercially successful. 'Alī Muhammad Nūrbakhsh's *Laylī va Majnūn* (*Layli and Majnun*, 1956) was another film that fit within the genre of historical films for its narrative, costumes and mise-en-scène; the film was based on the popular story of Layli and Majnun, which had previously been made into a film in Iran. While produced by some of Iran's cosmopolitan cultural trendsetters, these historical films continued the tradition of cosmo-national films of the 1930s by glorifying the heroes of an ancient Persianate culture and/or Islamicate society. Some Iranian-Turkish co-productions in the 1970s such as *Hak Yolu* (1971) and *Shirin and Farhad* (1970) could also be considered as part of the category of pre-revolutionary historical (and mythological) films, in that they touched upon historical and mythical narratives of Persian and Turkic dynasties in the region. However, as Iranian cinema consolidated, the production of historical films decreased in number until the post-revolutionary era when television and cinema institutions began producing a large number of historical films.

4.3.2 Rural-Urban Migration Films

In contrast to historical narratives, "rural-urban migration" was one of the most common themes or tropes in the commercial film industry. These films depicted the increasingly common migration of ruralists to big cities for work and prospects of a better life in an industrialising and modernising Iran. While painting a pure and naïve picture of country folk, the films of this category praised the overall modest, mentally gratifying and comfortable life in rural parts. Such representations were portrayed against the dystopic urban life and the greedy, distressed and degenerate city inhabitants. The theme of these films arguably echoed the kind of sentiments that were evoked in the first cosmo-national films of the 1930s, namely *Mr Haji*, *The Cinema Actor* and *The Lur Girl*.

The musical/comedy/drama, *The Farm's Nightingale* (*Bulbul-i Mazra'ah*, 1957), written and directed by Majīd Muhsinī, tells the story of a farmer boy, Shīrzād, and his sister, Gulnāz, who are in love with their landlord's city-dwelling daughter (Shuhrah) and son (Cyrus) respectively. Although the two couples have grown to love one another,[96] their marriage is seen as impossible by the landlord given their different social

---

[96] The landlord and his family used to live on the farm before they moved to the city.

backgrounds and the landlord's concern over his family's reputation.
Since as an educated man Cyrus could afford life in the city and could
change his new wife's rural mores, he receives his father's permission to
marry Gulnāz; Shuhrah and Shīrzād's marriage, however, remains an
unthinkable affair, given Shīrzād's poor and rural circumstances. Disappointed in her father's decision, love-stricken Shuhrah becomes seriously
ill – a situation that obliges her father to agree to her marriage with
Shīrzād. *The Farm's Nightingale* was screened in Russia at the Moscow
International Film Festival.[97] Similar to other films by Majīd Muhsinī,
The Farm's Nightingale was a discourse on displacements and changes
that made an impact on the moral fabric of a society in transition. While
capturing Persian norms and traditions that had disappeared in city life –
such as rural wedding traditions, folk dances and religious sentiments
that were still honoured in rural areas – the need for social reform also
loomed large. Traditional practices such as arranged marriages were
questioned and the alternative modern forms of love were encouraged.
Denoting class conflict and cultural differences, the film represented
villagers as honest, generous, trustworthy and "unaffected by civilisation," and city-dwellers as conniving, phony and soulless.

A *Vent of Hope* (*Rawzanah-'i Umīd*, 1958) tells the story of a poor
rural man in a city that is governed by money. Muhsin, from Isfahan,
wins the lottery and travels to Tehran to claim his prize. When he
arrives in busy Tehran, his luggage is swapped with the luggage of a
cabaret singer/dancer, Nasrīn, who then uses the prize money to buy
her own cabaret venue. Penniless in the city, Muhsin first finds employment in a stockyard and then as a busboy at the cabaret venue owned
by Nasrīn. An independent woman, Nasrīn is first portrayed as cold
and insensitive, but Muhsin's innocence and goodness win her over.
Upon hearing his misfortunes and overcome with guilt, Nasrīn writes
Muhsin a cheque for the money he won at the lottery. *A Vent of Hope*
included scenes conveying Iranian sensibility, which arguably ensured
commercial return and audience satisfaction. In a social realist turn,
the film includes footage from the stockyard where real labourers
are depicted in action, accompanied by Muhsin performing a song.
The lyrics read, "God is the one who protects and provides for people
in miraculous ways," implicitly broaching the subject of government
incompetency in responding to the needs of the poor in the country.

[97] Naficy, *A Social History of Iranian Cinema*, vol. 2, 154.

The song further calls on Iranians to work hard, for "Iran is needless of the world" and its soil is made of "gold," therefore stirring patriotic sentiments and criticising reliance on international forces, especially in a post-Mossadegh setting.

Tongue-Tied (*Zabūn-Bastah*, 1965) symbolised all Iranian characteristics that were deemed sacred in a rapidly changing society. The film tells the story of Safar-'Alī, a landless farmer who lives an arduous but happy life with his wife, Leila, in a small village. The master of the farm, however, has his eye on Leila, and makes numerous attempts to dispose of Safar-'Alī. Highlighting the power of money among city-dwellers, the film attends to drug-dealing and gangs in the city. In contrast, highlighting Safar-'Alī's respect for honour (at times above the law), naïveté, honesty, cooperation with the government authorities, hatred for drugs, his regard for family values (which were depicted on the brink of destruction due to the rampage of drugs and drug-dealers in the cities) and modesty, the film alludes to virtues that were slowly disappearing in urban Iran. In other words, Safar-'Alī represented the nostalgia for the "ideal Iranian" who no longer was. Touching upon the conflict between private and official law, this film valorises personal justice above the law, since "among villagers, the tradition is to counter force (zūr) with force."[98] The film further attends to socio-political conditions of the time in a satirical tone, especially the 1963 land reforms of the White Revolution. When in the presence of gang members Safar-'Alī proudly remarks that he owns some land that spans "two and a half metres," he becomes the source of the gang members' ridicule, who then sarcastically remark that with "all the commotion that has been made" about the land reforms, "the circumstances of villagers have gotten much better." The White Revolution (1962–1963), led by the Pahlavi government, was aimed at reducing the influence and power of large landowners and gaining the support of peasants through the redistribution of lands among the less fortunate. Produced after the revolution, the film aimed to tap into the social discourses and national debates that attended to the outcomes of the reforms. While promoting the cooperation of villagers and the government, *Tongue-Tied* subverted the official state discourse and actions by ridiculing the state's bureaucratic inefficiency

---

[98] Although Safar-'Alī imposes his own sense of justice, he respects the law and law enforcement.

that took advantage of the peasantry's honourable attributes. Similar to *Tongue-Tied*, other films such as *The Naïve* (*Hālū*, 1959)[99] and *The Legend of the North* (*Afsānah-'i Shumāl*, 1959) also explored the conflicting characteristics of salacious urban dwellers and moral rural people; the struggles between these polar opposites almost always ended with the triumph of the villagers, and the conquest of a rural lifestyle over an urban culture.

Swallows Will Return to the Nest (*Parastūhā bah Lānah Bāz-Mīgardand*, 1963) revolves around the story of 'Alī, a pious farmer,[100] who loses two of his children due to the lack of medical facilities in an Iranian village. After his loss, 'Alī realises that many of the problems in his village result from people's illiteracy, belief in superstitions and lack of educational facilities. In order to provide a better life for his own family and possibly other villagers, 'Alī, sells his property, moves to Tehran and works endlessly as a labourer until he succeeds in sending his son to a medical school in Paris. After a series of events that highlight decadence in Tehran and self-indulging lifestyles in Europe, 'Alī's son succeeds in finishing his studies abroad and moves back to Iran. Meanwhile, 'Alī persuades the villagers – who understand the urgency of establishing a medical facility – to come together and build a medical institute in the village. The actions of 'Alī, his son and other villagers to serve the community stem from their unconditional love for their village or in abstract, the nation, in the absence of governmental and external help. *Shamsī, the Champ* (*Shamsī Pahlivūn*, 1966), by Sīyāmak Yāsamī, also attends to the adventures of two sisters who move from Shiraz to Tehran for work. Faced with unemployment in the big city, one sister becomes a cabaret dancer (a recurrent theme in many Persian films), while the other disguises herself as a man and becomes a personal chauffeur. While situating Tehran as a liminal space that enables shifts and ambiguities in gendered roles, the film criticises the government's projects of modernisation and grand narrative of development by addressing the deceit and hardship endured by the sisters in Tehran, albeit in a light, romantic and comedic manner. Other films such as

---

[99] Not to be confused with Dariush Mehrjui's *Āqā-yi Hālū* (*Mr Naïve*, 1971).

[100] 'Alī's piety is characteristically made clear by the filmmaker as the first scene in the movie shows 'Alī praying on his farm.

The Misguided Child (Farzand-i Gumrāh, 1955), *The Sun Glistens* (*Khurshīd Mīdirakhshad*, 1956) and *A Friendship Pact* (*Paymān-i Dūstī*, 1959) also explore the lives of individuals who move to Tehran to leave their destitution and misfortune, only to find themselves in a relentless and cruel city that is riddled with poverty, debauchery and drugs.

4.3.3 *"Social-Urban" films*

In the above-mentioned examples, it is evident that the theme of rural-urban migration was mostly coupled with notions related to unpleasant urban experiences, occurrences that were marked by unfamiliarity and injustice in the city. In fact, the majority of commercial films that were made from the 1950s to the 1970s – most of which were hybrids of comedy and melodrama genres – explored new and unprecedented social problems that stemmed from urbanisation and modernisation. In their intertextual and multi-generic content, the "social-urban films" examined themes related to women and prostitution, corruptive cabarets, unemployment, poverty, class division, pickpocketing and the emergence of new societal classes (such as "New Money" people) – problems that were perceived to arise or to have increased dramatically with the advent of Iran's urbanisation, modernisation and industrialisation.

Sa'īd Nayvandī's *Eve's Daughters* (*Dukhtarān-i Havvā*, 1961) attends to issues of overpopulation in Tehran and its associated problems such as overpriced and overcrowded apartment buildings. At the beginning of the film, a voiceover accompanies panoramic shots of "the bride of Iranian cities," Tehran, and describes how the "large squares, wide streets, and modern buildings" lure villagers into the "beautiful and mythical" city, in search of "better wages" and "better lives." The issues of population influx are to such an extent, according to the voiceover, that new buildings can no longer meet the demands of the people, therefore creating "housing and rent problems." As the story revolves around the interconnected lives of a group of tenants in a building, the film depicts the conflicts between old and young generations, villager and urban lifestyles, traditional and new social norms, and the ways in which the tenants themselves create means to solve problems arising from urbanisation – again in the absence of a working government.

Figure 4.4 A poster for *Soirée in Hell* (1956)

Soirée in Hell (*Shab Nishīnī dar Jahannam*, 1956),[101] produced by
Mīsāqīyah Studio, was an Iranian attempt at making a high-budget
film that included an elaborate decor unprecedented in Iranian cinema
(Figure 4.4). Directed by Iranian-Armenian filmmakers, Samuel
Khāchīkīyān and Mūshiq Sarvarīyan (or Sarvarī), the film attests to
the interplays between official/unofficial, modern/traditional and
moral/immoral mores, and gives fluidity to the instances of national

---

[101] In a conversation with the author, Arby Ovanessian, an Iranian-Armenian
theatre and film director of the pre-revolutionary era, has mentioned that *Soirée
in Hell* is in fact an adaptation of an Armenian story.

identification in that period. Mesmerised by the idea of acquiring more wealth, Hājī Jabbār, a traditional, rich and stingy father, wants to marry off his "modern" (mutijadid) daughter, Parvīn, to a much older, wealthy man, with no regard for the love that exists between Parvīn and her cousin – indeed, a modern form of love that seemed insignificant to Parvīn's father. One day, however, Hājī Jabbār falls ill. While sleeping, he dreams that he has been taken to hell. Many unusual events happen to Hājī Jabbār in hell before he awakes from his nightmare, including encounters with characters such as Genghis Khan, Napoleon and Hitler, as well as being tormented by unfamiliar (and unacceptable) dance scenes such as the rock and roll dances of Iranian gigolos. The dissolution of order during the liminality of Hājī Jabbār's dream allows for more fluid sentiments to emerge and new customs to be established. Feeling as if he had been given a second chance in life, upon waking up, Hājī Jabbār acquires the favourable traits of "the Average Haji of Bazaar" typecast that had been circulated in the press; a man of good conscience who distributes his wealth among his friends and family, allows his daughter to marry the man of her choice and then peacefully passes away, possibly to heaven. Revolving around themes of benefaction, the film evokes moral lessons that are contextualised in competing and overlapping themes. In 1960, Mūshiq Sarvarīyān made another film entitled *Haji Jabbār in Paris* (*Hājī Jabbār dar Pārīs*) which featured the same character, played by the same actor. In the form of a ghost, Hājī Jabbār, who has taken a one month leave from hell comes to the help of Hassan, a poor but love-stricken man, to convince his girlfriend's stingy father to approve of their marriage. In a dream-like adventure, Hājī Jabbār and Hassan travel to Paris and encounter unfamiliar buildings, café customs, foreign foods, European dances, and practices such as the hula hooping tricks of kids. Muhammad Rizā Zandī's *Stingy* (*Khasīs*, 1955), made prior to both of the above-mentioned films, explored the same subject of materialistic Hajis. In the film, Hājī Hussayn, a stingy and greedy man, does not give permission to his daughter to marry the indigent man with whom she is in love. After a series of events that test the Hājī's moral principles, the father transforms into the religiously moral and rational Haji of the Bazaar who allows the marriage to take place.

New Money (*Tāzah bah Dawrān Rasīdah*, 1961), produced by Media Film, addresses economic inequality in the 1960s, when a number of people became excessively rich while others moved down the social ladder, alluding to the post-war social prototypes discussed in Chapter 3. The film tells the story of a seamster, Mīrzā Nusrat (played by the prominent stage actor, Taqī Zuhūrī), and his family who acquire a fortune in just a few months through the selling and buying of lands outside the city. With their new money, the family acquires new personalities, extravagant living spaces, new etiquettes and a newfound disdain for anything that represents their old lives. First, the names of family members change: Mihrī, the daughter, representing the characteristics of "the Average Lālahzārī Woman," goes by the "Western" name of "Mimi" to better fit her new image, clothing, hairstyle and accent. The once-veiled mother trades her modest outfits for the latest fashions of Tehran. "Blinded by money," as Mihrī's old suitor once remarks, Mīrzā Nusrat becomes unsympathetic to those in need. In attempts to become "an Average Gigolo," he attends dance classes such as tango and waltz, instructed by a European dance instructor. Having distanced himself from what the film visualises as "Iranian ethical values," the capricious father even takes on a young and conniving second wife, who attempts to steal his money. By including multiple personalities found in urban Iranian society, such as Mihrī's suitor as an honest hardworking labourer, a rich and greedy Mīrzā Nusrat, and his lover as the shrewd, modern, urban gold-digger woman, the film attests to existing social class conflicts and criticises the fast-paced flow of money into the country due to the processes of industrialisation in the 1960s. The presence of Europeans and rich European "wannabes" was intended to ridicule and criticise the emergent new class who were gaining prestige in a society still dominated by vernacular traditions. The film thus imagines "Iranianness" in the grey areas of national/international and low/high social class national imaginations.

Moreover, films such as *The Ladder of Progress* (*Nardibān-i Taraqqī*, 1957), *Mr Banknote* (*Āqā-yi Iskinās*, 1958) and *A Million Dollar Cheque* (*Chik-i Yik Mīlyūn Dulārī*, 1959) by the Iranian-Armenian director, Henrik Stepanian, *The Millionaire Groom* (*Dāmād-i Mīlyūnir*, 1959) (an adaptation of the British film, *The Million Pound Note*, 1954) and the much-celebrated film, *Qarun's Treasure* (*Ganj-i Qārūn*, 1965) all address themes of poverty, social class conflicts and the decadence of the rich in urban centres. *The Starless* (*Bī-Sitārah-hā*, 1959) by Khusraw Parvīzi portrays the rising unemployment rate in cities against the desires and attempts of the youth to live a good life. Despite its comedic tone, the film explores the miserable lives of three "vagabonds" who, at the end of the film, declare that it is better for them to die than live a life they cannot afford. In attempts to win the love of an "Average Lālahzārī Woman," the three vagabonds disguise themselves to resemble "the Average Lālahzārī Gigolo," although to no avail. Sīyāmak Yāsamī's *Wicked* (*Varparīdah*, 1962) also revolves around issues related to class conflicts by depicting the love story between an "Iranian Female Typewriter" who pretends to be an "Average Lālahzārī Woman," and an average white-collar worker who pretends to be an "Average Lālahzārī Gigolo," in order to win each other's love.

Aside from poverty, the theme of "a deceived girl in need of rescue" also featured prominently among many commercial urban commentary films in the 1950s – namely, *For You* (*Barā-yi Taw*, 1955), *The Last Night* (*Ākharīn Shab*, 1955) and *Conspiracy* (*Dasīsah*, 1955) and *The Chivalrous Villain* (*Lāt-i Javānmard*, 1958). *The Chivalrous Villain*, directed by Majīd Muhsinī, depicts Dāsh-Hasan as a renowned and chivalrous Jāhil of his neighbourhood who finds Fātī, a lonely woman, at the scene of a car accident. Having realised that she has attempted to commit suicide because of a broken heart, Dāsh-Hasan adopts Fātī as a sister and takes her to his home, where he and his mother care for the fragile woman. In the film, Dāsh-Hasan gets into a fight with a conniving gigolo from a rich part of the city named Khusraw, whom he accidentally murders. As a result, Dāsh-Hasan is arrested by the authorities and faces execution for murder. However, in his trial it becomes clear that Khusraw had shamelessly deceived many women. Considering Khusraw as "evil" and "degenerate" in comparison to Dāsh-Hasan, who defends women and the honour of his family and the neighbourhood, Dāsh-Hasan is acquitted by the justice system that pays tribute to a patriarchal system. He then marries Fātī, with whom he has fallen in love. Jamal Umid, a scholar of Iranian cinema, considers *The Chivalrous Villain* to lack the qualities of "pure Iranianness" to which Iranians had grown accustomed.[102] In an interview with Jamal Umid, the director believed that the "failure of the film" at the box office was due to the fact that "the Jāhil that people expected to see" on screen could not be envisioned in the

---

[102] Refer to Umid's discussion on *The Chivalrous Villain*, in Jamal Umid, "*Lāt-i Javānmard*" [*The Chivalrous Villain*], in *Tārīkh-i Sīnamā-yi Īrān*, 307. Umid refers to a conversation that he had with Majīd Muhsinī in the summer of 1976.

small "stature and physique" of the protagonist, played by the director himself.[103] Moreover, the film lacked "the necessary song-and-dance" numbers that ensured commercial success according to the director, such as "the dancing of Mahvash and Āfat"[104] (famous dance stars of the time).

Feminising the nation, the film depicts Fātī as mother-nation, deceived by men – or traitors of the nation – who create "nests of evil,"[105] men who cheat women/Iran by their empty promises of love.[106] On the other hand, Dāsh-Hasan resembles the hero that saves mother-Iran from the hands of evil. When Dāsh-Hasan accidentally drowns Khusraw, a dishonourable man who had invaded women's bodies, Fātī proclaims that he had taken revenge on "non-men," men who deceived innocent women with promises of marriage, but instead abandoned them in the streets. In the film, Dāsh-Hasan represents the hero who sacrifices his honour – the most valuable possession of a Jāhil – to marry Fātī and to raise her unborn child as his own; Dāsh-Hasan is thus depicted as a national hero. The "morality" depicted in films such as *The Chivalrous Villain* stems from religious notions, strongly informed by the urban culture of "Lūtī-garī" (folk-gallantry) which was attributed to the socially conservative southern neighbourhoods of Tehran. *South of the City (Junūb-i Shahr*, 1958), discussed in more length below, *The Neighbourhood's Jāhil (Jāhil-i Mahal*, 1964), *Lūtī* (1971) and *Men and Non-Real Men (Mard-hā va Nāmard-hā*, 1973) were among the many films that explored themes of folk-gallantry popular among the public, particularly in the southern parts of the city, a less wealthy and more religious and conservative settlement, where gallantry still served a social purpose.

The character of Jāhil was an intertextual icon. Demonstrating traditional Persian values of masculinity, embodied by a tall and strong physique, the Jāhil displayed a unique moustache, a modern dark suit, a chapeau hat that resembled the clothing of gangsters in 1940s and 1950s American mob films and a distinctive accent spoken in a raspy voice, as well as a bad temper. While some early commercial films included the character of the Jāhil, at times also referred to as a Lūtī, by

---

[103] Umid, *"Lāt-i Javānmard,"* 307.   [104] *Ibid.*
[105] This quotation is from the dialogues in the film.
[106] Interestingly, this rhetoric is very similar to the kind that was used by secular and religious intellectuals to describe "the United States" just before and after the 1979 revolution.

the late 1950s and early 1960s, films increasingly examined the conflicts between the good and the bad Jāhil. The good Jāhil embodied virtues such as purity, self-sacrifice, honesty, true-heartedness and, most importantly, empathy for those in need (especially in the name of Shi'ism). The bad Jāhil, on the other hand, was envisioned as oppressive, tyrannical, shrewd, corrupt and governed by money. The prototype of Jāhil and the culture surrounding his identity was a contentious one. The Jāhil, who usually engaged with the religiously-endowed traditional sports of zūrkhānah (the House of Strength, a traditional Iranian athletic facility for physical and moral training), was considered as chivalrous within a socially and culturally distinct moral code that belonged mostly to the more socially conservative parts of the city. As many films suggest, the Jāhil's philosophy was conceived as tacky, ignorant and cheap by Iran's educated and "cultured" middle-class. However, it seems that in "Film-Farsi" productions, the character of the good Jāhil replaces the character of the villager as one moves from rural-centred films toward the urban-centred commercial films (especially made in the 1960s and 1970s), particularly in terms of the purity and heroism showcased by the Jāhil. In line with this observation, famous actors such as Nusrat Malik-Mutī'ī, who first emerged on cinema screens in the 1950s and earned a reputation for their role as the clean-cut, honest, educated, modern, progressive and trustworthy hero (usually with modest origins), started to play the role of the good Jāhil – the chivalrous gallant of the dystopian southern parts of the city in the early 1960s. Another reason for this transformation could also be attributed to the popular rise of other young actors such as Fardīn, who arguably replaced Malik-Mutī'ī onscreen as the young and honest protagonist.

In *Lūtī* (by Khusraw Parvīzī, 1971), for example, Nāsir Malik-Mutī'ī plays the role of Lūtī Asad, an older folk-gallant, who has relinquished the Jāhilī (ignorant) ways of his youth and gained much reputation as a chivalrous man through honest work. While trying to persuade Bilqays, the daughter of Ilyās, the wine-seller, to stop hosting his son at her wine-house (where Bilqays dances and serves wine for guests), he falls in love with the woman himself. Upon discovering the companionship, the men of the city start calling Asad "a non-Lūtī" (Lūtī-yi nā-Lūtī). Here, Bilqays's house becomes a liminal space that signals a shift in Lūtī's way of life. Fellow honourable gallants paint Asad as losing his religiously endowed chivalry for drinking wine and taking a "devil" as his woman – notions that he himself had previously disapproved of. In contrast with the "loose" lifestyles of the youth in cities, the film depicts virtues and traditions that were disappearing among modern-day Jāhils, namely, bravery in the name of love. When Bilqays kills her long-time lover and client who had made fun of Asad (with whom she has fallen in love), Lūtī Asad claims the crime charge and flees from the town. When he returns after a couple of years, he finds Bilqays laughing in the arms of another man. Blinded by jealousy, and in an attempt to regain his hyper-masculine chivalrous attributes, Lūtī Asad kills both Bilqays and her lover, only to discover Bilqays's lover to be his own only son. The theme of a father killing his son revokes the old *Shahnamah* tale of Rustam and Suhrab, where Rustam, the father, unknowingly kills his son, Suhrab, in a battle. Ali Hatami's *Qalandar* (1972) also explores the inner conflicts of a Pahlivān (Champion) in old Tehran, which signified both a champion of zūrkhānah and a champion of gallant attributes in life – attributes that were embodied in the good Jāhil of the mid twentieth century. Aside from showcasing the contradictory relationship between the good and bad Jāhil or the struggles of gallantry in modern life, many films displayed the incompatible relationship of Jāhil – namely, the traditional gallant, and the "Fukulī," the modern, "Europeanised" Iranian, represented in the character prototype of the gigolo. The film *Jāhils and Gigolos* (*Jāhilhā va Zhīgūlhā*, 1964), by Hussayn Madanī, is a good example of a depiction of a stand-off between the Jāhils and gigolos of a southern neighbourhood, and the prototypical representations of each group commonly used in the visual culture, novels and stories published in magazines and newspapers of the time.

From the late 1950s onward, more films started to take on a noticeably serious and critical tone toward cultural change, as well as social and political conditions that complicated people's allegiances with families and social networks. Although these critical films still included cinema stars and scenes of bar fights, dance numbers and famous singers that had become the signifiers of popular cinema, they had a more critical outlook on Iranian everyday lives. *South of the City* (*Junūb-i Shahr*, 1958),[107] directed by Farrukh Ghaffari, an internationally educated film critic and director, is a film that can also be

---

[107] *South of the City* was based on a story written by Jalāl Muqaddam, a prominent director of this period.

categorised as one of the early pioneers of the Iranian alternative cinematic movement – a cinematic trend that, as Chapter 5 will discuss, took on a more distinctive shape in the 1960s. *South of the City* was banned after just a few days of screening in 1958. In order to reobtain a screening permit, the film had to omit certain parts and insert new scenes.[108] In 1964, after a number of scenes were reportedly added to the beginning and end of the film, *South of the City* was again screened in Tehran under a different title, *Competition in the City*. The film revolves around the story of 'Iffat, a widower who starts working at a cabaret venue in order to make a living for herself and her young son. 'Iffat eventually meets two contender Jāhils who fall madly in love with her. 'Iffat takes a liking to Farhād, the kind, empathetic and honourable Jāhil, rather than Asghar, the cruel, violent and oppressive one, who creates many obstacles for the two lovers. The film ends with 'Iffat and Farhād marrying and living a middle-class life; at the end of the film, 'Iffat becomes a housewife, while Farhād becomes a white-collar worker who leaves behind his Jāhilish appearance and attitude. *South of the City* was arguably one of the first films that displayed actual scenes from slums and southern parts of Tehran, depicting in a more realistic light the hardship and difficulties of the downtrodden sections of society.

South of the City embodied the aspirations of many film critics who in the 1950s protested against Persian films as "cheap" copies of "international popular flicks" that "lacked technical superiority," and who promoted the production of technically and visually advanced films that depicted real Iranian lives.[109] The film includes Persian percussion music (zarbī) in the background, which endows it with a distinct Persian sound. The rhythmic beats of Tunbak[110] played at the beginning and throughout certain parts of the film, which conveys a sense of apprehension and foreshadowed ominous events, also resembles the sound and feel of zūrkhānah. The setting of the film also has a very distinct urban feel; the opening scenes include shots from different parts of Tehran – a practice that became common in the

---

[108] For an alternative account of the commotion and discourse surrounding *South of the City* (1958), see Naficy, *A Social History of Iranian Cinema*, vol. 2, 188–190.

[109] Although the film was well received by some critics, it was disliked by others, such as Hūshang Kāvūsī.

[110] A percussion instrument prevalent in Iranian traditional music.

production of many subsequent films.[111] Song-and-dance numbers included in the film resemble the music and performances played at traditional cafés (mutribī or minstrel music). In fact, the film represents a stark contrast between the setting of a café and a cabaret venue, especially in terms of audience, taste and the kinds of songs, dances and activities that each featured. The cafés are depicted as distinctively "Iranian" spaces, represented through traditional instruments, minstrel music, singing and Naqqālī (storytelling based on Persian epic poems or Islamic traditions). The scenes from the café also include Persian paintings from the *Shahnamah*. Worthy to note is that the intertextual plot of the film subverts and undermines ancient Persian virtues. In a traditional Naqqālī (storytelling) scene in the café, for example, the storyteller's recounting of the tale about a Persian hero (pahlivūn) is superimposed on the image of Asghar's entrance (a virtueless Jāhil) into the café, a subversive vision in the film that ridiculed changes and conditions that came with modernisation and that lamented the disappearance of traditional Persian virtues.

The film uses a voiceover to convey a broader picture and meaning to the audience. Surprisingly, the voice of a woman (played by Fakhrī Khurvash as 'Iffat) is used, which bestows upon her some form of agency in the plot and centralises her role in the film by focusing on her perspective – especially since the storyline explores issues related to a single woman's motherhood and unemployment in Iran. 'Iffat conveys her frustration with the image that is associated with her as "a woman of the café," an image that allows men such as Asghar to do as they wish with her. The film also touches upon the social mobility of different classes; for example, at the end of the movie, the couple are shown as successful middle-class citizens who have undergone major transformations in terms of their clothing, attitude, taste and, as one might presume, social standing. *Stranger* (*Gharībah*, 1972) also

---

[111] Aside from the opening scenes that convey the familiarity, hustle and bustle, and hum of the city, the film also portrays a traditional café in the southern parts of the city, where 'Iffat works. The café features a miniature painting of a Qajar woman dancing in the background. The long shot of the camera that attempts to capture the painting is important, since this points to the significance of the old traditions of *Mutribī* (minstrel) music and dancing that were dominant in the early and mid-Qajar era, but were eventually replaced by new music recordings and European-style spectacles.

examined themes related to women's lack of voice in southern (and more traditional) parts of the city. Coming from a conservative family, Zarī is depicted as a voiceless figure in a family dominated by cultural traditions. She is, moreover, portrayed as an invisible woman in a love dynamic governed by a culture that allows men to impose themselves on women in the name of love, representing traditional societies such as Iran, where patriarchy prevails to this day.

Mixing themes of poverty, class division, social mobility, urbanisation, rural-urban migration, the plight of women and unemployment, many films started casting international figures who were visiting or living in Iranian cities as performers (especially in dance and music troupes) or tourists. *The Frankish Bride* (*'Arūs-i Farangī*, 1964), made by Nusratullāh Vahdat, is one of the first films of its kind that uses non-Iranian characters in its main plot as a means to highlight honourable virtues of average Iranians, especially the working class. In this film, Hussayn Turmuzī (Hussayn-Brake Hitter) is a poor taxi driver in Tehran who cannot afford to marry his cousin, Mahīn. One day, Hussayn picks up a young European woman named Maria, who is lost in the city. Maria stays with Hussayn for a couple of days until she is able to find her Iranian relatives. During this period, she falls in love with Hussayn for his chivalry and kindness – feelings that Hussayn does not necessarily reciprocate. Hussayn disapproves of Maria's "European" behaviour and liberal attitude (i.e. what Hussayn describes as "loose behaviour"). Maria eventually finds her relatives and Hussayn marries his cousin, who embodies all the qualities of an "Iranian woman" of which he approves.

The Frankish Bride uses Maria's character as a foolish and "wanton" European woman to draw a comparison between traditional Iranian criteria for women's moral conduct (modesty and reservation) and what was perceived as European conduct (loose and ill-mannered behaviour). Although Maria was not necessarily portrayed as "vulgar" or as a "prostitute" (i.e. the way in which free-living Iranian women were frequently depicted in Persian films), her conduct was portrayed as different, unfamiliar and thus undesirable for an ordinary Iranian man. The film further touched upon the increasing presence of European tourists in an industrialising Iran that had become a tourist attraction. Like many other Persian films of its time, *The Frankish Bride* also addressed class division and the living conditions of those from lower social strata, while at the same time valorising their honest and big-hearted personalities. Considered as a "critical comedy," *The Frankish Bride* was inspired by a news article in one of the daily newspapers of the time. Informed by the everyday lives of Iranians, the film revealed difference by representing locality within a global order.[112]

Similar to *The Frankish Bride*, *The Love Taxi* (1970) played with the subject of "international" characters in Iran, while at the same time addressing widening social and economic inequality. The storyline of the Iranian musical, *The Love Taxi*, briefly discussed in Chapter 3, is closely related to its Egyptian version of the same title. Habīb, a tourist taxi driver, encounters an Iranian man who disguises himself as a "foreigner" and attempts to deceive a woman, Parvīn, with his "Western" accent and attitude. Habīb reveals the true identity of the man and saves Parvīn from falling for the wrong man. Habīb eventually falls in love with Parvīn. However, once he discovers that Parvīn comes from a rich family, Habīb distances himself from her, knowing that their social class would pose a challenge in a future marriage. Toward the end of the film, nevertheless, Habīb realises that Parvīn's uncle has gambled away all the money that belonged to her and, as such, marries her without the need to worry about clashes in their social class standing.

The honest attributes of Habīb are depicted as distinctively Iranian in *The Love Taxi* – his modesty, morality and religiosity, adorned with his distinct Isfahani accent. Habīb's love for Parvīn blooms when he sees her as an equal in social status, or when she exhibits her Iranianness by eating Kallah Pachah, a traditional stew of boiled cow's feet, tongue and intestines. Habīb further demonstrates his nationalist sentiments in his pride for Persian heritage through his job as a tour guide. Habīb's distinctive Isfahani accent, simple clothing and classic urban folk songs which addressed the everyday experiences of his life as a taxi driver in minstrel performances resonated with the popular taste of the audience. Habīb and his musical performances (which he

---

[112] It should be mentioned that as early as 1959, Iranian directors had started to explore the conflicts and cultural contradictions that had emerged in major cities as a result of the presence of European women and the subsequent intermingling of Iranians and Europeans in a modernising Iran. *Ms Older Sister* (*Shābājī Khānūm*, 1959), by Sādiq Bahrāmī, was one of the first films that examined the incompatibility of Iranian and European cultural values in a traditional Iranian family that disapproved of the modern and "Frankish" lifestyle of their son's European fiancée.

addresses as "national music") are posed in stark contrast to the
character of Jingo, a European-looking, bow-tie-wearing cabaret singer,
who claims to sing "Iranian jazz" – a gigolo resembling the "Average
Lālahzārī Gigolo," who deems Habīb to be "incognizant of the New
Wave" music.

The two films below will examine in more detail the ways in which
social and cultural differences were negotiated on the Iranian silver
screen. *The Home-Wrecked* (Khānah-Kharābhā, 1975) critiqued and
warned against the new money that poured into the country through
foreign investments and allowed for rapid urbanisation and cultural
changes. Directed by Nusratullāh Karīmī and casting some of Iran's
most prominent actors and persona of pre- and post-revolutionary
Iran, *The Home-Wrecked* displayed the conformist tendencies of the
masses in pursuing the consumer culture that had become fashionable
in the pre-revolutionary era. In particular, it represented the conflicts
between and within various social strata. Situating the desire of Iranian
middle-class for new and individualised buildings and a modern lifestyle against a nostalgia for old houses and their associated communal
lifestyles, the film displays Nawrūz Khān deliberating over the selling
of the old house that he has inherited from his ancestors. Once convinced by his children and in-laws to sell the house, Nawrūz Khān is
tricked into buying a piece of land in a desolate area outside the city to
start constructing a new apartment building. The construction of the
new building, supervised by his son-in-law's shrewd and rich father,
however, costs much more than Nawrūz Khān could afford. His debt,
the family's expensive lifestyle that partly results from their interaction
with the ("new money") in-laws and complications in the construction
process lead Nawrūz Khān to regret his hurried decision to sell the old
house. At the end of the film, he sells his incomplete new building
project and purchases his old house for a much higher price than he
had initially sold it for. Regardless of the price, though, Nawrūz Khān
returns to the tranquil life that he had earlier lost when he began to live
a "modern" lifestyle.

Petty Fukulī (*Jujah Fukulī*, 1974), a lampooned version of *Qaysar*
(1969), is particularly interesting in the ways in which it juxtaposes the
old and new and traditional and modern.[113] Submerged in conscious
deconstruction of social norms, highlighting the social contradictions

---

[113] *Qaysar* (1969) will be discussed in more detail in the following chapter.

and urban contestations that were especially heralded by a "new time," the film cleverly touches upon the changing conditions of the time. Farmān, the most renowned Jāhil of the neighbourhood, wishes for his son, Firaydūn, to become a doctor rather than a Jāhil like him.[114] Years after his father's death, Firaydūn is shown to have become a singer in one of Tehran's popular clubs, indeed a modern occupation, despite the wishes and cries of his mother, Aqdas. Disgraced by her gigolo son who calls her "Mommy" rather than Nanah (the traditional Persian name for mother), Aqdas thinks that the best way for her son to snap out of being a *Jujah Fukulī* (petty bow-tie-wearing kid) is to marry him into a traditional family like that of Haydar Khān. However, Haydar Khān does not view Firaydūn (with his unorthodox appearance) as a good match for her daughter, Shīrīn. Unbeknown to the two families, Firaydūn and Shīrīn, a beautiful, modern and obstinate woman, fall in love and decide to get married – again representing the blossoming of a modern love. To convince Shīrīn's father to approve their union, Firaydūn decides to become a celebrated Jāhil in the neighbourhood by taking classes in jāhilīyyat (traditional gallantry) at the newly established "Institution for Jāhilī" (Anstītū Jāhilī), instructed by Hussayn "the Golden Heel" (Hussayn Pāshnah Talā). Jāhilī is a tradition acquired through years of building a chivalrous reputation in a neighbourhood, or alternatively, it is passed on from generation to generation. What is ironic here, however, is that, in the modern times of 1970s, even jāhilīyyat (albeit in a superficial form) could be *bought* with money at a school. The institution's instructor, known as "a tactful Jāhil" (Jāhil-i bā Tiknīk), succeeds in turning Firaydūn into a reputable neighbourhood jāhil who eventually earns the respect of Shīrīn's father. The interplay of the characters of Jāhil/Fukūlī, modern/traditional, low culture/high culture, schooled/unschooled and so on points to the plethora of imaginations that constituted Iranian modernity and highlight hybrid national sensibility.

---

[114] It is interesting to note here that the fact that a Jāhil decides that his son will be a doctor in the future is a contradictory phenomenon itself in the tradition of jāhilīyyat, since the good Jāhil figures of the era were depicted to be involved in the bazaar and the bad Jāhil was portrayed as involved in illegal work. The virtues of Jāhil, in Jāhilī commercial films, were thought to be passed from father to son. Thus, the fact that Farman chose a different path for his son than the one he had chosen for himself suggests another cultural change depicted in the film.

Through such a blending, the film was able to sublimate the social tensions associated with Iran's cosmopolitan and changing culture in an entertaining cinematic form.

Films such as *Ibrām in Paris* (*Ibrām dar Pārīs*, 1964), *Three Smarties in Japan* (*Sah Nāqulā dar Jāpun*, 1966), *Hungry Millionaires* (*Mūūnir-hā-yi Gurusnah*, 1967), *An Isfahani in New York* (*Yik Isfahānī dar Nīyaw Yurk*, 1972) and *Eastern Man, European Woman* (*Mard-i Sharghī, Zan-i Farangī*, 1975) highlight the contradictions through which Iranian commercial films of the time simultaneously imagined and unimagined national identity and defined a new form of Iranian-ness against European norms and lifestyles. Moreover, films such as *The Hero Bum* (*Vilgard-i Qahrimān*, 1965), *Tehran's Poor* (*Gidāyān-i Tihrān*, 1966), *The Bums* (*Vilgard-hā*, 1967), *Treasure and Sufferance* (*Ganj va Ranj*, 1967) and *The Starless Man* (*Mard-i Bīsitārah*, 1967) further attest to the ways in which film narratives were not only concerned with issues of poverty and unemployment, but also with moral lessons that could be told through the ordinary lives of the masses in entertaining or song-and-dance cinematic forms.

By concentrating on family values and social normatives, this popu-lar cinema evoked everyday moral substance. "Film-Farsi" cinema, furthermore, conjured principles that, according to the character of Ibrām in the film *Ibrām in Paris*, "conformed to Iranian standards." Sīyāmak Yāsamī, one of the most notable directors of "Fīlm-Fārsī," explained the popular attraction of the masses to this cinema as resulting from their "strong tendency to watch films that are inspired by their own lives."[115] The announcement for the film *Eastern Man, Western Woman* (1975) described it as "a tale about modern (imrūzī) life for modern people," with "a new interpretation of all the standards and traits of a traditional Eastern family."[116] Such local differences, however, were already embedded in the cinematic grammar of "Film-Farsi" that was informed by Hollywood, Indian, Egyptian and other popular cinematic cultures – already hybrid, multi-cultural and multi-ethnic. The encounters of Iranians with the global, through cinema and the everyday space of living in urban centres, was further facili-tated by the Iranian popular film industry, which in turn represented

---

[115] *Fīlm va Hunar* [Film and Art], no. 441 (Tir 21, 1352 [July 12, 1973]).

[116] "*Mard-i Sharqī, Zan-i Farangī*" [*Eastern Man, Western Woman*], accessed April 27, 2014, www.youtube.com/watch?v=K3Wi1qZbBao.

and further prompted the shaping of a commercial cosmopolitan culture in the Iranian imagination. Thus, although Hollywood, Egyptian and Indian popular cinemas had set the standard style against which the stylistic accomplishments of Iranian directors could be analysed, the efforts of the indigenous directors, in the words of Miriam Hansen, "to forge idioms of their own," "were crucially inflected by a larger vernacular-modernist culture at once cosmopolitan and local."[117]

While Persian-language films addressed cultural changes and tensions arising from rapid processes of modernisation, they embodied cosmopolitan outlooks – visions acquired by the industry through a half-century encounter with international films and/or through incorporating cosmopolitan figures in its productions. Iranian directors, critics and cineastes closely followed global cinematic events, the emergence of new technologies and the production of new films, and assimilated that information into their filmmaking. As mentioned above, popular movies had become so engaged with international films – especially in terms of content – that critics started to take issue with what they perceived as Iranian cinema's "imitation" of foreign films. The nationalist discourse of Iran had for many years associated national advancement with the denunciation of European lifestyles and Iranian imitation of Europe.

4.4 The Global in Local Persian-Language Films

By the 1960s, as briefly mentioned above, the presence of international characters had become widespread in Iranian films. Whether included in the plot as main characters or as extras, as unfamiliar characters that could be ridiculed or as positive characters, international figures had a palpable presence in the films of the commercial cinema industry. The dance and performance of numerous international artists and global figures, such as Marina in *The Frankish Bride*, Gregory Mark (Marcos Grigorian) in *The Calm before the Storm* (1960) and *White Gold* (1962), "Justine" who played the character of "Barbara" in *Eastern Man, Western Woman*, Vahan Aghamalian in *The Storm in Our Town*

---

[117] Miriam Hansen, "Vernacular Modernism: Tracking Cinema on a Global Scale," in Nataša Ďurovičová and Kathleen Newman (eds), *World Cinemas: Transnational Perspectives* (New York: Routledge, 2010), 295.

(1958), Antonella De Paolis in *Storm's Bellow* (*Na'rah-'i Tūfān*, 1969) – who played the role of a foreign woman who "steals" a married Iranian man – and other characters who imitated European and American stereotypes were included in many of the popular films of the era. As early as 1955, *Sitārah-'i Sīnamā* reported on the participation of "German dancers in a Persian film."[118] Alex and Lisa, "the famous ballet dancers of Germany," who had performed in Farhang Hall in Tehran, had been invited by Caravan Film to perform a few dances in *Bloody Moonlight* (*Mahtāb-i Khūnīn*, 1955).[119] Mentioning that for the first time performances that could "truly be called dance" were included in the film, the report encouraged other Persian films to cast experts in the field of dance if they needed to include dance scenes in their films.[120] In 1968, however, *Firdawsi* magazine criticised the creators of Persian films for relying on international actors such as Nancy Kovack and Marlene Schmidt to "boost" their industry.[121] Some critics preferred to rely on "local" actors rather than "no-grade actors from Italy, Greece, Lebanon and Israel."[122]

Aside from involving international figures as actors or in plots, members participating in film production were highly diverse. Similar to the late 1920s and early 1930s, a large number of Iranian-Armenian community members were involved in Iran's commercial film industry. Sanasar Khāchatūrīyān (producer and manager of Diana Film Studio), Samuel Khāchīkīyān (director and owner of Āzhīr Film Studio), Mūshiq Sarvarīyān (director), Serzh Āzarīyān (writer and director), Sīmīk Konstāntīn (Simik Constantin), Johnny Bāghdāsārīyān and Vāhān Tirpānchīyān (the three of whom opened Alborz Film Studio), Rubik Dizāduīyān (dubbing), Anik and Henrik Uvidīsīyān (studio owners/producers), Babken Āvidīsīyān (producer), Robert Ekhart (journalist, critic and director), Aramais Āghāmālīyān (director) and Arkadi Bughusīyān (dubbing) were among Armenian descendants who

---

[118] "Raqqāsah-hā-yi Ālmānī dar yik Fīlm-i Fārsī Shirkat Kardand" [German Dancers Participated in a Persian Film], *Sitārah-'i Sīnamā*, no. 25 (Bahman 13, 1333 [February 2, 1955]), 3.
[119] *Ibid.*   [120] *Ibid.*
[121] Māsīs, "'Khudimānī-hā' rā Daryābīd" [Discover "Our Own"], *Firdawsī*, no. 892 (Day 9, 1347 [December 30, 1968]), 39.
[122] *Ibid.*

were involved in Iranian film production, dubbing and television pro-
jects.[123] Aside from Armenians, Jewish Iranians such as 'Azizullāh
Kardavāni, Habībullāh Hakīmīyān, Farajullāh Nasīmīyān, Natail
Zebulānī, the cinematographer, Georges Lichenski, the successful
Bahai' studio owner, Mihdī Mīsāqīyyah and the Indian director,
Sardār Sākir, further diversified the field of film production in Iran,
making post–World War II cinema culture a multi-confessional enter-
prise.[124] Prominent cinematographers such as Boris Matveyev (Būrīs
Mātvāyif) were also among the diasporic members who were involved
in the commercial film industry.

Moreover, commercial films were often based on Iranian adaptations of international literary and filmic works. *Ashamed* (*Sharmsār*,
1950), directed by Ismā'īl Kūshān and starring Delkash (an Iranian
singer) and Hossein Dānishvar, was based on 'Alī Kasmāyī's adaptation of a story by a Scottish writer, Vālkin.[125] *Mashhadī Ibād* (1953),
written and directed by Samad Sabāhī (an Iranian Azerbaijani) and the
first production of Golden Age Studio ('Asr-i Talāyī), was an adaptation of an early-twentieth-century operetta of the same name written
by Uzeyir Hajibeyov (Hājībayglū), a prominent Azerbaijani composer
and playwright. The voiceover of the Iranian production pays tribute
to "the famous composer of the East" at the beginning of the film, and
remarks that the original story had occurred outside Iran. The original
play, also known as *O Olamasın, bu Olsun* (*If Not That One, Then
This One*), had been adapted and performed on stage in Iran many
times. The two Azerbaijani film adaptations of the story were also
screened in Iran in the early twentieth century and in the post–World
War II era. The Egyptian, Nuri Habib, was the cameraman of the
Iranian version of the film which was made in 1953.[126] Mihdī Ra'īs-
Fīrūz's film, *A Slip* (*Laghzish*, 1953), was based on Alexandre Dumas's
La Dame aux Camélias (*The Lady of the Camellias*).[127] *The Miser*
(1955), by Muhammad Rizā Zandī, was based on Molière's comedy of
the same name. 'Attaullāh Zāhid directed *A Mother's Kiss* (*Būsah'i*

---

[123] Naficy refers to the involvement of some of these figures in pre-revolutionary
cinema in more detail. See Naficy, *A Social History of Iranian Cinema*, vol. 2,
169–170.

[124] *Ibid.*, 170–172.

[125] Umid, *Tārīkh-i Sīnamā-yi Īrān*, 202. The author has been unable to locate the
works of this writer.

[126] *Ibid.*, 231.   [127] *Ibid.*, 233.

Mādar, 1955), based on the play (and film) *Sevil*, by the Azerbaijani writer and playwright, Jaffar Jabbarli (1899–1934).[128] Shapūr Yāsamī's *The Twins* (1959) was a loose visual adaptation of the Italian film *Padri e Figli* (*Fathers and Sons*, 1957), by Mario Monicelli.[129] *Dead-End* (1964), directed by Mihdī Mīr-Samadzādah and adapted for the screen by the prominent Iranian poet, Ahmad Shamlu, was based on a story by the British author, James Hadley Chase (1906–1985).[130] Aside from drawing on international literature, many other Persian films borrowed from contemporary Persian literature for their scenarios. Chapter 5 will discuss some of the films of the 1960s and 1970s that were visual adaptations of such national literary works.

4.5 Commercial Co-Productions

Starting in the 1960s, the Iranian film industry embarked upon commercial collaborations with other countries in the region and beyond. *Ibrām in Paris*, which depicted a traditional Jāhil, Ibrāhīm (also known as Ibrām), visiting the unfamiliar city of Paris, was an Iranian-French production. *An Isfahani in New York* (1972), an Iranian-American production, yet again depicted the contrasts between the promiscuous lifestyle of New Yorkers (both Iranian and non-Iranian) and the traditional attitude of an Iranian man who visits the city; the Isfahani in the film is shown to be lured into what is represented as a rootless and vulgar Western lifestyle due to momentary moral weaknesses that were imagined to be prevalent in the American society. Moreover, Iran and Turkey had collaborated on a number of popular films in the 1960s, when both the Turkish Yeşilçam (the Turkish commercial film industry, literally translated as Green Pine) and Iranian industry were both at their productional peaks. As mentioned above, *Hak Yolu* (1971) – an Iranian-Turkish co-production – involved both Turkish and Iranian actors, such as Jahāngīr Ghaffārī and Nilūfar. *Melişah* (*Malikshah*, 1969), a historical film about Malik Shah of the Seljuqid Dynasty, was a co-production of Erler Film and Pars Film Studios, directed by Ismāʿīl Kūshān, released in Iran under the name *The Generation of the Brave* (*Nasl-i Shujāʿān*). *Güzel Şoför* (*Shūfir Khushgilah*, 1970) – a story about a woman who moves from Tehran to Istanbul to find her

---

[128] *Ibid.*, 277.   [129] *Ibid.*, 318.
[130] This information is mentioned in the title sequence of the film.

uncle who has stolen her dead family's fortune – was also an Iranian-Turkish co-production by the Iranian director, Mahmūd Kūshān. *The Three Gallants* (*Sah Dilāvar*, 1971), a Persian film released in Iran, was directed by the famous Turkish Yeşilçam director, Türker Inanoğlu, and written by Muhammad Mutivassilānī and Türker Inanoğlu. *Shirin and Farhad* (*Ferhat ile Şirin*, 1970), an Iranian-Turkish remake of the famous Persian love story which was directed by Ismāʿīl Kūshān and written by Turkish Bülent Oran, cast both Iranian and Turkish actors. *The Heroes* (*Qahrimānān*, 1969) was the first Iranian-American production, sponsored by Moulin Rouge studio. The film, according to *Firdawsi* magazine, had a "European" (farangī) plot that took place in Iran. The assistant director of the film was the famous director of Iranian alternative cinema, Masʿūd Kīmīyāyī, who will be discussed in greater detail in Chapter 5.[131] Iranian commercial film producers also engaged with Arab filmmakers, including the Egyptian-born Lebanese director, Faruk Agrama, who directed *A Man from Tehran* (*Mardī az Tihrān*, 1966), starring the popular Iranian film stars Mohammad Ali Fardin and Furūzān.[132] Naficy refers to other international film studios with which Iranians worked, including Lebanese Orient Film, which produced *Fate* (*Sarnivisht*, 1967), starring the film's Armenian director, and Indian Ganesh Prasad Movies, which produced *The Bird of Happiness* (*Humāy-i Saʿādat*, 1971), starring many Iranian actors.[133]

✳ ✳ ✳

The sustained Persian-language cinema industry that emerged in the late 1940s was the industrial re-enactment of cinematic aspirations of the 1930s that called for the establishment of a sovereign cinema. This national enterprise, which came to be derogatively known as "Film-Farsi," ordained a continuous unveiling of chaotic social relations, and registered Iran's processes of self-invention and modernisation through its vernacular offerings. "Film-Farsi" constructed the Iranian imaginary by negotiating the complex and conflicting experience of

---

[131] "Dar Yingah-'i Imām Ittifāq Uftād!" [It Happened at Imam's Yingah!], *Firdawsī*, no. 881 (Mihr 22, 1347 [October 14, 1948]), no page number available.
[132] Naficy, *A Social History of Iranian Cinema*, vol. 2, 334.
[133] *Ibid.*, 334–335.

modernity, in accepting or rejecting it, or responding to it in multifaceted ways. Covering themes related to social conditions of the time, namely rural-urban migration, or challenges associated with urban life such as theft, cheating, the widening gap in class divisions and pollution, popular films were national offerings that depicted and unfolded tensions associated with the social processes of urbanisation and modernisation. As "Film-Farsi" national cinema solidified, it increasingly rebranded international cinematic narratives and/or content in its vernacular offerings and included an increasing number of global and multi-ethnic presences in its productions, hence creating a commercial vernacular-cosmopolitan cinema. While incorporating Hollywood, Hindi, Arab and international figures, subjects and narratives into its films, the "Film-Farsi" industry attempted to define itself as a national industry that promoted "Iranian" attributes (Persianate, Islamic and/or both). In other words, "Film-Farsi" became a national industry by assimilating cosmopolitanism and yet distancing itself from "foreign" influences.

The commercial qualities and hybrid entertainment genres of "Film-Farsi" – while evocative of cultural change – were regarded as cheap and imitative by the elite. Soon, many internationally educated critics realised that the popular cinema industry was not the national industry they had hoped for throughout the last two decades. The cinematic public opinion built around this industry through various publications and debates surrounding films allowed for a shift in the modes of filmmaking in the Iranian film industry. As the following chapter demonstrates, such discussions facilitated the emergence of an alternative cinema, derived from the very familiar themes, social commentaries and tropes of "Film-Farsi." The alter(native) cinema that took shape in the late 1950s and coagulated into a movement in the 1960s incorporated the popular film tropes (such as the song-and-dance numbers), social criticisms and Iranian vernacular life, but instead crafted a cinema that was artistic, philosophical, intellectual and politically charged. In that respect, the socially and nationally conscious grotesque forms of the Iranian commercial cinema of the 1950s to the 1970s, I argue, preceded, overlapped and juxtaposed the more politically explicit and arthouse cinematic developments that came to occupy the place of a "proper" national cinema in cinematic discourses of the pre-revolutionary era.

5 | Cinematic Revolution
Cosmopolitan Alter-Cinema of Pre-Revolutionary Iran

"Our age is a martyred age" (sinn-i mā sinn-i shahīd shudah īst), claimed Mas'ūd Kīmīyāyī, a prominent pre- and post-revolutionary Iranian filmmaker in an interview in 1978; "[v]ery soon, those which we knew, recognised and had aged with, were swept away and were instead replaced by dance, car brands and jeans ... we were the ones most affected by moving from [houses with large] backyards to apartment buildings."[1] Although popular cinema drew on the quotidian of Iranian life, its "entertaining" cinematic form was disapproved by many. Objections to "Film-Farsi," which gave rise to a cinematic horizon of expectation, paved the way for the emergence of an artistic counter-culture. By the late 1950s, there was a nostalgic consensus among many filmmakers to record on celluloid a "real" image of Iran; to resuscitate the disappearing cultural norms and social relations in a rapidly changing society, also observed by Kīmīyāyī above, in a social realist cinematic language. The attempts of a group of internationally educated filmmakers to create a visual repository of the changing conditions of the country facilitated the engendering of a cinematic movement in the late 1950s that was socially and politically charged – a cinematic revolution that presaged the political Revolution of 1979.

As discussed in previous chapters, the space of cinema, as a heterotopic space, both in its concrete site and on screen, brought the global into local Iranian urban neighbourhoods. The development of cinema and its propagation across the country elicited various reactions from the religious establishment, intelligentsia, political activists, cinema enthusiasts and the general public. In this chapter, I re-read artistic and intellectual cinematic developments from the late 1950s to the late 1970s to elucidate a cinematographic cosmopolitanism in Iranian

---

[1] Īraj Sābirī, "Safar-i Harf bā Mas'ūd Kīmīyāyī" [A Journey of Words with Masūd Kīmīyāyī], Sīnamā 56–58, no. 33 (Day–Bahman 1356 [January–February 1978]), 10.

national cinema that did not easily correspond to Kasravi's claims of Europeanism (urūpāyī-garāyī) in 1931 and Jalal Al-i Ahmad's 1962 analysis in Westoxication (Gharbzadigī). Rather than a retrospective examination of artistic productions of the time, I will investigate and contextualise the production and reception of an alternative cinematic movement that distanced itself from the "Film-Farsi" industry. Starting to emerge in the late 1950s, the periodicity of alternative cinema productions overlapped with that of the commercial cinema industry for the most part. Nevertheless, this cinematic trend solidified in the post-professional era of the 1960s – an era that allowed for counter-normative cinematic visions, activities and expectations to emerge in the arts, and especially cinema. I suggest that international cinematic liaisons of pre-revolutionary cinema infused the global and local, and thus crafted an alternative vernacular-cosmopolitan cinema that was "different," artistic and intellectual. In this inquiry into a multi-layered history with plural, alternative and non-synchronic temporalities, I argue that this socially geared cinema fostered a revolutionary cinematic imaginarium, which was temporally autonomous from and yet indispensable to the political and revolutionary goings-on of 1977–1979 – a cinematic revolution that presaged the 1979 revolution.

5.1 The 1960s: Cinema or the "Locus of Corruption" (kānūn-i fisād)

The ripple effect of global social movements and revolutions of the 1960s that accompanied decolonising movements across the world were felt in Iran too. Political discontent and social demands gave rise to the emergence of various political groupings that aimed to fight against the Pahlavi state; such concerns were also manifested in the cinema of the period. By the 1960s, popular cinema continued to be perceived by social critics as a corruptive site of sociability, dominating over the traditional, religious and local aspects of Iranian life. The high taxes imposed on international films propelled film companies to import yet more international commercial films, which ensured maximum profitability. Having perceived Iran's "space of experience" as different from that depicted on the movie screens, many members of the religious establishment and social thinkers used an anti-imperialist discourse that critiqued films featured in Iranian movie theatres, and sought to purify them from foreign socio-political interventions. For many in the religious establishment and intellectual circles, cinematic heterotopia or cinematic deterritorialisation, which involved a weakening of local, spatial and cultural ties and an expansion of imaginations, collapsed with what was perceived as socio-cultural colonisation by the West, especially heightened after the 1953 coup d'état and the Shah's White Revolution. Films were perceived as capitalist commodities that colonised cultural imaginations. Writing in 1965, Muhammad Taqī Tabātabāyī, for example, regarded cinema as "a locus of corruption and prostitution" (kānūn-i fisād va fahshā).[2] The dystopic imaginary visualised through films, in addition to the dark ambience rendered by the movie theatres, were argued to foster irreligious deeds, and disseminate psychological corruption and social crimes. In 1962, the Islamic monthly periodical, *Maktab-i Islām* (The School of Islam), also attacked cinema as a "cultural institution" for "the dissemination of prostitution and immorality."[3] Arguing that it was irrational to "cure a dangerous disease with poisonous ... palliatives," the author urged that the source that led to the youth's "moral collapse" had to be sought out and cured so that the youth did not join various political groupings (such as "the communists")[4] or lose their "moral principles" and "faith."[5]

In 1960, in an article entitled "Cinema in Iran, or One of the Technical and Practical Schools of Corruption," Mahmūd Afshār also expressed his discontent with "American and European films," which had been produced "for environments other than our [own] environment."[6] In his 1962 critical essays about Westoxication, Jalal Al-i Ahmad criticised cinemas as the "piggy banks" of the principal stockholders of Metro-Goldwyn Mayer, and spaces that were open to the cultural intrusion of such profit-seeking companies.[7] Writing from

---

[2] Muhammad Taqī Tabātabāyī, "Sīnamā yā Kānūn-i Fisād va Fahshā" [Cinema of the Locus of Corruption and Prostitution], *Kānūn*, yr 9, no. 9 (Āzar 1344 [November 1965]), 77.

[3] "Tafrīhāt-i Sālim!" [Healthy Recreations!], *Maktab-i Islām*, yr 4, no. 8 (Shahrīvar 1341 [September 1962]), 3–4.

[4] *Ibid.*, 5.   [5] *Ibid.*, 6.

[6] Mahmūd Afshār, "Sīnamā dar Īrān: Yā Yikī az Madrasah-hā-yi (Fannī) va 'Amalī-yi Fisād" [Cinema in Iran: Or One of the Technical and Practical Schools of Corruption], *Āyandah*, no. 4 (Isfand 1338 [February 1960]), 227.

[7] Jalāl Āl-i Ahmad, *Occidentosis: A Plague from the West*, trans. Robert Campbell (Berkeley, CA: Mizan Press, 1984), 105. Occidentosis is another common translation for Āl-i Ahmad's *Gharbzadigī* or Westoxication.

West Germany for *Maktab-i Islām* monthly in 1961, an author who only used his initials, A. J., took issue with Western states that saw themselves as "exemplars of advancement and civilisation" in comparison to the East.[8] Contending that "economic and technological advances" did not justify the perpetuation of the "Western" perception that Eastern countries were "backward,"[9] the author specifically criticised the West's "gift of civilisation" that brought "unwarranted freedom and moral degeneration," which were then disseminated through communication media among the youth from a very early age.[10]

Confronting "Western intrusion" by targeting cinema, these thinkers played a disciplinary role in the orientation that the Iranian cinema industry was to take (Figure 5.1). The remedy for the social maladies manifested in cinema and the unfamiliar habits of cinema-goers could be "learned from the progressive path of Islam,"[11] or by propagation of beneficial communication media, such as educational films that depicted and promoted Iranian traditions and vernacular practices. While the "Film-Farsi" national cinema attended to the lived experience of Iranians – as well as national moral norms and religious ethics – the commercial language of the films that fed capitalist modes of production and consumption, and the industry's manifold similarities with international popular cinemas, did not make the "Film-Farsi" industry a desirable enterprise in the eyes of the critics and elites.

5.2 On a Path toward Cinematic Redemption

"Contrary to those" who considered the art of cinema in Iran "to digress day by day," in 1954, Hasan Shīravānī, a film critic, believed "the industry of film-recording (san'at-i film-bardārī)" and cinema enterprise to have actually improved in the country.[12] Entertaining a different viewpoint, Hūshang Kāvūsī, who had become the Head of the Office of Supervision and Theatres and contributed much to the

---

[8] A. J., "Māhīyat-i Vāqi'ī-yi Tamaddun-i Gharb" [The True Essence of Western Civilisation], *Maktab-i Islām*, yr 3, no. 5 (Tīr 1340 [June 1961]), 41.

[9] *Ibid.*, 39–40. [10] *Ibid.*, 44.

[11] M. Vā'izī-Tabrīzī, "Dastūrāt-i Akhlāqī-yi Islāmī" [The Ethical Guidelines of Islam], *Parcham-i Islām*, yr 3, no. 1 (Farvardīn 12, 1327 [April 1, 1948]), 2.

[12] Hasan Shīravānī, "San'at va Hunar-i Fīlm-Bardārī dar Īrān" [The Industry and Art of Video-Recording in Iran], *Sitārah-'i Sīnamā*, no. 18 (Ābān 19, 1333 [November 10, 1954]), 6.

یك بررسی درباره وضع سینماهای پایتخت و فیلم‌هائی
که نشان میدهند ومقرراتی که باید رعایت کنند ونمی‌کنند.
دراین طرح باطنزی گرچه ساده ومعمولی ولی
جمشید لیثی دقیق وعمیق دیدگاه خودرا ازاین بررسی ابراز
میدارد.

Figure 5.1 A cartoon published in *Bāmshād* about cinema, sex and violence (1967)

revision of cinema regulations and censorship in the mid-1960s, still regarded the Iranian motion picture industry in 1968 as a "Chaotic Cinema."[13] "From twenty years ago, hundreds of thousands of kilometres of film have been used, millions have been spent, thousands of hours have been wasted," and still Iranian cinema had been unable to find a rightful place in world cinema; according to Kāvūsī, Iranian cinema still had not become a "classic" cinema.[14] In 1969, Kāvūsī questioned whether "vulgarity" and cultural products such as films, theatrical plays and music that are "reflections of hollow and ignorant minds" are a source of pride "for a society that is in [a state of] progress and evolution."[15] Perceiving the Iranian public's disposition for "the bazaar of vulgarism" as a grave "danger," Kāvūsī called for "an artistic revolution."[16]

In an article in *Nigīn* (*Jewel*) publication, Kāvūsī noted the course taken by Iranian post–World War II cinema over the years; films had gone from "hollow melodramas" that depicted "village girls" who moved to the city and started singing in cabaret venues until they were saved from the "shadows of the cabaret" by men and then taken to "the warmth of family" life, to "police films" with shallow narratives, to films that attempted to embody a "critical-social" undertone and were supposed to speak for the plight of the people.[17] Kāvūsī conceived the latter films, too, to suffer from "poor expression" and to be "completely primitive."[18] Kāvūsī believed that Iranian cinema had good actors, writers, technicians and topics; what it lacked, however, were producers – people who would use their economic learning and knowledge not only to make money, but also to add to the "industrial and productional economy" of the country.[19] The film critic and director then remarked that Iran would only have a real cinema when films were produced that were painted "with the colour of Iran"; this colour, for Kāvūsī, was not characterised by the "reading of [Persian] sonnets," "eating beef stews" or speaking in a slow and stretched manner.[20] The "authentic cinema of a nation" (sīnamā-yi 'asīl-i yik millat), the author

[13] Hūshang Kāvūsī, "Sīnamā-yi Bī Sāmān" [Chaotic Cinema], *Nigīn*, no. 34 (Isfand 1, 1346 [February 20, 1968]), 8.
[14] *Ibid.*
[15] Hūshang Kāvūsī, "Gandāb-i Rūbirū" [The Wasteland Ahead], *Nigīn*, yr 4, no. 44 (Day 30, 1347 [January 20, 1969]: 6.
[16] *Ibid.*   [17] Kāvūsī, "Sīnamā-yi Bī Sāmān," 8.   [18] *Ibid.*   [19] *Ibid.*, 9.
[20] *Ibid.* These were common tropes that characterised "Film-Farsi."

believed, reflected the "psychological and spatial characteristics and the social climate" that surrounded the filmmaker.[21] In other words, the critics endorsed the making of a realist cinema that attended to the social quotidian – a cinema that lent itself to global filmmaking techniques and topics that were in line with the widespread social and political movements of the 1960s and 1970s. The artistic social realist cinema envisioned by Kāvūsī was one that avoided hotchpotch genres of "Film-Farsi," followed certain universally recognised filmic genres and used cosmopolitan outlooks that made it conversant with international cinemas. Kāvūsī's proclivity for realist films, rather than films defined by their excess and exaggeration, was not an uncommon sensibility during this period. As Geoffrey Nowell-Smith argues, the Free Cinema of Britain, the New Wave of France, the Young German Cinema and the "Polish School," which flourished in Poland and other parts of East Central Europe in the 1960s, all shared an inclination toward realism and everyday life.[22]

In 1970, Sīyāvash Farhang, who wrote in the cinematic publication of the Film Society of Pahlavi University of Shiraz, the *Book of Cinema* (*Kitāb-i Sīnamā*), believed that the "extensive and deep impact" of cinema and its widespread accessibility bestowed "a heavy duty and responsibility upon filmmakers."[23] Any form of "distorted thinking" (kazh-andīshī) or vulgarity (ibtizāl) in film, the author believed, would leave a surprisingly strong impact on the audience.[24] According to Farhang, only a film that had a "rich cinematic language," one that considered the "social human" as its central tenet and attended to human issues "within a large and global aspect" could be "applauded and regarded as art."[25] Only an attendance to "the suffering of people and a critique of inhumane systems," he believed, would create an artist such as Charlie Chaplin and a cinema with a lasting impact. Such statements pointed out, once again, a responsibility for the young directors of Iranian cinema industry to stay away from recreating

---

[21] *Ibid.*
[22] Geoffrey Nowell-Smith, *Making Waves: New Cinemas of the 1960s* (New York: The Continuum International Publishing Group, 2008), 12.
[23] Sīyāvash Farhang, "Sīnamā: Mahdūdīyat-i Vāqiʿīyyat va Bī Intihāyī-yi Takhayyul" [Cinema: Limitation of Reality and Limitlessness of Imagination], *Kitāb-i Sīnamā* [Book of Cinema], no. 1 (Mihr 1349 [September 1970]), 4.
[24] *Ibid.*   [25] *Ibid.*, 4–5.

"the bourgeois atmosphere of entertaining films,"[26] and demonstrate their social commitment by addressing humanism and the societal issue of the environment they lived in. Such cosmopolitan cinematic visionaries that hesitated on cinematic realism were in line with the global socialist outlooks in filmic trends, such as the Japanese and French New Wave cinemas.

In 1968, Reza Barahani, a writer and critic, held that "artistic criticism" had a direct impact on the "creation of an artistic work."[27] An art critic, according to Barahani, was a "warner" and a "preventer of the spread of degradation."[28] In an era when "the bad is juxtaposed with the good, ugly with beautiful . . . deceptions mixed with truth, and foolishness with genius," Barahani declared, the critic must "explore," "comprehend," "distinguish" and use his or her "sharp and relentless pen" as a "sword" to discern "the boundary between estheticism and ugliness."[29] As technocrats of cinema, critics and the professional elite in this group considered it to be their prerogative to play a crucial role in the shaping of the cinematic culture in Iran. "Criticism," Hūshang Kāvūsī also maintained, automatically presented "a direction"; even though the direction was "abstract" to an extent, its guiding substance could be "extracted from in between the lines."[30]

Some critics deemed the creation of a "Third Cinema" to have been necessary in the Iranian film industry. Sh. Nāzirīyān stated that he disapproved of both the "old cinema," which consisted of "imitation and repetition, dishonesty, [and] degenerate subjects," and the new cinema, which "was removed from people, cinema, and commerce" and was "very private."[31] Instead, Nāzirīyān chose a "Third Cinema" that was neither "private or intellectual, nor necessarily commercial."[32] A Third Cinema, according to him, allowed filmmakers to unite, despite

---

[26] Suhrāb Dārā, "Antunīyunī: Fīlm-sāz-i Barguzīdigān?" [Antonioni: The Filmmaker of the Chosen Ones?], *Kitāb-i Sīnamā*, no. 1 (Mihr 1349 [September 1970]), 7.

[27] Reza Barahani, "Sunnat-Zadigī va Vazīfah-'i Muntaqid" [Traditionoxication and the Role of the Critic], *Firdawsī*, no. 855 (Farvardīn 27, 1347 [April 16, 1968]), 33.

[28] *Ibid.*   [29] *Ibid.*

[30] "Mīzigird-i Sīnamā-yi Īrān (1)" [Iranian Cinema Roundtable (1)], *Farhnag va Zindigī* [Culture and Life], no. 18 (1975), 55.

[31] "Sīnamā-yi Sivvum-i Īrān" [The Third Cinema of Iran], *Firdawsī*, no. 926 (Shahrīvar 10, 1948 [September 1, 1969]), 41.

[32] *Ibid.*

their differences, to save the industry from "the dead-end of Persian cinema."[33] Proclamations against the extant popular cinema of the time and demands for "an artistic revolution" which would give rise to a new cinema thus helped lay the perspectival foundation for the shaping of an alternative filmmaking that spoke to an informed, educated, middle-class, politically aware and cosmopolitan audience.

5.3 Alter-Cinema: The Horizon of an Alternative Cinematic Imagination

Before elaborating on the shaping of an alternative cinematic movement in Iran, it is perhaps more revealing to provide a general perspective on waves of new cinema movements that were concurrently forming in other parts of the world. Nowell-Smith argues that in Europe of the late 1950s, there were signs that a number of "new cinema" trends were already underway, although these signs pointed "in a number of different directions."[34] One sign was the emergence of an international audience that was interested in seeking out artistic films – an audience that had already been exposed to art films made in Europe in the 1950s.[35] Nevertheless, in order to tap into the general commercial market which sustained new cinema trends, directors started making films that followed specific genres, in particular varieties of the crime genre, and/or international quality productions; these films then provided the directors with more financial support to experiment.[36]

Film criticism, according to Nowell-Smith, was an important contributor to the formation of waves of new cinema. The 1960s demanded new productions that necessitated "new thinking and new modes of experience" which elaborated on the relationships between art and politics.[37] As such, film critics and political cinephiles came to claim the position of culture-makers and trendsetters. Most of the new cinema filmmakers were, in fact, critics who not only rejected old cinema (Hollywood), but denounced it as well. Aside from the bolstering of a culture of criticism, film festivals also came to play an important role not only in creating the categories of "New Wave" or "new cinema," but also in making them accessible to an international

---

[33] *Ibid.*   [34] Nowell-Smith, *Making Waves*, 23.   [35] *Ibid.*
[36] *Ibid.*, 24–25.   [37] *Ibid.*, 28.

audience. Although branding a new cinema as a "national" one is questionable due to the difficulty in delineating a cinema's nationality, Nowell-Smith argues that much of the new cinema movements in Europe were rooted in particular places of origin, and could thus be regarded as national cinemas.[38] While Nowell-Smith overlooks Iran's new artistic movement in his examination of global new waves in the 1960s, as the following paragraphs demonstrate, new patterns of filmmaking emerged in Iran in the late 1950s and early 1960s that resembled the global trends that, similar to political and student movements, were concurrently underway in different parts of the world. These new styles, patterns, narratives and attributes solidified the Iranian new artistic visions into an alternative vernacular-cosmopolitan cinema.

In the mid-1950s, a group of young Iranian journalists, film critics, directors, activists and actors emerged who, in attempts to distance the art of cinema from the debilitating charges of moral corruption and Westoxication, envisioned a different path for Iranian cinema. Starting in the late 1950s and early 1960s, many of the film magazines and cultural periodicals which were edited and run by these cosmopolitan intellectuals, writers and critics, increasingly focused on international New Wave cinematic trends. These periodicals also published detailed analyses and critiques of films, as well as numerous articles on the operation of new cinema technologies and concepts that would be of use to those in the industry or general cinema enthusiasts. Moreover, they featured articles on political currents in the world that bore Marxist and socialist tendencies. Most of these pieces were written in a sublimated literary language to avoid censorship – a trend that many of the alternative film productions of the time also followed.

Feeling the need for organised decision-making bodies to lobby for the promotion of a national cinema, a number of renowned film critics and intellectuals created several cinema associations in Iran. "The Society for Iranian Cinema and Theatre Writers" (Anjuman-i Nivīsandigān-i Sīnamā va Tiātr-i Īrān), established in 1956, for example, was one of the independent associations that organised weekly meetings and cinema screenings for the promotion of a critical

---

[38] *Ibid.*, 112.

cinema and theatre culture in Iran.[39] Government officials also sensed
the urgency in investing in the national film industry, which would
produce revenue, promote national pride and challenge international
cultural exploitation. In 1966, Ibrāhīm Khāwjah-Nūrī – a notable
writer, translator and politician of the time – published an article
entitled "A Big Plan for the Cinema of Iran," in which he outlined
the measures deemed necessary by the Supreme Council of Performative Arts (of the Ministry of Art and Culture) for the "encouragement
and improvement of Persian Films" in a time of "modernisation."[40]
Some of these recommended steps included "the creation of an association of film critics," "finding suitable evaluation techniques for the
identification of good and bad scenarios," "designating annual awards
and other prizes for the best annual productions" and "the establishment of Persian film festivals" – endeavours that, in fact, soon
followed.[41] In 1968, the Iranian Prime Minister, Amir Abbas
Huveyda, also announced that a sum of 10 million tomans would be
allocated to the film industry as part of the fourth national development plan.[42]

It was amid such cinematic dynamism in metropolitan centres that a
group of young directors in the late 1950s sought to craft an arthouse
cinema as an alternative to the mainstream "Film-Farsi" industry. The
professionalisation of the industry, the aspirations of filmmakers and
critics, and demands for the establishment of a socially committed art
cinema in the 1940s and 1950s propelled the crafting of a cinema in
the late 1950s that spoke to the perspectives circulated in Iranian
intellectual and critical milieus; this cinema could best be defined by
its visual, textual and productional alterity and self-distantiation from
the popular cinema. The professional and industrialised cinema of the
1960s coincided with Muhammad Reza Shah's White Revolution, a
series of educational and land reforms that aimed to reduce the power
of large landowners, the religious establishment and the premiership of

---

[39] "Asās-Nāmah va Nizām-Nāmah-'i Anjuman-i Nivīsandigān-i Sīnamā va Tiātr-i
Īrān" [The Society for Iranian Cinema and Theater Writers], *Sitārah-'i Sīnamā*,
yr 3, no. 81 (Mihr 8, 1336 [September 30, 1956]), 11.
[40] Ibrāhīm Khāwjah-Nūrī, "Tarh-i Buzurg Barā-yi Sīnamā-yi Īrān" [A Big Plan for
the Cinema of Iran], *Masā'il-i Īrān*, yr 4, no. 7 (Isfand 1345 [February 1966]), 13.
[41] *Ibid.*, 14.
[42] Hamid Naficy, *A Social History of Iranian Cinema*, vol. 2: *The Industrializing
Years, 1941–1978* (Durham, NC: Duke University Press, 2011), 328.

Amir Abbas Huvayda. During this period, the government exerted less pressure on cinema and started to support the arts more than ever; these measures provided conditions for more artistic and alternative creations in cinema.[43] The Centre for the Intellectual Development of Children and Young Adults, established in 1967 as a semi-government institution, and the Cinema Industry Development Company of Iran (Shirkat-i Gustarish-i San'at-i Sīnamāyī-yi Irān) were among institutions that supported and promoted filmmaking in the country.[44] Governmental agencies such as the Ministry of Culture and Arts and National Radio and Television Organisation (NRTO) also fostered the production of a variety of visual offerings through the employment of a number of film production centres and civil servant filmmakers.[45] In the 1960s, a culture of festivals also started to take form that worked to showcase prominent international films, namely, Italian neorealist, Japanese and French New Wave films, as well as Iranian arthouse productions.

In 1969, Nasīb Nasībī – a director, film critic and poet – remarked that by that time Iranian filmmakers had been engaged in the making of "an alternative cinema" (Sīnamā-yī Dīgar) for at least "six or seven years," a "cinema that was on a par with good filmic works of other countries."[46] A "merely 'narrative' cinema" (sīnamā-yi faqat "qissah-gū") now belonged to the past and a cinema that escaped popular imagination belonged to the future.[47] This "far-from-vulgarity-cinema" (Sīnamā-yi dūr az Ibtizāl),[48] where "the form of the film, similar to its content," was conceived as "modern,"[49] was extensively elaborated

---

[43] 'Ali Asghar Kīshanī, *Farāyand-i Ta'āmul-i Sīnamā-yi Īrān va Hukūmat-i Pahlavī* [*The Processes of Interaction of Iranian Cinema and Pahlavi Regime*] (Tehran: Islamic Republic Documentation Centre Publications, 2007), 265–266.

[44] Naficy, *A Social History of Iranian Cinema*, vol. 2, 330–331. The Cinema Industry Development Company of Iran was headed by Mihdī Būshihrī, the husband of Ashraf Pahlavī (Reza Shah's twin sister).

[45] Naficy, *A Social History of Iranian Cinema*, vol. 2, 330.

[46] "Naqd-i Fīlm dar Īrān: Guzārishī az Yik Guftugū, bā Shirkat-i Nasīb Nasībī . . . Hūshang Hisāmī . . . Basīr Nasībī . . . Mīnāsīyān" [Film Critique in Iran: Report of a Discussion, with the Participation of Nasīb Nasībī . . . Hūshang Hisāmī . . . Basīr Nasībī . . . Mīnāsīyān], *Nigīn*, no. 54 (Ābān 1348 [October 1969]), 60.

[47] Nasīb Nasībī, "Fīlm-i *Sarzanish-i Rasmī*" [The Film, *Reprimand*], *Nigīn*, no. 43 (Āzar 1347 [December 1968]), 71.

[48] This description had been used to describe Javād Tāhirī's film, *Reprimand* (*Sarzanish-i Rasmī*, 1968). See *ibid.*

[49] Nasībī, "Fīlm-i *Sarzanish-i Rasmī*," 71.

through a range of terminologies: "Young Cinema" (Sīnamā-yi Javān),[50] "Indigenous Cinema" (Sīnamā-yi Būmī),[51] "New Cinema of Iran" (Sīnamā-yi Jadīd),[52] "Cinema of Necessity" (Sīnamā-yi Zarūrat),[53] "Pure Intellectual Cinema" (Sīnamā-yi Nāb-i Rushanfikrānah), "Public Artistic Cinema" (Sīnamā-yi 'Umūmī-yi Ārtīstī)[54] and a "Socially-Oriented Cinema" (Sīnamā-yi Jāmi'ah Garā)[55] were among the expressions used by the people in the guild to describe a cinema that desired to highlight its distance from the popular film industry, and underline its realist cinematic language and novel techniques in filmmaking. Jamshīd Mashāyikhī, a prominent pre- and post-revolutionary actor, for instance, clearly distinguished between films that were made for "an intellectual class" and those projected for the general public. The films of "the critically acclaimed Persian cinema," he stated in 1971, would succeed in superseding the "vulgar" (mubtazal) cinema of "Film-Farsi" only if the "young directors" of the new movement worked together, without concern for monetary gains.[56] Drawing on Iranian cinema's cosmopolitan pedagogy and everyday societal concerns, the trendsetters of this new movement sublimated social, political and ideological tensions, altered cinematic imaginaries and aroused intellectual debates.

What the critics expressed as the signifying character of this alternative cinematic movement was the youthfulness of its filmmakers, in both physical and metaphorical form. In 1976, Firaydun Rahnama, a prominent pre-revolutionary director and social critic, claimed that the

---

[50] *Ibid.*

[51] "Sīnamā-yi Būmī" [Indigenous Cinema], *Rūdakī*, nos 37–38 (Ābān–Āzar 1353 [October–November 1974]), 21.

[52] Bihzād 'Ishqī, "Sīnamā-yi Jadīd-i Īrān" [New Cinema of Iran], *Rūdakī*, nos 39–40 (Day–Bahman 1353 [December 1974–January 1975]), 36.

[53] Bihzād 'Ishqī, "Sīnamā-yi Zarūrat" [Cinema of Necessity], *Rūdakī*, nos 39–40 (Day–Bahman 1353 [December 1974–January 1975]), 36.

[54] These terms were specifically used to describe the cinema of Kamran Shirdel (and his film, *The Night It Rained* [*Ūn Shab kah Bārūn Ūmad*, 1967–1974]). See Parī Safā, "Nishastī bā Kāmrān Shīrdil" [A Conversation with Kamran Shirdel], *Rūdakī*, nos 39–40 (Day–Bahman 1353 [December 1974–January 1975]), 13.

[55] Bihzād 'Ishqī, "Sīnamā-yi Jāmi'ah Garā" [Socially-Oriented Cinema], *Rūdakī*, no. 48 (Mihr 1353 [September–October 1974]), 14. Bihzād 'Ishqī, interestingly, further divided the socially oriented cinema of the pre-revolutionary era into the two categories of "Reformist Socially Oriented Cinema" and "Revolutionary Socially Oriented Cinema."

[56] "Dar Justujūy-i Yik Sīnamā-yi Sālim va Tafakkur-Angīz" [In Search of a Healthy and Thought-Provoking Cinema], an interview with Jamshīd Mashāyikhī by H. Rafī', *Nigīn*, no. 78 (Ābān 1350 [October 1971]), 35.

"only hope" for Iranian cinema rested in the hands of "the youth."[57] This movement, pioneered by young, cosmopolitan directors, evoked a fresh beginning – a new spirit that inevitably did not fear commercial failure and artistic experimentation. Labels such as "Avant Garde Cinema" or "New Cinema," Rahnama remarked, had been used flippantly to designate this cache of films; the use of the title "alternative cinema" (sīnamā-yi dīgar), however, was more appropriate in the opinion of the author, as it denoted a trend that was far from the "common concept of cinema."[58] The title of "alternative cinema," Rahnama claimed, no longer referred to the cinema of "the youth of New York" alone, but also to the youthful trend of filmmaking in Iran; he thereby linked the young cinematic trend in Iran to the international cinema.[59] In a 1996 retrospective interview, Farrukh Ghaffari, an influential critic and director of the pre-revolutionary era, also contended the term "New Wave Cinema" (sīnamā-yi Mawj-i Naw) to be an "erroneous" (ghalat) label for this new pre-revolutionary cinematic trend. Instead, he proposed "Alternative Cinema" (Sīnamā-yi Mutifā-vit) as a novel title for the collection of films that were made by the young generation of filmmakers.[60] Alter(native) cinema was, therefore, seen as a different trend from the commercial movie industry of the time, in both technique and content.

Alter-cinema responded to the national sensorium that was imagined by social critics – a body of imaginings and realities that they perceived as being occluded by earlier and commercial cinematic conventions. Inspired by French New Wave films, Hūshang Hisāmī, a film critic, claimed that unlike countries such as France where, for a large number of people, spectatorship was considered as a "thought-stimulating" activity, film-watching in Iran was solely conceived as "one hundred percent entertainment."[61] The writer stressed that the alternative film industry needed to divert its direction from the entertainment cinema.

---

[57] Firaydun Rahnama, "Javānān Tanhā Umīd-i Sīnamā-yi Mā Hastand" [The Youth Are the Only Hope for Our Cinema], Kāvah [Munich], no. 60 (Summer 1355 [1976]), 28.
[58] Ibid.   [59] Ibid.
[60] Farrukh Ghaffari, "Sīnamā-yi Īrān az Dīrūz tā Imrūz" [Iran's Cinema from Yesterday to Today], Īrān Nāmah, yr 14, no. 3 (Tābestān 1375 [Summer 1996]), 350.
[61] "Barrisī-yi Naqd-i Fīlm dar Īrān (2)" [An Examination of Film Criticism in Iran (2)], Nigīn, no. 56 (Day 1348 [December 1969]), 38.

At a time when social, political, economic and cultural contradictions were at their height and leftist and socialist ideologies deemed
change as necessary, the young directors demanded a push for a visual
revolution by incorporating realism and socially committed themes
into their own visual offerings. In their attempts, they at times
employed Iranian modernist literary works that entertained critical
and philosophical questions and concerns. In fact, collaboration
among modernist writers such as Ghulamhussayn Sa'edi and Hushang
Gulshiri and the new group of filmmakers, Naficy argues, drew them
closer as an oppositional assembly of cultural trendsetters. Some
members of this young group of writers and filmmakers founded the
Writers' Association of Iran (Kānūn-i Nivīsandigān-i Īrān) which, despite its intermittent lifespan, aimed to recognise and acknowledge the
entitlements of writers who wrote for publications, theatre, cinema,
radio and television.[62] Most members of this young community of
filmmakers and writers belonged to leftist intellectual groups who
expressed their political views, albeit in symbolic forms, in literary
and filmic productions.[63] Some filmmaker-writer members of this
association included Bahram Bayzayi and Nādir Ibrāhīmī.[64]

In 1969, underscoring the philosophical conundrums that critics
expected in the new movement, Hūshang Hisāmī remarked that "the
Iranian critic awaits the presentation of a philosophical question in a
movie theatre."[65] The philosophical analysis of films, in the words of
another author, Nasīb Nasībī, required extensive "knowledge and a
cognition of cinematic expression," a task that only a limited number
of people with the necessary skills were fit to carry out.[66] Some critics,
therefore, prompted alter-cinema directors to make films that spoke to
a larger audience and were also commercially successful. In a public
letter to Firaydun Rahnama, a critic, poet and avant-garde director,
Kāvūsī mentioned that Iranian cinema had "two poles": one was the
pole with "big money and small thinking," and the other the pole with
"small money and big thinking."[67] The first pole, Kāvūsī believed, had
dominated the field and would not be deterred by "the usual means,"

---

[62] Naficy, *A Social History of Iranian Cinema*, vol. 2, 403.   [63] *Ibid.*
[64] *Ibid.*   [65] "Barrisī-yi Naqd-i Fīlm dar Īrān (2)," 35.   [66] *Ibid.*
[67] Hūshang Kāvūsī, "Yik Nāmah bah Firaydūn Rahnamā" [A Letter to Firaydun
Rahnama], *Nigīn*, no. 29 (Mihr 1346 [September 1967]), 16.

unless there was a change "in the way of thinking and in public taste."[68] Kāvūsī encouraged Rahnama, whose films were artistic and philosophically inclined, to make films that would divert the capital that had wrongfully gone into the pockets of commercial filmmakers for years to the place where it belonged: in the cinema of the likes of "Rahnama, Gulistān and Gulah."[69] Such assertions demonstrate that directors were encouraged to make films that were not only esthetically and thematically fitting for international festivals, but also suitable for Iranian masses.

The pleas of the critics prompted alternative filmmakers to draw on unconventional styles of filmmaking and to create socially committed esthetic expressions. The reason for such attention to the social and filmic realism, according to Dariush Ashoori, was to be found in history. Writing in 1965, Ashoori, a writer and intellectual, considered the arts in Iran to be going through "an age of crisis," riddled with "confusion" and "chaos."[70] Very few Iranian works of art, in his opinion, were considered valuable on an international level. Ashoori considered historical and social constraints to account for an artist's inability to gain international recognition; while the artist was unable to change these factors, Ashoori contended, an "awareness" of such limitations was an effective solution for the artist to liberate him- or herself.[71] After a golden cultural age, the author continued, civilised societies of Asia experienced an age of stagnation, during which these civilisations were subject to the invasion of Western culture, importation of machinery and the kind of lifestyle that such new modes of interaction gave rise to. This cultural invasion overthrew the foundations of ancient civilisations and pushed them into an "intense social, economic, political, and cultural revolution."[72] This revolution, Ashoori thought, was still in progress at the time of his writing, and it was for this reason that Iranian contemporary art could not escape from social fever and turbulence.[73] Everything, according to him, was "in a stage of transformation and change."[74] Although the Iranian artist was dependent on the "foreigner," he or she still had "roots" within his or her ancestral land.[75] The film directors of the alternative movement embodied the revolutionary fervour and social disquiet

---

[68] *Ibid.*   [69] *Ibid.*
[70] Dariush Ashoori, "Mushkil-i Hunarmand-i Imrūz" [The Problem of Today's Artist], *Ārash*, no. 10 (Ābān 1344 [October 1965]), 120.
[71] *Ibid.*   [72] *Ibid.*, 121.   [73] *Ibid.*   [74] *Ibid.*   [75] *Ibid.*, 122.

spoken of by Ashoori. They took their cameras to the streets and recorded the vernacular of Iranians in sophisticated and internationally recognised cinematic forms.

The emerging alter-cinema was not necessarily an industry that was financed by independent and non-governmental institutions – in fact, many films of this cinema were funded by governmental or semi-governmental agencies, such as the NRTO, the Ministry of Culture and Arts and the Institute for the Intellectual Development of Children and Young Adults. While the first two institutions were part of the state ideological apparatuses, they were not homogeneous in their control and disciplining of the industry.[76] These agencies entertained different ideologies and were shaped by the personal philosophies of their administrators. The NRTO, for example, according to Nasībī, had been "with no doubt" effective in the development of Iran's "Young Cinema."[77] Films such as *Reprimand* (1968) by Javād Tāhirī, for example, were made possible through the facilities provided by NRTO for the young directors of the time. The Ministry of Culture and Art, on the other hand, was perceived as a more conservative organisation.[78]

Despite the efforts of the religious establishment and social critics who sought to discipline and purify cinema from the socio-political and cultural interventions of the West, as the previous chapters have demonstrated, Iranian cinema was already riddled with heterogeneity, transnational imaginings and cosmopolitan visions. In its dialogic cultural interactions, alter-cinema did not annihilate "Western cinema" or "Film-Farsi," but it rather worked toward their incorporation, humiliation, critique and commendation. While the eclectic alter-cinema highlighted Iranian "values" or what can be regarded as the Iranian vernacular, this cinematic movement as a whole did not seek to posit Iran as necessarily unique or exceptional in relation to its global counterparts; and while it attempted to separate itself

---

[76] Naficy, *A Social History of Iranian Cinema*, vol. 2, 331.

[77] Nasībī, "Fīlm-i *Sarzanish-i Rasmī*," 71.

[78] This observation is based on Mahnaz Afkhami's interview with the Minister of the Culture and Arts, Mehrdad Pahlbod, as part of the Oral History Project of Foundation for Iranian Studies. This is also quoted in Naficy, *A Social History of Iranian Cinema*, vol. 2, 331. See Mehrdad Pahlbod, "Oral History Interview: Mehrdad Pahlbod," interview by Mahnaz Afkhami, Oral History Project, Foundation for Iranian Studies, May 25 and 30, 1983, accessed April 20, 2018, http://fis-iran.org/en/content/pahlbod-mehrdad.

ideologically, its productions overlapped with those of the popular film industry as it drew on motifs such as song-and-dance numbers, fight scenes and the vernacular of southern Tehran. In other words, this cinematic movement's "imaginary coherence," to borrow from Andrew Higson, that categorised it as national cinema was, in fact, pluralistic and international in character.[79]

Films of alter-cinema presented a sense of familiarity, in both content and structure, with global cinemas of the time. Many directors within the alter-cinematic movement had studied cinema and film studies abroad. To name a few: Sohrab Shahid Sales (1943–1998) studied cinema in both Vienna and Paris; Kamran Shirdel (b. 1939), an acknowledged documentary maker, finished his studies in Rome under the instruction of directors such as Nanni Loy (1925–1995); Dariush Mehrjui (b. 1939) studied at the Department of Cinema at UCLA under the instruction of directors such as Jean Renoir (1894–1979); and Parviz Kimiavi (b. 1939) studied film and photography in France. Those not educated abroad had engaged with French, American, Azerbaijani, Soviet Russian, Indian, Turkish, German, Egyptian and Italian films that had been circulating in Iranian movie theatres and film associations for years. Having integrated an international cinematic visual archive, the young filmmakers reformed extant Iranian cinema so as to account for their cosmopolitan experiences in the making of modern Iranian identity. Farrukh Ghaffari's *South of the City* (*Junūb-i Shahr*, 1958), discussed at length in Chapter 4, was arguably the first alternative film that borrowed visual and narrative elements from the "Film-Farsi" cinema.[80] The following paragraphs will explore a number of other films that were considered to be part and parcel of this new cinematic trend.

Sīyāvash in Persepolis (*Sīyāvash dar Takht-i Jamshīd*, 1967), directed by Firaydun Rahnama (1930–1975), who had studied film at the Sorbonne in France, was arguably one of the first arthouse films of the Iranian alternative movement that had a postmodern approach to story-telling. Funded by the NRTO, the feature film showcased an ancient Iranian legend in a novel cinematic form. The film was shot on the site of the ancient Persepolis ruins in the suburbs of the city of Shiraz, which

---

[79] Andrew Higson, "The Concept of National Cinema," *Screen* 30(4) (1989): 38.

[80] *South of the City* was based on a story written by Jalāl Muqaddam, a prominent director of this period.

provided the film with historical significance. The film is based on *Shahnamah*'s story of Sīyāvash, a prince who tries to create peace in the land of his father, the King of Iran. Rejecting the advances of his father's first wife and thus provoking her contempt, Sīyāvash becomes the victim of lies that his stepmother schemes for him. Sīyāvash's step-mother tells the King of Iran that she and Sīyāvash had had an affair, resulting in several children who had all been murdered. Enraged by the news, the king orders his son to be burned to death; Sīyāvash's inno-cence, however, is proven by the fact that he miraculously walks out of the fire alive. Having performed a miracle, Sīyāvash becomes the leader of Iran's army against the rival country, Turan (Tūrān). The ruler of Turan offers Sīyāvash a peace treaty, in addition to 100 hostages – a deal refused by the king. Disagreeing with his father, Sīyāvash flees to another country and, on his travels, he marries the daughter of another ruler in Turan despite his uncle's disapproval. To take revenge, the uncle orders the killing of his nephew. Throughout the story, Sīyāvash is depicted as a just, pure and innocent son of Iran, whose heart beats for peace and justice. The story of Sīyāvash is revered in many Persian literary works and theatrical performances.

At the beginning of Rahnama's *Sīyāvash in Persepolis*, Sīyāvash, Kāvūs (the king), Sūdābah (the stepmother) and Afrāsīyāb (the future father-in-law), dressed in the attire of the Sassanian Dynasty (224–651 CE), are depicted as walking amid the ruins of Persepolis without any form of extravagant décor and stage set. While on a stroll, they encounter a few people with cameras and recording equipment whom, according to one member of the entourage, are tourists who have travelled to this land to make reports. Just as the people from the past are bewildered by the filmmaking crew and their Jeep automobile, the modern people are perplexed by the attire of the people of the past. Rahnama thus effaced the boundaries of time, bringing the past of Iran to its present. While merging fact and fiction to allude to the imaginary nature of pseudo-historical narratives, Rahnama reminded the viewer of and critiqued the Pahlavi Dynasty's appropriation of historical accounts to justify the government's increasingly nationalist ambitions that accompanied huge investments in a large army and attempts to return Iran to its ancient imperial past. Interestingly, in the same year, Mohammad Reza Shah coronated himself and Farah Pahlavi in a lavish ceremony held in Tehran, while he adopted the title of *Shāhanshāh* ("King of Kings"). In a different section of the film, Rustam, the champion of the ancient land of Iran and arguably the most famous hero of the *Shahnamah*, is depicted in a rather comical armour, playing a popular Iranian game (nūn bīyār, kabāb bibar) with a young child. Rustam, who is idolised in Persian literature for his corporeal strength and visionary capabilities, is subverted in Rahnama's film to become an everyday man, stripped of his fame, masculinity and reputation. Another scene in the film shows an archeologist and a woman dancing the tango on a platform in Persepolis when, suddenly, they both turn their gaze toward the viewer and stare at the camera. The film not only recalls the orientalist gaze of Europeans in its depiction of the exotic fables of *Shahnamah*, but also allows for the Iranian gaze to be fixated on Europeans amid the ancient ruins of Iran, unironically destroyed at the hands of Europeans. In merging old and new, past and present, fact and fiction and local and global in the desolate ruins of what was once the emblem of ancient Persian glory, Rahnama provides a postmodern outlook on the history of modern Iran.

In 1971, after the screening of *Sīyāvash in Persepolis* at Free Cinema festival, Nasīb Nasībī wrote a review in the *Free Cinema* publication.[81] Claiming Rahnama's film to embody a "poetic and knowledgeable architecture," Nasībī believed a "secret" to be hidden in the film, a "secret of humanity ... love, and existence."[82] "While watching the film," Nasībī remarked, "we are no longer earthbound. We are freed, able to fly."[83] The author believed the film had a connection with the future – "to a thousand years ahead" – in the same way that Rahnama connected the ancient story of Sīyāvash to "today's people" and showed that "today, too, Sīyāvash still exists."[84] Nasībī remarked that Rahnama mixed myth and reality, and used "a completely Eastern and spiritual technique" in his filmmaking.[85] Nasībī believed that Rahnama was about to establish a "school" of filmmaking in the country. In the same year, *Free Cinema* magazine published a translation of Henri Langlois's commentary on Rahnama's film after its screening at Paris Cinémathèque.[86] After praising the film, Langlois specifically pointed

---

[81] It should be noted that the film was first screened at Paris Cinémathèque in 1966.

[82] Nasīb Nasībī, "*Sīyāvash dar Takht-i Jamshīd*" [Siavash in Persepolis], *Sīnamā-yi Azād: Kitāb-i Avval* [Free Cinema: First Book] (Tehran: Azad Cinema Publishing Centre, Āzar 1350 [November 1971]), 63–64.

[83] *Ibid.*, 63.   [84] *Ibid.*   [85] *Ibid.*, 65.

[86] "Harfhā-yi Hānrī Lāngluwā Mudīr-i 'Sīnamā-tik'-i Pārīs dar Shab-i Namāyish-i Fīlm-i *Sīyāvash* dar Sīnamā-tik" [The Comments of Henri Langlois, the

out the "fourth dimension" of the film to be his favourite aspect – a
dimension that "destroyed time in the film and changed many
things."[87] Thus, the film signalled a significant turn in the history of
Iranian cinema's alternative movement; while it embodied elements that
spoke to the notion of Iranianness, it resonated with the sentiments of
postmodern literature and global avant-garde filmmaking – which in
turn led to the positive reception of the film by cinephiles in Paris and
art milieus in Iran.

Mrs Ahu's Husband (*Shawhar-i Āhū Khānūm*, 1968) directed by
Davūd Mullāpūr (b. 1938), a narrative film that combined popular
sentiments with new cinematic forms, was considered by the film critic,
'Abdulrizā 'Attār, as a "good film" made on a limited budget – a
worthwhile project that was undertaken at a time when cinema in Iran
had "become the carcass-eater of an abundant number of" foreign
movies and "Film-Farsi" productions.[88] For 'Attār, this was a film that
presented "what Persian cinema ought to be."[89] Based on a popular
book by 'Alī Muhammad Afghānī (b. 1925) published in 1960, the
film depicts the life of a married, middle-aged, religious man, Sayyid
Mīrān, who after meeting Humā, a young widowed woman, finds
himself struggling with his carnal desires. Sayyad Mīrān finally gives
in to his lust at the expense of losing his moral ways; violating the
ethical and cultural conventions of the time, tarnishing his reputation
and breaking his wife's heart, Sayyid Mīrān takes Humā as his second
wife. The book and the film both seem to challenge such patriarchal
polygamous practices that are sanctioned by Shi'i laws – but are
arguably uncommon among the urban public – and depict them as
immoral on a social level. At the end of the film, Sayyid Mīrān, who
has already experienced considerable hardship, both emotional and
financial, finds himself back with his first wife, Āhū Khānum, when
Humā, the symbol of sin-enticing evil, abruptly decides to leave her
new husband; Sayyid Mīrān looks at his first wife and smiles at her,

Manager of Paris "Cinémathèque" on the Night of the Screening of the Film,
Siavash, at the Cinémathèque], *Sīnamā-yi Azād: Kitāb-i Avval* (Āzar
1350 [November 1971]), 69. Henri Langlois was a co-founder of Cinémathèque
Française and a friend of Firaydun Rahnama.
[87] "Harfhā-yi Hānrī Lāngluwā Mudīr-i 'Sīnamā-tik'-i Pārīs," 71.
[88] 'Abdulrizā 'Attār, "*Shawhar-i Āhū Khānum*: Fīlmī Tahsīn Bar-Angīz" [*Mrs
Ahu's Husband*: An Admirable Film], *Nigīn*, no. 43 (Āzar 30, 1347 [December
21, 1968]), 59–60.
[89] *Ibid.*, 59.

a gaze and smile that she returns, alluding to a happy ending in the film. Praising the film for having used an Iranian literary work and departing from the common themes of Iranian commercial films (including scenes of "eating beef stew," "belly dancing" and "fight scenes" in café-bars),[90] 'Attār stated that *Mrs Ahu's Husband* had used cinematic allegories that were employed by international filmmakers.

Like many other filmmakers of the time, Dāvūd Mullāpūr, the director of *Mrs Ahu's Husband*, had received his higher education outside Iran. He first came upon Afghānī's book, *Mrs Ahu's Husband*, in London, suggested to him by Arbi Ovanessian, an arthouse filmmaker and theatre director, who initially intended to direct the film.[91] Due to some miscommunication between Mullāpūr and Ovanessian, however, Mullāpūr decided to direct the film himself. According to an interview in *Firdawsi* magazine, Mullāpūr wanted to make a film "for Iran," while Ovanessian intended to make a film "for outside Iran."[92] Directing a film that did not necessarily have an "intellectual" dimension to it – unlike the approach that Ovanessian would have taken – Mullāpūr aspired to produce a film that was to the taste of the "market" and did not require "people to think a lot." The film was perceived as a well-made alternative film, perhaps partly because it was based on a literary work.[93] "National features," "presentation of native thoughts" and common "expectations of the audience" were a number of factors that were taken into account in the making of *Mrs Ahu's Husband*.[94] The film was especially praised by critics and intellectuals for representing the "oppression of women" on the Iran screen (Figure 5.2).[95] Claiming the film to be "hundred per cent Iranian," another film critic in *Firdawsi* magazine commended the director for

---

[90] Hūshang Kāvūsī considered scenes of eating "beef stew" (ābgūsht – a traditional Iranian dish), "belly dancing" (raqs-i shikam) and "fight scenes" (kutak-kārī) to be common motifs in all "Film-Farsi" movies. See Basīr Nasībī's interview with Hūshang Kāvūsī in 1968: Basīr Nasībī, "Fīlm va Sīnamā va Fīlm Fārsī" [Film and Cinema and Film-Farsi], *Nigīn*, no. 39 (Murdād 31, 1347 [August 22, 1968]), 10.

[91] "Musāhibah bā Dāvūd Mullāpūr Kārgardān-i Fīlm-i Shawhar-i Āhū Khānūm" [An Interview with Dāvūd Mullāpūr the Director of *Mrs Ahu's Husband*], *Firdawsī*, no. 889 (Āzar 18, 1347 [December 9, 1968]), 42. This article is an interview with Dāvūd Mullāpūr by Kamran Shirdel, Muhammad Ali Sepanlu, Ahmad Rizā Ahmadī, Nūrī 'alā and Firaydūn Mu'izī Muqaddam.

[92] *Ibid.*, 43.   [93] *Ibid.*   [94] *Ibid.*

[95] Although this was a task that had also been undertaken in many "Film-Farsis" of the time.

Figure 5.2 A report on *Mrs Ahu's Husband* (1968) in *Firdawsi* magazine

refraining from contributing to the "nauseating imitations" that are "Film-Farsi" and for making a "national" film.[96]

Similar to *Mrs Ahu's Husband*, Dariush Mehrjui's *The Cow* (*Gāv*, 1969) was also based on a literary work – a screenplay by Ghulamhussayn Sa'edi. The film was praised by film critics as a film with global sentiments, as it suggested universal themes of hopelessness, marginalisation and loss. Comparing Mehrjui's stories to modern tales of Kalilah and Dimnah,[97] Zīyā Razavī praised the humanism of *Gāv* in that it portrayed the narration of "human in the name of human, free from the mask of animalism."[98] The protaganist of the film, Mashdī Hassan, lives in a remote, impoverished village, where the means of his subsistence are reduced to a single cow. The passing away of the beloved cow stimulates a series of mysterious events, the most significant of which is the metamorphosis of Mashdī Hassan into the character of the cow, itself. Screened at the Berlin, Cannes and Moscow film festivals, *Gāv*, according to Razavī, a film critic, was especially noted for its depiction of "the various faces of imperialism," "socially constructed relations and interests of humans" and its "critique of property" and superficial "aims of people" in life – topics that were of utmost importance in the political discussions of the late 1960s.[99] The physical and visual alienation of Mashdī Hassan, the sense of despair and overall grim spirit of the film conveyed imaginaries that resonated with educated and socio-politically conscious audiences.

As soon as it was released in 1969, *Qaysar* (1969), by Mas'ūd Kīmīyāyī (b. 1941), was critically acclaimed as one of the formative films of Iranian national cinema.[100] What was important for the film critic, 'Alī Hamadānī, was that *Qaysar* "brought tidings from the

---

[96] Al'ām, "'*Shawhar-i Āhū Khānūm:*' yik Āghāz-i Sitāyish-Āmīz" ["*Mrs Ahu's Husband:*" An Applaudable Beginning], *Firdawsī*, no. 889 (Āzar 18, 1347 [December 9, 1968]), no page numbers available.

[97] *Kalilah va Dimnah* is a collection of ancient Indian tales in Sanskrit which was first translated to Pahlavi Persian during the Sassanian Empire (224–651 AD). The animal fables of this collection were used as a treatise for political and human conduct during various dynasties in the Middle East.

[98] Zīyā Razavī, "Fistīvāl-i Sīnamāyī-yi Birlīn, 1972" [Berlin Film Festival, 1972], *Kāvah* (Munich), nos 41–42 (Pāyīz va Zimistān 1350 [Fall and Winter 1972]), 304.

[99] *Ibid.*

[100] In fact, according to 'Alī Hamadānī, the film was claimed to be "the first" or "second" film of Iranian cinema industry at the time of its production in 1969.

confines of our own four-walls (chāhār-dīvārī)."[101] The film was conceived as particularly "Iranian" in that it (re)presented "the blind rebellions and ubiquitous dead-ends" that were seen every day "protruding from the four-walls" of Iranian private lives in the southern parts of Tehran.[102] A girl is raped and, to save herself from the public embarrassment of unchastity, she attempts suicide by poisoning herself. With the violation of her virtue, the honours of her brothers and family are also marred. In the hypermasculine society of southern Tehran where the impaired honour of men must be amended, the brothers, Farmān and Qaysar, set out to take revenge by themselves. Farmān, a Jāhil who has relinquished his knife for a reformed life, is killed by the rapist's brothers. In the absence of social justice, Qaysar, who now needs to avenge both his sister and his brother, redefines universal ethics according to his own personal context, namely his dissatisfaction with the status quo. "If you don't strike first, they will strike you," says Qaysar to his mother as he prepares to embark on his vendetta. In his quest for justice, he engages in conflict with the police and law enforcement, who fail in fulfilling their responsibility to implement justice in his impoverished community.[103] Qaysar perhaps evokes Nietzsche's character, Ubermensch, as he who creates new values, independent of others, for the enhancement of humanity. The popular reception of the film by the Iranian audience points to the welcoming of such new values in the society of the time.[104] Hamadānī compared the film's theme of vice/virtue to the genre of Western films; while "[Andre] Bazin considered Western film as the American epic," Hamadānī considered *Qaysar* as the Iranian "epic," one that in its imitation of Western films, "if there is any imitation," was better than the original.[105]

See 'Alī Hamadānī, "Hamāsah-'i Qaysar va Sīm-i Ākhar" [The Epic of Qaysar and Madness], *Nigīn*, no. 56 (Day 1348 [December 1969]), 68.

[101] *Ibid.*, 69.   [102] *Ibid.*

[103] It is interesting to compare Qaysar's scuffle with the police in *Qaysar* (1969) with Safar-'Alī's struggle in *Tongue-Tied* (1965), a popular film that was discussed in Chapter 4, where the latter respects the law even though he pursues his own sense of justice. *Qaysar* encompasses a robust revolutionary spirit and social angst that is less prominent in *Tongue-Tied*.

[104] Qaysar had a following outside movie theatres, as some people started dressing and carrying themselves like him.

[105] Hamadānī, "Hamāsah-'i Qaysar," 69.

Taking issue with the "folkloric" elements of *Qaysar*, Hūshang Kāvūsī wrote an unfavourable review of the film in *Nigīn* cultural magazine, in reaction to the positive appraisal of *Qaysar* by the prominent filmmaker, Ibrāhīm Gulistān.[106] Desiring a national cinema that distanced itself from "Film-Farsi" productions, Kāvūsī ridiculed *Qaysar* for its employment of everyday practices and vernacular language of the south of Tehran – a neighbourhood which was widely invoked in "Film-Farsi" motion pictures. "When I watch *Qaysar*," Kāvūsī mentioned, "I clearly see its connection to 'Film-Farsi.'"[107] The author mocked how scenes from traditional "coffee houses" (qahvah-khānah), "Nāyib Gurbah Shopping Centre" (Bāzārchah Nāyib Gurbah), an old-fashioned neighbourhood in southern Tehran where the most important events of the film take place, outmoded public "bath houses" and "prayer veils" (chādur namāz) supposedly added elements of "pure folklore" (fulklur-i khālis) to the film and made a "pure cinema" (sīnamā-yi ʿasīl).[108] This was how, in the sardonic words of Kāvūsī, "Film-Farsi" was suddenly "transformed into pure Iranian cinema" which apparently had "a second birth after many years of waiting."[109] Such comments shared by Kāvūsī allude to two points: (1) that alter-cinema films borrowed from elements of popular film productions that were successful at the box office and that spoke to everyday Iranians; and (2) that critics had differing viewpoints on what constituted an alternative cinema.

Tranquillity in the Presence of Others (Ārāmish dar Huzūr-i Dīgarān), made by Naser Taghvayi (b. 1941) in 1970 and screened in 1973, depicted the mechanical lives of a people and a lifestyle that reflected otiose human values and a lack of motivation for continued existence. Recalling it as "Tranquillity in the presence of a *catastrophe*," Gītī Vahīdī believed Taghvayi to have effectively "accessed the culture of his society," a culture that had "polluted" (ālūdah kardah) urban city-dwellers and "brought them to a state of dreadfulness."[110] The film

---

[106] Hūshang Kāvūsī, "Az ʿDāj Sītī' tā Bāzārchah-'i Nāyib Gurbah" [From "Dodge City" to the Bazaar of Nayib Gurbah], *Nigīn*, no. 56 (Day 1348 [December 1969]), 23.

[107] *Ibid.*   [108] Kāvūsī, "Az ʿDāj Sītī' tā Bāzārchah-'i Nāyib Gurbah," 23–24.

[109] *Ibid.*, 44.

[110] Gītī Vahīdī, "Ārāmish dar Huzūr-i Fāji'ah" [Tranquility in the Presence of a Catastrophe], *Nigīn*, no. 96 (Urdībihisht 1352 [April 1973]), 56 (emphasis added).

portrays a retired colonel who, after moving to a village and marrying a simple woman, Munirah, decides to sell everything and move back to his house in the city. To his surprise and denial, however, his two daughters Malihah and Mahlaqā – whom he had left in the city – have changed significantly since he saw them last; so has the colonel himself, now that he has lost his former power and glory. The loneliness of all characters in the deceitful and trivial world outside heralds a disastrous ending for the film. "Pregnant with catastrophe," in the words of Vahīdī, the film was a metaphor for a universal tragedy, and it called for a return to "virginal traditions" (sunnat-i bikr) and the "pure ... culture" of ruralism.[111]

Sohrab Shahid-Sales's *A Simple Event* (*Yik Ittifāq-i Sādah*, 1973), screened at numerous film festivals, is arguably a spaceless and timeless allegory for marginalised classes, as well as a symbol for the crushed dreams of the Iranian underclass. The slow tempo and visual esthetics of the film set *A Simple Event* in stark contrast with the commercial films of the time. The film revolves around the life of a young village boy in the northern parts of Iran who struggles to catch up with his studies at school and help his father in illegal fishing, while taking care of his ill mother in the evenings. The eventual death of his mother is a quiet catastrophe in the life of the boy, who is a mere bystander as the world around him continues unchanged. In the words of A. H. Weiler (1975), an editor and critic from the *New York Times* who reported on the screening of the film at the Museum of Modern Art's New Directors/New Films series in New York City, the "documentary-like authenticity" of the film portrayed the global "tragedy of isolation, poverty and hopelessness" localised in the "daily life of a [ten year old] boy" in the Persian hinterland.[112]

Henry Chapier of the journal *Le Quotidien de Paris* conceived of *The Beehive* (*Kandū*, 1975), by Firaydūn Gulah, as a film with a "global subject."[113] In this film, the case of an Iranian unemployed

[111] *Ibid.*, 55.
[112] A. H. Weiler, "The Screen; A Simple Event," *New York Times*, April 8, 1975, accessed February 21, 2013, www.nytimes.com/1975/04/08/archives/the-screen-a-simple-event-from-iran-at-modern-art.html.
[113] "Gulah, Mahbūb-i Sīnamāgarān-i Īrān" [Gulah, Popular among Iranian Filmmakers], *Sīnamā 54*, no. 21 (Day–Bahman 1354 [December 1975–January 1976]), 8. This film review is published in Persian in Tehran International Film Festival journal, *Sīnamā 54*, in a column under the name of the French journal, *Le Quotidien de Paris*. I have not consulted the original review in French.

young man in a rapidly developing society is globalised through the universal themes of estrangement, desperation and insubordination, present throughout the film. The local traditional coffee-house where the protagonist, Ebi (Ibī), spends most of his time becomes the locale of such transcendental motifs. In the film, Ebi makes a bet to pass through seven café-restaurants devouring food and drink without paying for them. The number of restaurants visited by Ebi is arguably an allegory for the seven passages of the Iranian mythological hero, Rustam, who appears in the book of *Shahnamah*. Donning the American outfit provided by his friend, Ebi begins his journey in dime-store cafés and makes his way up to the more upscale bars, where his obtrusive appearance is no longer invisible among their middle- and high-class customers. Along the way, he is relentlessly beaten – acts that symbolise the suppression and isolation of marginalised voices.

Masʿūd Kīmīyāyī's *Soil/Land* (*Khāk*, 1973) was perceived to have a "historical and thus, inevitably humanist" feel, arising from the director's established style of filmmaking.[114] Hassan Asadī believed that Kīmīyāyī's films depicted "the bitter lives" of people – the "internal contradiction" of the lives of Iranians.[115] The title of the film, according to Asadī, alludes to a critical item that connects humans to life: "land."[116] *Khāk* was another literary film of its period based on Mahmud Dawlat Abadi's story, *The Legend of Baba Subhan* (*Usnah-'i Bābā Subhān*, 1967). The film depicts how the widowed "Frankish" (European) wife of the lord of a village attempts to take over the land on which Baba Subhan's sons, Sālih and Musayyib, have worked as farmers for a long time. The land, which had been given to the sons by the lord himself, represents all that the two young men have owned and lived for their whole lives; it is the land where they work and invest their time, the land they financially depend on, feed from and pray on. The struggle over the land leads to the killing of Musayyib and the injuring of Sālih – who then attempts to take revenge for his brother, his land and the life that he once had. Themes of injustice imposed upon the brothers and their inability to change their fates evoke themes of marginalisation and inequality present in many other films of altercinema. Such themes are localised in the context of an Iranian village

---

[114] Hassan Asadī, "Naqdhā-yi darbārah-'i Film-i *Khāk*: Tārīkh bar Zamīnah-'i 'Khāk'" [Comments about the Film, *Soil/Land*: History Based on "Land"], *Nigīn*, no. 101 (Mihr 1352 [September 1973]), 14.
[115] *Ibid.* [116] *Ibid.*, 15.

by depicting traditions of carpet weaving and farming, as well as clothing, village accent and local customs. The subject of the film, according to Asadī, spills over into the "reality" of Iranian everyday life and "conforms" to universal themes.[117] Khāk or land in this film stands for mother Iran. While the "Frankish" woman represents the international political forces that exploited Iranian land and national resources, the two sons of Baba Subhan symbolise mother nation's sons who fought for their home land and brought honour to their family and village. The European wife, dressed in city women's clothing, exemplifies wickedness, shrewdness and injustice. She is placed in stark contrast to Musayyib's wife, dressed in simple white clothes, who represents a nurturing mother, modest wife and support-ive sister for the sons of Iran. Baba Subhan's remark that "having your eye on somebody else's food spread constitutes a dishonour" could likewise be interpreted as a call for objection against American imperi-alism in Iran. Baba Subhan's family demonstrates the "oppression of the working people" and Musayyib's death represents the honour in becoming a martyr; drawing on Shi'ite traditions in glorifying and idealising martyrdom, Asadī praised Musayyib's death, especially since the defence of land, the "source of economic life, and spring of culture and morality," required martyrdom.[118]

The pre-revolutionary alter-cinema was an attempt to redefine "Iran-ian cinema" and create a visual depository that portrayed the vernacu-lar and Iranian experience of modernity in politically and ideologically sublimated forms. Parviz Kimiavi's *Excavations at Qaytariyyah* (*Haf-fārī dar Qaytarīyyah*, 1969) was considered by Nasībī to be "an alternative film from an alternative cinema" (fīlmī dīgar az sīnamāyī dīgar).[119] Kimiavi, a filmmaker who in the words of Nasībī "spoke consciously," had a cinematic vision that was "special" and that could not be defined within a single framework; when he moved his camera, it was as if he discovered "another world."[120] Mehrjui's *The Postman* (*Pustchī*, 1972) represented "the labouring class," and, more specific-ally, the "transformation of the rural order into an industrial one" in a

---

[117] *Ibid.*   [118] *Ibid.*
[119] Nasīb Nasībī, "*Haffārī dar Qaytarīyyah*: Fīlmī Dīgar az Sīnamāyī Dīgar" [*Excavations at Qaytarīyyah*: An Alternative Film from an Alternative Cinema], *Nigīn*, no. 31 (Murdād 1348 [July 1969]), 69.
[120] *Ibid.*, 73.

rapidly industrialising Iran.[121] In its visual grammar, social hierarchies are concretely demonstrated through the framing of the postman's small house, which stands isolated in stark contrast to the master's mansion. On the other hand, the physical struggle of the postman with impotency, while his rival engages in an affair with his wife, exemplifies his castration at the hand of a Europeanised enemy. The postman's sexual illness arguably symbolised the incapability of the Shah of Iran to stand up to American influence and intervention. Upon learning of his wife's affair, the postman attacks his rival with a knife and kills him. *Prince Ihtijab* (*Shāzdah Ihtijāb*, 1974) drew from the monarchical history of Iran to narrate "the decline of an aristocratic family in the context of an end of an era," perhaps signifying the end of a monarchical Iran.[122] In his numerous films before the revolution, such as *Hassan Kachal* (*Hassan, the Bald*, 1971), *Bābā Shamal* (1972) and *Sattār Khān* (1972), 'Alī Hātamī dramatised Iranian folklore, rituals and historical events into popular motion pictures that explored themes of vernacular idioms and nationhood.[123] Hātamī's *Tūqī* (1970) drew on the practices and customs of traditional families who, instead of trusting the state, relied on honour and their own definition of Shari'a (Islamic law) to settle disputes. Although such topics also circulated in the commercial comedies of the time, Hātamī's film was an alternative and grim demonstration of voicelessness and personal justice in a city with high unemployment rates.

The Spring (*Chishmah*, 1971), directed by Arby Ovanessian, an Armenian-Iranian filmmaker who had studied film at the London School of Film Technique, and theatre in America, was a poetic and philosophical rendering of two tragic interconnected love stories. Taking place in an Iranian village, the film, in the words of Bihzād 'Ishqī, represented "the dialectic of existence and non-existence," where "existence is inevitably tied to non-existence" in the conclusion of the film.[124] In his film, Ovanessian drew on familiar Iranian social

[121] Bihzād 'Ishqī, "Tazādhā-yi Ijtimā'ī dar Fīlm-i *Pustchī*" [Social Conflict in the Film, *The Postman*], *Nigīn*, no. 90 (Ābān 1351 [October 1972]), 49.

[122] Jamshīd Akramī, "Mīrās-i Tabāh Kunandah" [Corrosive Legacy], *Rūdakī*, nos 37–38 (Ābān–Āzar 1353 [October–November 1974]), 21.

[123] For more information about Ali Hatami's films, see Hamid Reza Sadr, *Iranian Cinema: A Political History* (New York: I. B. Tauris, 2006), 152–153.

[124] Bihzād 'Ishqī, "*Chishmah*" [*The Spring*], *Nigīn*, no. 94 (Farvardīn 1352 [March 1973]), 60.

norms and religious sentiments, namely, feelings of dishonour associated with a Christian woman's love affair outside her marriage, the
guilty conscience of a man who falls madly in love with a Christian
woman outside his marriage and the villagers' verdict to stone the
woman for enticing lust and breaking Iranian moral order. Ovanessian
incorporated a strongly symbolic language in his film; the spring, for
example, could metaphorically and physically stand for the female sex
as a source of love, lust and fertility.

   Bahram Bayzayi's *The Stranger and Fog* (*Gharībah va Mah*, 1974),
a depiction of "the disappointing philosophy of existence" that, like
many other films of its time, sublimated political sentiments of the
period, in the words of Akramī, bore "the aroma of Khayyam's
poems."[125] Filmed in a village in the north of Iran, the camera follows
everyday activities and rituals of the region's people. Expressing the
region's cultural and religious beliefs, the film amplifies Iranian motifs
and folkloric traditions in a surreal setting. One could argue that
although Hollywood and internationally prominent cinemas had set
standard styles that directors and spectators, everywhere, believed to
be modern, as the ground against which the stylistic accomplishments
of Iranian directors could be analysed, the efforts of the indigenous
directors to fashion Iranian idioms, "were crucially inflected by a
larger vernacular-modernist culture at once cosmopolitan and
local."[126] What was intrinsic to the cinematic temporality of alter-
cinema, one could therefore argue, was a complex network of cosmopolitan and vernacular elements that sublimated socio-political tensions of the society of the time (Figure 5.3).

5.4 The Branching of the Alternative Cinema: Azad Cinema

The alternative cinematic movement was not only limited to the filmic
offerings that were featured in Iranian movie theatres, television and
international festivals. Free Cinema (Sīnamā-yi Āzād), considered as
the "experimental" (Tajrubī) cinema of Iran, was an avant-garde
movement that distanced itself far from the narrative commercial

---

[125] Jamshīd Akramī, "Jahd dar Gharībah Namāyī" [Efforts in Defamiliarisation],
Rūdakī, nos 37–38 (Ābān–Āzar 1353 [October–November 1974]), 24.
[126] Miriam Hansen, "Vernacular Modernism: Tracking Cinema on a Global
Scale," in Nataša Ďurovičová and Kathleen Newman (eds), *World Cinemas:
Transnational Perspectives* (New York: Routledge, 2010), 295.

and alternative cinema. Free Cinema was first founded through the collaboration of a number of young directors. With the financial support of the National Television, according to Jamal Umid (a film-maker and co-founder of Free Cinema), Free Cinema took a more solid form.[127] The group showcased their own short films, mostly made as amateur school projects and theses, and later on – after they became better known among the public and cineastes – they started holding screening and discussion programs about prominent filmmakers. Eventually, the group also established a film festival and journal publication by the same name. In 1969, *Firdawsi* magazine supported Iran's "amateur cinema" that had recently found the opportunity to screen a number of its films at Iran's Kānūn-i Fīlm (Film Association), "the only healthy cinematic environment" in Iran.[128] In a report on an "amateur film" entitled *The Eyes* (*Chashmhā*, 1969), Basīr Nasībī reveals to the reader that the amateur cinema of Iran, which resembled an avant-garde (pīshraw) cinema, had begun with the short film, *The Blood of a Memory* (*Khūn-i Yik Khātirah*). *The Eyes* by Ibrāhīm Vahīd-Zādah included "new thoughts in a new form," "a subjective ambience" and "a symbolic expression"; overall, it was a film that, according to the author of the article, demonstrated the director's "hatred for a 'story-telling' cinema."[129] In an interview with the director in *Nigīn* magazine, Arby Ovanessian and Basīr Nasībī also praised the film for its new form amid "the vexatious bazaar of Film-Farsi."[130]

In 1970, after almost two years since its establishment, Basīr Nasībī commended the Free Cinema institution (in collaboration with Screening Workshop, another institution that projected and promoted amateur films) for showcasing experimental films for three consecutive

---

[127] Jamal Umid, *Tārīkh-i Sīnamā-yi Īrān: 1279–1357* [*The History of Iranian Cinema: 1900–1979*] (Tehran: Rawzanah Publications, 1995), 1035.

[128] Basīr Nasībī, "'*Chashmhā*' va Sīnamā-yi Ghayr-i Hirfah-yī" ["*The Eyes*" and the Non-Professional Cinema], *Firdawsī*, no. 914 (Khurdād 19, 1348 [June 9, 1969]), 37. It's very probable that Nasībī was making a reference to the Kānūn-i Millī-yi Fīlm (National Film Association), which showcased alternative and avant-garde Iranian and international films.

[129] *Ibid.*

[130] Arby Ovanessian, Ibrāhīm Vahīdzādah and Basīr Nasībī, "Harfhā-yī darbārah-'i yik Fīlm – (*Chashmhā*)" [Words about a Film – (*The Eyes*)], *Nigīn*, no. 49 (Khurdād 31, 1348 [June 21, 1969]), 25.

Figure 5.3 A film poster from the 1970s (*Journey of the Stone*, 1978)

nights, which helped to consolidate the movement in the country.[131]
The young filmmakers – who had recently learned how to use 8mm for
their films – organised the first festival of 8mm films in Iran.[132] Suhayl
Sūzanī, Humāyūn Pāyvar, Bihnām Jaʻfarī, Shahrīyār Pārsīpūr and Fīrūz

---

[131] Basīr Nasībī, "Sīnamā-yi Tajrubī: Chihrah-ʾi Dīgar-i Sīnamā-yi Īrān"
[Experimental Cinema: Another Face of Iranian Cinema], *Nigīn*, no. 68 (Day
1349 [December 1970]), 47.

[132] Umid, *Tārīkh-i Sīnamā-yi Īrān*, 1036. This is according to a report in the
Tehran International Film Festival publication (*Sīnamā 53* or *Cinema 1353*
[1974]) by Muhammad Haqīqat, which had not been published.

Guharī were among the number of young directors who were involved in this cinematic field. According to Nasībī, some of the films that were shown in the screenings were avant-garde with abstract subjects, while others explored historical and philosophical themes.[133] Shahrīyār Pārsīpūr, for example, drew from the *Epic of Gilgamesh* in the making of an experimental film by the same title, while Suhayl Sūzanī's *Loyalty 9 Take 171 (Ma'rifat 9 Take 171)* made "a conscious use of light" as the means to portray its content.[134] Despite their qualities, what Basīr believed to be "valuable" in experimental films related to their "freedom" and "liberation" from conventional methods of filmmaking and their "unpretentiousness." The "hope" for the future of Iran's cinema, the author believed, rested in the hands of the youth.[135] In a matter of a few years, Azad Cinema, or Iran's experimental cinema, had gained such momentum that it organised a film festival that would feature the short films made by Azad young directors.

5.5 Film Festivals and the Staging of an Alternative Vernacular-Cosmopolitan Cinema

Still zealous to watch internationally acclaimed art films, starting in the late 1940s and early 1950s, cinema enthusiasts, filmmakers, critics and university students organised numerous screening venues in various Iranian cities. In 1954, for example, the "biggest cinema festival of the year" was organised in Tehran, which was solely dedicated to the "great masterpieces of Italian cinema," including films such as Vittorio De Sica's *Bicycle Thieves* (1948) and Alberto Lattuada's *The Overcoat* (1952).[136] Similarly, the National Film Association (Kānūn-i Millī-yi Fīlm), which was established in 1949 and was later changed to the National Film Archive of Iran,[137] organised many film-screening events and festivals that showcased Iranian and international films usually not featured in commercial movie theatres.[138]

---

[133] Nasībī, "Sīnamā-yi Tajrubī," 47.   [134] *Ibid.*   [135] *Ibid.*
[136] "Buzurgtarīn Fistīvāl-i Sīnamāyī-yi Sāl az Shāhkārhā-yi Buzurg-i Fīlm-hā-yi Ītālīyāyī" [The Biggest Cinema Festival of the Year (Showcasing) the Great Masterpieces of Italian Films], *Sitārah'i Sīnamā*, no. 16 (Mihr 28, 1333 [October 20, 1954]), 25.
[137] Ghaffari, "Sīnamā-yi Īrān," 346.
[138] For more information about the National Film Association, see Ghaffari, "Sīnamā-yi Īrān," 343–352.

The National Art Association and Ciné Club (Kānūn-i Millī-yi Hunar va Sīnah Kulūb) was established in 1954 by a group of cinema, music, painting and literature experts, to serve as a forum for people to "assemble" in "social institutions, art associations ... and cultural agencies" in order to "exchange opinions on the advancement and expansion of art" in Iran.[139] The Association's mandate called for the organisation of "film festivals and theatres," "lectures on the topics of art and literature" and the "creation of a groundwork to counter the commercial aspects of art."[140] Various university student groups around the country also organised and publicised film events on university campuses and in art houses. In 1969, for example, Pahlavi University Film Association and Āryāmihr University held film nights on their campuses that showcased famous international intellectual and arthouse films.[141]

Starting in the early 1960s, Iran hosted many international artists, actors/actresses, directors and performing art groups who visited the country, especially Tehran, Mashhad, Isfahan and Shiraz, and staged their national artistic offerings. "The Week of Hungary's Art in Tehran," which took place in April 1968 at Hilton Hotel, is one such example; according to *Firdawsi* publication, Hungarian "artistic shows," "historical artifacts" and "folkloric art" were showcased in the capital during that week.[142] In order to create more familiarity and stronger rapport between the two countries, the exhibition included a selection of folkloric songs played by a group of Hungarian musicians, a gypsy troubadour who performed Hungarian folk music, a film about the country and ceramics and paintings, as well as Hungarian cuisine prepared by professional chefs.[143]

Numerous international festivals were also organised in Iran that acted as hubs of artistic diversity, spaces of heterogeneity that brought celebrated artists, actors, directors and films from around the globe

---

[139] "Kānūn-i Millī-yi Hunar va Sīnah Kulūb" [National Art Association and Ciné Club], *Payk-i Sīnamā*, yr 1, no. 9 (Āzar 6, 1333 [November 27, 1954]), 22.
[140] *Ibid.*
[141] "Kūshish dar Rāh-i Namāyish-i Fīlmhā-yi Khūb-i Sīnamāyī" [Attempts at the Screening of Good Cinema Films], *Nigīn*, no. 56 (Day 1348 [December 1969]), 49.
[142] "Haftah-'i Hunar-i Majāristān dar Tihrān" [The Week of Hungarian Art in Tehran], *Firdawsī*, no. 854 (Farvardīn 20, 1347 [April 9, 1968]), page not clear.
[143] *Ibid.*

to the country; these festivals and the cultural exchanges that ensued further facilitated the making of a macaronic cosmopolitan cinema culture. In 1959, Unifrance, an institution established for the promotion of French films outside France, in collaboration with Mr Ashtīyānī, organised a "French Cinema Week" as part of the French Film Festival in Tehran, which showcased seven major French feature productions and seven short films, including François Truffaut's *Les 400 Coups* (1959), Jacques Tati's *Mon Oncle* (1958) and René Clair's *Porte des Lilas* (1957).[144] Examples of other film festivals included the Tehran International Festival of Films for Children and Young Adults (starting in 1966), Shiraz Persepolis Arts Festival (Jashn-i Hunar-i Shīrāz, 1967–1977), Gratitude (Sipās) Film Festival (1969–1974), the critically acclaimed Tehran International Film Festival (1972–1979), Free Cinema Film Festival (starting in 1970) and Tūs Festival (starting in 1975).

Within two years of its inception, Tehran International Film Festival succeeded in becoming a Class A festival, and according to *Screen International*, was on its way to rank second after the renowned Cannes Festival.[145] *Variety* magazine, in fact, published a poster for the Tehran festival in 1976 that cited it as "the biggest film event after the Cannes Film Festival."[146] Tehran International Film Festival was a highly reputable event – at least in its early phase – that benefitted from the participation of many international actors, producers and filmmakers, namely Michelangelo Antonioni, Frencesco Rosi, Grigori Kozintsev, Alain Tanner, Pietro Germi, Nikita Mikhalkov, Lina Wertmüller and Georgian prominent filmmaker, Nana Mchedlidze, along with their films. "Is there a reason for one to bear the trouble of travelling such a long distance to Tehran?" asked a European reporter who had published an article in the Tehran International Film Festival publication in 1975 (Figure 5.4). In his reply, he named the

---

[144] Jalal Muqaddam, "Fistīvāl-i Fīlm-i Farānsah dar Tihrān" [French Film Festival in Tehran], *Fīlm va Zindigī*, no. 5 (1338 [1959]), 55–62.

[145] "Screen International: Īnjā Suhbat az Buland Parvāzī Ast" [Screen International: Here There Is Talk of Ambition], *Sīnamā 54*, no. 21 (Day–Bahman 1354 [December–January 1975]), 4.

[146] "Tehran International Film Festival," *Variety (Archive: 1905–2000)* 283, no. 2 (May 19, 1976): 77, accessed April 20, 2018, retrieved from http://search.proquest.com/docview/1285983144?accountid=14771.

Figure 5.4 An image from Tehran International Film Festival in 1975

Tehran festival as *the* reason for taking on such an endeavour.[147]
International critics regarded the festival to be an opportunity where
the "fixed ideas of the West [about Iran] would be brought to the table
for re-evaluation."[148] The critics believed that through the festival's
Iranian productions, filmmakers "attempted for the first time to present
a realist image of the everyday life of Iranians," which was, for them,
"completely different from the mythical picture of the East."[149]

After having visited the Tehran International Film Festival, Lina
Wertmüller, a prominent Italian director, spoke about the "tremendous
passion of Iranians in communicating and receiving information on a
cultural level," as well as their zeal for knowing about "all the events
that occur in the West."[150] Considering the special geopolitical position
of the country, Hazhīr Dāryūsh, the General Director of the Festival,

---

[147] Forslund, "Matbū'āt-i Jahān va Sivvumīn Jashnvārah-'i Jahānī-yi Fīlm-i
Tihrān" [World Publications and the Third Tehran International Film Festival],
Sīnamā 54 (Shahrīvar 1354 [September 1975]), 65.
[148] *Ibid.*   [149] *Ibid.*
[150] "Il Tempo," *Sinamā 54*, no. 21 (Day–Bahman 1354 [December–January
1975]), 8.

held that Iran played the "role of a bridge between the Western countries that had a long history of filmmaking" and the "new movements of filmmaking in the third world countries."[151] Aside from the foreign audience assembled by the festival in Tehran, the local Iranian audiences were also eager participants in film screenings. In his trip to the festival in 1976, the BBC film critic, Alexander Walker, remarked that he had not seen any other festival to have been "welcomed by the local population" to the same extent as in Tehran.[152] In an interview about Tehran International Film Festival, Bahman Farmān-Ārā, a filmmaker and producer who had studied drama in London and film in the United States, specifically stated that in the creating of artistic works, "one must think of the masses, and not only a few intellectual friends."[153] The film productions of the new movement and the festivals of the time, according to Farmān-Ārā, worked to "enhance the mindset of the people" and "boost their expectations of cinema," through interaction with the world beyond, hence fashioning a "revolution of thought," or a revolution of expectations in pre-revolutionary Iran.[154] All of these are indicative of a cinematic revolution, or a revolution of artistic thought that pre-dated the 1978–1979 political revolution, the history and temporality of which could not be studied in isolation from literary, ideological, cultural and political instances before and after it. It would be accurate to say that the films of alter-cinema both shaped and *were* shaped by Iranian experiences within the context of a globally embedded imaginarium; these films, then, worked to further inspire the ideologically and politically revolutionary sentiments of the public during this period – feelings that were manifested in political contestations from the 1960s to the late 1970s and exhibited in the 1979 revolution.

By a "process of incorporation," or creative dialogic processes, the alter-cinema of Iran integrated international cinematic elements as well

---

[151] "Screen International," 4.

[152] Alexander Walker, "Ingilistān, Firistandah-'i Tilivīzīyunī-yi B.B.C.: Jashnvārah-'i Chahārum, Fursatī Barā-yi Īrānīhā-yi Javān" [England, BBC Television Channel: The Fourth Festival, An Opportunity for Iranian Youth], *Sīnamā 55*, no. 22 (Farvardīn 2535 [March 1976]), 55. This article is based on an interview with Alexander Walker and an interviewee with regard to the film festival.

[153] Īraj Sābirī, "*Sāyah-hā-yi Buland*: 'Chūn' va 'Chirā' bā Bahman Farmān-Ārā" [*The Tall Shadows*: "Question" and "Answer" with Bahman Farman-Ara], *Sīnamā 56–58*, no. 36 (Murdād–Shahrīvar 1357 [August–September 1978]), 30.

[154] *Ibid.*, 34.

as the commercial Film-Farsi industry, and engendered a macaronic visual articulation that was implicitly, and at times explicitly, political.[155] Regardless of the cultural particularities expressed within these films, foreign film critics compared the productions of alter-cinema to those of world-renowned directors. Many international film critics, including the prominent British John Gillett, contended that Iran's new cinema was under the influence of international filmmakers – ranging from François Truffaut to Akira Kurosawa.[156] The techniques of Shahīd Sālis – named as the Chekhov of cinema – were reminiscent of Truffaut's *The 400 Blows* (1959), as well as the productions of Italy's neorealist movement;[157] Mehrjui's *The Postman* was believed to delineate "human irrationality and fallibility" as seen in Luis Buñuel's cinema;[158] Parviz Kimiavi's "strongly national" film, *The Mongols* (*Mughulhā*, 1973), was thought to be informed by the cinemas of Godard and Pudovkin.[159] Furthermore, Shirdel's documentary *That Night That Was Raining* (*Ūn Shab kah Bārūn Ūmad*, 1967–1974) was conceived to be charmed by hints of Italian neorealism;[160] and Bahman Farmān-Ārā's *Prince Ihtijab* was evocative of expressionist horror films.[161] Such proclamations were not indicative of an imitative cinema that mimicked cinemas of the West, whether commercial or avant-garde. Rather, in its artistic creation, this internationally engaged alternative cinema gave esthetic expression to the extant Iranian socio-political tensions, sublimating them into visual offerings that spoke to informed international audiences.

On the one hand, one could argue that the likening of the films of alter-cinema and/or their filmmakers to international (and especially European) filmmakers was reposed on an orientalist viewpoint that considered the industry of filmmaking in Iran to have been static; many critics were startled to witness such filmic creativity pouring forth in

[155] Peter McGee, *Cinema, Theory and Political Responsibility in Contemporary Culture* (Cambridge University Press, 1997), 26.
[156] John Gillett, "Dar Hāshīyah-'i Jashnvārah-'i Kan: Dar Intizār-i Zuhūr-i Āsārī Buzurg az Sīnamā-yi Īrān" [On the Sidelines of the Cannes Film Festival: In Anticipation of Great Works from Iranian Cinema], *Sīnamā 54*, no. 18 (Murdād–Shahrīvar 1354 [August–September 1975]), 60. This citation is based on an article that was published in *Sīnamā 54* in Persian under the name of John Gillett, most probably translated from an English article that he wrote. The original article by John Gillett has not been located by the author.
[157] Bengt Forslund, "Matbū'āt-i Jahān va Sivvumīn Jashnvārah-'i Jahānī-yi Fīlm-i Tihrān" [World Press and the Third Tehran International Film Festival], *Sīnamā 54*, no. 18 (Murdād–Shahrīvar 1354 [August–September 1975]), 68.
[158] *Ibid.*   [159] *Ibid.*, 69.   [160] *Ibid.*, 66.   [161] *Ibid.*

the span of just a few years. One could even contend that such comparisons by Europeans and Americans were premised on the uninformed perspective that Iranian filmmakers had no creativity or filmmaking tradition of their own, and their artistic creations had to be defined in terms of renowned directors of already prominent and recognised cinemas. While these arguments may hold substance with regard to how international film critics watched, analysed and studied the Iranian cinema of the pre-revolutionary era, a close reading of the history of Iranian cinema reveals that Iran had a long-standing relationship with cinema and that, by the 1970s, it had already registered a *tradition* of filmmaking – one that from its beginning encompassed a cosmopolitan outlook. It is also worthy to note that the Iranian reception of global cinematic cultures and international films did not inevitably lead to imitations of international films, but gave rise to artistic creations that were also "Iranian," in that they conversed with national debates and everyday life.

As Iran gained a more prominent position in international politics in the 1960s, and as the national film industry took a more critical turn, an increasing number of Iranian films began to be featured in global festivals. As early as the 1960s, the Pahlavi government, which still attempted to use films as propagandist tools, sent three films to be included in the second International Film Festival of Moscow, held from July 18 to 23, 1961. Based on a report by Bahrām Būshihrī-pūr, the representative of the Ministry of the Press and Radio in Moscow to the Deputy Prime Minister, and the Head of the Office of the Press and Radio, Mr Mu'īnīyān, the three films of *Tehran*, *Isfahan* and *Persepolis* were selected to be sent to the Moscow film festival, of which only *Tehran* and *Isfahan* were screened. The Iranian entourage to the festival included Majīd Muhsinī, whose *The Farm's Nightingale* (*Bulbul-i Mazra'ah*, 1957) was also screened in Moscow, Ismā'īl Kūshān and a few other people.[162] *Tehran* was screened for

---

[162] "Guzārish-i Vābastah-'i Matbū'ātī-yi Īrān dar Muskaw Rāji' bah Shirkat-i Fīlmhā-yi Īrānī dar Duvvumīn Fistīvāl-i Baynulmilalī-yi Sīnamāyī-yi Muskaw: Sanad-i Shumārah 171/3" [Report of the Press Representative of Iran in Moscow in Regard to the Participation of Iranian Films in the Second International Cinema Festival of Moscow: Document Number 171/3], in *Asnādī az Mūsīqī, Ti'ātr va Sīnamā dar Īrān (1300–1357)* [*Documents on Music, Theatre and Cinema in Iran (1921–1978)*] (Tehran: The Press and Publication Organisation of the Ministry of Culture and Islamic Guidance, 2000), vol. 2, 801–808.

an audience of 2,000 people at the festival, then projected twice in
Modern Cinema of Moscow for a total number of 5,000 people and
then at Lenin Stadium (Luzhniki Stadium).[163] *Isfahan* was screened
at Cinema Russia for 2,500 people and was well received by the jury
and the audience.[164] *Tehran*, which was produced by the National
Office of the Press and Radio (no year indicated), touched upon the
"advancement" of the country and "the unfounded claims of Russian
radio's propaganda"; the film's "screening at the heart of international communism," therefore, according to the Office of the Press
and Radio, was a great victory for Iran.[165] *Isfahan* also showcased
the "improvement in the lives of workers and matters of social
insurance," which again aimed to "refute the propaganda of the
Soviet Union against" Iran.[166] The two films, reportedly, were well
received by Russian audiences.[167] According to the report, the representative of Soviet Film had suggested to arrange for a "cinematic
week for Iranian films in Moscow," which would include the
screening of seven artistic films and seven documentary films within
a week.[168] On April 8, 1963, Ibrāhīm Gulistān (b. 1922), the
renowned writer and filmmaker, sent a letter on behalf of his production company, Gulistān Film Unit, to the Office of the Prime Minister,
indicating his wish for the Iranian government to submit his production company's films to be included at the Moscow International

[163] *Ibid.*, 804.   [164] *Ibid.*, 804–805.
[165] "Guzārish-i Vābastah-'i Matbū'ātī-yi Īrān dar Muskaw Rāji' bah Shirkat-i
    Fīlm-hā-yi Īrānī," Document Number 171/2, 799. A number of films under the
    title of "Tehran" or including the word "Tehran" were produced in the 1950s
    and 1960s by filmmakers such as Ibrāhīm Gulistān and those who were trained
    and supervised by the Syracuse University Team advisers. It is not clear when
    this film was produced and who the director was. See M. Ali Issari, *Cinema in
    Iran: 1900–1979* (London: The Scarecrow Press, 1989), 346–347 and App. G.
[166] "Guzārish-i Vābastah-'i Matbū'ātī-yi Īrān dar Muskaw Rāji' bah Shirkat-i
    Fīlmhā-yi Īrānī," Document Number 171/2, 799. A number of documentaries
    were produced in Iran with Isfahan as their setting. Based on this report, it is
    not clear who made the film and when it was produced. For a list of
    documentaries that were based in Isfahan, see Issari, *Cinema in Iran*, 346–347
    and App. G.
[167] "Guzārish-i Vābastah-'i Matbū'ātī-yi Īrān dar Muskaw Rāji' bah Shirkat-i
    Fīlmhā-yi Īrānī," Document Number 171/2, 800.
[168] "Guzārish-i Vābastah-'i Matbū'ātī-yi Īrān dar Muskaw Rāji' bah Shirkat-i
    Fīlmhā-yi Īrānī," Document Number 171/3, 807. It is not clear if this Iranian
    Cinema Week was ever organised in Moscow.

Film Festival.[169] According to Gulistān, documentaries such as *A Fire* (*Yik Ātash*, 1961) which had won an award at the Venice Film Festival in 1961,[170] and his other short films which were screened at international film festival, were all films that had been produced without the "financial" or "psychological" help of the government.[171] No Asian or Middle Eastern country, the author remarked, "other than Japan and India," had achieved such success and international recognition.[172] Now, with the upcoming Moscow festival in 1963, Gulistān asked the government to arrange to send his films to the festival, films which demonstrated "the human work, efforts and advancement of our country" and "had artistic value."[173]

The dialogic interaction of Iranian films with global cinemas could also be witnessed at other international film festivals, where many alter-cinema film directors attempted to showcase their works. *Dawn of Capricorn* (*Tulū'-i Jiddī*, 1964)[174] by Ahmad Fārūqī (1938–1993), *The Cow* by Dariush Mehrjui, *Rhythm* (*Rītm*, 1971) by Manūchihr Tayyāb (b. 1937), *The Experience* (*Tajruabah*, 1973) by Abbas Kiarostami (1940–2016), *The Stranger and Fog* by Bahrām Bayzāyī (b. 1938) and *Prince Ihtijab* and *The Tall Shadows of the Wind* (*Sāyah-hā-yi Buland-i Bād*, 1979) by Bahman Farmān-Ārā (b. 1942) were among the films that were screened at the Cannes Film Festival throughout the pre-revolutionary era. Furūgh Farrukhzād's (1934–1966) *The House Is Black* (*Khānah Sīyāh Ast*, 1962) was showcased and won an award at Oberhausen International Short Film Festival in 1962.[175] Other films, such as *The Face of 75* (*Chihrah 75*, 1965)[176] by Hajīr Dāryūsh (1938–1995), and Sohrab Shahid Sales's

---

[169] "Darkhāst-i Ibrāhīm Gulistān Mabnī bar Irsāl-i Ti'dādī az Fīlmhā-yi Vay bah Fistīvāl-i Muskaw: Sanad-i Shumārah-'i 192" [Ibrāhīm Gulestan's Request in Regard to the Sending of a Number of his Films to Moscow Festival: Document Number 192], in *Asnādī az Mūsīqī, Ti'ātr va Sīnamā dar Īrān (1300–1357)*, vol. 2, 907–908.

[170] Gulistān's *A Fire* (1961) had won two awards at the Venice Film Festival. See Issari, *Cinema in Iran*, App. G.

[171] "Darkhāst-i Ibrāhīm Gulistān Mabnī bar Irsāl-i Ti'dādī az Fīlmhā-yi Vay bah Fistīvāl-i Muskaw," Document Number 1921/1, 909.

[172] *Ibid.*   [173] *Ibid.*

[174] Fārūghī's documentary, *Dawn of Capricorn*, had won two awards at the 1964 Cannes Film Festival. See Issari, *Cinema in Iran*, 188.

[175] Ghaffari, "Sīnamā-yi Īrān," 344.

[176] *The Face of 75* won an award at Berlin International Film Festival in 1965. See Issari, *Cinema in Iran*, App. G.

films, *A Simple Event* (*Yik Ittifāq-i Sādah*, 1974), *Still Life* (*Tabī'at-i Bījān*, 1974) and *In Exile* (*Dar Ghurbat*, 1975), in addition to Parviz Kimiavi's *The Stone Garden* (*Bāgh-i Sangī*, 1976), were featured at Berlin International Film Festival and won awards as artistic, ambitious films that contributed to what Peter W. Jansen remarked as "a festival forming an almost integrated whole."[177] Ibrāhīm Gulistān's *The Hills of Marlik* (*Tappah-hā-yi Mārlīk*, 1964) also won an award at the 1964 Venice Film Festival.[178] Iranian films were, moreover, well known at Asian film festivals such as the "Tashkent Asian Festival" in Uzbekistan, where Bahrām Bayzayī's *The Stranger and Fog* was featured in 1975.[179] *The Dead-End* (*Bunbast*, 1977) by Parvīz Sayyād (b. 1939) was also showcased at Moscow International Film Festival in 1977.[180]

Through their participation in international film festivals, Iranian films were now increasingly watched and analysed by an international audience. According to the publication, *Sīnamā 5*, the Festival of Iranian Films in America, which included "ten feature films and eighteen short films," was to take place in Washington and sixteen other cities in the United States.[181] Moreover, The Week of Iranian Cinema in Paris – which, based on a 1973 article, took longer than one week – showcased twelve Iranian films and some short films in two movie theatres and the French Cinémathèque in Paris.[182] Not everyone believed in the global acknowledgment of Iranian films. Dāvūd Īpakchī reported that "Iranians residing in Paris" constituted "the majority of the audiences for the films"; this in itself, the author believed, was reflective of "Iranian cinema's need to make a name for itself on a

[177] This is quoted in "24th Berlin International Film Festival June 21–July 2, 1974," *Berlinale*, accessed February 21, 2013, www.berlinale.de/en/archiv/jahresarchive/1974/01_jahresblatt_1974/01_Jahresblatt_1974.html.

[178] See Issari, *Cinema in Iran*, 190.

[179] Hūshang Shaftī, "Guzārishī Kūtāh az Chahārumīn Jashnvārah-'i Āsīyāyī-yi 'Tāshkand'" [A Short Report on the Fourth Asian Festival of "Tashkent"], *Sīnamā 55*, no. 24 (Tīr–Murdād 2535 [June–July 1976]), 65.

[180] Bihrūz Tūrānī, "Fīlm-i '*Bunbast*' Asar-i Parvīz Sayyād dar Jashnvārah-'i Muskaw" [The Movie "*The Dead-End*" by Parviz Sayyad in Moscow Festival], *Bunyād*, no. 6 (Shahrīvar 2536 [September 1977]), 64.

[181] "Jashnvārah-'i Fīlmhā-yi Īrānī dar Āmrīcā" [The Festival of Iranian Films in America], *Sīnamā 55*, no. 24 (Tīr–Murdād 2535 [July–August 1975]), 57.

[182] Dāvūd Īpakchī, "Nigāhī bah Sīnamā-yi Javān-i Īrān dar Pārīs" [A Look at the Young Iranian Cinema in Paris], *Nigīn*, no. 99 (Murdād 1352 [August 1973]), 48.

global level."[183] The presence of these films in theatres outside Iran, and the rising number of films that were distributed to the international market, however, were evocative of a growing cinematic interaction and exchange between Iran and prominent cinemas of the world.

In the 1970s, some pre-revolutionary directors and producers participated in collaborative projects that usually involved European and North American producers and film companies. Cinema Services Company (Shirkat-i Khadamāt-i Sīnamāyī), managed by Bahman Farmān-Ārā in 1975, for example, was responsible for the reviewing of some collaborative film projects with other countries. In addition to the co-productions mentioned in the previous chapter, *The Desert of Tartars* (*Il Deserto dei Tartari*, 1976)[184] by Valerio Zurlini, was another co-produced film that was shot in Arg-i Bam.[185] *Caravans* (*Kāravānhā*, 1978), by James Fargo, was another Iranian-American co-production shot in Iran in 1976.[186]

Aside from co-productions, a number of prominent international directors also made films in Iran. In 1967, Albert Lamorrise, a French filmmaker and producer, directed the documentary *Le Vent des Amoureux*, or *The Lovers' Wind* (*Bād-i Sabā*, 1969) – a documentary shot from a helicopter, where the camera, personifying the wind, filmed various beautiful landscapes of Iran. The original film made in 1967, however, was not to the liking of the General Office of National Cinematic Administration and was thus not approved. In 1969, Lamorisse travelled to Iran again to add new scenes to his documentary in order to attain the approval of the Iranian Administration; however, his helicopter crashed due to technical defects and he died at the scene.[187] Claude Lelouch, a renowned French filmmaker, directed a short film in 1971 by the title *Iran*, which he allegedly dedicated to the Shah's wife, Farah Pahlavi. The film won six international awards after its release – for the geographical footage and amazing editing of the film, which juxtaposes modern and traditional Iranians in a poetic visualisation of modern (and modernising) Iran. In 1977, the prominent French filmmaker and anthropologist, Jean

---

[183] *Ibid.*
[184] "Fīlmhā-yi Mushtarak" [Co-produced Films], *Sīnamā 54*, no. 18 (Murdād–Shahrīvar 1354 [August–September 1975]), 61.
[185] Arg-i Bam was the largest brick-walled building in the world located in the Iranian province of Kirman. Announced as a World Heritage Site by UNESCO, Arg-i Bam was destroyed in 2003 by an earthquake.
[186] "Fīlmhā-yi Mushtarak," 61. It should be noted that Iran has not been credited for many of these collaborative projects in the film credits.
[187] "Khabarhā-yi Tāzah az Sīnamā-yi Īrān," page number not available.

Rouch, directed a 16mm 40-minute film by the title *La Mosque du Chah à Ispahan* (*The Shah Mosque in Isfahan*), which depicts the meeting of Jean Rouch and his Iranian filmmaker friend, Farrukh Ghaffari, at the Shah Mosque in Isfahan. The film shows Ghaffari walking Rouch through the different sections of the mosque, exploring the geometric shape of the building and the ways in which light finds its way through different angles of the architecture. While studying the beauty of the monument, the two filmmakers discuss the relationship between Islam and death, as well as sex and cinema.[188]

5.6 Revolution Onscreen: A Cinematic Revolution before the Political Revolution

As the cinematic movement of the time captured the growing mood of political dissent in the late 1960s and 1970s, the socially conscious cinematic content of Iran's alternative cinema also transformed into a more revolutionary one – a cinematic language that at times also illustrated religious undertones as part of the culture and society that it attempted to capture. In the 1970s, the revolutionary content of films, therefore, arguably caught up with the revolutionary sentiments brewing among the public. Mas'ūd Kīmīyāyī's *Qaysar* (1969) symbolised the subversive geist of alternative voices in a traditional community that still valued religious morale; voices that seek virtue through vengeance – albeit with a single knife – in a rapidly changing society full of vice. On the other hand, Amīr Nādirī's *Tangsīr* (1974) portrayed the struggle of one man's honest attributes, aroused by his religious ethics, against a corrupt social system. Based on a novel by Sādiq Chūbak, the story takes place in southern parts of Iran inhabited by the Tangsīrī people and in the port city of Būshihr. Zā'ir Muhammad is an honest man whose life's savings, which he had bestowed to some powerful men in Būshihr as a form of investment, are taken from him. Zā'ir Muhammad, a veteran who had previously engaged in battle with British forces, is now compelled to work as a well-digger in his village. Outraged by the injustices in his city

---

[188] I originally found this film on the website for the French National Centre for Scientific Research (Le Centre national de la recherche scientifique). The description of the film and information relating to it can be found at http://videotheque.cnrs.fr/index.php?urlaction=doc&id_doc=2216&rang=1 (accessed April 20, 2018). The film has alternatively been titled *Ispahan: A Persian Letter*.

where, according to him, "its governor is a thief, its lawyer is a thief, and its Sayyid[189] is a thief," Zā'ir Muhammad decides to take justice into his own hands. After paying a visit to the mosque and the shrine of his village, gaining the blessing of the village's religious leader, drinking holy water from the mosque's water reservoir and reminiscing over a painting of the Shi'i saint, Imam Hussain, which altogether reminds one of the events of the Battle of Karbala, Zā'ir Muhmmad starts his journey against injustice. Digging out his gun and axe, Zā'ir Muhammad takes revenge against those who have oppressed the villagers for years, acts that people of his village see as courageous and righteous. The valorisation of Zā'ir Muhammad and his course of action propels the villagers to follow in his footsteps, to revolt and fight the injustice imposed upon them. The film thus projects a struggle that ends in a widespread provocation of popular sentiment against tyranny – arguably, a filmic revolution that occurred before the political revolution of 1979.

Parviz Kimiavi's *The Stone Garden* (*Bāgh-i Sangī*, 1976) illustrated the negotiations of various aspects of modernity such as individuality and personal religion against "tradition," as exemplified in established religion and inherited customs and patterns of life in a remote Iranian village. While the film revolves around the story of a shrine constructed by Darvīsh Khān, the protagonist, following a revelation, it criticises the Iranian pre-revolutionary state bureaucracy and the corruption of religious establishment in Iran. Similarly, Mas'ūd Kīmīyāyī's *Journey of the Stone* (*Safar-i Sang*, 1978) called for rebellion against injustice and tyranny brought upon a master in a remote village. The arrival of a gypsy, a timeless and placeless roamer, a righteous man with Persian literary and mythical attributes who holds religious beliefs, stirs revolutionary fervour in the hearts and minds of the villagers. The master, who has monopolised the millstones in the area, does not allow other villagers to make and own a millstone as a means to their economic independence. The presence of the gypsy and his desire for justice for human kind as dictated in the Quran, a copy of which he keeps attached to his arm, inspires a group of men in the village to stand up to the master and attempt to bring a millstone to the village. The film draws on religious faith as an antidote against oppression and a means to organise the proletariat against capitalist aspirations. Interestingly, this revolution also involves the mobilisation of women, who accompany the group of men as they carry the millstone to their village.

---

[189] A title given to the descendants of the Prophet in Shi'i Islam.

Bahman Farmān-Ārā's *The Tall Shadows of the Wind* examined the "religious tendencies" of people and analysed their emergence "in different social strata."[190] Based on a short story by Hushang Gulshiri by the title *The First Innocent (Ma'sūm-i Avval,* 1970), the film is about a scarecrow created by the superstitious people of a village to protect them against bad omens. The scarecrow, however, soon gains an identity of its own and becomes more powerful than people had ever expected. In other words, in pursuit of protection and security, villagers erect an idol that eventually takes over the village and terrorises its people. The scarecrow arguably allegorised the Shah, who had exchanged his role as the good "shepherd" for absolute power and capitalist ambitions. The film drew on symbolisms such as the scarecrow and colours such as red, a socialist indication, to demonstrate the resistance of villagers against the oppression of a human-made idol. The film depicts the uprising of villagers that is inspired by a saviour from outside the village, someone who could possibly stand for the character of Ayatullah Ruhullah Khomeini, the leader of the 1979 political revolution. Farmān-Ārā's film was caught in the turmoil of goings-on before the 1979 revolution and was thus banned by the government. After the revolution, the film was screened for a few days before it was banned by the Islamic Republic. The violent and vengeful actions present in these films represented evocations of anger and a cry for a new order. In other words, the alter-cinema directors brought the content of films in the late 1970s into concord with the political revolution that was concomitantly brewing. Muhsin Yalfānī, a renowned author and playwright, remarked on this observation a few days before the toppling of the Pahlavi Dynasty: "the art of resistance" manifested in various forms, he believed, "had engaged in a struggle against the dictatorship" in the era immediately before the revolution.[191]

* * *

The alter-cinematic movement of pre-revolutionary Iran and the scope of the movies produced by it, coupled with film journal and cinema publications, cinema spaces, Iranian festivals and their various channels of cultural exchange, instigated the formation of a heterogeneous

---

[190] Sābirī, "*Sāyah-hā-yi Buland,*" 35.
[191] Muhsin Yalfānī, "'Hunar-i Muqāvimat' bah Sitīz-i Dīktāturī Pardākht" ["The Art of Resistance" Engaged in a Struggle against Dictatorship], *Āyandigān,* no. 3281 [Bahman 16, 1365 [February 5, 1979]), 4.

Figure 5.5 The burning of Sīnamā Kāprī during the revolutionary period

Iranian imaginarium that was informed by a global nexus. Alter-cinema was a cinematic journey that, in its variegated collection of experiences, challenged the hegemonic image of progress and prosperity presented by the state to the outside world. One can see a cogent argument for the fact that, in the making of vernacular cosmopolitan films, directors and audiences, the alter-cinema of Iran disturbed national boundaries and presented a new national sensorium. This plural national image, which embodied a visualisation of everyday life, evoked a horizon of expectation for the future of Iran – one that was moral, sovereign, anti-imperialist, anti-capitalist and anti-oppression; it was arguably a visual horizon of expectation that in its temporality preceded the political revolution. In the 1970s, in the words of an author in March 1979, people were experiencing "cinema in the streets."[192] Interestingly, Iranian movie houses became targets of revolutionary angst as many cinemas were set on fire in the weeks prior to the 1979 revolution (Figure 5.5). Most damaging of these was the

---

[192] Hasan Tihrānī, "Mardum dar Khīyābān Sīnamā rā Tajrubah Mīkunand" [People Are Experiencing Cinema on the Streets], *Āyandigān*, no. 3297 (Isfand 16, 1357 [March 7, 1979]), 6.

burning of Cinema Rex in Abadan, where 400 people, who were reportedly trapped in the cinema, died in the fire (see book cover).

Sublimating social and political tensions in its vernacular and yet cinematically cosmopolitan design, alter-cinema corresponded to a cinematic temporality that was autonomous and yet related to the political temporality of pre-revolutionary Iran. As such, one can observe that the protentional subject of alter-cinema founded on ideals of a cinematic revolution, a revolution of thought, cinematic vision and expectations, in fact preceded the actual political revolution of 1979.

Conclusion

"Although more than half a century has passed since its propagation," 'Alī Assadī, a scholar and writer, concluded in a mid-1970s issue of *Culture and Life* magazine, "Iranian cinema has not yet reached a stage of self-actualisation." "In other words," Assadī continued, "Persian film has not yet developed its own identity."[1] The relation of Iranian films to the society, national culture and its values and traditions, the author believed, was yet "insufficient" and "superficial." The future of Persian cinema, Assadī stated, depended on its evolution.[2] The future of the cinema that Assadī spoke of in the pre-revolutionary era has not only achieved a self-actualisation in the post-revolutionary era, but it has gained widespread international recognition in festivals and academia – to an extent that it has been called a "true 'world cinema.'"[3] Based on a report by the Iranian Farabi Cinema Foundation in 2004, the number of short and feature-length Iranian films screened in international film festivals grew from "88 appearances in 1989 to 980 in 2000."[4] Regarded as "Iranian New Wave" cinema (sīnamā-ye mawj-e naw), or "New Cinema" (sīnamā-ye naw), this post-revolutionary project has been distinguished from what was – and still is – perceived as the "degraded" (*fāsid*) industry of the pre-revolutionary era in much of the extant literature on the history of Iranian cinema.

---

[1] 'Ali Assadī, "Darāmadī bar Jāmiʻah-shināsī-yi Sīnamā dar Īrān"
[An Introduction to the Sociology of Cinema in Iran], *Farhang va Zindigī* [Culture and Life], nos. 13–14 (Zimistān 1352–Bahār 1353 [Winter 1973–Spring 1974]), 15.

[2] *Ibid.*

[3] Richard Tapper, *The New Iranian Cinema: Politics, Representation and Identity* (London: I. B. Tauris Publishers, 2002), 3.

[4] The increasing number of awards won by these films also attests to the eminence of Iranian cinema's profile on an international level. Shahab Esfandiary, *Iranian Cinema and Globalization: National, Transnational, and Islamic Dimensions* (Bristol: Intellect, 2012), 69.

The reasons as to why the post-revolutionary cinema has achieved prominence on the international scene following the 1979 Revolution and the Iran–Iraq war (1981–1989) have been argued to be manifold, mainly expressed on the grounds of financial and ideological rationale following the revolution. The control and monopoly on the importation of foreign films by the Ministry of Culture and Islamic Guidance, the increasing participation of government, semi-government agencies and public-sector organisations in film productions, municipal tax increases on film imports and a decrease on local cinema tickets, and the new Islamic guidelines for film productions, some contend, have led to the blooming (as well as Islamising) of the local cinema industry.[5] Such explanations alone, however, do not adequately account for the global prominence of this industry today.[6] To be more specific, analytical approaches that take for granted and amplify ruptures, such as the break from the pre-revolutionary to the post-revolutionary era, are often grounded in a homogeneous conception of historical time that does not distinguish the temporality of the political from the temporality of cinema. The conventional homogeneous time works to anchor and legitimise a historical amnesia that constitutes post-revolutionary cinema as a product of the 1979 political revolution. Such conjecture allows for the political events of 1979 to overdetermine the history of cinema, and thus to overlook highly diverse and creative pre-revolutionary experiments that gave rise to an Iranian cosmopolitan cinematic imaginary, still in play in the post-revolutionary era. What is sure about the Iranian post-revolutionary "New Cinema" or the cinema that lends itself to more "universalist" constructions (i.e. New Cinemas around the world) is

---

[5] See Hamid Naficy, "Islamising Film Culture in Iran: A Post-Khatami Update," in Richard Tapper (ed.), *The New Iranian Cinema: Politics, Representation, and Cinema* (New York: I. B. Tauris, 2002), 35–50. See also Esfandiary, *Iranian Cinema and Globalization*, 69–70.

[6] In his book, Blake Atwood also argues that the direction and fruition of the post-revolutionary cinema cannot be defined in terms of the political rupture that happened during the 1979 revolution. Instead, he considers the reformist movement of the Iranian president Mohammad Khatami (1997–2005) to have been a transformative period in the history of contemporary Iranian cinema. Examining the cultural changes, esthetic standards and technological practices in Iranian cinema from the late 1990s to the present, Atwood argues that the reformist movement and the Iranian film industry supported, criticised and shaped one another. See Blake Atwood, *Reform Cinema in Iran: Film and Political Change in the Islamic Republic* (New York: Columbia University Press, 2016).

that it speaks to an international audience – a trait that also identified the pre-revolutionary alternative cinema, naturally based on its cosmopolitan outlook.

In its broadest sense, this book is about the ways in which visions transform. What I have attempted to show in the preceding pages are the transformations of the faces of cosmopolitanism in Iran from a cosmopolitan cinematic culture in the early twentieth century – informed by social cosmopolitanism – to a cinema that conveyed visual cosmopolitanism in its films in the late 1970s. Exploring the contours of diversity in social and cultural practices in the late nineteenth and early twentieth centuries, I argue for the fashioning of a social cosmopolitanism that significantly informed the cinematic culture of the time. Members of the Armenian, Azerbaijani and Georgian communities, in addition to cosmopolitan Iranian merchants who by virtue of their trade engaged international communities inside and outside Iran, were among the first people who made use of their trade spaces as venues for film screenings and became the first cinematograph owners and operators in Iran. Such cinematic practices, in addition to other cultural activities that involved the collaboration of international communities and Iranians in Tehran, created a dynamic cosmopolitan culture in the first three decades of the twentieth century.

The heterotopic qualities of cinema and the space of interaction that it facilitated also contributed to social and cinematic cosmopolitanism. Its technology, heterogeneous space and the competing imaginaries that it impelled were constituent of a cinematic modernity. As part and parcel of an Iranian urban modernity, Iran's cinematic modernity could not be studied in isolation from the cosmopolitan society that prompted its materialisation and the cosmopolitanism that it further shaped. The early cinema films imported to Iran were European actualités and short films that were translated and explained for audiences by diasporic communities and cosmopolitan residents of Iran. With their multilingual intertitles, the silent films of the 1930s also aimed to target Persian-speaking as well as Russian- and French-speaking audiences.

With the brewing of nationalist sentiments in the 1910s and 1920s, cinema was increasingly accepted and promoted by urban tradespeople, artists and intellectuals for the advancement and progress of the nation. In other words, these cosmopolitan residents took part in engendering patriotic feelings and nationalist aspirations. "Iran's salvage" was perceived to be possible through a rectification of "morals" – especially by turning Iranian "ancestors" into "role models," rather than "imitating" Europeans.[7] Cinema, as a visual and public mode of communication, played an important role in restoring social morality and advancing the nation. Morality, in fact, became a central tenet in the classification of films and their promotion by cosmopolitan practitioners from very early on.

Seen as an effective medium in public enlightenment and national propaganda, especially considering the political goings-on and influx of international films during the interwar period, by the early 1930s the newly established Pahlavi Dynasty co-opted cinema as an extension of the government's technologies of power and discipline. The Pahlavi state institutionalised cinema by issuing a set of codes for filming, screening and regulating the space of cinema. Cinema and educational international films were now more than ever promoted in school pedagogy and public discourses. The overdetermining nationalist discourse of the 1920s and 1930s was accompanied by aspirations for cinematic sovereignty on the part of thinkers, cinema enthusiasts and the government – aspirations that eventually materialised in the form of a Persian-language cinema that emerged in the late 1920s. While the language of the emergent films was considered as a "national" signifier of a sovereign industry, the cinema that emerged was a cosmo-national construct, in that it relied on international studios and cosmopolitan figures for its productions. Iranians were eager to stage this "sovereign" cinema on an international level, perhaps partly because major powers of the time were making propagandist newsreels or orientalist feature films that had biased views of the life and history of Iran, situating the country at the centre of international ideological and political debates.

Because of World War II, international politics and domestic conditions, the cosmo-national cinema of the 1930s entered a decade of inactivity in terms of feature-film production until the late 1940s, when a commercial film industry commenced its activities. This period, however, involved dynamic cultural activities that paved the way for the emergence of Iran's sustained national cinema in the late 1940s. It also witnessed the professionalisation of theatre (and later cinema)

---

[7] "Nijāt-i Īrān" [Iran's Salvation], *Īrān-i Bāstān*, no. 32 (Shahrīvar 25, 1312 [September 16, 1933]), 3.

actors, critics and writers, the opening of studios that dubbed international films into the Persian language and made them more accessible to audiences and critics, an increase in the number of movie theatres that featured dubbed international films (namely Italian and Egyptian films following World War II), and the publishing of a large number of film journals and cultural magazines that explored national and international cultural trends. The national cinema that began its productions in the late 1940s arguably relied on the actors, film dubbers, movie theatres, cultural magazines and the image culture that was fostered during this period.

The initial high aspirations of critics about the emergent "national" cinema of the late 1940s as representative of Iran turned into criticisms in the 1950s that were aimed at what was perceived as an "imitative," "vulgar" and "artistically inferior" cinema. The smorgasbord of low-brow films derogatively termed as "Film-Farsi" by the critics, however, proved to be popular among the Iranian masses. This commercial industry drew from social contestations that defined the everyday lived experience of Iranians, while borrowing from international popular cinematic trends, namely, Hollywood, Indian and Egyptian cinemas, with which Iranian audiences were already familiar. In the commercial industry that boomed in the 1950s, cosmopolitanism was a style of national imagination. While incorporating a cosmopolitan cinematic language, the "Film-Farsi" enterprise created films that stimulated Iranian sensibilities and explored social concerns through a sustained national industry. In this book, I have explored some of the recurring themes and motifs of popular films and have treated them as openings into the larger social and political debates of the time.

As discussed above, critics did not hold a favourable view toward this vernacular cosmopolitan cinema industry and initiated a discourse that inspired a revolution of expectations, a revolution of thought or, arguably, a *cinematic revolution*. A group of young directors in the late 1950s and early 1960s materialised this cinematic revolution in a cache of films that increasingly spoke to the viewpoints of the Iranian elite and international critics. Sharing much in common with inter-national cinematic trends such as Italian neorealism, French New Wave and Third World Cinema, especially in terms of technique and visual language, this alter(native) cinema was also concerned with the "lived experience" of Iranians, albeit in social-realist and artistic forms. This vernacular cosmopolitan alternative cinema – which was at times supported by the government and official agencies – was increasingly committed to painting a realist image of everyday life in Iran and sublimated political objections within allegorical and symbolic cinematic languages. As revolutionary fervour grew stronger among the public in the 1970s, the films of alter-cinema also incorporated more revolutionary themes. At times, in fact, alternative films visualised uprisings against injustice, social oppression and imperialist aspirations. The visual revolution of the alter-cinematic movement, then, presaged the political revolution of 1979, once again indicating the autonomy of cinematic temporality and yet its interconnectedness to social and political temporalities.

The history of cinema that has been captured in the preceding pages can be summarised as a history of cinematic cosmopolitanism in three broad stages: a pre-professional era that was characterised by a cosmopolitan cinema culture, but one that was not yet fully capable of sustaining a cinema industry; a professional era, which started in the interwar period, extended to the post–World War II era and coincided with a bolstering of cinema establishments, the professionalisation of the guild, the creation of cinematic platforms, societies and festivals and the emergence of Iran's "Film-Farsi" industry; a post-professional era, the periodisation of which allowed for counter-normative cinematic visions, activities and expectations, which were manifested in arthouse and alternative films and Azad (Free) cinema productions. Needless to say, the above-mentioned eras were not necessarily demarcated by temporal boundaries, separated and non-integrated; rather, they were overlapping and strongly informed by and in dialogue with one another.

Miriam Hansen argues that Russian cinema "became Soviet cinema by going through a process of Americanisation," namely through the adoption of American montage and through its fascination with lower genres.[8] Following Hansen, the main question that the book at hand has attempted to tackle is whether the distinctively "Iranian" cinema of the pre-revolutionary era emerged through a process of cosmopolitanism. Being conversant with heterogeneous post–World War II international film cultures, the preceding pages demonstrate that

---

[8] Miriam Bratu Hansen, "The Mass Production of the Senses: Classical Cinema as Vernacular Modernism," *Modernism/Modernity* 6(2) (1999): 61.

pre-revolutionary Iranian cinema worked as "the basis of the plurality of imagined worlds"[9] – a hybrid space in which the Iranian self could be reimagined and restaged in various ways on the global screen. Whether or not the cinematic cosmopolitanism of pre-revolutionary Iran was extended to the post-revolutionary era and transformed into variant forms is a worthwhile inquiry that requires much filmic scrutiny and close reading of film reception. Considering its success at international festivals, however, what is sure is that the post-revolutionary construct, the so-called "New Cinema,"[10] is still in conversation with international critics and is actively seeking a place in international markets. Christopher Gow states that the post-revolutionary cinema has been regarded as a "quintessential 'art' cinema in Europe and North America."[11] This, in the view of Azadeh Farahmand, is related to an ongoing economic crisis, which has then led to the deterioration of local filmmaking in Iran,[12] and instead, an increase in international investments and international co-productions.[13] According to Farahmand, in the early 1990s, the removal of government subsidies in filmmaking, higher production costs, less governmental support and growing inflation increasingly compelled many Iranian filmmakers to consider using international markets mediated through film festivals.[14] The popularity of Iranian films at international festivals has also led to an increase in the chance of foreign investment in local (and diasporic) film production.[15] International co-productions, then, as Gow discusses, restrict the variety of Iranian films that are accessible to the international audiences, and therefore skew the overall picture of Iranian filmmaking (as an art cinema).[16] In fact, with a tighter grip on cultural products in the second half of the 2000s, and especially after the controversial

[9] Arjun Appadurai, *Modernity at Large: Cultural Dimensions of Globalisation* (Minneapolis, MN: University of Minnesota Press, 1996), 5.

[10] Scholars argue for this New Cinema to have emerged after the end of Iran–Iraq War and to have taken shape in the 1990s.

[11] Christopher Gow, *From Iran to Hollywood, and Some Places in between: Re-Framing Post-Revolutionary Iranian Cinema* (London: I. B. Tauris, 2011), 3.

[12] Azadeh Farahmand, "Perspectives on Recent (International Acclaim for) Iranian Cinema," in Richard Tapper (ed.), *New Iranian Cinema: Politics, Representation and Identity* (London: I. B. Tauris, 2002), 87.

[13] Gow, *From Iran to Hollywood*, 4.

[14] Farahmand, "Perspectives on Recent (International Acclaim for) Iranian Cinema," 93.

[15] *Ibid.*, 93–94.   [16] Gow, *From Iran to Hollywood*, 5.

2009 Presidential elections, some filmmakers who relied on private and personal funding were compelled to distribute films (sometimes surreptitiously) at international festivals that had not obtained the mandatory filming permission from the government. While one can trace breaks between pre-revolutionary and post-revolutionary cinema, one can also see clear continuities between the two in light of their cosmopolitan outlooks. The breaks between the two cinematic periods are especially noticeable due to post-revolutionary governmental policies that have impacted visual motifs and content in films – what Negar Mottahedeh calls "a system of modesty."[17] This book has been an attempt to employ "cosmopolitanism" as a new mode of thinking to re-examine and represent the transmutation of cinematic visions and imaginaries in pre-revolutionary Iran. I hope this project's original reading of the transformative contours of Iranian cinema has been a small and yet unique contribution to the field of Iranian cinema, Middle-Eastern cosmopolitanism and historiography of modern Iran and early cinema.

[17] Negar Mottahedeh, *Displaced Allegories: Post-Revolutionary Iranian Cinema* (Durham, NC: Duke University Press, 2008), 2.

Index